THE
SCIENCE
OF
MIRACLES

INVESTIGATING
THE INCREDIBLE

JOE NICKELL
The World's Only Professional Paranormal Investigator

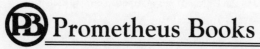

59 John Glenn Drive
Amherst, New York 14228–2119

Cover design by Nicole Sommer-Lecht
Cover image © 2012 iStockphoto

Inquiries should be addressed to
Prometheus Books
59 John Glenn Drive
Amherst, New York 14228–2119
VOICE: 716–691–0133
FAX: 716–691–0137
WWW.PROMETHEUSBOOKS.COM

17 16 15 14 13   5 4 3 2 1

Library of Congress Cataloging-in-Publication Data forthcoming

Printed in the United States of America on acid-free paper

CONTENTS

ACKNOWLEDGMENTS   9

INTRODUCTION: TOWARD A
SCIENCE OF MIRACLES   13

PART 1: MIRACULOUS EFFIGIES

Chapter 1. Miracle Idols   19

Chapter 2. Miracle Statue of Belgium   23

Chapter 3. The Idol of Pachacamac   27

Chapter 4. The Holy Image of Guadalupe   31

Chapter 5. The Painting That Performs a Miracle   35

Chapter 6. Jesus under the Microscope   41

Chapter 7. Snapshot Miracles   45

Chapter 8. Grilled-Cheese Madonna   51

Chapter 9. Animated Images: The "New" Idolatry   57

Chapter 10. A Weeping Icon and the Crime Laboratory 65

Chapter 11. The Case of the Miracle Oil   71

Chapter 12. Hindu Statues That Drink Milk   79

Chapter 13. The Statues That Glow   83

PART 2: MAGICAL RELICS

Chapter 14. The True Cross: Chaucer, Calvin, and Relic Mongers   91

Chapter 15. The Holy Blood   101

Chapter 16. The Image of Edessa Revealed   105

Chapter 17. The Holy Mandylion: A Déjà-View   111

Chapter 18. Miracle or Fraud? The Turin Shroud   119

Chapter 19. Artistry and the Shroud   129

Chapter 20. Oviedo's Holy Sudarium   133

Chapter 21. Miraculous Relics   139

Chapter 22. In Search of the Emerald Grail   149

Chapter 23. St. James's Miraculous Relics   157

Chapter 24. "Incorruptible" Corpses   169

PART 3: MIRACLE HEALINGS

Chapter 25. Jesus' Healings   175

Chapter 26. Lourdes and Other Healing Waters   183

Chapter 27. The Belgian Lourdes   187

Chapter 28. Miracle Dirt of Chimayó   191

Chapter 29. Peter Popoff's "Gift of Knowledge"   197

Chapter 30. Benny Hinn's Miracle Crusades   205

Chapter 31. Spiritist Healer: "John of God"   213

Chapter 32. Healings by a "Victim Soul"   219

PART 4: VISIONARY EXPERIENCES

Chapter 33. Jesus' Resurrection Apparitions 225

Chapter 34. "Visions" behind The Passion 233

Chapter 35. Eucharistic Signs 241

Chapter 36. The Secrets of Fatima 249

Chapter 37. The Medjugorje Phenomenon 257

Chapter 38. Guardian Angel Encounters 261

Chapter 39. Heaven's Stenographer 269

Chapter 40. The Mormon Seer 277

Chapter 41. Visits from the Beyond 285

PART 5: SAINTLY POWERS

Chapter 42. Miracles—or Parables? 297

Chapter 43. Miracle Worker of Amsterdam 309

Chapter 44. Mysteries of Popular Saints 315

Chapter 45. Tijuana's Murderer "Saint" 319

Chapter 46. Stigmata: Wounds of Christ 323

Chapter 47. The Case of Padre Pío 335

Chapter 48. Stigmata of a Convert 341

Chapter 49. Taking Up Serpents 347

Chapter 50. Additional Pentecostal Powers 355

Chapter 51. Loretto Staircase: St. Joseph's Miracle Carpentry? 359

PART 6: THE DEVIL'S WORK?

Chapter 52. Exorcising Demons   369

Chapter 53. Horror at Amityville   381

Chapter 54. Demon Victims I Have Known   385

Chapter 55. Satan's Step   391

Chapter 56. Footprints of the Devil?   395

Chapter 57. Fire from Heaven—or Hell?   403

NOTES   407

REFERENCES   410

INDEX   442

ACKNOWLEDGMENTS

I am grateful to the numerous people who helped to make this book possible.

Paul Kurtz (1925–2012), chairman and founder of Prometheus Books, believed in this project, and the skilled staff members at Prometheus were again a pleasure to work with, including Steven L. Mitchell, Cate Roberts-Abel, Brian McMahon, Jade Zora Scibilia, Melissa Shofner, and Nicole Sommer-Lecht.

At the Center for Inquiry I am grateful to Timothy Binga, director of the Center for Inquiry Libraries, for research assistance, aided by Librarian Lisa Nolan; Paul E. Loynes for typesetting; Thomas Flynn for photographic expertise and other advice; my assistant, Ed Beck, for many efforts, including scanning and organizing illustrations; and indeed the entire CFI staff for help at all levels—especially Ronald A. Lindsay, president and CEO; Barry Karr, executive director of CFI's Committee for Skeptical Inquiry; Kendrick Frazier, editor of *Skeptical Inquirer* (CFI's science magazine); and Patricia Beauchamp, Chris Fix, Julia Lavarnway, and many others.

I especially want to thank John and Mary Frantz for their generous financial assistance, which helped make many of my investigations possible.

I am also grateful to my wife Diana Harris for her assistance, and the support of my daughter, Cherie Roycroft, and grandchildren Chase, Tyner, and Alexis Jo.

In addition to those mentioned in the text, I am also indebted to the many scholars, scientists, popular writers, and other generous folk who assisted me at numerous sites around the world over the many years of this investigative effort. To all I am most appreciative.

In memory of Paul Kurtz
(1925–2012)
humanist philosopher,
founder of the worldwide skeptics movement,
mentor, and friend.

This book is only one
of countless ways
he lives on.

INTRODUCTION: TOWARD A SCIENCE OF MIRACLES

D o miracles actually occur? Certainly, miracle claims abound. Miraculous healings are reported at various holy shrines, like Lourdes in the French Pyrenees, and New Mexico's Chimayo, where a unique "Holy Dirt" is said to effect inexplicable cures. Some scientists have suggested that the image on the Shroud of Turin, the reputed burial linen of Jesus, could only have been produced by a miraculous burst of radiant energy at the moment of his resurrection. Again and again, statues and icons weep or bleed, potential saints exhibit the stigmata (the bleeding wounds of Christ) and other phenomena, visionaries receive prophetic messages that appear to come true, and myriad signs and wonders appear. All these are held to be miraculous.

But what exactly is a miracle? In Latin the word is *miraculum*, from *mirari*, "to wonder at." The term has been defined in many ways. For example, *Webster's New Universal Encyclopedia* describes a miracle as "an event that cannot be explained by the known laws of nature and is therefore attributed to divine intervention" (McGlynn 1997, 771). But this is a most unsatisfactory definition, since it depends not on positive evidence for an event, but on its being inexplicable. Such a claim is based on a logical fallacy called arguing from ignorance; that is, from a lack of knowledge. One cannot insist, for example, that we don't know what caused someone's cancer to go into remission and then conclude that therefore we do know that the remission was caused by "a miracle from God."

The Anglican writer C. S. Lewis (1898–1963) succinctly defined a miracle as "an interference with Nature by supernatural power" (Lewis 1947, 15). But this begs the question, what supernatural power? One cannot explain one mystery by invoking another.

In his treatise "Of Miracles," philosopher David Hume (1711–1776) argued that miracles did not in fact occur. He stated (1777 [1902, 114–16]):

A miracle is a violation of the laws of nature; and as a firm and unalterable experience has established these laws, the proof against a miracle, from the very nature of the fact, as is entire as any argument from experience can possibly be imagined. . . .

The plain consequence is (and it is a general maxim worthy of our attention), "That no testimony is sufficient to establish a miracle, unless the testimony be of such a kind, that its falsehood would be more miraculous, than the fact, which it endeavors to establish; and even in that case there is a mutual destruction of arguments, and the superior only gives us an assurance suitable to that degree of force, which remains, after deducting the inferior." When anyone tells me, that he saw a dead man restored to life, I immediately consider with myself, whether it be more probable, that this person should either deceive or be deceived, or that the fact, which he relates, should really have happened. I weigh the one miracle against the other; and according to the superiority, which I discover, I pronounce my decision, and always reject the greater miracle. If the falsehood of his testimony would be more miraculous, than the event which he relates; then, and not till then, can he pretend to command my belief or opinion.[1]

C. S. Lewis (1947, 11–12) begged to differ, insisting that

If immediate experience cannot prove or disprove the miraculous, still less can history do so. Many people think one can decide whether a miracle occurred in the past by examining the evidence "according to the ordinary rules of historical inquiry." But the ordinary rules cannot be worked until we have decided whether miracles are possible, and if so, how probable they are. For if they are impossible, then no amount of historical evidence will convince us. If they are possible but immensely improbable, then only mathematically demonstrative evidence will convince us: and since history never provides that degree of evidence for any event, history can never convince us that a miracle occurred. If, on the other hand, miracles are not intrinsically improbable, then the existing evidence will be sufficient to convince us that quite a number of miracles have occurred. The result of our historical enquiries thus depends on the philosophical views which we have been holding before we even began to look at the evidence. The philosophical question must therefore come first.

However, I have taken a very different approach than these philosophers. Now in my fifth decade of examining miracle claims, I have avoided putting the proverbial cart before the horse; that is, I have refused to decide, antecedent to inquiry, whether or not a miracle could exist. I have therefore tried to avoid the approach of "believers" and "debunkers" who may start with the desired or expected answer and work backward to the evidence. Instead, I have determined to investigate specific cases, trying to discover the best evidence and let it lead to the most likely solution, using established principles of scientific inquiry.

One such principle is the old skeptical maxim that "extraordinary claims require extraordinary proof"—that is, that evidence must be commensurate with a given claim. Another principle, established in science as well as in law and scholarship, is that the person who asserts a claim has the burden of proof, not someone who questions it—it being difficult or even impossible to prove a negative. The person who proclaims, "Well, I may not be able to prove this is a miracle, but you can't prove it isn't" has just lost the argument. Yet another principle is known as Occam's razor (named for William of Ockham, the fourteenth-century philosopher). This holds that the simplest tenable explanation—that is, the hypothesis with the fewest assumptions—is to be preferred.

I began investigating alleged supernatural and other paranormal claims in 1969 while working as a stage magician. I went on to become a private investigator for a world-famous detective agency, and still later a scholar with a doctorate in English (specializing in literary investigation and folklore). In 1995 I became senior research fellow for the organization now known as the Committee for Skeptical Inquiry, publishers of *Skeptical Inquirer* science magazine. In this role I am, apparently, the world's only full-time professional paranormal investigator. Much of that work has been as a "Miracle Detective," as chronicled in my book *Looking for a Miracle* (1993) and on numerous television documentaries. The character played by Hilary Swank in the 2007 movie *The Reaping* was based partially on me. (Warner Brothers even invited me onto the movie set to watch some of the filming and to meet the engaging Hilary.)

So here is much of the fruit of my more than forty years of labor, *The Science of Miracles*. I have grouped the chapters into six parts as follows:

Part 1, "Miraculous Effigies," presents alleged miracle figures of every kind: idols, icons and statues that "weep" and exhibit other remarkable phenomena, images that appear spontaneously, "miracle" photographs, and so on.

Part 2, "Magical Relics," scrutinizes such holy relics as the Shroud of Turin, pieces of the True Cross, the Holy Grail, the reputed blood of Christ at Bruges, and many more, including allegedly miraculous relics of saints.

Part 3, "Miracle Healings," examines the claims for various healing shrines and the reputed miracles worked by the hands of such faith healers as Peter Popoff, Benny Hinn, and Brazil's John of God.

Part 4, "Visionary Experiences," treats the holy visions and paranormal phenomena reported at sites like Fatima, Portugal; Medjugorje, in the former Yugoslavia; and Conyers, Georgia. Events such as near-death experiences and angelic encounters are also examined.

Part 5, "Saintly Powers," investigates reputed wonderworking abilities of saints, including glossolalia, stigmata, fire immunity, and other feats.

Finally, Part 6, "The Devil's Work," discusses those allegedly supernatural phenomena attributed to Satan or to demons—notably various devil's footprints, cases of demon possession, and outbreaks of phenomena such as those reported as the "Amityville Horror."

So turn the page and come with me on this around-the-world adventure to investigate strange mysteries at the interface of science and religion. Let us dare to check our emotions and rely on reason and evidence, seeing, as I have long held, that the progress of science is a series of solved mysteries.

PART 1
MIRACULOUS EFFIGIES

Chapter 1

MIRACLE IDOLS

Effigies that worked apparent miracles were reported in ancient cultures. The operative word here is apparent. What can we learn about wonderworking idols that credulous folk of yore did not know? We begin with the sensational mystery of a Babylonian figure worshipped for its demonstrable appetite!

THE IDOL OF BEL

During the reign of Cyrus, the Babylonians persuaded the Persian king to worship their idol Bel (or Baal), which was set up in a temple. Each day the priests placed before the figure twelve bushels of flour, forty sheep, and fifty gallons of wine (figure 1.1). Then the temple doors would be closed. Yet when the doors were opened in the morning, the entire meal would have been devoured!

These events are told in relation to the Old Testament prophet Daniel, who, encountering the priests, soon uncovered the secret of the devouring, imbibing idol. The story is found in chapter fourteen of the Book of Daniel (in Catholic Bibles, Daniel 14:1–21).

Daniel, a wise counselor to Cyrus, advised him on many matters, but the king demanded to know why Daniel refused to worship the deity. Daniel responded by stating that he believed in a living God. Cyrus pressed him further: Was not Bel a living God? Did Daniel not see how much the effigy ate and drank each day? Daniel, laughing, cautioned the king not to be deceived. He observed that the idol was merely a brass-over-clay statue and therefore incapable of eating or drinking anything.

SECRET REVEALED

For this perceived blasphemy, King Cyrus grew angry. Summoning the seventy priests of Bel, he proposed a test between them and Daniel. The loser—or losers—would be put to death. And so Cyrus ordered the food and wine to be placed before the statue once again, but this time the temple doors were not just closed; they were sealed as well. This way, no one could gain entry without revealing the fact.

The following morning the seals were unbroken, yet the food was gone. However, Daniel had set a trap to reveal possible trickery. According to the account, he had instructed his servants to scatter ashes upon the floor of the temple before it was sealed. When the doors were opened, Daniel restrained the king from entering the temple and called attention to the unmistakable footprints—of men, women, and children—preserved in the ashes.

Thereupon, the priests confessed. They revealed the secret doors by which they and their families had entered and partaken of the daily feast. Although the legend is not known to have a historical basis, it no doubt helped motivate the Jews to resist idolatry. We can also appreciate it as a model of critical thinking—especially one among the earliest reports of paranormal investigation.

FIRE FROM HEAVEN

Another magical feat is associated with Bel (or Baal), although it does not directly involve an idol; this time, however, the deity is trumped by an apparent miracle from God. This story, which is related in 1 Kings (18:19–39), features a sort of duel between the prophet Elijah and 450 priests of Baal. Each side is to invoke his deity in an attempt to receive, as a sign, fire from Heaven.

After the priests fail, Elijah builds an altar of twelve stones surrounded by a trench, places on it wood and pieces of a sacrificial bull, and then (as if to make the test more difficult?) drenches the whole with four jars of water, repeated two more times. Finally, Elijah invokes the Lord: "Then the fire of the Lord fell, and consumed the burnt sacrifice, and the wood, and the stones, and the dust, and licked up the water that was in the trench" (1 Kings 18:38).

However, a clue as to what could have occurred (if such an event actually happened) is found in a similar account, recorded in 2 Maccabees 1:19–36 (Catholic Bibles). In this account a "thick liquid" is described rather than water, and it is called "nephthar" (similar to naphtha)—obviously a flammable petroleum product.

How the liquid could have been ignited is suggested in the account (1:22) that tells how at first the sun was clouded over. Then, when the sun finally shone, the fire blazed forth and everyone marveled. This could be consistent with a small, concave "condensing" mirror, or possibly a "burning glass," having been secreted among the petroleum-drenched sticks of wood to trigger the fire when the sun's rays were focused on it.

Of course this incident might never actually have happened. When I researched it many years ago, one scientist cautioned that the Maccabean account was apparently written about a century after the events it describes and so may have been little more than a pious legend (Stavroudis 1979). The same may be said of the version involving Elijah, as well as of many other such "miracle" tales.

OTHER TEMPLE IDOLS

Additional stories of ancient wonderworking—in Greek and Roman temples—survive. The great mathematician, engineer, and inventor Hero of Alexandria provided some detailed evidence in his treatise *The Pneumatics* (ca. 62 CE).

Complete with schematic drawings, Hero describes the mechanistic works of some of his predecessors as well as his own modifications and original inventions. Hydraulics and pneumatics, along with concealed tubing, effected the mechanical miracles.

For example, Hero mentions an ingenious idol used by the ancient Egyptians, described as "Libations on an Altar produced by Fire." The altar was a heavy pedestal upon which stood the idol, the statue of a goddess holding a vase. When a fire was built upon the altar, presently the figure would—seemingly miraculously—pour out the customary libations upon it. Hero explained that under the fire bowl was an airtight chamber, the air of which expanded as it was heated. This forced the wine from a hidden reservoir up a tube inside the figure and out the vase. As the wine extinguished the fire, the flow stopped (Gibson 1967, 21–22).

He also cited various remarkable automata, for example one that would drink any quantity of liquid presented to it (Hero n. d.; Nickell 1993, 46). As well, he described several magical vases capable of producing miracle effects, like Moses's bowl that turned water to blood (Exodus 4:9), Elijah's cruse that repeatedly refilled itself with oil (1 Kings 17:8–16), and the water pots in which Jesus turned water to wine (John 2:1–11). Possibly, these "miracles" only represent well-known magical effects having been incorporated into the legends of those who supposedly worked miracles.

Figure 1.1. Artist's conception of what the Idol of Bel might have looked like. (Drawing by Joe Nickell)

CHAPTER 2

MIRACLE STATUE OF BELGIUM

Belgium's most frequented pilgrimage site is Scherpenheuvel (Dutch for "sharp hill"), in the north-central part of the country. There, in the Middle Ages, stood a great, solitary oak that was visible from all around. The spot was a center of superstitious practices and pagan worship until, in the fourteenth century, a small wooden figure of the Virgin Mary was affixed to the tree, and the makeshift shrine began to gain fame. In time, miracles began to be attributed to the little statue (see figure 2.1).

LEGENDS

The first reputed miracle occurred in 1514, when, according to a pious legend, a shepherd or shepherd boy discovered the figurine lying on the ground and intended to take it home. However, the Virgin Mary miraculously transfixed him—froze him in place—preventing the statue's removal. Subsequently, the shrine became more widely known.

In 1602, a little wooden chapel was built at the site, and the following year a new miracle was reported: the statue wept bloody tears, reportedly in protest over the religious schism then plaguing the Low Countries.

Still another miracle was said to have occurred in 1604 when troops of Archduke Albert (the Spanish-appointed governor of the Low Countries) routed the Protestants and retook Ostend. Albert and his wife, Archduchess Isabella, determined to thank God by commissioning the erection of a monumental baroque basilica at the site, inaugurated in 1627. Albert died in the meantime, but Isabella walked to the inauguration, giving rise to pilgrimages that have continued ever since, supplicants seeking their own miracles in the form of healings and other blessings (*Scherpenheuvel* n. d.; *Scherpenheuvel-Zichem* n. d.).

What are we to make of the alleged miracles of Scherpenheuvel? First, we should remember that the site was considered magical before it was taken over by Catholic Christians, part of a common process known as syncretism in which one religion is grafted onto another. (For example, Catholic conquistadors in Mexico erected a shrine to the Virgin Mary on a hill where the Aztecs had a temple to their virgin goddess Tonantzin [Mullen 1998, 6; Smith 1983, 20; Nickell 1993, 29–34; Nickell 2004, 51–55].) In short, one may ask, are the alleged miracles of Scherpenheuvel attributable to the statue of the Virgin, and the power of the Virgin herself, or to pagan deities? Or might there have been no miracles at all?

The story of the transfixed shepherd boy is one of those vague, pious folktales that lack any supporting evidence. If we are prepared to believe a shepherd boy considered taking the statue, we can also believe it was only an attack of conscience that stayed his hand, and the rest of the tale is attributable to exaggeration.

BLOODY TEARS

As to the statue's bloody tears, that figurine was not the same one that had transfixed the shepherd boy. The original had been stolen in 1580, when the region was pillaged by Dutch Protestant iconoclasts (those hostile to the worship of images). In other words, the statue that legendarily saved itself from a shepherd's grasp was unable to stave off marauding anti-idolaters, suggesting that its powers were limited at best. Thus the bloody tears were produced by a *replacement* statue, and in any case, the phenomenon—judging from numerous modern examples (see chapter 9)—was likely a pious fraud.

The 1604 military victory at Ostend does not seem so miraculous if one adopts the perspective of the Protestants or if one wonders why we should think statues miraculous when desirable things happen (a statue's theft is prevented, a battle won) but not unmiraculous when bad things occur (a statue is stolen, marauders overrun the land).

CONCLUSION

Given the image of the Virgin Mary as healer and protectress (Mullen 1998, 10), it is not surprising that desperate people still seek miracles at Scherpenheuvel, where I have witnessed the votive candles, the fervent prayers, the posted notes beseeching "Moeder Maria" for supernatural assistance. Such help may seem to come to those who count only the good luck; otherwise they discount the bad or even—sad to say—blame themselves for not praying hard enough.

Figure 2.1. This little statue of the Virgin at Belgium's most-frequented pilgrimage site is said to be miraculous despite being a replacement. (Photo by Joe Nickell)

CHAPTER 3

THE IDOL OF PACHACAMAC

P eru, like all the Americas, was relatively recently settled (an occurrence made possible by the last Ice Age, which allowed humans to cross the now-inundated Bering Land Bridge between present-day Russia and Alaska). A succession of native cultures flourished in various regions and eventually metamorphosed into the Inca Empire. This began in the Andean highlands circa 1200 CE and—by the Spanish Conquest of the 1530s—ranged from Ecuador south to Chile.

Ancient mysteries abound in Peru, several of which I was able to look into prior to speaking at the Second Ibero-American Conference on Critical Thinking held in Lima, August 3–5, 2006. Here I report on the remarkable oracle at the stepped-pyramid complex of Pachacamac.

ORACLE AT PACHACAMAC

In the Lurín Valley, about thirty kilometers south of Lima, stands the sacred citadel of Pachacamac. An extensive archeological site, it is a complex of adobe-brick buildings and pyramids, spanning various ancient cultures. Pachacamac was the dominant pilgrimage center on Peru's central coast and "home to the most feared, and respected, oracle in the Andes" (Wehner and Gaudio 2004, 283).

On August 2, I commissioned a personal tour of the citadel, enlisting a driver and professional guide. Like countless pilgrims of the Wari-Ishmay and later Inca cultures, I walked the sandy streets, climbed the stepped pyramids, and gazed from the heights of Pachacamac (figure 3.1). Albeit for different reasons, I, too, was in quest of the mysterious oracle.

At this Andean citadel, the god Pachacamac—whose name in the Incan language, Quechua, means "Lord of the World"—reigned supreme. According to native mythology, Pachacamac, the Creator, took as his wife Urpiwachak, who was goddess of fish and birds. (A pyramid temple with her name stands in the northwest part of the city near a now-dry lagoon.) Among Pachacamac's countless roles were protector of food, controller of earthquakes, and healer of diseases (*Pachakamaq* n. d., 35).

Few details are known about the oracle, but one naturally thinks of Ancient Greece's Oracle of Delphi. There, worshipers believed, the Pythian priestesses channeled the god Apollo after inhaling the fumes and drinking the waters of a bubbling spring that ran beneath the temple. According to Owen S. Rachleff, in his *The Occult Conceit* (1971, 137),

> It is quite obvious that the Oracle was simply intoxicated by some form of narcotic that had been naturally or artificially dissolved in the waters of the spring. The pertinent factor, however, especially as it concerns modern precognition, is the subsequent interpretation given her ravings by the Delphic priests. Most often these interpretations were offerings of good advice on matters of war, marriage, finance, and the like. But when the priests were asked for specific predictions—the bane of all seers— they cloaked their reports in clever ambiguities that, coupled with the ambiguous condition of human life, served as an effective ploy. Thus the name of a king or prince babbled by the Oracle might mean prosperity or calamity for the kingdom or personal harm (or fortune) for the king. If the king was later involved in a crisis, either good or bad—as kings or rulers are wont to be—the priests could take credit for a significant prophecy; something, they would say, was in the air concerning their king.

The wooden idol of Pachacamac (now in the on-site museum but "probably a replica" [Wehner and Gaudio 2004, 283]) was carved with various figures and symbols representing "a cosmic vision of the Andean world" of the twelfth century (Pachakamaq n. d., 11). At the top of the long, cylindrical idol stands, Janus-like, a two-faced figure, apparently representing Pachacamac's oracular ability. This is evident in the deity's being able to see in opposite directions and so, symbolically, to divine the past and future. According to chroniclers, copies of the idol were placed in several different parts of the city (Pachakamaq n. d., 11).

ENTER PIZARRO

As we now know, the oracle met its match in the two-facedness of Francisco Pizarro (ca. 1471–1541). Searching for gold and other riches, Pizarro spent nearly two years traveling across South America's mountains and deserts to locate the heart of the great Inca Empire. The Inca king Atahualpa had received assurance from the oracle at Pachacamac that he would be victorious against the bearded white men who ventured into his land. He expected to sacrifice most to the sun god, keeping only a few as castrated servants, while capturing and breeding the Spaniards' remarkable horses.

Pizarro had ideas of his own. He sent a friendly invitation to Ata-hualpa to join him at Cajamarca, the Incan gold-production center, in mid-November 1523. Arriving early, Pizarro stationed his 170 men in three empty warehouses that flanked the main square. Atahualpa arrived with five thousand warriors; he was so confident of supremacy that they were cere-monially dressed and only lightly armed. The king was ostentatiously borne on a litter by eighty Inca officials.

Under Pizarro's direction, a Dominican friar approached Atahualpa and explained that he had come to spread the Catholic faith, offering the king a little breviary (a book of instructions for the recitation of Catholic daily services). Outraged at this presumption, Atahualpa flung the book to the ground, whereupon the conquistadors launched a surprise attack with trumpets blaring, cannon blazing, and armored men on horseback charging with swords and lances. The Incans panicked and fled but were slaughtered in great numbers while many others were suffocated in the crush of bodies.

Captured and imprisoned, Atahualpa bitterly complained of the Pacha-camac oracle's false prediction that he would prevail over the Spaniards. He soon offered the Spaniards a king's ransom: in return for his freedom, he would fill a big room (almost eighty-eight cubic meters) with gold and two more with silver. Pizarro agreed, and, as the sacred and other priceless items arrived, he had nine furnaces run continuously to convert them into bars—an estimated 13,420 pounds of 22-karat gold and 26,000 of good-quality silver.

Despite the ransom, a majority of the Spanish officers decided to execute Atahualpa anyway, fearing he was plotting against them. The king agreed to a last-minute baptism—apparently to avoid an infidel's fate of being burned at the stake—and was hanged (Wehner and Gaudio 2004, 283,

460). The oracle of Pachacamac had failed to see not only the ruler's defeat, but his death as well.

Now Pizarro was drawn to the citadel by Atahualpa's accounts of golden treasures there. He and a troop of his soldiers made a three-week ride to the site. Shoving the Incan priests aside, the conquistador strode to the top of the stepped pyramid where he found a building fashioned of cane and mud, its door adorned with gemstones. In its dark interior he found the roughly carved effigy of Pachacamac. As he wrote, "Seeing the filth and mockery of the idol, we went out to ask why they thought highly of something so dirty and ugly" (quoted in Wehner and Gaudio 2004, 283).

Pizarro should have looked critically at his own situation. Living by the sword and failing to follow many of the commandments of his own professed faith, he quarreled with his officers over power, had one executed, and was in turn assassinated by that man's followers—a sordid episode in the sordid history of religious conquest

Figure 3.1. Peruvian guide helps identify one of the stepped pyramids at Pachacamac. (Photo by Joe Nickell)

CHAPTER 4

THE HOLY *IMAGE* OF *GUADALUPE*

Mexico's *Image of Guadalupe* is a sixteenth-century depiction of the Virgin Mary that, according to pious legend, she imprinted miraculously on an Aztec convert's cloak. The Indian, Juan Diego, was canonized as a saint, although new evidence confirms skeptics' claims that the image is merely a native artist's painting, the tale is apocryphal, and "Juan Diego" is probably fictitious.

The story of Juan Diego, related in the *Nican Mopohua* ("an account"), which was written in the native Aztec language, is sometimes called the "gospel of Guadalupe." According to this account, in early December of 1531 (some ten years after Cortez's defeat of the Aztec Empire) Juan Diego was a recent convert who supposedly left his village to attend Mass in another. As he passed the foot of a hill named Tepeyac he encountered a young girl, radiant in golden mist, who identified herself as "the ever-virgin Holy Mary, mother of the true God" and asked that a temple be built on the site. Later, as a sign to a skeptical bishop, she caused her self-portrait to appear miraculously on Juan's cactus-fiber cloak.

The legend obviously contains a number of motifs from the Old and New Testament as well as statements of specific Catholic dogma. Indeed, the tale itself appears to have been borrowed from an earlier Spanish legend in which the Virgin appeared to a shepherd and led him to discover a statue of her along a river known as Guadalupe ("hidden channel"). Moreover, the resulting shrine at Tepeyac was in front of the site where the Aztecs had had a temple for their own virgin goddess Tonantzin (Smith 1983). Thus the Catholic tradition was grafted onto the Indian one, a process folklorists call syncretism.

The image itself also yields evidence of considerable borrowing. It is a traditional portrait of Mary, replete with standard artistic motifs (see accompanying illustration) clearly derived from earlier Spanish paintings. Yet some proponents of the image have suggested that the obvious artistic elements were later additions and that the "original" portions—the face, hands, robe, and mantle—are therefore "inexplicable" and even "miraculous" (Callahan 1981) (see figure 4.1).

Actually, infrared photographs show that the hands have been modified, and close-up photography shows that pigment has been applied to the highlight areas of the face heavily enough to obscure the texture of the cloth. There is also obvious cracking and flaking of paint all along a vertical seam, and the infrared photos reveal in the robe's fold what appear to be sketch lines, suggesting that an artist roughed out the figure before painting it. Portrait artist Glenn Taylor has pointed out that the part in the Virgin's hair is off-center; that her eyes, including the irises, have outlines, as they often do in paintings, but not in nature, and that these outlines appear to have been done with a brush; and that much other evidence suggests the picture was probably copied by an inexpert artist from an expertly done original. (Again, see figure 4.1.)

In fact, during a formal investigation of the cloth in 1556, it was stated that the image was "painted yesteryear by an Indian," specifically "the Indian painter Marcos." This was probably the Aztec painter Marcos Cipac de Aquino who was active in Mexico at the time the *Image of Guadalupe* appeared.

In 1985, forensic analyst John F. Fischer and I reported all of this evidence and more in "a folkloristic and iconographic investigation" of the *Image of Guadalupe* in *Skeptical Inquirer* (figure 4.1). We also addressed some of the pseudoscience that the image has attracted. For example, some claim to have discovered faces, including that of "Juan Diego," in the magnified weave of the Virgin's eyes—evidence of nothing more than the pious imagination's ability to perceive images, inkblot-like, in random shapes (Nickell and Fischer 1985).

Later our findings were confirmed when the Spanish-language magazine *Proceso* reported the results of a study of the *Image of Guadalupe*. It had been conducted—secretly—in 1982 by art restoration expert José Sol Rosales.

Rosales examined the cloth with a stereomicroscope and observed that the canvas appeared to be a mixture of linen and hemp or cactus fiber. It had been prepared with a brush coat of white primer (calcium sulfate), and the image was then rendered in distemper (i.e., paint consisting of pigment, water, and a binding medium). The artist used a "very limited palette," the expert stated, consisting of black (from pine soot), white, blue, green, various earth colors ("tierras"), reds (including carmine), and gold. Rosales concluded that the image did not originate supernaturally but was instead the work of an artist who used the materials and methods of the sixteenth century ("El Vaticano" 2002).

In addition, new scholarship (for example, Brading 2001) suggests that, while the image was painted not long after the Spanish conquest and was alleged to have miraculous powers, the pious legend of Mary's appearance to Juan Diego may date from the following century. Some Catholic scholars, including the former curator of the basilica Monsignor Guillermo Schulemburg, even doubt the historical existence of Juan Diego. Schulemburg said the canonization of Juan Diego would be the "recognition of a cult" (Nickell 1997).

However, the skeptics are apparently having little if any effect on the Church, which canonized "Juan Diego" as a saint, fictitious or not.

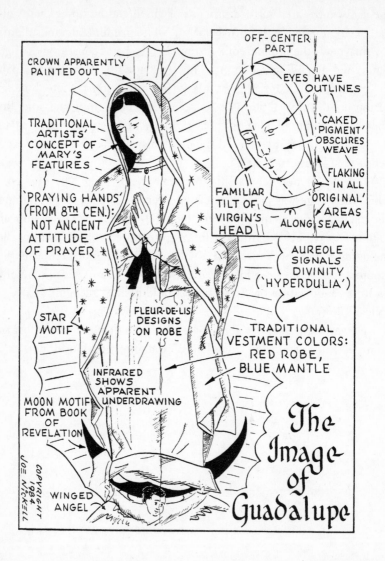

Figure 4.1. Supposedly a "miraculous" portrait of the Virgin Mary, the *Image of Guadalupe* actually exhibits artistic motifs and evidence of painting, even its "original" areas. (Forensic illustration by Joe Nickell)

CHAPTER 5

THE PAINTING THAT PERFORMS A MIRACLE

An enigmatic painting is exhibited at the church of San Francisco de Asis (St. Francis of Assisi) at Ranchos de Taos, New Mexico (figure 5.1). It depicts a barefoot Jesus standing by the Sea of Galilee; however, when the lights are extinguished, the background luminesces, as if the sky and sea were shining in moonlight, and the figure becomes silhouetted, a cross appearing at the left shoulder and a halo appearing over the head (Michell 1979, 94; Colombo 1999, 70–72) (see figure 5.2). Other mysterious effects are sometimes reported as well.

BACKGROUND

Known as "The Shadow of the Cross," the life-size painting was created in 1896 by an obscure French-Canadian artist named Henri Ault (d. ca. 1912), who had a studio in the Cobalt, Ontario, region (Rawson 1914, 615–16). Ault is said to have denied being responsible for the effect, which he claimed to have discovered (quite fortuitously) upon entering his studio one night. "He believed he was going mad, and he was never able to explain the reason for the transformation," states writer John Michell (1979, 94).

Reportedly, British scientist and gullible Spiritualist William Crookes (1832–1919) was the first to attempt—unsuccessfully—to explain the painting (Michell 1979, 94), which toured Europe and was supposedly an attraction at the 1904 World's Fair in St. Louis. A church brochure claims: "It is not known what causes the background to be luminous. It was painted before radium was discovered and when tested with Geiger counters the results have been negative" (*Shadow of the Cross* n. d.).

Sources even allege that more extensive scientific examinations have been conducted, utilizing "Geiger counters, light tests and scrapings"—all to no avail (Michell 1979, 94). However, as reported by *New Mexico Magazine*, while a church archivist claimed the painting had once been analyzed "for all known luminescent substances," she conceded "she had no documentation of the testing and was not sure who did the test or when" (Gaussoin 1998). Such alleged analyses appear to be apocryphal, representing attempts to convince the credulous that science is trumped by supernatural mystery.

In 1948 the picture was donated to the church, and in the early 1980s it was relocated to a room of the adjacent parish hall, furnished with folding chairs. A videotape provides an introduction to the local parish.

When the lights are turned out and the background begins to glow, subjective impressions can prevail. Observes one source (Crystal 2003): "Soon the silhouette of Jesus grows three-dimensional and appears more like a dark statue than flat image. His robes seem to billow in the breeze."

The church takes a cautious view of the phenomenon, and there are no reported healing cures associated with the painting. Pilgrims' reactions vary. Some exclaim "It's a miracle!" says archivist Corina Santistevan. "There are those who are very touched and very moved and very reverent," she says. "And those who continue to be skeptical. And those who are curious and want a scientific explanation" (Chavez 2002).

INVESTIGATION

I was among the latter group. I visited the historic church on October 27, 2003, accompanied by colleague Vaughn Rees. While photographs—and certainly actual examinations of the painting—are not permitted, we managed to get a close look by staying for two showings and the interval between.

Some of the picture's touted mysteries are easily explained, such as our docent's claim that Jesus' eyes follow the viewer wherever he or she stands. That is merely the result of a three-dimensional view being "fixed" in a two-dimensional representation, and any such portrait in which the subject's eyes gaze directly at the viewer will produce the same effect (Nickell 2003).

The picture is also said to appear more intense the longer one views it, but that would be expected due to the viewer's eyes becoming accustomed to the dark. In the mottled background of the painting, some see a boat, angels, or other images, but these are simply simulacra: pictures perceived, Rorschach-like, in random patterns. Some people report seeing the image of Jesus "vibrate," the docent told us; however, that is attributable to the well-known autokinetic effect by which a stationary light in the dark appears to be moving due to slight, involuntary eye movements (Schick and Vaughn 1999, 45). All such effects may be augmented by the power of suggestion.

Regarding the appearance of the halo and cross, it must be noted that—contrary to some sources (for example, Michell 1979, 94; Crystal 2003)—the halo is *always visible*, consisting of a simple outlined ellipse. It merely becomes silhouetted when the background luminesces. Such an effect—as my own experiments demonstrated—could easily be created by painting the halo outline with ordinary, opaque paint over a background rendered with a phosphorescent (glow-in-the-dark) one.

The same principle could explain the appearing-cross effect, except in that case the phosphorescent paint would need to *visibly match* that of the nonglowing background areas—something easy for an artist to accomplish. This was my preferred hypothesis to explain the mystery, after I first learned of it from Canadian writer John Robert Colombo (1996).

Supporting this hypothesis is the observation that the painting's background—in contrast to the other areas—is badly cracked and flaking, consistent with its having a different composition. (Underneath, where the upper layer has flaked off, is a very bright blue, whose presence suggests the picture was repainted—as with a phosphorescent paint.)[1] Further corroborative evidence comes from the fact that the glowing of the paint begins to diminish after a few minutes—just like phosphorescent paint—and must be re-exposed to light for the effect to continue (Casper 2004).

Proponents' insistence that the picture was created before radium was discovered (by Pierre and Marie Curie in 1898) is largely irrelevant, since nonradium luminous paints had long been available commercially. The first, Balmain's paint (a calcium sulfide phosphor to which was added a small amount of a bismuth compound as an "activator") appeared in 1870 ("Phosphorescence" 1911; "Luminescence" 1960). In 1879 an English patent was awarded "for the use of phosphorescent salts, such as sulphid [sulfide] of lime, of strontium, barium, etc., for the purpose of illumination by mixing them with paint or varnish." ("Phosphorescent Paint Patented" 1879).[2]

Although in 1896 Ault's "The Shadow of the Cross" was a novelty, some modern artists now produce luminous paintings as a special genre (Duffy 1995), and there are commercial transformational pictures (such as a "daylight" seascape, using four glow-in-the-dark colors, that, in the dark, becomes a "sunset" scene [Spilsbury 1997]).

CONCLUSIONS

Evidence suggests that despite his reported protestations to the contrary, artist Henri Ault deliberately and cleverly created "The Shadow of the Cross" effects. Just such a metamorphosing picture could have been accomplished using glow-in-the-dark pigments or paints that were well known and even commercially available at the time the painting was produced. It is no longer much of a mystery and certainly no miracle, notwithstanding the disingenuity with which the painting's custodians claim science is baffled while at the same time avoiding the testing that could lay the matter to rest.

Figure 5.1. Historic mission church of San Francisco de Asis in Ranchos de Taos, New Mexico, is home to a "mystery painting." (Photo by Joe Nickell)

Figure 5.2. Before-and-after photos of the transformational painting, "The Shadow of the Cross," illustrate a mystery that supposedly baffles science. (Photos reproduced courtesy of Sarbo Photography, Albuquerque, NM)

CHAPTER 6

JESUS UNDER THE MICROSCOPE

It has long been common, especially within the Catholic tradition, to discover faces of holy personages in random patterns and to suggest these are miraculous. In my book *Looking for a Miracle* (Nickell 1993), and in an article in *Free Inquiry* magazine (Nickell 1997), I recounted several of these including the famous image of Jesus discovered in the skillet burns on a New Mexico tortilla in 1978. Usually, these simulacra are the result of the ink-blot or picture-in-the-clouds effect: the mind's tendency to create order out of chaos. On occasion, however, they are faked.

On Good Friday, 1995, when I appeared on a special live episode of *Oprah* to discuss miracles, I met a daughter of Maria Rubio, the woman who had discovered the tortilla Jesus mentioned in chapter 8. Afterward, as we were waiting in a limousine for a ride to the airport, I also talked with a self-styled visionary who had been on the show. She showed me a "miraculous" rose petal that bore a likeness of Jesus, one of several such items that supposedly came from the Philippines. Examining the petal with my illuminated Coddington magnifier (a pen-lighted loupe), I was suspicious and asked to borrow the object for further study (see figure 6.1).

I subsequently examined the rose petal by viewing it with transmitted light, using a fluorescent light box and a stereomicroscope (figure 6.2). I noted that everywhere there were markings there was damage to the rose petal, resembling hatch marks made with a blunt tool (figure 6.3). In contrast, ordinary rose petals had no such markings (see figure 6.4, top right).

However, I found that faces could easily be drawn with a blunt stylus (figure 6.4, top left). I obtained dried rose petals, rejuvenated them with boiling water, then smoothed out the wrinkles on the surface of a light box and drew the requisite pictures. They have characteristics similar to the "miraculous" one.

As this case shows, paranormal claims are not solved by assumptions (for example, that rose petals have mottled patterns that could yield a facial image) but rather by investigation on a case-by-case basis.

Figure 6.1. Rose petal with "miraculous" portrait of Jesus. (Author's photo)

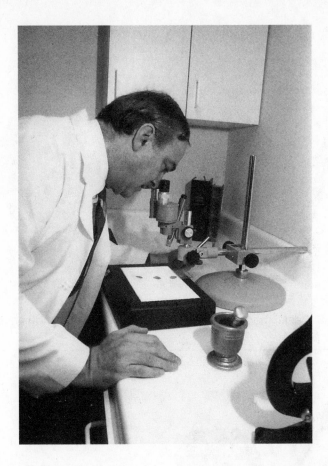

Figure 6.2. Author examines rose petals in his paranormal laboratory. (Author's photo)

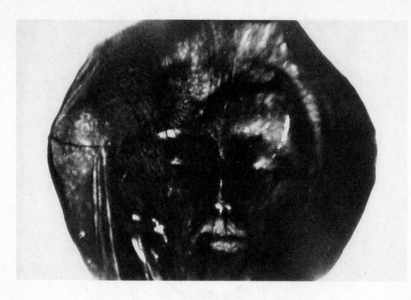

Figure 6.3. Facial markings constitute damage, resembling stylus marks. (Author's photo)

Figure 6.4. An ordinary rose petal (*top right*) lacks markings, but a stylus (*top left*) can be used to produce faces such as the three shown (*bottom*). (Author's photos)

CHAPTER 7

SNAPSHOT MIRACLES

On Friday, October 27, 1995, the television program *Unsolved Mysteries* aired a segment, "Kentucky Visions," that included investigative work by the Committee for the Scientific Investigation of Claims of the Paranormal (now Committee for Skeptical Inquiry [CSI]). The popular, prime-time television series had requested CSICOP's opinion of some "miraculous" photographs taken at a recent Virgin Mary sighting at a hillside spot in central Kentucky. This was my first significant case as senior research fellow—or as the narrator termed me, "Paranormal Investigator" (a "P. I." nonetheless).

The photographs were made by a Sunday school teacher who had visited the Valley Hill site (near Bardstown, Kentucky) with eight girls from her class. I did not see the photographs until the day I was brought on location for filming, but I was sent color photocopies of them in advance. The lack of reproductive quality put me at more of a disadvantage with some photos than with others. I did recognize that the claimed "faces of Jesus and Mary" in one photo were simply due to random, out-of-focus patterns of light and shadow caused by mishandling of the film pack (more on that later).

I also recognized in another photo the now common effect at Marian apparition sites, a phenomenon known as the "golden door." This is an arched door shape, filled with golden light, that is believed by some to be the doorway to heaven mentioned in Revelation 4:1. In fact, as explained in an earlier *Skeptical Inquirer* (Winter 1993), it is simply an artifact of the Polaroid OneStep camera, which, when flooded with bright light, as when pointed at the sun or a halogen lamp, produces a picture of the camera's own aperture (Nickell 1993a) (figure 7.1). This was codiscovered by Georgia

Skeptics members Dale Heatherington and Anson Kennedy, who tutored me in making such photos. (Together we have wasted much Polaroid film, all in the interest of scientific experimentation.)

I telephoned Kennedy about two of the other "miracle" effects, and he was already familiar with one of them. Sight unseen, simply from my description of the alleged "angel wings," he diagnosed light leakage into the Polaroid film pack. My subsequent experimentation confirmed his explanation and showed how the leakage could have occurred (figure 7.2).

Fortunately, my experimentation also provided an explanation for the remaining effect—one that had at first puzzled both Kennedy and me, as well as some professional photographers and film processors I consulted. The effect was that of a chart superimposed on one picture. The chart was slightly out of focus, but nevertheless unmistakable. One of the girls at the site thought she could see in the blurred printing the name of a deceased friend. Where had the chart come from? It appeared to have resulted from a double exposure, although the Polaroid OneStep camera should not ordinarily permit that to occur.

Suddenly, I realized that the card atop the film pack, which protects the film from light and is ejected when the pack is first loaded into the camera, has a chart printed on its underside! Indeed, that was clearly the mysterious chart in question, somehow appearing in mirror image in the photograph taken by the Sunday school teacher. But how had it gotten onto one photo? My subsequent experiments showed it was possible to produce such an effect by light leakage (the same culprit that produced the "angel wings"). The light had leaked in, between the card and the first potential photograph, bouncing off the white card and onto the light-sensitized surface of the film, thus making an exposure of a portion of the chart. In this way it was superimposed on the first photograph made from that pack (figures 7.3 and 7.4).

Taken together, the evidence from all four photographs, some of which had multiple effects, provided corroborative evidence that the film pack was somehow mishandled and admitted light, maybe by the front having been pulled down with the thumb on being inserted into the camera, or maybe by someone having sat on the pack. Since the other major effect, the golden door, was due to the construction of the camera, there was therefore no indication of hoaxing with any of the pictures.

On the television program, my comments were edited down to very brief but sufficient explanations. The treatment of the photographs was uneven from a skeptical point of view. The "faces" were greatly enhanced to make them look more realistic. Commendable was the use of an effective graphics technique whereby the chart was placed on the screen beside the chart-bearing photo, then flopped so as to superimpose it on the photo.

Skeptics who watched the segment with me laughed loudly at the conclusion of my interview when the narrator commented, "Rational explanations may satisfy *some* people, but. . . ." This comment was followed by various "miracle" claims that went unchallenged. I had not only explained how the "golden door" photos are made; I had also showed several of them for the *Unsolved Mysteries* camera (figure 7.1); but this was omitted from the program even though such photos were described as "mysterious." Also omitted were my explanations for silver rosaries supposedly turning to gold—either due to tarnishing or the rubbing off of the silver plating to expose the copper or brass beneath (Nickell 1993b). I included an explanation for a new claim: glass-beaded rosaries were supposedly turning, momentarily, a golden color; I theorized that the faceted beads were reflecting the golden light of the sun.

Much was made about people reportedly seeing the sun pulsate, spin, or exhibit other phenomena—all due to optical effects resulting from staring at the sun, which I discussed at some length in my *Looking for a Miracle* (1993b). Many pilgrims also had claimed to see showers of golden flakes, which I attributed to their having looked at the bright sun (even though some insisted they had not looked *directly* at the sun), or to a dappling of sunlight through the canopy of tree leaves, or to the power of suggestion—or a combination. All of my comments about such other phenomena, including faith healing, ended up on the cutting-room floor.

The program did end on a rather skeptical note, with program host Robert Stack stating, "It is interesting to note that the local Catholic church has declined to recognize Valley Hill as anything out of the ordinary. The rest of us will have to decide for ourselves." Unfortunately, they will have to decide without the benefit of all of the skeptical evidence. That's why I sometimes refer to the television show as "Unsolving Mysteries."

Figure 7.1. "Golden door" photo. (Experimental photo by Joe Nickell)

Figure 7.2. "Angel wings" effect. (Experimental photo by Joe Nickell)

Figure 7.3. "Miracle" chart. (Experimental photo by Joe Nickell)

Figure 7.4. Detail of chart superimposition. (Experimental photo by Joe Nickell)

CHAPTER 8

GRILLED-CHEESE MADONNA

S ince it came to light in 2004, it has become the quintessential holy image to appear on an item of food: the face, many say of the Virgin Mary, on a grilled-cheese sandwich. While it has sparked little piety— the Catholic church has not sanctioned it as divine—it has become the subject of controversy and ridicule and has even suffered insinuations of fakery. I once had custody of the curious item, and I was actually able to photograph and examine the image under magnification (figures 8.1–8.2). Here are my findings.

BACKGROUND

The image reportedly appeared ten years earlier in the Hollywood, Florida, home of Gregg and Diana Duyser. Mrs. Duyser, fifty-two, said she had grilled the sandwich without butter or oil and had just taken a bite when she noticed—staring back at her—the image of a woman's face in the toasting pattern. She perceived it as the face of "the Virgin Mary, Mother of God." Placing it in a plastic box with cotton balls, she kept it enshrined on her nightstand.

Duyser was impressed that the sandwich never molded. However, toast and hardened cheese that are kept dry naturally resist molding.

The Duysers received $28,000 when they auctioned the sandwich on the Internet site eBay. The site had initially pulled the item—which supposedly broke its policy of not allowing "listings that are intended as jokes"—

but the couple insisted that the item was neither a joke nor a hoax. Soon the "'Virgin Mary' sandwich" was back, attracting bids. It was purchased by an online casino—GoldenPalace.com—whose CEO, Richard Rowe, stated that he intended to use the sandwich to raise funds for charity ("'Virgin Mary' Sandwich" 2004).

SIMULACRA

The image-bearing sandwich received—possibly outdistanced—the notoriety accorded other sacred food icons. They include Maria Rubio's famous 1977 tortilla that bore the face of Jesus, also in the pattern of skillet burns; a giant forkful of spaghetti pictured on a billboard in which some perceived the likeness of Christ; and the image of Mother Teresa discovered on a cinnamon bun (see Nickell 2004).

Queried by the Associated Press during the holy-grilled-cheese brouhaha, I explained that such images are nothing more than evidence of the human ability—termed *pareidolia*—to interpret essentially random patterns, such as ink blots or pictures in clouds, as recognizable images. The most famous example is the face of the man in the moon.

Perceived pictures of this type are called *simulacra*, and many are interpreted as religious images (a female face becoming "Mary," for example). These are perhaps most often associated with Catholic or Orthodox traditions, wherein there is a special emphasis on icons or other holy images (Nickell 2004; Thompson 2004).

In the wake of the grilled-cheese image came others, one on a fish stick hailed as "the son of Cod" ("It's the Son of Cod" 2004), another a pair of images on a pancake. A woman interpreted the latter duo as Jesus and Mary, while her mother, the actual flapjack flipper, thought they resembled a Bedouin and Santa Claus (Nohlgren 2004). The grilled-cheese icon even helped inspire an entire book: called *Madonna of the Toast* (Poole 2007), it treats both "Secular Sightings" (for example, Myrtle Young's famous collection of pictorial potato chips) and "Forms of Faith" (including the previously mentioned Mother Teresa "Nun Bun"—missing since it was stolen in 2005).

A HOAX?

The Duysers' grilled-cheese Madonna was lampooned on the *Penn and Teller: Bullshit!* series on the Showtime network ("Signs from Heaven" 2006) and elsewhere by other debunkers (Stollznow 2008). Some of them found clever ways to make fake images on toast. One method involved a custom cast-iron skillet molded with Jesus' face, another a yeast extract used to paint pictures on bread before toasting (Poole 2007, 88–89). A Holy Toast!™ "miracle bread stamper" was even marketed in 2006.

But was the image due to possible trickery, as some implied? The rush to suggest fakery antecedent to inquiry is a most unfortunate approach. It is certainly not the method of a serious, intellectually honest investigation.

As it happens, I was able to examine the grilled cheese in question in 2005. I had custody of it for the better part of a day, January 14, courtesy of its Las Vegas–based owners who loaned it to Penn and Teller's producer, who in turn entrusted it to me. I was in Las Vegas to tape segments for that popular program, the timing of which coincided with the James Randi Educational Foundation's annual conference, The Amaz!ng Meeting 3 (held at the Stardust Resort and Casino). There, I shared the framed pop icon with other skeptics who eagerly posed with it, including Michael Shermer and Steve Shaw (also known as the mentalist Banachek). No one thought the image looked like the Virgin Mary (as her visage is imagined in art); instead some suggested it resembled Greta Garbo, Marlene Dietrich, or other celebrities.

Eventually I retired to a suite where I could study the controversial sandwich. It was in what appeared to be its original plastic box, surrounded with cotton balls, and set in a deep frame. I placed a forensic centimeter scale thereon and photographed the sandwich using a 35mm camera and close-up lenses (again, see figures 8.1 and 8.2). I also examined it macroscopically, using a 10x Bausch & Lomb illuminated Coddington magnifier.

I observed that the surface had a spotty, heat-blistered appearance (again, see figure 8.2). The spots making up "eyes," "nose," and "mouth" are similar to those elsewhere on the toasted bread. There was no apparent difference or incongruity with regard to hue, sheen, form, or indeed any other characteristic. That is to say, there were no facial areas that seemed more linear or in any way drawn or added (as by, say, use of a wood-burning tool or by any of various other means I considered). Therefore, it is consistent with a genuine (accidentally produced) simulacrum rather than a faked one.

Moreover, a careful close-up look at the "face" reveals it to be far less perfect than it may at first sight appear. (Those who suggest that hoaxing may have been involved, please take notice.) The features really consist only of some squiggles, a fact perhaps best appreciated by turning the picture ninety degrees. The nostrils are missing, yet the mind—"recognizing" a face—fills them in. Again, there is a pronounced extraneous, curved mark on the lady's right cheek, yet the mind tends helpfully to filter it out (or perhaps interpret it as, say, a curl of hair). In short, the image seems a rather typical simulacrum.

Nevertheless, Diana Duyser certainly acts as if she believes that the "Virgin Mary" image on the grilled cheese is, as she says, "a miracle." No longer owning the sandwich, she has had its image tattooed onto one of her ample breasts (pictured in Poole 2007, 86). She thus demonstrates that with simulacra, belief—as well as beauty—is often in the eye of the beholder.

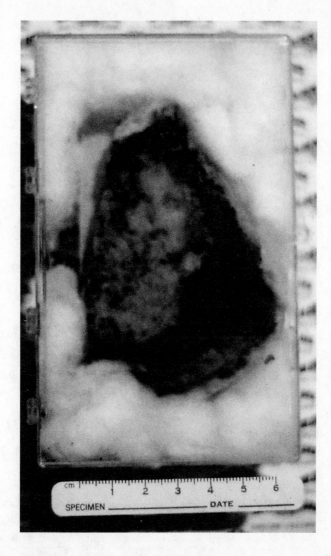

Figure 8.1. The famous face-bearing grilled-cheese sandwich has been kept in a plastic case since its creation in 1994. (Forensic scale added; photo by Joe Nickell)

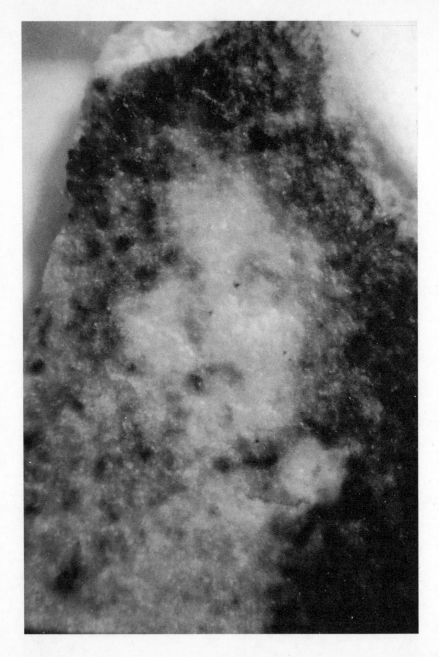

Figure 8.2. Close-up photograph reveals spotty, accidental nature of image: a simulacrum. (Photo by Joe Nickell)

CHAPTER 9

ANIMATED IMAGES: THE "NEW" IDOLATRY

For a live, prime-time television program, I was asked to evaluate claims that a statue in Sacramento streamed tears of blood. The case prompted me to take a retrospective look at a wide variety of related phenomena, ranging from weeping icons to perambulating statues, many of which I personally investigated over the years.

IDOLATRY

Belief that an effigy is in some way animated (from *anima*, meaning "breath") not only challenges science's naturalistic worldview; it also crosses a theological line. It moves from *veneration* (reverence toward an image) to *idolatry* (or image worship) in which the image is regarded as the "tenement or vehicle of the god and fraught with divine influence" ("Idolatry" 1960).

Religious prohibitions of idolatry are ancient. In the Old Testament, the second commandment is an injunction against "graven images," but only those that were to be adored or served (Exodus 20:4–5); others were explicitly allowed (Exodus 25:18). Influenced by Islam and Judaism, a movement of iconoclasts (Greek "image-breakers") sought to carry out the injunction between about 723–842 CE, destroying countless religious works and persecuting those who made and venerated them. In the ninth century, iconoclasm was declared a heresy.

Images proliferated, being widely used for ornamental, instructional, and devotional purposes. In the Orthodox Church image veneration largely focused on icons (wood panels painted in the Byzantine tradition) and was generally more elaborate than the veneration in Roman Catholicism, which tended to favor statues ("Images" 1993).

A new iconoclasm arose during the Protestant Reformation in sixteenth-century Europe. Reformers like Martin Luther and John Calvin listed image worship among the Church's excesses.

Ironically, Catholic Bibles (as related in chapter 1), unlike Protestant ones, contain an extra, fourteenth chapter of Daniel that condemns idolatry with a story.

ANIMATED STATUES

Roman Catholicism yielded several modern instances of allegedly animated statues. In 1981, for example, in a church at Thornton, California, a sculpted Virgin Mary not only altered the angle of her eyes and the tilt of her chin, churchgoers reported, but also wept and even strolled about the church at night. Although no one ever actually witnessed the latter, the statue was frequently found several feet from its usual location, standing at the altar.

A bishop's investigation, however, failed to support the miracle claims. Investigating clerics determined that the purported movement of the statue's eyes and chin were merely due to variations in photographic angles. Worse, they branded the weeping and perambulations a probable hoax. For their efforts, the investigators were denounced by some believers, even called "a bunch of devils" (Nickell 1998, 67).

In 1985 came reports that a figure of the Virgin in a grotto at Ballinspittle, Ireland, began to sway gently. Thousands of pilgrims, eager to witness the phenomenon, flocked to the village to view the statue, which was adorned with a halo of blue lights.

It remained for a group of scientists from University College, Cork, to discover the truth about the statue. They, too, saw the figure sway, yet a motion-picture camera revealed that no such movement had occurred. They soon determined that the effect was an illusion. According to the science magazine *Discover* ("Those Who Sway Together" 1985, 19):

> It is induced when people rock gently back and forth while looking at the
> statue. At dusk, when the sky is grey and landmarks are obscured, the eye

has no point of reference except the halo of blue lights. Therefore, say the scientists, the eye is unable to detect the fact that one's head and body are unconsciously moving. The viewer who sways is likely to get the impression that not he but the statue is moving.

Other phenomena were reported in Pennsylvania in 1989. The case began on Good Friday at the Holy Trinity Church in Ambridge, a quiet Ohio River mill town fifteen miles northwest of Pittsburgh. During the service a luminous, life-sized crucifixion figure of Christ reportedly closed its eyes. At first, no one claimed to have seen the eyelids actually moving, only that the eyes had been about one-third open when the statue was relocated in January, and that during the special three-hour prayer meeting the eyes were observed to be shut. However, the pastor of the church was soon reporting additional claims: "At times the eyes seem to be opening and a little later seem to close again."

Soon, an investigation was launched by the diocese, with a commission appointed to examine the evidence and report on the astonishing phenomena. After careful study of the before-and-after videotapes, the commission found "no convincing evidence" that the statue closed its eyes during the Good Friday service. When close-up views of the face from each videotape showed the eyes in a similar, partially open position, the commission rejected claims that a miracle had occurred. Commission members stated that they felt the witnesses were sincere but could have been deceived by the church's lighting and by the angles of viewing. In the wake of the commission's report, the pastor was barred from celebrating Mass, and he responded by resigning (Nickell 1998, 65–66).

But if that statue's eyes did not close, what about another's that allegedly opened? They belonged to a "sleeping" figure of Jesus that a Hoboken, New Jersey, street "preacher" had once rescued from a garbage bin. He claimed in July 2005 that while he was cleaning the figurine it opened its right eye. Stories soon spread of the statue "blinking" its right eye, turning its head, and performing other unverifiable feats.

Actually the statue's eyes were never closed. I studied high-resolution photos of the figure and determined that it had glass eyes and that portions of its upper and lower right eyelids had been broken off, the explanation for the opening-eye effect (Nickell 2005).

Other statue animations have been reported, including chameleonesque effects. For example, the previously mentioned 1989 eye-closing statue at Ambridge, Pennsylvania, also reportedly changed color—from vivid tones on Good Friday to dull ones after. However, these were attributed to the lighting and to pious imagination.

Similar explanations applied to a thirty-inch figure of Mary in a church at Patterson, New Jersey, that reportedly changed color in 1992. One witness saw the base of the statue turn a "dark, dark pink," while another said the figure once "turned the brightest blue." The statue was actually white with pink and blue tones, and the effect appeared to correlate with the emotive force of the believers. Not surprisingly, therefore, many people were unable to witness the color change and went away disappointed (Nickell 1998, 66–67).

Still other statues were supposedly even more remarkably alive: they were said to have heartbeats! The statues were at a Marian apparition site in Conyers, Georgia. Asked by an Atlanta television station to investigate the claims (and others), I found that there were no heartbeats detectable by stethoscope (figure 9.1). In fact, people were reaching up to feel the throb-bings and were instead either feeling the pulse in their own thumbs or once again suffering the effects of pious imagination (Nickell 1996).

EXUDING EFFIGIES

Not only statues but also icons and other images may seemingly become animated. (Icons are common in Orthodox churches.) According to D. Scott Rogo, in his *Miracles: A Parascientific Inquiry into Wondrous Phenomena* (1982, 161),

> Cases of religious statues, paintings, icons, and other effigies that sud-denly begin to bleed or weep have been documented throughout history. Before Rome was sacked in 1527, for instance, a statue of Christ housed in a local monastery wept for several days. When the city of Syracuse in Sicily lay under Spanish siege in 1719, a marble statue of St. Lucy in the city cried continually.

Similar manifestations have been increasingly reported in modern times. Interestingly, Syracuse was the site of another "weeping" statue in

1953. It was reported that the liquid was consistent with real tears, although doubts were raised about the scientific competency and impartiality of the investigators. The woman who owned the original statue had received it as a wedding gift in March, and it began to weep in her presence in late August, the culmination of several weeks of upheaval in her household. She was pregnant, and for several weeks she had been suffering "seizures," fainting spells, and attacks of blindness. Local doctors were unable to diagnose her condition, and she may have been seeking attention. The case was followed by an epidemic of similar manifestations across Roman Catholic Italy. Rogo (1982, 178) remarked that they were "no doubt spawned by wide press coverage of the Syracuse miracle."

Two other Italian cases are especially instructive. In one, which took place in Pavia in 1980, no one witnessed the initial weeping, and the woman who owned the plaster bas-relief was soon caught surreptitiously applying "tears" with a water pistol! In 1995 an epidemic of crying effigies followed one that began weeping in Sardinia. However, tests on the blood were clinically analyzed and the DNA was shown to be that of the statue's owner. Her attorney explained, "Well, the Virgin Mary had to get that blood from somewhere" (Nickell 1997).

Another instructive case transpired in 1985 when a statue of the Virgin began first weeping then bleeding in the home of a Quebec railroad worker. Soon the phenomenon spread to other nearby icons, statues, and crucifixes. Thousands of pilgrims waited in the brutal winter cold to view the "miracle"—as many as twelve thousand in a single week. The local bishop went largely ignored as he implied that the affair was a false miracle. Then, suddenly, the Associated Press reported that the affair was "all a hoax—not even a very clever hoax." Newsmen from the Canadian Broadcasting Corporation had been permitted to borrow an icon and had had it examined. The blood had been mixed with animal fat so that, when the room warmed from the body heat of pilgrims, the substance would liquefy and flow realistically. The owner confessed that he had used his own blood to produce the effects (Nickell 1998, 58).

There are not always such definitive results. An icon I investigated in Astoria, Queens, New York, May 11, 1991, was no longer weeping and my stereomicroscopic examination showed little. However, a videotape of the earlier weeping revealed that the "tear" rivulets flowed from *outside the eyes* and were greatly disproportionate to the diminutive size of the saint's face, observations that suggested a rather crude hoax (Nickell 1998, 54). Later, the priest who had presided over the Astoria church when it was visited by the weeping phenomenon was presiding over a Toronto church with an icon that had also begun to weep, as discussed in the next chapter.

An interesting feature of the exuding icons is the variety of substances involved, together with some apparent trends. In Catholicism the images tended to yield watery tears or blood, until relatively recently when— seeming to tap the Greek Orthodox tradition that has received media attention—there has been an occasional shift to oil. And in the Russian Orthodox tradition, the icons tend to exude myrrh (a fragrant resin) or myrrh-scented oil—as in a case I investigated in Moscow. The "myrrhing" involved an icon of the assassinated czar Nicholas II and occurred at a time when there was a campaign to bestow sainthood on him and his family (Nickell 2002).

INVESTIGATIVE APPROACH

As these examples show, more and more frequently we are seeing news reports of "weeping" and other animated effigies. Not one has ever been authenticated by science. However, rather than simply dismiss such claims, I actually investigate them—whenever possible.

Sometimes I am contacted on short notice, as when CNN asked me to assess the case of the Sacramento statue that appeared to be crying blood. Fortunately, I had been able to see photos and videos of the supposed weeping. I observed that the streams of "blood" came only from Mary's left eye, and that one of the rivulets in fact began above and outside the eye itself. Moreover, the streams were not flowing but rather remained static, as if there had merely been an *application* of the red substance. These observations led me to tell Paula Zahn when I appeared on her show (*Paula Zahn Now*, CNN, December 2, 2005) that I had good news and bad news: the bad news was that the weeping was fake; the good news was that few of the faithful would believe me.

I told the *Sacramento Bee* (Kollars and Fletcher 2005) that the weeping was a "clumsy, obvious hoax." When a church spokesperson, Reverend James Murphy, said there were no plans to investigate the incident, I responded, "If a statue is a fraud or a hoax, or even just a mistake, it should be determined and that should be that. If it's a fake, then it should be repudiated."

However, Reverend Murphy expressed an all-too-typical attitude, stating, "If people view this as a miracle and it brings them closer to God, then that's a good thing" (Milbourn 2005). But such an end-justifies-the-means approach is untenable—especially given the seriousness of the matter: an affront to science, religion, ethics, and good sense, as well as truth, all in one.

Figure 9.1. At a Marian apparition site at Conyers, Georgia, the author examines a statue of the Virgin Mary that some pilgrims claim exhibits heartbeats. (Author's photo by William Evans)

CHAPTER 10

A WEEPING ICON AND THE CRIME LABORATORY

O n September 3, 1996, at the request of the *Toronto Sun*, I traveled
to Canada to investigate the world's latest "weeping icon." I was
to meet with reporters at the newspaper's King Street offices and
from there be escorted to a Greek Orthodox church in Toronto's East York
district. Church officials had promised staffers at the *Sun* that they would be
able to examine the icon at 11 p.m., and I was enlisted for that purpose. In
addition to my overnight bag, I also packed a "weeping icon kit" consisting
of a camera and close-up lenses, a stereomicroscope removed from its base,
and various vials, pipettes, bibulous paper, and other collection materials.

THRONG OF PILGRIMS

As we arrived in the neighborhood, however, I saw not the nearly deserted
church I had expected to be awaiting our special appointment but rather
traffic congestion and a line of pilgrims stretching far off into the night.
I waited outside with my conspicuous case while reporters went to learn
that the promise of an examination had been retracted. I was determined
to proceed anyway and to do the best I could. A *Sun* reporter of Greek
extraction feared I might start a riot, but his colleague, Scot Magnish, who
had brought me there, was only concerned for my safety. (It was not wise
for him to go inside, given rumored responses to his critical article on
the phenomenon published in the latest edition of the newspaper.) After
retrieving some essentials from my kit, which I stuffed into my pockets, I

handed Scot my case, turned, and bounded up the steps of the little church. Behind me, *Sun* photographer Craig Robertson rushed to keep up. We passed a lady who shouted the admission price ("two dollars fifty cents") at us; I shouted back, "*Toronto Sun!*" and kept going.

Inside, the church was swelteringly hot. Nevertheless, people milled about for a time after viewing the controversial icon of the Madonna and Child, while new pilgrims passed before it. A table filled with candles and a crude sign that read "PLEASE DO NOT TOUCH THE ICON OF VIRGIN MARY" kept the curious at bay. An attendant refused my request for a sample of the tears and pretended to ignore me when I asked again, in a louder voice.

OILY TEARS

A hanging oil lamp partially obscured the face of the Madonna, but by moving my head from side to side and thus catching the light on the surface of the picture, I made several important discoveries. First, the icon itself was a fake—not an original wood-panel painting at all but merely a color photographic *print*. In addition, the "tears" did not emanate from the eyes but from somewhere near the top of the Virgin's head, and so, by definition, the image was not "weeping." Moreover, one of the four tear rivulets was smeared and looked "suspiciously oily" (as I told the *Sun*).

The latter point was quite significant, since real tears, or even mere water, would quickly dry in the hot atmosphere of the church. But a nondrying oil (such as olive oil) would remain fresh and glistening for hours or days—just the trick for "weeping" icons and one apparently more commonly used than the hidden tubes and special chemicals so often proposed by theorists. During the quarter of an hour or so that I observed the image, there was no fresh flow of "tears"—just the same unchanging rivulets I saw at the beginning. (There were also fine droplets between the streaks, as if the painting had been spattered on, possibly from the oil lamp that almost touched the print.)

After lengthy appeal, I persuaded the priest, Reverend Ieronimos Katseas, to provide a better view—at least for the photographer. Katseas pulled the lamp away with one hand while holding a candle close to the Madonna's face with the other. Photographer Robertson clicked away.

In the subsequent article by Magnish and two colleagues, I was quoted as saying that the phenomenon was "more carnival sideshow than miracle" and that I was troubled by the withdrawal of the promise to allow the icon to be examined. "It would seem to me a miracle could withstand a little skepticism," I stated, complaining further about being kept at a distance and being refused a sample of the "tears" (Magnish et al. 1996).

REVELATIONS

In the meantime, reporters learned that Katseas had been embroiled in considerable earlier controversy. It turns out that he had also preached at a Greek Orthodox cathedral in Queens, New York, when an icon there—that of a mid-nineteenth-century nun, St. Irene—began crying and drawing hundreds of thousands of pilgrims, some from as far away as India and Japan. More than a year later, after I had investigated that icon with the New York Area Skeptics and concluded that the phenomenon was bogus (Nickell 1993), the icon was stolen at gunpoint. Supposedly, Katseas refused to cooperate in producing the key to the case that housed it and was pistol-whipped, after which the bandits broke the lock and made off with the "miraculous" icon. It was subsequently returned—minus $800,000 in gems and golden jewelry that decorated it—under conditions that remain controversial (Christopoulos 1996).

Katseas was also defrocked in 1993 when it was learned he had previously worked in a brothel in Athens. A church document on the priest's excommunication states that a New York ecclesiastical court found him guilty of slander, perjury, and defamation, as well as being "in the employ of a house of prostitution" (Goldhar 1996). In fact, in 1987, in sworn testimony before a Greek judge, Katseas admitted he had been so employed (Magnish et al. 1996).

A rumor I heard from neighborhood residents was soon confirmed by a newspaper report, namely that the Toronto icon began weeping after the East York church found itself financially strapped with an accumulated debt from mortgages of almost $271,000. In June, in response to the debt situation, the church dispatched Father Archimandrite Gregory from Colorado with instructions to evict Katseas from the church, but the matter became mired in the courts. After the icon began "weeping," Gregory cast doubt on the phenomenon, stating in a letter, "It would not be surprising if this were a hoax, in order to attract people to spend money" (Goldhar 1996). Such revelations and opinions, however, had no effect on some pilgrims. Said one woman: "I don't care if there's a pipe and a hose behind that picture. I don't care if the Virgin Mary jumps right out of the painting. You either believe in miracles or you don't. I believe" (DiManno 1996). On the other hand, a woman living in the neighborhood stated, "We all need something to believe in, but this is preying on those who really need a miracle" (Goldhar 1996).

LABORATORY TESTS

Subsequently, on August 27, 1997, I returned to the church, invited by attorneys for the parent Orthodox Church authority. Attended by a police guard stationed outside, a detective from the police fraud squad, and members of the Canadian news media (figure 10.1), I examined the icon carefully. (For the purpose, a carpenter assigned to assist me dismantled the frame the icon had acquired.)

This time putting my "weeping icon kit" to good use, I took samples of the oil and signed them over to the detective for testing by the police crime laboratory (Kudrez 1997). Later, at a forensic conference in Nova Scotia (where I was a lecturer), I learned that the oil had indeed proved to be of a nondrying variety. However, since obviously there was no one to say who put it on the icon, the case went nowhere.

Figure 10.1. Joe Nickell closely examines the "weeping" icon in a Greek Orthodox church before taking samples for analysis by a crime laboratory. (Author's photo)

CHAPTER 11

THE CASE OF THE MIRACLE OIL

For a new television series on the Oprah Winfrey Network (OWN) called *Miracle Detectives*, I was invited to a home in Northern California where myriad icons, statues, and other religious effigies were "miraculously streaming oil"—"healing" oil, some claim. There I joined cohosts Randall Sullivan (whose book *The Miracle Detective* [2004] prompted the series) and Indre Vískontas (a neuroscientist and skeptic) (figure 11.1). Indre introduced me on the show by announcing: "Joe Nickell is one of the most prominent debunkers of purported miraculous or supernatural events in the country—maybe even the world." As it happened, I had long ago suggested the case was one of pious fraud (Fernandez 2001). What would an on-site investigation reveal?

BACKGROUND

The home I visited in Union City, California, belonged to a diminutive Philippine American woman named Cora Lorenzo. There, in 1991, she hung by the front door in her living room a holy-water font she had bought on a trip to Lourdes, the French healing shrine. One November evening in 1995, Lorenzo noticed that the water had dried up. The next morning, however, which happened to be the Catholic feast of the Pentecost, the font had mysteriously been refilled with scented oil. Both her husband and twenty-four-year-old son denied that they had placed it there.

Soon, word of the "miracle" spread, and visitors—mostly the Catholic faithful—began to come in swarms. Some left their own icons and holy figurines overnight, only to retrieve them the next day drizzled with oil. Claims of healings—from headaches to rashes to arthritis—began to be reported. More visitors came from as far away as Indonesia, Australia, Holland, and Nigeria.

In 2001, the *San Jose Mercury News* featured the oil story but included more than a trickle of skepticism. A spokesperson for the Diocese of San Jose urged that such claims should be given "great caution." Described as "a professional debunker," I was quoted in observing that nondrying oils like olive oil could remain fresh looking for long periods of time. (Since they do not evaporate like water, such oils have become favored for weeping-icon trickery.) I mentioned other cases of "miraculous" oily or bloody effigies that ranged from those that remain unproven to those that have been determined to be fraudulent. Moreover, although there were unverified claims of the oil samples miraculously increasing in quantity (rather like the self-replenishing jar of oil in the Old Testament [2 Kings 4:1–7]), the *Mercury News* reported that this did not happen to the vial of oil the newspaper received from Cora Lorenzo (Fernandez 2001).

INVESTIGATING ON SITE

When I met Lorenzo at her home on May 24, 2010, she hugged me and said she had wanted to meet me ever since I appeared on a Discovery Channel special on miracles some ten years before (figure 11.2). The home was filled with effigies, including statues of the Virgin and the children of Fatima, multiple copies of the *Image of Guadalupe* and the Shroud of Turin, and other such reproductions.

Initially puzzled by the proliferation of oil, Vískontas nodded understandingly as we toured the display and I pointed out, using a magnifier, how the oil was often suspiciously placed (figure 11.3): it was spattered onto a mirror, placed above or outside the eyes of statuary for an unconvincing "weeping" look, separately placed (not dripped from the eyes) onto hands, and indeed was indistinguishable from careless human placement. In addition, Vískontas wondered aloud why the oil would appear not only on religious items but also on walls, door jambs, and the like.

The *Miracle Detectives* segment on the case, "Mysterious Oils" (the second part of the January 5, 2011, episode), featured a forensic construction expert, Robert G. Cox, who has fifty years' experience in building inspection. Cox's findings matched my own. Demolishing the idea that the oil was somehow seeping into the room from outside—as by Lorenzo possibly having "leaky oil tanks in her attic" (Fernandez 2001)—Cox pointed out that the gypsum drywall was covered with enamel paint, which he observed "is a fairly dense material." Using a pocket microscope he observed "dots" of oil, indicating it had been splattered onto the wall—similar to the spatter patterns I had noted here and there. Cox concluded the oil was therefore appearing from inside the room.

But was the oil freshly flowing, as some people believed? It was never doing so, apparently, when the scene was properly observed. As the *Mercury News* reported nearly a decade earlier (Fernandez 2001), "During a reporter's two visits to Lorenzo's house, oil was present on the walls and statues, but did not flow on either occasion." I showed Vískontas how a trickle that is already on a statue or icon could go unnoticed from one low-light vantage point, then, as the viewer moved, catch light and glint as if it had suddenly appeared. (I have been at sites where flickering candles placed before an oil-streaming icon could cause the trickles to seem to be moving—flowing—although they were actually static.) There were no unambiguous fresh flows during the two days I was on site.

Still, we agreed to test the issue using video surveillance, although Sullivan was somewhat uneasy, feeling it amounted to "testing God." However, he said to me, "That's what you're here to do is test God, so, yeah." Lorenzo gave her permission to do whatever we wanted, so we wiped down a large oil-exhibiting statue of the Virgin, emptied the Lourdes font, and then trained a surveillance camera on each. We also placed a small statue in a plastic bag, which Vískontas and I heat sealed to prevent tampering, and (although not shown on the program) I took custody of another that I monitored overnight in my hotel room. The next day the three of us reconvened at the Lorenzo home to check the results of our tests. Not a single trace of fresh oil had appeared anywhere, as far as we could tell—certainly not on the effigies and font we had under observation. Things were not looking very miraculous.

HEALING OIL?

Nevertheless, how do we explain the reported healings? First of all, they are just that: reported. Besides, claims of "miraculous" healing are invariably predicated on being medically inexplicable, so claimants are simply engaging in a logical fallacy, *argumentum ad ignorantiam* (an "argument from ignorance")—that is, drawing a conclusion based on a lack of knowledge.

In fact, there are many potential explanations. For example, some illnesses, such as multiple sclerosis, are known to exhibit spontaneous remission. Other reputed cures may be attributable to such factors as misdiagnosis, prior medical treatment, psychosomatic conditions, the body's own natural healing mechanisms, and other factors. For such reasons, the international panel of physicians appointed by the Catholic Church to identify "miracles" at Lourdes, the French "healing" shrine, announced in 2008 that it would end the practice. Now the panel will only indicate that some cases are "remarkable." And remarkable healings may happen to anyone—independent of supposedly magical oil (Nickell 2008).

Miracle Detectives examined the claim of Marlene Alberto, a woman who reported having been miraculously healed of an eye ailment. Her "symptoms suggested" that she had a macular hole in her left eye. Reportedly, doctors recommended she have surgery; she preferred not to accept the risk, instead anointing her eye with oil from the Lorenzo home, whereupon the hole surprisingly closed. The show consulted Ronald P. Gallemore, MD, PhD, who pointed out that "spontaneous closure" sometimes occurs in such cases, with the opening filling in with scar tissue as a result of the body's own healing processes. Although such spontaneous closures are rare, they are not medically inexplicable and do not warrant the term *miracle*.

A CASE OF DECEPTION

When we emptied the Lourdes font using a syringe, we filled some flint-glass vials with the oil—one of which I kept while two others were sent to Flora Research Laboratories for testing. Meanwhile, the show consulted David Stewart, author of *Healing Oils of the Bible* (2002)—which is published by an aromatherapy company and touts the inclusion of God and his creations (such as oil-producing plants) in healthcare. Stewart sniffed a sample of the Lorenzo oil and found it to have a "spiritual" quality. However, he did suggest that analysis of the oil could be significant, since, as he told *Miracle Detectives*, "God's oils are not synthetic by definition."

Often, the testing of substances from weeping icons is of little benefit because, presumably, a deity could use any substance it wished and, anyway, it is the question of how the substance got on the effigy in the first place that matters. For example, actual "salty tears" were reported to flow from a plaster bas-relief in Pavia, Italy, but then the owner was secretly observed applying the liquid with a water pistol (Nickell 1997). Nevertheless, in several cases tests have been revelatory. In 1913 a color print that "bled" was exposed when the substance failed tests for human blood; in 1985 a bleeding statue of the Virgin at a home in Quebec was exposed as a hoax when the blood was tested and found to be mixed with animal fat (so that when the room warmed from pilgrims' body heat the substance would liquefy and flow realistically); and a case in Sardinia in 1995 was solved when DNA tests showed the blood was that of the statue's owner (chapter 9). In yet another instance, involving a home with statues on which oil appeared in the presence of a comatose girl, the substance proved to be 80 percent vegetable oil and 20 percent chicken fat, consistent with the use of kitchen drippings (Nickell 1999).

With such cases in mind, I was happy that the Lorenzo oil was to be tested. The laboratory report was instructive. While the substance was a vegetable oil, tests also revealed the presence of a glycol ether—a synthetic compound used as a fixative by the perfume industry ("in order," Vískontas explained, "to keep elements together"). Sullivan agreed with Stewart that it was unlikely that God would need to use a synthetic material.

With regard to the other evidence (especially the placement of the oil), he said to Vískontas that although he was disappointed, "You and I both agree, I think, that somebody's putting that oil there." That had always seemed likely to me, but now there was a preponderance of scientific evidence to that effect thanks to the *Miracle Detectives* investigation.

Figure 11.1. The cohosts of *Miracle Detectives* examine effigies with trickles of "miraculously" appearing oil at a home in Northern California. (Photo by Joe Nickell)

Figure 11.2. The author poses with Cora Lorenzo, whose home is famous as a shrine that pilgrims visit for "healing" oil. (Author's photo)

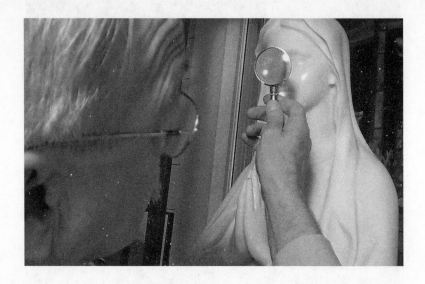

Figure 11.3. The author examines an oil-weeping Madonna on the porch of the Lorenzo home. (Author's photo)

CHAPTER 12

HINDU STATUES THAT DRINK MILK

Throughout the Hindu world on September 21, 1995, statues of Indian deities, seemingly miraculously, sipped spoonfuls of milk in supposed fulfillment of a devotee's dream.

As the phenomenon progressed, it spread from the deity Lord Ganesh, the elephant-headed, multihanded, Hindu god, to other idols, including Nandi the Bull and statues of Lord Shiva, who is often depicted in human form with a serpent around his neck. Spreading across India, the milk-sipping phenomenon soon extended to other parts of the Asian continent as well as to Europe and North America, where it was duly noted on television and in newspapers.

EXPLANATION

An Indian psychiatrist explained: "All people are vulnerable to such credulousness. Hindus were especially susceptible because this was the season of *pitr baksh*, when the devout offered milk for the souls of their ancestors" (cited in Nickell 1996). So many Hindus were caught up in the mass hysteria that milk supplies were depleted and prices soared—even for canned and powdered milk, although only "Kachcha," unboiled milk, was supposed to be accepted by the deities.

Skeptics pointed out that many of the statues were made of baked clay, which absorbs liquids prodigiously by capillary attraction. States Julia Higgins, professor of polymer chemistry at London's Imperial College,

"Break a flowerpot, dip it in water, and the water disappears like mad" (Nickell 1996). With glazed statues, only a bit of the glaze need be absent, say from a tooth (as indeed seemed the case in one statue), for capillary attraction to work.

But what about relatively nonporous materials like marble, or even nonporous ones such as brass and other metals? Some people noticed milk pooling at the bottoms of such statues but could not explain how it was getting there. The secret was discovered by India's Department of Science and Technology in New Delhi. Researchers there offered a statue milk mixed with a red dye and observed that while the milk quickly disappeared from the spoon, it soon coated the statue due to surface tension. Explained the secretary of the Indian Rationalists' Society, Sanal Edamaruku, when a spoonful of milk is offered to a "wet idol" (many of the idols had been ritually washed) the spoon is naturally tilted a bit and the milk imperceptibly drains over the idol in such a thin layer that is virtually transparent, especially on marble or other white or light-colored surfaces. "The basic principle behind it," says Edamaruku, "is that when two drops of a liquid are brought together it leads to the formation of one drop" (Nickell 1996).

Hoaxing was apparently responsible in a few cases. For example, *India Abroad* reported, "At a temple in the Bengali Market area of the capital, canisters with pipes running into them were found in the backyard. The canisters had gathered the milk fed by the devotees." And at a temple in Toronto investigated by CSICOP Fellow Henry Gordon, a well-known magician and author in Canada, the attendants refused to allow him to lift the small, thirsty idol from its large base. (He was also refused the opportunity to give the idol water and thus test the claim that it drank only milk.)

Although the widespread phenomenon reportedly ceased after one day, possibly due to official expectations, it continued in some homes in New York City for a time. Reported the *Miami Herald*, "It took 'the miracle' exactly eight days to reach Miami from India." On the other hand, at certain sites, such as the Ganesh temple in Toronto's Richmond Hill suburb, nothing ever happened.

Nature magazine reported that "science took a hammering from religion" over the affair, but it did so only on the propaganda level. *Nature* seemed heartened by the statement signed by prominent scientists in Madras. It called on educated Indians to help ensure "that primitive obscurantism and superstition did not hold sway over a society on the threshold of the 21st century" (Jayaraman 1995).

My initial involvement with the phenomenon was to monitor developments and answer news queries as well as to write an article about the events for *Skeptical Inquirer* magazine. At the end of May 2001, however, I had an opportunity to study the phenomenon with Indian skeptic Vikas Gora, who was visiting the Center for Inquiry, home of my office and paranormal-investigation lab. We spent a profitable afternoon replicating and discussing the milk-drinking effect. Vikas had actually witnessed the original "miracle" and had considerable first-hand knowledge about the entire matter, which he was eager to share.

Our experiments confirmed that it does not matter what effigy is used, although white is obviously best if milk is to be the beverage. When a colored figurine is used, water may be substituted for the milk. Although the statue does need to be wet for the first demonstration, thereafter each successive dribbling prepares the figure for the next apparent sipping. Also, the effect works best if the spoon is filled to the brim with liquid.

CHAPTER 13

THE STATUES THAT GLOW

T
wo women noticed it first, about August 4, 2003: the eyes of the Virgin Mary statue on the church's bell tower had begun to glow; so had the statue's halo and Sacred Heart. Subsequently the same features of a Jesus statue on the tower's opposite side were also observed to shine mysteriously.

Soon, thousands of pilgrims and curiosity seekers had flocked to the site, St. Joseph the Provider Catholic Church in Campbell, Ohio, just south of Youngstown (Horton 2003; Kubik 2003).

ON SITE

I decided to take in the spectacle and conduct an investigation. Donning a suitable disguise as a pilgrim, which included an ostentatious cross hung from my neck, I drove to Campbell on Saturday, August 16, 2003. As I neared the site I occasionally stopped to ask for directions and thus get feedback from local residents.

At my first stop, a fast-food restaurant in nearby Hubbard, Ohio, I asked a workman about the "miracle statues." Climbing down from his stepladder he said that he had not heard about them and cautioned, "I wouldn't put much faith in statues." Closer to the church, a convenience store clerk was familiar with stories about the supposedly miraculous phenomenon but offered a condescendingly skeptical smile while giving directions.

Arriving at the church in the afternoon, I decided to change quickly into the persona of investigative journalist—complete with photographer's vest, camera, and notebook. In this way I could freely go about my business of taking numerous photographs, making experiments (more on this presently), and conducting interviews.

As luck would have it, I was able to catch St. Joseph's busy young priest, Michael Swierz, as he was hurrying into the church. I identified myself as a writer with "*Skeptical Inquirer*, the science magazine." He flashed a smile and repeated what he had recently told the Associated Press, that there was a ready explanation for the phenomenon. He stated that during the 1970s the pair of statues had their halo, eyes, and hearts covered with gold leaf. He thought that rain might have washed away the grime or that some chemical reaction might have taken place, causing the gold to shine more brightly ("Priest Offers Explanation" 2003; Swierz 2003).

Reverend Swierz told me the real miracle was that the phenomenon—which had apparently only been noticed recently—had brought together so many diverse people from various places.

EXAMINATION

It seemed easy to confirm the priest's basic explanation. During the afternoon I was able to observe that the gilded areas, especially those of the Sacred Heart of Mary statue (which faces west) were shining brightly while the sun was out, but they dimmed whenever clouds obtruded. Several other statues on the grounds—all lacking gilding—failed to shine. (Local photographer John Yavorsky shared my observation and, equipped with a telephoto lens, kindly shot an extra roll of film for me [see figure 13.1].)

A few people were insistent that the phenomenon occurred even at night, supposedly disproving the shining hypothesis and indicating that the statues were indeed glowing. I resolved to return in the evening, when a crowd would be expected to gather.

After securing lodging and eating supper, I returned for the evening gathering—or "show," as the *Cleveland Plain Dealer* termed it (Horton 2003). I brought along a pair of binoculars and a flashlight and joined the latest crowd of pilgrims trampling the grass of the church's east and west courtyards.

After dark, the two statues continued to shine much as before (albeit without the fluctuations caused by waxing and waning sunlight). However, there were obviously streetlights and church security lights as sources of illumination as well as significant ambient light. I observed that the shining changed with the angle of viewing. Also, when I played the beam of my flashlight across each statue's gilded areas, there were distinct flashes of light. These practical experiments clearly demonstrated that the light was being *reflected*, not *transmitted*. In other words, there was no *glowing*, only the *shining* expected from the areas covered with gold leaf.

The following day, I made my third visit to the church grounds. I talked with a volunteer who was loading a vehicle with supplies for a church picnic. He said the gilding on the statues dated from about 1973 or 1974. He had thought it might have been redone about 1991, but said he was told that that had been judged too costly and had not been carried out. He stated that he had noticed the effect for years but thought nothing of it until it began to receive attention.

He thus confirmed the suggestion of Monsignor Robert Siffrin, vicar-general of the Youngstown, Ohio, Catholic diocese. Monsignor Siffrin said that the shining areas of the statues may have always reflected light and that some people had previously noticed it without drawing attention to it. He agreed with Father Swierz "that light is reflected off the gold leaf" (Kubik 2003).

FURTHER OBSERVATIONS

I spent much time studying the two statues with binoculars, which gave me a good look at the shining areas. Having been a professional sign painter in my youth (Nickell 2001), with hands-on experience in applying gold leaf, I recognized its distinctive appearance on the church statues. It was surely genuine gilding and not the "gold leaf paint" mentioned in some news accounts (see Kubik 2003). ("Gold" paint is typically made with bronze powder as a pigment, and it soon tarnishes [Owen 1958]. Only genuine leaf has the look and brilliance of gold like that on the church's statues, and it is widely used for such outdoor applications, including the famous gold dome of the Denver, Colorado, capitol [Green 2003].)

A brief discussion of the process of surface gilding (distinct from glass—or window—gilding) will be instructive. The process involves the use of either a "quick" (varnish-based) or "slow" (linseed-oil-based) size, the latter permitting "a more brilliant burnish" and enhancing durability. The size is brushed over a suitably primed surface and allowed to dry to "a hard, dry-feeling tack," whereupon incredibly thin squares of beaten gold are then laid on (Owen 1958, 57). The leaves may be purchased "loose" (interleaved between the pages of a book) or in "patent" form (lightly adhered to a paper backing); patent gold is preferred for gilding in the wind (Owen 1958, 57–59; Duvall 1952, 52, 65–66; Sutherland 1889, 6–7).

Finally, after the leaves have been applied in overlapping fashion, they are burnished and then covered with a protective coat of varnish. "This will cut down on the brilliance of the leaf somewhat," notes one authoritative text (Owen 1958, 59), "but durability will be insured."

My observations of the supposedly glowing statues in Campbell revealed that, not unexpectedly, the gold was missing in places, and where it was present some areas were brighter than others. I suspect that some of the protective overcoating is still on the duller areas, but that it has largely worn off the rest, causing them to shine even more brightly.

CONCLUSIONS

I found nothing that seemed even remotely supernatural at the site, although much miracle mongering was going on. Some people claimed, for example, that reddish streaks below the Jesus statue were evidence of miraculous "blood," even though these came not from the body (for example, the heart or areas of Jesus' crucifixion wounds) but from the very bottom of the box-like base. I thought it much more likely that they were rust stains from the hardware that secured the statue to the bell tower.

Emotional belief is not easy to counter with dispassionate reason and evidence, however. One woman, who saw me taking photographs and scribbling notes, asked my opinion of the "glowing" phenomenon. When I explained my findings and concluded that the gold was merely shining, she managed a smile and said, "I prefer not to believe that." Such is the way some minds are inoculated against disproof.

Figure 13.1. One of two supposedly miraculous statues at an Ohio Catholic church whose eyes, halo, and Sacred Heart reportedly began "glowing." (Author's photo by John Yavorsky.)

PART 2
MAGICAL RELICS

CHAPTER 14

THE TRUE CROSS: CHAUCER, CALVIN, AND RELIC MONGERS

Although there is little justification in either the Old or the New Testament to support what would become a cult of relics in early Christianity, such a practice did develop. And relics were typically said to have miraculous properties.

The earliest veneration of Christian relics can be traced to about 156 CE when Polycarp, the bishop of Smyrna, was martyred and his burned remains were gathered for veneration. In time, the distribution and veneration of packets of dust, tiny fragments of bone or cloth, and the like—associated with martyrs and saints—became common. At about 400 CE, St. Augustine deplored the excesses and outright fraud of the relic business, disparaging "hypocrites in the garb of monks for hawking about the limbs of martyrs," adding skeptically, "if indeed of martyrs" (*Encyclopedia Britannica* 1978, s.v. "Relics").

Among other, later critics was Geoffrey Chaucer (ca. 1340–1400), whose great unfinished work *The Canterbury Tales* contains a satirical attack on relic mongering. An even more scathing condemnation comes from John Calvin (1509–1564), the Protestant reformer, whose *Treatise on Relics* is a surprisingly modern look at the Roman Catholic Church's veneration of relics. Both Chaucer and Calvin weighed in on those most quintessentially Christian relics, fragments of the reputed Holy Cross itself. Here is a summary of their views, supplemented by my own investigations and research on the cross, which according to legend was discovered in the fourth century by St. Helena.

CHAUCER'S "PARDONER'S TALE"

The Canterbury Tales (ca. 1386–1400) is Geoffrey Chaucer's fictional classic compilation of stories told by traveling pilgrims, including the host of the Tabard Inn in Southwark, England, from which said pilgrims set out, wending their way to Canterbury Cathedral. "The Pardoner's Tale" satirizes phony relics in a classic of skepticism worthy of a brief retrospective here. The pardoner—one who sells the church's forgiveness of sins—is a pretentious fellow, as hinted in the opening lines (in quaint Middle English):

> "Lordynges," quod he, "in chirches whan I preche,
> I peyne me to han an hauteyn speche,
> And rynge it out as round as gooth a belle,
> For I kan al by rote that I telle.
> My theme is alwey oon, and ever was—
> '*Radix malorum est cupiditas.*'"

That is, as I translate it (and all that follows) into modern English:

> "My Lords," said he, "in churches when I preach,
> I do take pains to have a high-toned speech,
> And ring it out as roundly as a bell,
> For I know by rote all that I tell.
> My theme's to be the same and always will
> That 'Greed is at the root of all evil.'"

But the pardoner is merely a hypocrite. First, he displays his letters of approval signed by the pope. Then he brings out his reliquaries, with bits of cloth and other alleged relics, including the shoulder bone of a sheep, and declares:

> "If when this bone be washed in any well,
> If cow, or calf, or sheep, or ox should swell
> From eaten worm, or by a snake's been stung,
> Take water of that well and wash its tongue,
> And it is healed forthwith; and furthermore,

Of poxes and of scabs and every sore
Shall every sheep be healed, that of this well
Drinks a draft; take heed of what I tell."

He adds that the relic-treated water will cause farm animals to multiply and will put an end to all human jealousy, including distrust of a wife's faithfulness—even if she has lain with two or three priests! Of another ruse, he admits,

"By this trick I've won, year by year,
A hundred marks since I was Pardoner.
I stand as if a cleric in my pulpit,
And when the common people down do sit,
I preach, so as you've heard me say before,
And even tell a hundred falsehoods more."

Acknowledging his hypocrisy, he states:

"Thus can I preach against the self-same vice
Which I do use, and that is avarice.
But, though I too am guilty of that sin,
Yet can I make other folk to turn
From avarice, and hurry to repent.
But that is not my principal intent."

The pardoner then goes on to tell his tale. (It features three young rogues who set out on a drunken quest to slay evil Death. An old man directs them to a spot where they instead discover a treasure of gold coins. Unfortunately, they end up killing each other out of avarice and so indeed find death.)

Finished with his morality tale, the pardoner makes a direct pitch to his host, who rails against the fraudulent relics while indicating his own belief in the relic of the True Cross. The pardoner begins the exchange:

"Come forth, sir host, and offer first then,
And you shall kiss the relics every one,
Yes, for fourpence! Unbuckle now your purse."

"Nay, nay," said he, "then I'd have Christ's curse!
It shall not be, however you beseech me.
You would have me kiss your old breeches,
And swear they were a relic of a saint,
Although they're stained with your own fundament!
But by the cross which Saint Helena found,
I'd like to have your bollocks in my hand
Instead of relics or reliquarium;
Let's cut them off, I'll help to carry them;
They shall be enshrined within a hog's turd."
This pardoner answered not a word.

(The Knight helps make peace between the two men, whereupon the pilgrims "rode forth on their way.")

Now, Chaucer's own view of the True Cross is unstated, but having it endorsed by his central character, a good Christian and a man of seeming integrity, suggests that Chaucer accepts the relic allegedly found by St. Helena as authentic. Nevertheless, if he does not condemn all relics outright, Chaucer does identify and disparage fraudulent relic practices. At the time he was writing, this was a bold stance for a writer to take. Reformist John Calvin, however, writing a century and a half later, took the matter several steps further.

CALVIN ON RELICS

John Calvin's condemnation of relics is sweeping. In his *Treatise on Relics* (1543), he observes that "the desire for relics is never without superstition, and what is worse, it is usually the parent of idolatry" (Calvin 1543, 218). He is unrelenting in his withering look at relics—from the reputed Holy Blood, "exhibited in more than a hundred places" (226), to the many bogus holy shrouds (including today's controversial one, which was kept at Nice in Calvin's time; it wasn't transferred to Turin until 1578 [Nickell 2009, 40]).

Calvin had much to say about the pieces of the alleged True Cross—the location of which was supposed to have been miraculously revealed to St. Helena in 326 CE. Calvin suggested that "if we were to collect all these pieces of the True Cross exhibited in various parts, they would form a whole ship's cargo." He also said that there were more relics of it "than three hundred men could carry," adding, "As an explanation of this, [the relic mongers] have invented the tale, that whatever quantity of wood may be cut off this true cross, its size never decreases. This is, however, such a clumsy and silly imposture, that the most superstitious may see through it" (233).

Calvin specifically refers to the alleged fragment known as the *Titulus Crucis* (cross title board). Bearing the inscription "This is the King of the Jews," the Titulus—with text in Greek, Latin, and Hebrew—was ordered by Pilate to be placed on the cross (Luke 23:38). Two churches, Calvin delights in observing, lay claim to this relic. Actually, Helena supposedly divided the Titulus into three pieces, only one of which now remains—kept, as Calvin noted (234), in Rome's Church of the Holy Cross.

Modern science has validated Calvin's skepticism of the Titulus. First, the artifact contains a number of anachronisms and other problematic elements that indicate it is a probable forgery (Nickell 2007, 86–90). For example, although the Hebrew (or Aramaic) letters are correctly written from right to left, so—incorrectly—are the Greek and Latin lines. Based on my research on the history of writing, as soon as I saw this error (see my drawing, figure 14.1), I thought it a prima facie indication of spuriousness (see my *Pen, Ink, and Evidence* [Nickell 1990]).

Another paleographic error is found in the Greek line. Although it is written in mirror-image fashion from right to left, one letter—the *z*—is not reversed. This further emphasizes the problematic nature of the writing and suggests that the writer may not have been familiar with the ancient languages. Unless we accept the rationalizations of the Titulus's defenders (Thiede and d'Ancona 2000, 96–100), spelling errors also cast doubt on the inscription. Another doubtful feature is the letters having not just been painted but first incised into the wood—a seemingly gratuitous enhancement—whereas one would instead expect a hastily prepared placard intended to be used quickly and then discarded.

Indeed, such suspicions are confirmed via radiocarbon dating. A sample of the walnut wood (*Juglans regia*) was taken from the back of the slab, cleaned to remove any contamination, and then subjected to the carbon-dating process. Control samples of varying ages were also included to confirm the accuracy of the process. The tests on the Titulus revealed that it was made between 980 and 1146 CE (Bella and Azzi 2002)—a date range incompatible with its alleged first-century origin but consistent with the period (1144–1145) when the artifact was apparently acquired (Nickell 2007, 86–90).

THE FRAGMENTS

Over the years I have encountered pieces of the alleged True Cross (figure 14.2), together with the pious legends of their acquisition. In my own collection are a pilgrim's token of the True Cross (reputedly made in the seventh century by mixing clay with some ash from a burned piece of the cross) and a small bronze Byzantine cross of about the same time period (Nickell 2007, 79, 93). The latter was a legacy of Constantine the Great (274–337), who issued an edict that tolerated Christianity after having a miraculous vision of a flaming cross in the sky—a vision that is both doubtful and of later vintage (Nickell 2007, 77–79).

It is another reputed vision—that of Constantine's mother, Queen Helena (later St. Helena)—to which is attributed the finding of the True Cross. In 326, nearly three centuries after the crucifixion, Helena went to Jerusalem, where she allegedly discovered the site of the cross's conceal-ment, supposedly with divine inspiration: either by heavenly signs, dreams, or the guidance of a Jew named Judas. In fact, she supposedly located, beneath rubble, three crosses—supposedly of Jesus and the two thieves crucified with him (Matthew 27:38)—but was unable to distinguish which was Jesus'. Each cross was then tested on a mortally ill woman, and one—according to the fanciful legend—miraculously healed her, thus proving it was the *Vera Crux*, the True Cross.

Supposedly a portion of the cross was given to Constantine while another was taken to Rome. The main portion remained in the custody of successive bishops of Jerusalem; it was captured by Persians in 614 but then victoriously returned in 627. Finally, in 1187 it was lost forever, after cru-sading Franks occupied Jerusalem.

Nevertheless, alleged fragments of the True Cross and Roman nails from the crucifixion proliferated. As early as the mid-fourth century, St. Cyril of Jerusalem (ca. 315–386) wrote that "already the whole world is filled with fragments of the wood of the Cross." From the fifth century on, a "cult of the Cross" developed and churches were erected in the True

Cross's name. In a letter, St. Paulinus of Nola (353–431) dared to explain (and Calvin would later satirize, as we have seen) the claim that, regardless of how many pieces were taken from the cross, it never diminished in size—a "fact" that has been compared with Jesus' Miracle of the Multiplying Loaves and Fishes (Cruz 1984, 39).

I was able to view a purported piece of the True Cross in Turin in 2004. It was set in a cruciform reliquary (along with a purported relic of the Holy Blood). The lighted reliquary is the focal point of a relic chapel—the crypt of the Church of Maria Ausiliatrice—which contains a fabulous collection of some five thousand relics of saints, exhibited in seemingly endless panels and display cases along the walls. Included are relics alleged to be from Mary Magdalene and, more credibly, St. Francis of Assisi.

In 2009 in Genoa I saw no fewer than four pieces of the "True Cross" arrayed in an elaborate reliquary cross (figure 14.2). The fragments were specifically claimed to be from the True Cross—or so "tradition has it." (Translation: "This is only a handed-down tale.") Known as *Croce degli Zaccaria* (or "cross of the Zaccaria"), it was formerly owned by a family of that name, who were among the major merchant traders of the eastern Mediterranean when Genoa was at its commercial and political peak. The reliquary was reportedly first commissioned in the ninth century, then remade in its present form (again see figure 14.2) between 1260 and 1283—a gilt and bejeweled cruciform artifact now displayed in the Museum of the Treasury of the Cathedral of San Lorenzo (St. Lawrence) of Genoa (Marica 2007, 6; "Museum of the Treasury," n. d.).

Again, the lack of any credible provenance (its traceability to some known point)—together with the incredible proliferation of such fragments and even the suspicious neatness of these four pieces of the "True Cross"—makes the Croce degli Zaccaria a piece to be entirely skeptical of, not revered.

CONCLUSION

There is no credible evidence that Helena, or anyone, found Jesus' cross (with or without accompanying crosses of the two thieves) in the fourth century—or at any other time for that matter. The provenance is laughable. Even more so is the absurd tale of its miraculousness: its infinite ability to restore itself no matter how many pieces were taken from it.

The proliferating pieces of the True Cross have been rivaled for out-landishness by many other bogus relics—such as over forty shrouds of Jesus and multiple corpses of Mary Magdalene (Nickell 2007, 40, 116). Geoffrey Chaucer and John Calvin were justifiably critical of relic hucksterism in their respective times, and we—with our modern scientific means of analysis, such as radiocarbon dating—must be no less so.

Figure 14.1. The Titulus Crucis, allegedly the placard on Jesus' cross, as mentioned in the Gospels, has now been radiocarbon tested. (Drawing by Joe Nickell)

Figure 14.2. Purportedly, the True Cross, "discovered" in the fourth century, could replenish itself miraculously—no matter how many pieces like these, mounted in a cross reliquary in Genoa, were removed. (Photo by Joe Nickell)

CHAPTER 15

THE HOLY BLOOD

A member of the European Union, Belgium is located between the Netherlands, Germany, and France. The country, which takes its name from its first recorded inhabitants, ancient Celts known as Belgae, has a rich history, having been a province of the Roman Empire, the heart of the Carolingian dynasty, and a celebrated medieval textile center. Today, among its many great attractions are such historic cities as Brussels, Ghent, and Bruges, together with museums of Flemish art. While it is a country of scientific advances (a world leader in heart and lung transplants as well as in fertility treatments [*World Desk Reference* 2000, 129]), it is also, according to many, a place of miracles.

I made my first investigative pilgrimage to Belgium in 1998 (accompanied by local skeptic Tim Trachet). I returned in 2006 (with Dutch science writer and translator Jan Willem Nienhuys) as a side excursion from travels in the Netherlands (Nickell 2007a). On both occasions, I looked at purported wonders such as the healing shrine known as the Belgian Lourdes (chapter 27), an ancient miracle statue (chapter 2), and a vial of the Holy Blood of Christ.

BLOOD OF CHRIST

John Calvin (1543, 226) critically observed that alleged blood of Jesus "is exhibited in more than a hundred places," one of the most celebrated being the Basilica of the Holy Blood in Bruges. I twice visited the site, and on the second occasion (October 25, 2006) I was able to hold in my hands the reliquary supposedly containing the very blood of Christ (figure 15.1). It has been called "Europe's holiest relic" (Coupe 2009, 132).

According to legend, the Bruges relic was obtained in Palestine in the mid-twelfth century, during the Second Crusade, by Thierry of Alsace. He allegedly received it from his relative Baldwin II, then King of Jerusalem, as a reward for meritorious service. However, chronicles of the crusades fail to mention the relic being present in Jerusalem (Aspeslag 1988, 10). Sources claim that Thierry, Count of Flanders, brought the relic to Bruges in 1150, while another source reports that it arrived in 1204. In any event, the earliest document that refers to it dates from 1270 (*Catholic Encyclopedia* 1913, s.v. "Bruges"; Aspeslag 1988, 9–11).

The reliquary, housed in the twelfth-century Basilica of the Holy Blood, is now brought out daily for veneration by the faithful. Although mistakenly characterized by at least one source as "a fragment of cloth stained with what is said to be the blood of Christ" (McDonald 2009, 145), it in fact consists of "clotted blood" contained in a vial set in a glass-fronted cylinder, each end of which is covered with gold coronets decorated with angels. The vial (made of rock crystal rather than glass) has been determined to be an eleventh- or twelfth-century Byzantine perfume bottle.

In 1310 Pope Clement V issued a papal bull granting indulgences to pilgrims who visited the chapel at Bruges and venerated the blood. At that time, believers claimed the blood miraculously returned to its original liquid state every Friday at noon. This not only sounds like a magic trick, but it evokes the similar suspect "miracle" of the blood of St. Januarius at Naples (discussed in chapter 21). (See also Nickell 2007b.)

Unfortunately, the Holy Blood at Bruges soon stopped liquefying, supposedly as the result of some blasphemy that occurred later in 1310. The miracle recurred only one more time, in 1388 (Aspeslag 1988, 11).

A CLOSE LOOK

Naturally, I wanted to get a good look at the "blood," so I twice stood in the pilgrims' line, supposedly to pray over the reliquary (again, see figure 15.1). In fact, although I bowed respectfully, I used the two brief occasions to scrutinize the substance. I observed that it had a waxen look and was bespeckled with "coagulated drops" that have suspiciously remained red (*Bruges Tourist Guide* 1998, 28) unlike blood, which blackens with age (Kirk 1974, 194–95).

In brief, the Holy Blood of Bruges lacks a credible provenance, since it has no record for a dozen centuries after the death of Jesus and is contained in a medieval bottle. It appeared with a profusion of other dubious blood relics, including several with which it had in common the property of liquefying and resolidifying, suggestive of a magic trick. Both that behavior and its current appearance are incompatible with genuine old blood and are instead indicative of a pious fraud.

Figure 15.1. Joe Nickell appears to be venerating the Holy Blood at Bruges but is really only getting a good look at it! (Author's photo by Jan Willem Nienhuys)

CHAPTER 16

THE IMAGE OF EDESSA REVEALED

Among certain reputedly miraculous images of Jesus—said to be *acheiropoietos* or "not made by hands"—was the Image of Edessa, known later to the Byzantines as the Mandylion (or "holy towel"). I was able to view this image, part of a traveling exhibition of "Vatican Splendors," in Cleveland, Ohio, on September 1, 2008. It bore the title "The Mandylion of Edessa," although the official exhibition catalog held some surprise revelations ("Mandylion of Edessa" 2008). I would discover others.

THE LEGEND

The story of the Edessan image is related in a mid-fourth-century Syriac text called *The Doctrine of Addai*. It tells how King Abgar of Edessa (now Urfa in south-central Turkey), afflicted with leprosy, sent a messenger named Ananias to deliver a letter to Jesus requesting a cure. In the letter (according to a tenth-century report [quoted in Wilson 1979, 272–90]), Abgar sends "greetings to Jesus the Savior who has come to light as a good physician in the city of Jerusalem" and who, he has heard, "can make the blind see, the lame walk . . . heal those who are tortured by chronic illnesses, and . . . raise the dead." Abgar decided that Jesus either is God himself or the Son of God, and so he entreats Jesus to "come to me and cure me of my disease." He notes that he has heard of the Jews' plan to harm Jesus and adds, "I have a very small city, but it is stately and will be sufficient for us both to live in peace."

Abgar, so the story goes, instructed Ananias that if he were unable to persuade Jesus to return with him to Edessa, he was to bring back a portrait instead. But while Ananias sat on a rock drawing the portrait, Jesus summoned him, divining his mission and the fact of the letter Ananias carried. After reading it, Jesus responded with a letter of his own, writing, "Blessed are you, Abgar, in that you believed in me without having actually seen me." Jesus said that while he must fulfill his mission on earth, he would later send one of his disciples to cure Abgar's suffering and to "also provide your city with a sufficient defense to keep all your enemies from taking it." After entrusting the letter to Ananias, "the Savior then washed his face in water, wiped off the moisture that was left on the towel that was given to him, and in some divine and inexpressible manner had his own likeness impressed on it." Jesus gave Ananias the towel to present to Abgar as "consolation" for his disease.

Quite a different version of the story (see Wilson 1979, 277–78) holds that the image was impressed with Jesus' bloody sweat during his agony in the Garden of Gethsemane (Luke 22:44). (This anticipates the still later tradition of Veronica's Veil, wherein Veronica, a woman from Jerusalem, was so moved by Jesus' struggling with his cross on the way to execution that she wiped his face on her veil or kerchief, thus imprinting it with his bloody sweat. Actually, the term *veronica* is simply a corruption of the Latin words *vera iconica*, "true images" [Nickell 2007, 71–76].) In this second version of the story, Jesus' disciple Thomas held the cloth for safekeeping until Jesus ascended to heaven, whereupon it was then sent to King Abgar.

Significantly, the earliest mention of the Abgar/Jesus correspondence—an account of circa 325 CE by Bishop Eusebius—*lacks any mention of the holy image* (Nickell 1998, 45). Also, in one revealing fourth-century text of *The Doctrine of Addai*, the image is described not as of miraculous origin but merely as the work of Hannan (Ananias), who "took and painted a portrait of Jesus in choice paints, and brought it with him to his lord King Abgar" (quoted in Wilson 1979, 130).

Historian Sir Steven Runciman has denounced all versions of the legend as apocryphal: "It is easy to show that the story of Abgar and Jesus as we now have it is untrue, that the letters contain phrases copied from the gospels and are framed according to the dictates of later theology" (quoted in Sox 1978, 52).

THE MANDYLION'S JOURNEY

Nevertheless, Runciman adds, "that does not necessarily invalidate the tradition on which the story was based" (quoted in Sox 1978, 52). The best evidence in the case would be the image itself, but *which* image? There have been several, each claimed to be the miraculous original. Obviously, only one could be authentic, but does it even still exist?

The Mandylion has a gap in its provenance (or historical record) of several centuries. It was reportedly transferred in 944 to Constantinople, capital of the Byzantine Empire, along with the purported letter from Jesus to King Abgar. The image may once have been incorporated into a triptych of the tenth century. Its side panels, now reposing in the monastery of Saint Catherine on Mount Sinai, illustrate the pious legend of Abgar receiving the image. Interestingly, the panels portray Abgar as having the features of Byzantine emperor Constantine VII Porphyrogenitos.

After the Venetians conquered Constantinople in 1204, during the Fourth Crusade, the Mandylion was reportedly transferred to the West, where its history becomes confused. Three traditions develop, each associated with a different "original" of the image:

1. *Parisian Mandylion.* Allegedly obtained by Emperor Baldwin II and sold or donated by him in 1247, this image was eventually acquired by King Louis IX (1214–1270), who had it installed in the Sainte-Chapelle in Paris. It was lost in 1792, apparently destroyed during the French Revolution ("Mandylion of Edessa" 2008; Wilson 1991, 129).

2. *Genoese Mandylion.* Although this image reportedly can be traced back to the tenth century, its verifiable history dates from 1362 when then Byzantine Emperor John V donated it to Genoa's Doge Leonardo Montaldo. After Montaldo died in 1384, the Mandylion was bequeathed to the Genoese Church of St. Bartholomew of the Armenians, arriving in 1388. It remains there, displayed in a gilt-silver, enameled frame of the fourteenth-century Palaeologan style. The image itself is on a cloth that has been glued to a wooden board ("Mandylion of Edessa" 2008; "Image of Edessa" 2008; Wilson 1991, 113–14, 137–38).

3. *Vatican Mandylion.* This image (figure 16.1) has no certain history before the sixteenth century, when it was known to be kept at the convent of San Silvestro in Capito. In 1517, the nuns were reportedly forbidden to exhibit it, so it would not compete with the church's Veronica. And in 1587 it was mentioned by one Cesare Baromio. In 1623 it received its silver frame, donated by Sister Dionora Chiarucci. It remained at San Silvestro until 1870 when, during the war that completed the unification of Italy, Pope Pius IX had it removed to the Vatican for safekeeping. Except when traveling, it still reposes in the Vatican's Matilda Chapel ("Mandylion of Edessa" 2008; "Image of Edessa" 2008; Wilson 1991, 139–40).

These are the three Edessan Mandylions that have been claimed as original. Others—such as a seventeenth-century Mandylion icon in Buckingham Palace in London, surrounded by painted panels (Wilson 1979, 111)—need not concern us here.

IMAGE ANALYSIS

The Vatican now concedes (in the words of the official Vatican Splendors exhibit catalog "Mandylion of Edessa" 2008]) that "the Mandylion is no longer enveloped today by any legend of its origin as an image made without the intervention of human hands."

In the summer of 1996, the Vatican Museum's chemistry and painting restoration laboratory analyzed their Mandylion. It was taken out of its baroque reliquary and removed from its silver-sheet frame (made in 1623). Glued to a cedar support panel was the linen cloth on which the face of Christ was clearly "painted," although the nondestructive tests were insufficient to specifically confirm that the painting medium was tempera.

While "the thin layer of pigment showed no traces of overpainting," there were nonetheless "alterations in the execution of the nose, mouth, and eyes" that were "observed in the x-rays and thermographic and reflectographic photographs." Specifically, the nose had once been shorter, "so that the image originally must have had a different physiognomy" ("Mandylion of Edessa" 2008, 57–58).

The museums' scholars learned (according to "Mandylion of Edessa" 2008, 56):

The version in the Vatican and the one in Genoa are almost wholly identical in their representation, form, technique, and measurements. Indeed, they must at some point in their history have crossed paths, for the rivet holes that surround the Genoese image coincide with those that attach the Vatican Mandylion to the cutout sheet of silver that frames the image. . . . So this silver frame, or one like to it, must also have originally covered the panel in Genoa.

ICONOGRAPHY

The Mandylion clearly has been copied and recopied, as if the different versions were just so many "icons" (as they are now called). It is not surprising that many of them appeared. According to Thomas Humber (1978, 92), "Soon the popular demand for more copies representing the 'true likeness' of Christ was such that selected artists were allowed or encouraged to make duplications." Indeed, "there was, conveniently, another tradition supporting the copies: the Image could miraculously duplicate itself."

Because icons were traditionally painted on wood, the fact that both the Vatican and Genoese Mandylions are on linen suggests that each was intended to be regarded as the original Edessan image. That image was described in the tenth-century account as "a moist secretion without coloring or painter's art," an "impression" of Jesus' face on "linen cloth" that—as is the way of legend—"eventually became indestructible" (quoted in Wilson 1979, 273).

While the original image appears lost to history, Ian Wilson (1979, 119–21) goes so far as to argue that the Edessan image has survived—indeed, that it is nothing less than the Shroud of Turin, the alleged burial cloth of Jesus! To the obvious rejoinder that the early Mandylions bore only a facial image whereas the Turin "shroud" bears full-length frontal and dorsal images, Wilson argues that the latter may have been folded in such a way as to exhibit only the face. Also there is an eighth-century account of King Abgar receiving a cloth with the image of Jesus' whole body ("Image of Edessa" 2008). Unfortunately, the Turin cloth has no provenance prior to the mid-fourteenth century when—according to a later bishop's report to the pope—an artist confessed it was his handiwork. Indeed, the image is rendered in red ocher and vermilion tempera paint—not as a positive image but as a negative one, as if it were a bodily *imprint.* Moreover, the cloth has been radiocarbon dated to the time of the forger's confession (Nickell 1998). (Another image-bearing shroud—of Besançon, France—did not come from Constantinople in 1204 as alleged but was clearly a sixteenth-century copy of the Turin fake [Nickell 1998, 64].)

The evidence is lacking, therefore, that any of these figured cloths ever bore a "not-made-by-hands" image. Instead, they have evolved from unlikely legend to Edessan portrait to self-duplicating Mandylions to proliferating "Veronicas" to full-length body image—all supposedly of the living Jesus—and thence to imaged "shrouds" with simulated frontal and dorsal bodily imprints. Finally, modern science and scholarship have revealed the truth about these pious deceptions.

Figure 16.1. This allegedly miraculous portrait of Jesus is actually a sixteenth-century painted fake. (Photo by Joe Nickell)

CHAPTER 17

THE HOLY MANDYLION: A DÉJÀ-VIEW

It was like déjà-vu. As discussed in the previous chapter, in 2008, in a traveling exhibition called "Vatican Splendors," I had seen the Holy Mandylion, also known as the Image of Edessa, which was once held to be the miraculous self-portrait of Christ (Nickell 2009). Now, in Genoa the following year, I was seeing another such image and recalling how in the Dark Ages the Image was said to be able to miraculously duplicate itself—one way to explain how there could be so many "originals."

PIOUS LEGEND

The original, according to legend, was produced for King Abgar of Edessa after he sent a messenger, Ananias, with a letter to Jesus requesting a cure for the king's leprosy. If Jesus was unable to come, Ananias was instructed, he was to bring the holy man's portrait instead. But as Ananias attempted to paint a picture Jesus himself intervened, washing his face in water and inexplicably imprinting his visage on a towel—hence the name *Mandylion*, a unique word of Byzantine Greek coinage describing a holy facecloth (Wilson 1979, 272–90; "Mandylion of Edessa" 2008).

Alas, this legend is unknown before the fourth century; moreover, there are conflicting versions. One attributes the image to the bloody sweat exuded by Jesus during his agony in the Garden of Gethsemane (Luke 22:44). A later legend holds that a woman named Veronica, who pitied Jesus as he struggled with his cross on the way to his crucifixion, gave him her veil or kerchief with which to wipe his bloody, sweaty face. In fact, however, this made-up tale obviously derives from the fact that Veronica is simply a corruption of *vera iconica*, medieval Latin for "true images" (Nickell 2007, 71–76). In one revealing fourth-century text of the Edessan legend, the image is not claimed as miraculous but instead merely the work of Hannan (Ananias), who "painted a portrait of Jesus in choice paints" and gave it to the king (quoted in Wilson 1979, 130).

Astonishingly, many Shroud of Turin devotees, following Ian Wilson (1979, 119–21), believe the "shroud" is the lost original of the Edessan image! How do they equate the latter's face-only image with the full-length, front-and-back bodily images of the Turin cloth? They imagine the shroud was folded so that only the face showed—never mind its lack of record for over thirteen centuries, a bishop's report of the forger's confession, pigments and paint that make up the image and "blood," and radiocarbon dating to the time of the forger's confession: about the middle of the fourteenth century (Nickell 1998; 2007) (see chapter 18).

COMPETING MANDYLIONS

According to the authoritative source *The Dictionary of Art* (Turner 1996), the Edessan image "entered Christian iconography during the 11th and 12th centuries, first in manuscript picture cycles that were elaborated to accompany narratives of the Edessan legend and then as part of a fixed scheme of images in church decoration." As we saw in the previous chapter, three of these "original" Mandylions have received the most attention, each supposedly having been the very one brought to Constantinople in 1204 by crusaders. One, the Parisian Mandylion, was acquired by King Louis IX in the thirteenth century and became lost in 1792, probably destroyed in the French Revolution.

Of the two surviving examples, the Vatican Mandylion has no certain history prior to the sixteenth century. In 1517 the nuns of San Silvestro in Capito were reportedly forbidden to exhibit it so that it would not compete with their church's "Veronica" (Wilson 1991). The Vatican now concedes (in the official Vatican Splendors exhibit text ["Mandylion of Edessa" 2008]) that "the Mandylion is no longer enveloped today by any legend of its origin as an image made without the intervention of human hands."

I understand this to be an admission not only that the Vatican version is merely an artist's rendering, but also that such is true of all Mandylions.

This brings us to the other surviving image, the Genoese Mandylion. It, too, lacks meaningful provenance. It is allegedly traceable to the tenth century, but its verifiable history dates only from 1362. At that time Byzantine emperor John V donated it to Genoa's Doge Leonardo Montaldo after whose death in 1384 it was bequeathed to the Genoese Church of St. Bartholomew of the Armenians. It arrived there in 1388; that is where it remains and where I photographed it (figure 17.1), displayed in a gilt-silver enameled frame of the fourteenth-century Palaeologan style.

Interestingly, fragments of ancient Persian and Arabian fabrics were found stuck on the back of the Genoese icon panel. The Arabian fragment is from the sixteenth century, whereas the figural silk Persian one has been attributed to the tenth century on stylistic grounds. However, radiocarbon testing of the wood gave a more reliable date range of 1240–1280 (Wolf 2005).

SIMILARITIES

Both the Vatican and the Genoese Mandylions are painted (the Genoese in egg tempera, the Vatican apparently the same) on linen cloth that has been glued to a wood panel ("Mandylion of Edessa" 2008; Church of St. Bartholomeo degli Armeni 2009; Wilson 1991, 113–14, 137–38). However, both X-rays and tomography (an X-ray technique whereby selected planes are photographed) reveal that the Genoese image-bearing cloth covers *an original image painted on wood* (Bozzo 1994). Also, the Vatican's on-cloth image shows alterations (in X-rays and reflectographic and thermographic photographs), especially in the nose, which was originally shorter, "so that the image originally must have had a different physiognomy" ("Mandylion of Edessa" 2008, 58).

In 1996, the Vatican Museum's experts concluded (according to "Mandylion of Edessa" 2008, 58):

> The version in the Vatican and the one in Genoa are almost wholly identical in their representation, form, technique, and measurements. Indeed, they must at some point in their history have crossed paths, for the rivet

holes that surround the Genoese image coincide with those that attach
the Vatican Mandylion to the cutout sheet of silver that frames the
image. . . . So this silver frame, or one like to it must also have originally
covered in the Genoa.

See my summary comparison of the two Mandylions (table 17.1 [based
on "Mandylion of Edessa" 2008; Bozzo 1974; Wolf 2005]).

Indeed, the images themselves, as they now appear to the eye, are
remarkably alike. Measurement ratios—involving the most critical areas:
the eyes, lengthy nose, and mouth—are strikingly similar. Therefore, when
photographs of the images are brought to the same scale (based on inter-
pupillary distance), those features effectively superimpose, as I determined
by using computer-generated transparencies. (These were prepared by CFI
Libraries Director Tim Binga using photos taken by art experts [Wilson
1991, plates 13 and 14]. However, the lack of a forensic scale in each pre-
vents reaching a definite conclusion as to whether tracing might have been
involved.)

CONCLUSIONS

Since the prototypical image for the later Mandylions and "Veronicas" first
appeared in Constantinople in the tenth century, many copies have been
made. In one known seventeenth-century instance, no fewer than six "exact"
facsimiles were carefully made. Such replicas could later be mistaken for or
misrepresented as the original, as happened, for example, with one that was
specially made and sent to plague-ridden Venice in the 1470s; it later became
known as the Holy Face of Alicante in Spain (Wilson 1991, 101–108).

Perhaps this is what occurred in the case of the two existing Mandylions. The Genoese image, with its older provenance and two-stage creation, appears to be the earliest. Its original image was certainly an artist's
copy, since it was painted not on cloth but directly on the wood panel. (One
source reports that it has the same dimensions as the missing central panel
of a triptych in the St. Catharine's Monastery at Mount Sinai [Wolf 2005].)

Vatican experts acknowledge the evidence suggesting that their Mandylion is "a later replica of the one now in Genoa; that it was produced
in the fourteenth century, when the Genoese version . . . was given its

existing Palaeologan frame; and that it was then placed in the silver frame of the older version," thus explaining the matched rivet holes ("Mandylion of Edessa" 2008, 57). Their main reservation is that the alterations in the Vatican image's features (especially the nose) may be inconsistent with a simple, direct copy. However, it would seem that the alterations might be due only to the image having been alternately painted and corrected in the freehand process of copying it. Expert examination, in fact, showed "no signs of overpainting" ("Mandylion of Edessa" 2008, 57).

In brief, then, the totality of evidence is most consistent with the hypothesis that the Genoan Mandylion is a replica, made no earlier than the thirteenth century, and that the Vatican Mandylion is a fourteenth-century copy of that replica. There is no proof that either was directly copied from the now-lost tenth-century "original," and instead there is proof against it. Neither is there any credible evidence that there was an authentic first-century image of Jesus—miraculous or otherwise. The Shroud of Turin is not such an original, having been proven to be the work of a confessed forger in the middle of the fourteenth century. Thus, the shroud image simply followed the traditional likeness and not the other way around.

Figure 17.1. The author poses with the Holy Face of Genoa—one of two said to be the Edessan Image, or Mandylion—an allegedly miraculous self-portrait of Christ. (Author's photo)

Table 17.1 Mandylions		
Criteria	Vatican	Genoese
Radiocarbon date	None	1240–1280
Verifiable provenance	From 1517	From 1362
Painting medium	Tempera (unconfirmed)	Egg tempera
Support	Linen affixed to wood panel (cedar)	Linen affixed to wood panel (cedar or poplar)
Process of execution	Has image corrections (e.g., nose once shorter)	Retouched image on cloth
	covers original painted on wood	
Inner frame measurements	About $11^1/_2$ x 8 inches.	About $11^1/_2$ x 8 inches.
Positions of rivet holes (despite different frames)	Match Genoese frame	Match Vatican frame
Date of frame	Uncertain; mounted in 1623 baroque reliquary (by Francesco Comi)	fourteenth-century style

CHAPTER 18

MIRACLE OR FRAUD?
THE TURIN SHROUD

T he Shroud of Turin continues to be the subject of media presentations that treat it as being so mysterious as to imply a supernatural origin. One recent study (Binga 2001) found only ten credible skeptical books on the topic versus over four hundred promoting the cloth as the authentic, or potentially authentic, burial cloth of Jesus—including a revisionist tome, *The Resurrection of the Shroud* (Antonacci 2000). Yet since the cloth appeared in the middle of the fourteenth century it has been at the center of scandal, exposés, and controversy—a dubious legacy for what is purported to be the most holy relic in Christendom.

BOGUS SHROUDS

There have been numerous "true" shrouds of Jesus—along with vials of his mother's breast milk, hay from the manger in which he was born, and countless relics of his crucifixion—but the Turin cloth uniquely bears the apparent imprints of a crucified man. Unfortunately the cloth is incompatible with New Testament accounts of Jesus' burial.

John's Gospel (19:38–42, 20:5–7) specifically states that the body was "wound" with "linen clothes" and a large quantity of burial spices (myrrh and aloes). Still another cloth (called "the napkin") covered his face and head. In contrast, the Shroud of Turin represents a *single, draped* cloth (laid under and then over the "body") without any trace of the burial spices.

Of the many earlier purported shrouds of Christ, which were typically about half the length of the Turin cloth, one was the subject of a reported seventh-century dispute on the island of Iona between Christians and Jews, both of whom claimed it. As adjudicator, an Arab ruler placed the alleged relic in a fire from which it levitated, unscathed, and fell at the feet of the Christians—or so says a pious tale. In medieval Europe alone there were "at least forty-three 'True Shrouds'" (Humber 1978, 78).

SCANDAL AT LIREY

The cloth now known as the Shroud of Turin first appeared about 1355 at a little church in Lirey, in north central France. Its owner, a soldier of fortune named Geoffroy de Charney, claimed it as the authentic shroud of Christ, although he never explained how he acquired such a fabulous possession. According to a later bishop's report, written by Pierre D'Arcis to the Avignon pope, Clement VII, in 1389, the shroud was being used as part of a faith-healing scam:

> The case, Holy Father, stands thus. Some time since in this diocese of Troyes the dean of a certain collegiate church, to wit, that of Lirey, falsely and deceitfully, being consumed with the passion of avarice, and not from any motive of devotion but only of gain, procured for his church a certain cloth cunningly painted, upon which by a clever sleight of hand was depicted the twofold image of one man, that is to say, the back and the front, he falsely declaring and pretending that this was the actual shroud in which our Savior Jesus Christ was enfolded in the tomb, and upon which the whole likeness of the Savior had remained thus impressed together with the wounds which He bore. . . . And further to attract the multitude so that money might cunningly be wrung from them, pretended miracles were worked, certain men being hired to represent themselves as healed at the moment of the exhibition of the shroud.

D'Arcis continued, speaking of a predecessor who conducted the investigation and uncovered the forger: "Eventually, after diligent inquiry and examination, he discovered the fraud and how the said cloth had been cunningly painted, the truth being attested by the artist who had painted it, to wit, that it was a work of human skill and not miraculously wrought or bestowed" (emphasis added).

Action had been taken and the cloth hidden away, but now, years later, it had resurfaced. D'Arcis (1389) spoke of "the grievous nature of the scandal, the contempt brought upon the Church and ecclesiastical jurisdiction, and the danger to souls."

As a consequence Clement ordered that, while the cloth could continue being exhibited (it had been displayed on a high platform flanked by torches), during the exhibition it must be loudly announced that "it is not the True Shroud of Our Lord, but a painting or picture made in the semblance or representation of the Shroud" (Humber 1978, 100). Thus the scandal at Lirey ended—for a time.

FURTHER MISREPRESENTATION

During the Hundred Years' War, Margaret de Charney, granddaughter of the Shroud's original owner, gained custody of the cloth, allegedly for safekeeping. But despite many subsequent entreaties she refused to return it, instead even taking it on tour in the areas of present-day France, Belgium, and Switzerland. When there were additional challenges to the Shroud's authenticity, Margaret could only produce documents officially labeling it a "representation."

In 1453, at Geneva, Margaret sold the cloth to Duke Louis I of Savoy. Some Shroud proponents like to say Margaret "gave" the cloth to Duke Louis, but it is only fair to point out that in return he "gave" Margaret the sum of two castles. In 1457, after years of broken promises to return the cloth to the canons of Lirey and later to compensate them for its loss, Margaret was excommunicated. She died in 1460.

The Savoys (who later comprised the Italian monarchy and owned the shroud until it was bequeathed to the Vatican in 1983) represented the shroud as genuine. They treated it as a "holy charm" having magical powers and enshrined it in an expanded church at their castle at Chambéry. There in 1532 a fire blazed through the chapel and before the cloth was rescued a blob of molten silver from the reliquary burned through its forty-eight folds. The alleged talisman was thus revealed as being unable even to protect itself. Eventually, in a shrewd political move—by a later Duke who wished a more suitable capital—the cloth was transferred to Turin (in present-day Italy) (see figure 18.1).

In 1898 the shroud was photographed for the first time, and the glass-plate negatives showed a more lifelike, quasi-positive image. Thus began the modern era of the shroud, with proponents asking how a mere medieval forger could have produced a perfect "photographic" negative before the development of photography. In fact the analogy with photographic images is misleading, since the "positive" image shows a figure with white hair and beard, the opposite of what would be expected for a Palestinian Jew in his thirties.

Nevertheless, some shroud advocates suggested the image was produced by simple contact with bloody sweat or burial ointments. But that is disproved by a lack of wraparound distortions. Also, not all imaged areas would have been touched by a simple draped cloth, so some sort of *projection* was envisioned. One notion was "vaporography," body vapors supposedly interacting with spices on the cloth to yield a vapor "photo," but all experimentation produced was a blur (Nickell 1998, 81–84). Others began to opine that the image was "scorched" by a miraculous burst of radiant energy at the time of Jesus' resurrection. Yet no known radiation would produce such superficial images, and actual scorches on the cloth from the fire of 1532 exhibit strong reddish fluorescence, in contrast to the shroud images that do not fluoresce at all.

SECRET STUDY

In 1969 the archbishop of Turin appointed a secret commission to examine the shroud. That fact was leaked, then denied, but (according to Wilcox 1977, 44) "at last the Turin authorities were forced to admit what they previously denied." The man who had exposed the secrecy accused the clerics of acting "like thieves in the night." More detailed studies—again clandestine—began in 1973.

The commission included internationally known forensic serologists who made heroic efforts to validate the "blood," but all of the microscopial, chemical, biological, and instrumental tests were negative. This was not surprising, since the stains were suspiciously still red and artistically "picturelike." Experts discovered reddish granules that would not even dissolve in reagents that dissolve blood, and one investigator found traces of what appeared to be paint. An art expert concluded that the image had been produced by an artistic printing technique.

The commission's report was withheld until 1976 and then was largely suppressed, while a *rebuttal* report was freely made available. Thus began an approach that would be repeated over and over: distinguished experts would be asked to examine the cloth then would be attacked when they obtained other than desired results.

SCIENCE VS. "SHROUD SCIENCE"

Further examinations were conducted in 1978 by the Shroud of Turin Research Project (STURP). STURP was a group of mostly religious believers whose leaders served on the executive council of the Holy Shroud Guild, a Catholic organization that advocated the "cause" of the supposed relic. STURP members, like others calling themselves "sindonologists" (i.e. shroudologists), gave the impression that they started with the desired answer.

STURP pathologist Robert Bucklin—another Holy Shroud Guild executive councilman—stated that he was willing to stake his reputation on the shroud's authenticity. He and other proshroud pathologists argued for the image's anatomical correctness, yet a footprint on the cloth is inconsistent with the position of the leg to which it is attached, the hair falls as for a standing rather than a recumbent figure, and the physique is so unnaturally elongated (similar to figures in Gothic art) that one proshroud pathologist concluded that Jesus must have suffered from Marfan syndrome (Nickell 1989)!

STURP lacked experts in art and forensic chemistry—with one exception: famed microanalyst Walter C. McCrone. Examining thirty-two tape-lifted samples from the shroud, McCrone identified the "blood" as tempera paint containing red ocher and vermilion along with traces of rose madder—pigments used by medieval artists to depict blood. He also discovered that on the image—but not the background—were significant amounts of the red ocher pigment. He first thought this was applied as a dry powder but later concluded it was a component of dilute paint applied in the medi-

eval *grisaille* (monochromatic) technique (McCrone 1996; cf. Nickell 1998).
For his efforts McCrone was held to a secrecy agreement, while statements
were made to the press that there was no evidence of artistry. He was, he
says, "drummed out" of STURP.

STURP representatives paid a surprise visit to McCrone's lab to con-
fiscate his samples. They then gave them to two late additions to STURP,
John Heller and Alan Adler, neither of whom was a forensic serologist or
a pigment expert. The pair soon proclaimed that they had "identified the
presence of blood." However, at the 1983 conference of the prestigious
International Association for Identification, forensic analyst John F. Fischer
explained how results similar to theirs could be obtained from tempera
paint.

A later claim concerns reported evidence of human DNA in a shroud
"blood" sample, although the archbishop of Turin and the Vatican refused
to authenticate the samples or accept any research carried out on them.
University of Texas researcher Leoncio Garza-Valdez, in his *The DNA of
God?* (1999, 41), claims it was possible "to clone the sample and amplify
it," proving it was "ancient" blood "from a human being or high primate,"
while Ian Wilson's *The Blood and the Shroud* (1998, 91) asserted it was "human
blood."

Actually the scientist at the DNA lab, Victor Tryon, told *Time* magazine that he could not say how old the DNA was or that it came from blood.
As he explained, "Everyone who has ever touched the shroud or cried over
the shroud has left a potential DNA signal there." Tryon resigned from the
new shroud project due to what he disparaged as "zealotry in science" (Van
Biema 1998, 61).

POLLEN FAKERY?

McCrone would later refute another bit of proshroud propaganda: the
claim of Swiss criminologist Max Frei-Sulzer that he had found certain
pollen grains on the cloth that "could only have originated from plants that
grew exclusively in Palestine at the time of Christ." Earlier Frei had also
claimed to have discovered pollens on the cloth that were characteristic
of Istanbul (formerly Constantinople) and the area of ancient Edessa—
seeming to confirm a "theory" of the shroud's missing early history. Wilson

(1979) conjectured that the shroud was the fourth-century Image of Edessa, a legendary "miraculous" imprint of Jesus' face made as a gift to King Abgar. Wilson's notion was that the shroud had been folded so that only the face showed and that it had thus been disguised for centuries. Actually, had the cloth been kept in a frame for such a long period there would have been an age-yellowed, rectangular area around the face. Nevertheless Frei's alleged pollen evidence gave new support to Wilson's ideas.

I say *alleged* evidence because Frei had credibility problems. Before his death in 1983 his reputation suffered when, representing himself as a handwriting expert, he pronounced the infamous "Hitler diaries" genuine; they were soon exposed as forgeries.

In the meantime an even more serious question had arisen about Frei's pollen evidence. Whereas he reported finding numerous types of pollen from Palestine and other areas, STURP's tape-lifted samples, taken at the same time, showed few pollen. Micropaleontologist Steven D. Schafersman was probably the first to publicly suggest that Frei might be guilty of deception. He explained how unlikely it was, given the evidence of the shroud's exclusively European history, that thirty-three different Middle Eastern pollens could have reached the cloth, particularly only pollen from Palestine, Istanbul, and the Anatolian steppe. With such selectivity, Schafersman stated, "these would be miraculous winds indeed." In an article in *Skeptical Inquirer* Schafersman (1982) called for an investigation of Frei's work.

When Frei's tape samples became available after his death, McCrone was asked to authenticate them. This he was readily able to do, he told me, "since it was easy to find red ocher on linen fibers much the same as I had seen them on my samples." But there were few pollen other than on a single tape that bore "dozens" in one small area. This indicated that the tape had subsequently been "contaminated," probably deliberately, McCrone concluded, by having been pulled back and the pollen surreptitiously introduced.

McCrone added (1993):

One further point with respect to Max which I haven't mentioned anywhere, anytime to anybody is based on a statement made by his counterpart in Basel as head of the Police Crime Laboratory there that Max had been several times found guilty and was censured by the Police hierarchy in Switzerland for, shall we say, overenthusiastic interpretation of his evidence. His Basel counterpart had been on the investigating committee and expressed surprise in a letter to me that Max was able to continue in his position as Head of the Police Crime Lab in Zurich.

C-14 FALSEHOODS

The pollen "evidence" became especially important to believers following the devastating results of radiocarbon dating tests in 1988. Three laboratories (at Oxford, Zurich, and the University of Arizona) used accelerator mass spectrometry (AMS) to date samples of the linen. The results were in close agreement and were given added credibility by the use of control samples of known dates. The resulting age span was circa 1260–1390 CE— consistent with the time of the reported forger's confession.

Shroud enthusiasts were devastated, but they soon rallied, beginning a campaign to discredit the radiocarbon findings. Someone put out a false story that the AMS tests were done on one of the patches from the 1532 fire, thus supposedly yielding a late date. A Russian scientist, Dmitrii Kuznetsov, claimed to have established experimentally that heat from a fire (like that of 1532) could alter the radiocarbon date. But others could not replicate his alleged results and it turned out that his physics calculations had been plagiarized—complete with an error (Wilson 1998, 219–23). (Kuznetsov was also exposed in *Skeptical Inquirer* for bogus research in a study criticizing evolution [Larhammar 1995].)

A more persistent challenge to the radiocarbon testing was hurled by Garza-Valdez (1993). He claimed to have obtained samples of the "miraculous cloth" that bore a microbial coating, contamination that could have altered the radiocarbon date. However, that notion was effectively disproved by physicist Thomas J. Pickett (1996). He performed a simple calculation that showed that for the shroud to have been altered by thirteen centuries (i.e., from Jesus' first-century death to the radiocarbon date of 1325±65 years) there would have to be twice as much contamination, by weight, as the weight of the cloth itself!

SHROUD OF RORSCHACH

Following the suspicious pollen evidence were claims that plant images had been identified on the cloth. These were allegedly discerned from "smudgy" appearing areas in shroud photos that were subsequently enhanced. The work was done by a retired geriatric psychiatrist, Alan Whanger, and his wife Mary, former missionaries who have taken up image analysis as a hobby. They were later assisted by an Israeli botanist who looked at their photos of "flower" images (many of them "wilted" and otherwise distorted) and exclaimed, "Those are the flowers of Jerusalem!" (Whanger and Whanger 1998, 79). Apparently no one has thought to see if some might match the flowers of France or Italy or even to try to prove that the images are indeed floral (given the relative scarcity of pollen grains on the cloth).

The visualized "flower and plant images" join other perceived shapes seen—Rorschach-like—in the shroud's mottled image and off-image areas. These include "Roman coins" over the eyes, head and arm "phylacteries" (small Jewish prayer boxes), an "amulet," and such crucifixion-associated items (see John 19) as "a large nail," a "hammer," "sponge on a reed," "Roman thrusting spear," "pliers," "two scourges," "two brush brooms," "two small nails," "large spoon or trowel in a box," "a loose coil of rope," a "cloak" with "belt," a "tunic," a pair of "sandals," and other hilarious imaginings, including "Roman dice," all discovered by the Whangers (1998) and their botanist friend.

They and others have also reported finding ancient Latin and Greek words, such as "Jesus" and "Nazareth." Even Ian Wilson (1998, 242) felt compelled to state: "While there can be absolutely no doubting the sincerity of those who make these claims, the great danger of such arguments is that researchers may 'see' merely what their minds trick them into thinking is there."

CONCLUSION

We see that "shroud science"—like "creation science" and other pseudosciences in the service of dogma—begins with the desired answer and works backward to the evidence. Although they are bereft of any viable hypothesis for the image formation, sindonologists are quick to dismiss the profound, corroborative evidence for artistry. Instead, they suggest that the "mystery" of the shroud implies a miracle, but of course that is merely an example of the logical fallacy called arguing from ignorance.

Worse, some have engaged in pseudoscience and even, apparently, outright scientific fraud, while others have shamefully mistreated the honest scientists who reported unpopular findings. We should again recall the words of Canon Ulysse Chevalier, the Catholic scholar who brought to light the documentary evidence of the shroud's medieval origin. As he lamented, "The history of the shroud constitutes a protracted violation of the two virtues so often commended by our holy books: justice and truth" (quoted in Nickell 1998, 21).

Figure 18.1. The author visits the Shroud of Turin casket, surmounted by a photograph of its facial image. (Author's photo)

CHAPTER 19

ARTISTRY AND THE SHROUD

S cience has established that the Shroud of Turin is a medieval artwork, even though devotees refuse to accept such findings. Much of the continuing debate centers on the question of how the image was formed and what artist could have produced such a work.

MAKING SHROUDLIKE IMAGES

Proponents have suggested that the quasi-negative image might have been the result of simple contact between cloth and a body covered with oils and spices used in the burial process. However, such imprinting would have resulted in severe wraparound distortions that are lacking in the shroud image. Moreover, not all of the features that printed would have been in contact with a simple draped cloth.

Recognizing these problems, proponent Paul Vignon proposed an imaging process that would have acted across a distance, what he called "vaporography." Supposedly, weak amoniacal vapors (from the fermented urea in sweat) interacted with spices on the cloth (likened to a sensitized photographic plate) to produce a vapor "photo." However, vapors do not travel in perfectly straight (vertical) lines; instead, they diffuse and convect, and therefore—as I showed experimentally in 1977—the result will simply be a blur (Nickell 1998, 77–84).

Undaunted, shroud proponents even invoked a miracle, suggesting a mechanism they called "flash photolysis"—described as a short burst of radiant energy at the moment of Christ's resurrection. It was at this point that skeptics began remarking sarcastically that proponents would need to develop a science of miracles. One problem is that real scorches on linen exhibit a strong reddish fluorescence, while the shroud images do not fluorescence at all. Moreover, there is no natural source for such radiation, but even if there were, it would have had to have been *focused* to produce an image like that on the shroud (Nickell 1998, 85–94). Besides, suggesting "flash photolysis" is rather like proposing an "x-factor": one cannot explain a mystery by invoking another mystery. In fact, shroud advocates have no visible hypothesis of image formation.

Microscopist Walter C. McCrone's discovery of red ocher and vermilion tempera paint on the shroud led him to conclude that the entire image had been painted, despite the problems artists have in creating quasi-negative images. As an alternative, some two years before McCrone published his findings I reported the results of my own experiments in creating shroudlike "negative" images. I molded wet cloth to a relief—a bas-relief to minimize distortions—and, when it was dry, I rubbed on powdered pigment using a dauber. This technique (similar to making a rubbing from a gravestone) automatically yields quasi-negative images that, since dry powder is used, do not soak into the cloth. It also produces encoded three-dimensional information and other shroud features (see figure 19.1).

REPLICA SHROUD

Using hypotheses I advanced in my *Inquest on the Shroud of Turin* (1998), my friend and colleague Luigi Garlaschelli, professor of organic chemistry at the University of Pavia, determined to reproduce the shroud as a full-size replica with the properties of the original. (For example, the shroud image has sparse red-ocher pigment confined to the tops of the threads, and an attendant yellowish stain of apparent cellulose degradation.)

He used specially hand-woven linen, laid over a volunteer, with a bas-relief substituted for the face to avoid critical wraparound distortions. He employed a version of my rubbing technique with my added hypothesis of an acidic pigment that, over time, mostly sloughed off but left behind a ghostly image due to the acid degrading the cellulose (Nickell 1998, 138–40). Garlaschelli artificially aged the result and then washed off the pigment. As he notes, the resulting image possessed "all the characteristics of the Shroud of Turin." He added, "In particular, the image is a pseudo-negative, is fuzzy with half-tones, resides on the topmost fibers of the cloth, has some 3-D embedded properties, and does not fluoresce" (quoted in Polidoro, 2010, 18).

I was on hand in the fall of 2009 when Garlaschelli presented his results in Genoa at Italy's largest science fair. He dedicated his illustrated lecture to me, too generously saying that I was "the brain" and he "only the hands." In fact I am humbled to have been mentioned regarding such a wonderful accomplishment. It shows shroud science trumped by real science.

NAMING THE SHROUD ARTIST

On occasion in the field of art history and criticism it becomes useful to assign a name to the unknown artist of a particular masterwork. Such is now the case with the medieval painting of the crucified Jesus known as the Shroud of Turin.

Long held to be the authentic burial cloth of Jesus, the "shroud" is now well established as the work of a mid-fourteenth-century French artist. As discussed in the previous chapter, the supposed relic first surfaced at a little church in the village of Lirey, in north-central France, about 1355. At that time it was being used in a faith-healing scheme to bilk pilgrims. Stylistic and iconographic elements provide corroborative evidence that the image is indeed the work of a medieval artisan, and "blood" flows on the image are also indicative of artistry, being suspiciously still red, "picturelike," and rendered in tempera paint.

This cumulative evidence for artistry is finally underscored by the radiocarbon dating. Provided by laboratories at Oxford, Zurich, and the University of Arizona, the results were consistent in dating the cloth to ca. 1260–1390 (or about the time the artist was identified, in 1355 [Damon et al. 1989]).

Who was this artist? As with so many of his fellow craftsmen, his name remains unknown to us. We are aware that he flourished in the 1350s in north-central France, probably living in the diocese of Troyes—possibly even in the city of Troyes itself—since he seems to have been accessible to the investigating Bishop of Troyes.

While the artist's genius has sometimes been exaggerated, he was certainly a skilled and clever artisan. He did make mistakes, such as depicting the hair as hanging rather than splayed (i.e., consistent with a standing rather than a recumbent figure). But he showed ingenuity, study, and skill in many ways, not the least of which was accurately distributing the darks and lights in a manner consistent with the bodily imprint that was supposedly represented. That he did not include the wraparound distortions a real body would have left is no doubt merely attributable to his overriding artistic sensibility.

The traditional way of naming an unknown but important artist is to designate him "Master," followed by an appropriate descriptor—such as place (for example, Master of Flémalle, or Master Honoré of Paris) or work of art (such as the Master of the Altar of St. Bartholomew or Master of the Castello Nativity). One fifteenth-century engraver is known as the Master of 1466, and a sixteenth-century Limoges enameller has been given a designation based on the monograms on his works: Master K. I. P. (Janson 1963; Davidson and Gerry 1939).

Following this tradition, we may now name the creator of the work presently known as the Shroud of Turin, or as the great French scholar Ulysse Chevalier termed it, the Saint Suaire de Lirey-Chambéry-Turin (i.e., the Holy Shroud of Lirey-Chambéry-Turin [Chevalier 1900]). This recognizes the cloth's first public appearance at Lirey as well as its subsequent homes. It also recognizes the tradition of naming a purported shroud by its place of display: for instance, the Shroud of Cadouin (after a cloth taken as crusader's booty from Antioch in 1098 to Cadouin, France), the Shroud of Besançon (considered a sixteenth copy of the Turin shroud, exhibited at Besançon, France), and the Shroud of Compiégne (an eight-foot shroud that surfaced in 877 and was venerated for eleven centuries at the St. Cornelius in Abbey Compiégne) (Nickell 1998, 53, 64).

In this light, it seems appropriate to use the original place name when referring to the artist, since that is the one connected with him historically. Therefore, the title, "Master of the 'Shroud' of Lirey," seems appropriate. The designation is not only useful but also helps to deemphasize the accusation of deliberate fraud against the artist. Although the cloth was originally misrepresented as the authentic shroud of Jesus, it is far from certain that the artist was initially aware of the intended deception. He could have been commissioned to make a symbolic shroud—albeit an unusually realistic one—for reputedly ceremonial purposes. In any event, such a skilled craftsman must have produced many additional works of art, all of which are part of his implicit legacy.

CHAPTER 20

OVIEDO'S HOLY SUDARIUM

While science has established the Shroud of Turin as a fourteenth-century forgery—rendered in tempera paint by a confessed forger and radiocarbon dated to the time of the forger's confession (Nickell 1998; McCrone 1996)—the propaganda offensive to convince the public otherwise continues. As part of the strategy, shroud proponents are now ballyhooing another cloth, a supposed companion burial wrapping that they claim helps argue for the shroud's authenticity.

"COMPANION RELIC"

At issue is the Oviedo Cloth, an 84×3×53-centimeter piece of linen, stained with supposed blood, that some believe is the *sudarium* or "napkin" that covered the face of Jesus in the tomb. As described in the New Testament (John 20:7) it was "about his head." Such a cloth was used in ancient Jewish burial practice to cover the face of the deceased (Nickell 1998, 33–34).

One reason for the interest in the Oviedo Cloth among Shroud of Turin advocates is to counter the devastating radiocarbon evidence. Three laboratories used sophisticated carbon-14 dating technology to test a piece of shroud cloth, the resulting origin was identified as being between 1260 and 1390 CE. In response, advocates hope to tie the shroud to the Oviedo Cloth, since, allegedly, "the history of the sudarium is undisputed" and it "was a revered relic preserved from the days of the crucifixion" (Anderson 2000).

Alas, however, the provenance (or historical record) of the Oviedo cloth, located in the Cathedral of Oviedo in northern Spain, is not nearly so definitive. Indeed, even most proauthenticity sources admit it cannot really

133

be established earlier than about the eighth century (Whanger and Whanger 1998, 56), and the earliest supposed documentary evidence is from the eleventh century. According to Mark Guscin in *The Oviedo Cloth* (1998, 17) (see figure 20.1), "The key date in the history of the sudarium is 14 March 1075." At that time an oak chest in which the cloth was kept was reportedly opened by King Alfonso VI and others, including the famed knight El Cid, and recorded in a document stating that the chest had long reposed in the church. Unfortunately, the original document is lost and only a thirteenth-century "copy" is found in the cathedral archives (Guscin 1998, 17).

However, an account of the cloth was penned in the twelfth century by a bishop of Oviedo named Pelayo, who claimed the sudarium had been kept in Jerusalem from the time it was discovered in the tomb until the seventh century, when Christians fleeing the Persian invasion took it to Spain (figure 20.2). But relic mongers typically fabricated stories about their bogus productions, and there were many allegedly genuine *sudaria*, just as there were numerous "true shrouds"—at least forty-three in medieval Europe alone (Humber 1978, 78). Yet there is not the slightest hint in the Christian Gospels or anywhere else in the New Testament that the burial wrappings of Jesus were actually preserved. Later, of course, certain apocryphal texts claimed otherwise. One fourth-century account mentioned a tradition that Peter had kept the sudarium, but what had subsequently become of it was unknown (Wilson 1979, 92–95).

Those who would try to link the questionable Oviedo sudarium to the Turin "shroud"—and vice-versa, in the hopes of mutual authentication—face a problem: the sudarium lacks an image like that on the shroud. Had such a cloth indeed covered the face of Jesus, "this would have prevented the image from being formed on the shroud, and it would presumably have caused it to be formed on the sudarium" (Guscin 1998, 33, 34). Proponents now postulate that the sudarium was used only *temporarily*, in the period after crucifixion and before burial, having been put aside before the body was wrapped.

But however clever this rationalization, John's Gospel states that Jesus was buried "as the manner of the Jews is to bury" (19:40), and the use of a kerchief to cover the face in burial is specifically mentioned in the Jewish Mishnah. Also, with regard to the burial of Lazarus (John 11:44), who was "bound hand and foot with graveclothes," we are told that "his face was bound about with a napkin."

Undaunted, shroud and sudarium advocates have joined forces and are now making the kind of outrageous and pseudoscientific claims that used to be made for the shroud alone, claiming that "blood" and pollen evidence link the two cloths. Unfortunately, the new claims come from many of the same dubious and discredited sources as before.

"BLOOD" STAINS

At an international congress in Oviedo, in October 1994, papers were presented focusing on the latest "investigations" of the supposed sudarium. One claimant was Pierluigi Baima Bollone, who purported to have established that the "blood" stains on the cloth not only were human blood but were of type AB, "the same group," according to Guscin (1998, 56), "as the blood on the shroud."

Actually the assertion that the shroud has type AB blood also comes from the same source, and Bollone's claims are baloney. Even one of the shroud's most committed defenders, Ian Wilson (1998, 89), merely remarks in passing that Bollone "claimed to" have made such a determination. A zealous shroud partisan and chairman of a shroud center, Bollone is a professor of legal medicine.

In contrast, internationally known forensic serologists, employing the standard scientific tests used in crime laboratories, were unable to find any evidence of blood on several "blood"-stained threads from the Shroud of Turin. The substance, which was suspiciously still red, failed sensitive tests for hemoglobin and hemoglobin derivatives, blood corpuscles, or any other identifiable blood components. The "blood" could not be identified as such, let alone by species or type, and it contained reddish granules that would not even dissolve in reagents that dissolve blood. Sophisticated further tests—including microspectroscopic analysis, thin-layer chromatography, and neutron activation analysis—were also negative. Subsequently, famed microanalyst Walter McCrone identified the "blood" as tempera paint containing red ocher and vermilion along with traces of rose madder—pigments used by medieval artists to depict blood (Nickell 1998, 127–31).

So when we are told that there is "human blood of the group AB" on the Oviedo "sudarium," and that the claim of such comes from Bollone, there is cause for skepticism. (Operating even further beyond his field of expertise,

Bollone "has also studied the fabric of the sudarium, and affirmed that it is typical of the first century" [Guscin 1998, 56]—never mind seeking the opinion of textile experts.)

Another alleged correspondence between the "shroud" and the "sudarium" is that the "blood" stains on the latter supposedly "coincide exactly with the face of the image on the Turin Shroud." Dr. Alan Whanger claims to have found numerous "points of coincidence" between the Oviedo stains and the Turin image by employing a dubious overlay technique. Guscin (1998, 32) describes Whanger as a "highly respected scientist." Be that as it may, he is a retired geriatric psychiatrist and former missionary who has taken up image analysis as a hobby.

Whanger's judgment in such matters should perhaps be viewed in light of his studies of the Shroud of Turin. As we have already seen, in that cloth's mottled image and off-image areas, Whanger has perceived such crucifixion-associated items as "a large nail," "hammer," "sponge on a reed," "Roman thrusting spear," "loose coil of rope," pair of "sandals" and numerous other imaginings—including "Roman dice"—that the good psychiatrist "sees," Rorschach-like, in shroud photos. He and a botanist friend have also "identified" various "flower" images as well as ancient Latin and Greek words such as "Jesus" and "Nazareth" (Nickell 2001).

POLLEN "EVIDENCE"

Still another purported link between the Turin and Oviedo cloths concerns pollen allegedly found on them. The shroud supposedly bears certain pollens characteristic of locales (Palestine, Constantinople, and ancient Edessa) that seemingly confirm a "theory" of the shroud's missing early history. Similarly, pollens supposedly discovered on the Oviedo Cloth seem to confirm its purported historical route (from Jerusalem through North Africa to Toledo and Oviedo), indeed to "perfectly match" the route (see figure 20.2) according to Guscin. But perhaps the match is too good to be true. As it turns out, the alleged pollen evidence that supposedly helps authenticate the Oviedo Cloth was also provided by Max Frei, whose questionable findings were discussed in chapter 18. In light of the suspicions raised about the shroud pollens, the Oviedo pollen claims should no longer be touted until an independent and impartial sampling is conducted.

CONCLUSIONS

As with the Shroud of Turin, the study of the Oviedo Cloth is obviously characterized by pseudoscience and possibly worse. The problems are symptomatic of bias that can occur when analyses of a controversial object are conducted not by independent experts, chosen solely for their expertise, but instead by committed, self-selected partisans who begin with the desired answer and work backward to the evidence—a profound example of what is called confirmation bias.

If reports that the Oviedo cloth has been radiocarbon tested are true, then the supposed relic is indeed a fake. The claim is that two laboratories have dated it to the seventh and eight centuries, respectively, devastatingly consistent with the historical record. (For more, see my *Relics of the Christ* 2007, 154–66, 177–79.)

Figure 20.1. *The Oviedo Cloth* by Mark Guscin.

Figure 20.2. Map of Spain shows the legendary journey of the sudarium to Oviedo; a later pilgrim's route is also shown. (Illustration by Joe Nickell)

CHAPTER 21

MIRACULOUS RELICS

In October 2004, after participating in the Fifth World Skeptics Congress in Abano Terme, Italy—near Padua, where Galileo taught and discovered Jupiter's moons (Frazier 2005)—I remained in the beautiful country for some investigative work. Here are some of my findings.

RELICS OF THE SAINTS

I was able to visit a number of churches containing alleged relics—objects associated with a saint or martyr. These may be all or part of the holy person's body (in Catholicism, a *first-class relic*) or some item associated with him or her (such as an article of clothing, a *second-class relic*). Venerated since the first century CE, relics were thought to be imbued with special qualities or powers—such as healing—that could be tapped by one touching or even viewing them (Pick 1979, 101).

As we saw in chapter 14, so prevalent had relic veneration become in St. Augustine's time (about 400 CE) that he deplored "hypocrites in the garb of monks" for hawking the bones of martyrs, adding with due skepticism, "if indeed of martyrs" (quoted in "Relics" 1973). About 403, Vigilantius of Talouse condemned the veneration of relics as being nothing more than a form of idolatry, but St. Jerome defended the cult of relics—on the basis of miracles that God reputedly worked through them ("Relics" 1967).

Here and there were such relics as the fingers of St. Paul, St. Andrew, and the doubting Thomas. There were multiple heads of John the Baptist. Especially prolific were relics associated with Jesus, whose foreskin was enshrined at no fewer than six churches. There were also his swaddling clothes, hay from the manger, and vials of his mother's breast milk. A tear that he shed at Lazarus's tomb was also preserved, along with countless relics of his crucifixion and burial (Nickell 1993, 75–76).

Italy is especially rich with relics. With the generous assistance of my Italian friends, who relayed me from city to city by train across the northern part of the country, I visited reputed holy relics in Vienna, Milan, and Turin (before later flying to Naples).

In Venice, beneath the high altar of the Basilica di San Marco (St. Mark's Basilica), supposedly lies the body of the author of the Gospel of Mark, martyred in Alexandria and later brought to the city by Venetian merchants. Some Italian colleagues and I visited the cavernous Byzantine basilica on October 11, first paying to see a collection of relics that included an alleged piece of the stone column of Jesus' flagellation, then paying again to pass by St. Mark's reputed remains.

Unfortunately, since the remains did not come to Venice until 829 CE (whereupon construction of the basilica was immediately begun to enshrine them), there is a serious question as to their provenance. Even accepting the substance of the story about their acquisition, one source notes that "the identity of the piously stolen body depends on the solidarity of the Alexandrine tradition" (Coulson 1958, 302). Moreover, according to a National Geographic Society travel guide (Jepson 2001, 143), "many claim the saint's relics were destroyed in a fire in 976."

In Milan, I visited the Basilica of St. Eustorgio, my guide being noted writer (and fellow *Skeptical Inquirer* columnist) Massimo Polidoro. In a dark recess of the church we read the inscription, "SEPVLCRVM TRIVM MAGORVM" (Sepulcher of the Three Magi). A carved stone slab nearby was accompanied by a sign that informed, "According to tradition this stone slab with the comet was on top of the Magi's tomb and was brought to Italy along with their relics." Actually the story is a bit more complicated.

Legendarily, the relics were discovered by St. Helena (248–328), mother of Constantine the Great. They were supposedly transferred to Milan by St. Eustorgio (d. 518), who carried them by ox cart. Then after Milan fell to Frederick Barbarossa in 1162, they were transported to Cologne two years later (Cruz 1984, 154; Lowenthal 1998).

It appears, however, according to an article by David Lowenthal titled "Fabricating Heritage" (1998), that the relics were never in Milan. Instead, it seems that the whole tale was made up by the Cologne archbishop, Reinald of Cologne. In any event, in 1909 some fragments of the alleged Magi bones were "returned" to Milan and enshrined in the church named for their legendary transporter, the sixth-century bishop of Milan.

In Turin, I visited important "relic" sites. One, the Cathedral of St. John the Baptist, houses the notorious Shroud of Turin, the supposed burial cloth of Christ that is actually a proven forgery, radiocarbon dated to the time of a confessed fourteenth-century artist. With a small group of Turin skeptics, I also studied the latest shroud developments at the Museo della Sindone (Holy Shroud Museum) along with many items associated with the cloth, including the mammoth camera with which it was first photographed in 1898. (For more on the shroud, see Nickell 1998; McCrone 1996).

Elsewhere in Turin, I visited the Church of Maria Ausiliatrice, whose crypt is a relic's chapel containing a fabulous collection: an estimated five thousand relics of saints! There are endless panels and display cases of them along the walls, including relics alleged to be from Mary Magdalene and, more credibly, St. Francis of Assisi.

The focal point of the chapel (figure 21.1) is a lighted cross containing, purportedly, a small amount of the Holy Blood of Christ. As with other such blood relics, however, there is no credible evidence to link it with Jesus or even with his time. With the blood is, purportedly, a piece of the True Cross discovered due to a vision by St. Helena in 326. Protestant reformer John Calvin, in his *Treatise on Relics* (1543, 61), stated that there were enough alleged fragments of the cross to "form a whole ship's cargo."

Because such relics were eagerly sought by noblemen and churches alike in order to enhance their influence, there were always those willing to supply them—even if by unholy means.

The Catholic Church has addressed the question of authenticity of relics in something less than a head-on fashion. It often sidesteps the issue by refraining from taking a position regarding the genuineness of a particular relic. The veneration of certain doubtful relics was permitted to continue on the grounds that, even if a relic was in fact spurious, God was not dishonored by an error that had been continued in good faith, whereas it was felt that a final verdict could not easily be pronounced in the case of many relics. Besides, it was argued, the devotions "deeply rooted in the heart of peasantry" could not lightly be dismissed ("Christian Relics" 2004). Thus, an end-justifies-the-means attitude—which helped create and promote fake relics in the first place—prevailed.

HOLY GRAIL, HOLY HOAX

In Milan and Turin I visited sites that have gained new interest due to the runaway popularity of Dan Brown's *The Da Vinci Code* (2004). The novel presents a modern-day quest for the Holy Grail, the legendary cup Jesus and his disciples drank from at the Last Supper, which was also subsequently used to catch and preserve his blood at the crucifixion (figure 21.2). That act was usually attributed to Mary Magdalene or Joseph of Arimathea. The original grail story is the French romance *Le Conte du Graal* (*The Story of the Grail*), composed about 1190 by Chrétien de Troyes (Barber 2004, 17–19).

Brown's novel is predicated on a conspiracy theory involving Jesus and Mary Magdalene. Supposedly the old French word *sangreal* is explained not as *san greal* ("holy grail") but as *sang real* ("royal blood"). Although that concept was not current before the Late Middle Ages, a source Brown drew heavily on, *Holy Blood, Holy Grail*, argues that Jesus was married to Mary Magdalene, with whom he had a child, and even that he may have survived the crucifixion. Jesus' child, so the "non-fiction" book claims, thus began a bloodline that led to the Merovingian dynasty, a succession of kings who ruled what is today France from 481 to 751 (Baigent et al. 1996).

Evidence of the holy bloodline was supposedly found in a trove of parchment documents, discovered by Bérenger Saunière, the priest of Rennes-le-Château in the Pyrenees. The secret had been kept by a shadowy society known as the Priory of Sion, which harked back to the era of the Knights Templar and claimed among its past "Grand Masters" Leonardo da Vinci, Isaac Newton, and Victor Hugo.

Brown seizes on Leonardo—borrowing from "The Secret Code of Leonardo Da Vinci," chapter one of another work of pseudohistory titled *The Templar Revelation*. This was coauthored by "researchers" Lynn Pick-nett and Clive Prince, whose previous foray into nonsense was their claim that Leonardo had created the Shroud of Turin—even though that forgery appeared nearly a century before the great artist and inventive genius was born!

Among the "revelations" of Picknett and Prince (1998, 19–21), adopted by Dan Brown in *The Da Vinci Code*, is a claim regarding Leonardo's fresco, *Last Supper*, which I visited in Milan with Massimo Polidoro. Supposedly, the painting contains hidden symbolism relating to the *sang real* secret. Picknett and Prince claim, for instance, that St. John in the picture (seated at the right of Jesus) is actually a woman—Mary Magdalene!—and that the shape made by "Mary" and Jesus is "a giant, spread-eagled 'M,'" allegedly confirming the interpretation. By repeating this silliness, Brown provokes critics to note that his characterizations reveal ignorance about his subject (Bernstein 2004, 12).

Alas, the whole basis of *The Da Vinci Code*—the "discovered" parchments of Rennes-le-Château, relating to the alleged Priory of Sion—were part of a hoax perpetrated by a man named Pierre Plantard. Plantard commissioned a friend to create fake parchments which he then used to concoct the bogus priory story in 1956 (Olson and Miesel 2004, 223–39).

Of course, Dan Brown—along with the authors of *Holy Blood, Holy Grail* and *The Templar Revelation*—was duped by the Priory of Sion hoax, which he in turn foisted onto his readers. He is apparently unrepentant, however, and his apologists point out that *The Da Vinci Code* is, after all, fiction, although at the beginning of the novel Brown claimed it was based on certain facts. Meanwhile, despite the devastatingly negative evidence, *The Da Vinci Code* mania continues, along with the quest for the fictitious Holy Grail.

BLOOD OF ST. JANUARIUS

Joined by paranormal investigator Luigi Garlaschelli (from the Department of Organic Chemistry at the University of Pavia), I flew from Turin to Naples to further investigate a miracle claim on which I had previously spent much time. It concerned the "blood" of the legendary martyr San Gennaro—St. Januarius—who was supposedly bishop of Benevento, Italy, in 305 CE when he was beheaded during the persecutions of Christians by Diocletian.

Eyewitnesses dating back to at least the fourteenth century reported that what is represented as the martyred saint's congealed blood periodically liquefies, reddens, and froths—in an apparent contravention of natural laws. The ritual takes place several times annually. According to tradition, if the phenomenon fails to occur, disaster is imminent (Nickell and Fischer 1992, 145–51).

Reasons for suspicions abound. First, the Catholic Church has never been able to verify the historical existence of San Gennaro. Moreover, there is absolutely no provenance for the saint's blood relics prior to 1389 (when an unknown traveler reported his astonishment at witnessing the liquefaction).

Another reason for suspicion is that there are additional saints, whose blood is said to liquefy—some twenty in all—and virtually every one of them is found in the Naples area. Such proliferation seems less suggestive of the miraculous than indicative of some regional secret.

It is important to note that no sustained scientific scrutiny of the blood relics has ever been permitted. Also, descriptions of the liquefaction vary, and it is not always easy to separate what may be permutations in the phenomenon's occurrence from differences attributable to individual perceptions. Assertions that the substance in the vials is genuine blood are based solely on spectroscopic analyses that employed antiquated equipment and were done under such poor conditions as to cast grave doubts on the results. (For a full discussion of the Januarian legend and phenomena, see Nickell and Fischer 1992, 145–64.)

Forensic analyst John F. Fischer and I offered a solution to the phenomenon, involving a mixture of olive oil, melted beeswax, and pigment. Only a small amount of the wax is added, sufficient that, when the whole is cool, the mixture is solid, but when slightly warmed (by body heat, nearby candles, and so on) the trace of congealing substance melts and—slowly or even quite suddenly—the mixture liquefies. As one authority states: "A very important fact is that liquefaction has occurred during repair of the casket, a circumstance in which it seems highly unlikely that God would work a miracle" (Coulson 1958, 239).

In 1991, before we could publish our research, a team of Italian scientists made international headlines with their own solution to the Januarian mystery. Writing in the journal *Nature*, Professor Garlaschelli and two colleagues from Milan, Franco Ramaccini and Sergio Della Sala, proposed "that thixotropy may furnish an explanation." A thixotropic gel is one capable of liquefying when agitated and of resolidifying when allowed to stand. The Italian scientists, creating such a gel by mixing chalk and hydrated iron chloride with a small amount of salt water, reported a convincing replication of the Januarian phenomenon (Garlaschelli et al. 1991).

In 1996, Garlaschelli was able to examine a similarly liquefying blood relic, that of St. Lorenzo (at the Church of St. Maria in Arnaseno, Italy). Using a test-tube mixer, he whirled the ampoule containing the "blood" to test the thixotropic-gel hypothesis, but there was no effect. He then immersed the ampoule in warm water to test the melting hypothesis, whereupon a "miracle" occurred: the contents liquefied and turned red—just like the Januarian phenomenon (Polidoro 2004).

In 2004, in company with Luigi Garlaschelli himself, I was able to visit the Italian sites that hold the reputed relics of San Gennaro. The sites included the Chapel of the Treasury, situated inside the Cathedral of Naples. This baroque chapel—rich in frescoes and marbles—holds the gilded silver bust of the saint and the ampulla of the "blood" that periodically liquefies and again coagulates. Garlaschelli (2004) cautions that the St. Januarius and St. Lorenzo "blood" relics do not necessarily work on the same principle, and he still believes the former may be a thixotropic substance.

We also visited the Church of Capuchin Monks at Pozzuoli, Italy, a short train ride from Naples. Here is the marble slab, installed in the church wall, reputed to be the stone on which Januarius was beheaded (figure 21.3). In the late 1980s, however, the stone was examined and determined to be a paleo-Christian altar, possibly dating from the seventh century (hundreds of years after the martyrdom). The red spots that were supposed to be the blood of the saint are believed to be traces from an old painting together with some candle drippings. According to Garlaschelli (2004), the church itself now discourages the cult of the Pozzuoli Stone, he says, "as a superstition originating from the wishful thinking and self-delusion of the worshippers." That could apply to many other miracle claims—throughout Italy and beyond.

Figure 21.1. A lighted-cross reliquary in a Turin church purportedly contains a piece of the True Cross and some of the Holy Blood of Christ. (Photo by Joe Nickell)

Figure 21.2. Statue of Faith holding the Holy Grail stands before the Gran Madre di Dio Church in Turin. According to legend, this is the site where the Holy Grail is hidden. (Photo by Joe Nickell)

Figure 21.3. Luigi Garlaschelli, intrepid Italian paranormal investigator, poses with the Pozzuoli Stone on which St. Januarius was legendarily beheaded. (Photo by Joe Nickell)

CHAPTER 22

IN SEARCH OF THE EMERALD GRAIL

I n the old-town portion of Genoa, Italy, the city where Christopher
Columbus was born, stands the great Romanesque-Gothic cathedral
of San Lorenzo (Saint Lawrence).[1] Here, in the subterranean Museum
of the Treasury—which houses reputed pieces of the True Cross, relics of
John the Baptist, and other religious objects—is displayed *Il Sacro Catino*,
"the Holy Basin." This is one of the most famous embodiments of the legendary "Holy Grail," and I was able to study both it and its legend there in
the fall of 2009 (figure 22.1), attempting to resolve some of the mysteries
and controversies concerning it.

GRAIL LEGENDS AND MIRACLES

Romantic stories about the quest for the *San Gréal*, or "Holy Grail"—
reportedly the cup used by Jesus at the Last Supper—have proliferated
for centuries. Popularly, the grail (originally the word meant "dish") is the
talisman sought by the knights of King Arthur's Round Table. The quest is
known to English audiences largely though French romances compiled and
translated by Sir Thomas Malory in his *Morte d'Arthur* in 1470. Therein the
grail is represented as the chalice from which Jesus and his disciples drank
at the Last Supper before it was subsequently used to catch and preserve
his blood from the crucifixion. This act was usually attributed to Mary
Magdalene or Joseph of Arimathea (the latter having claimed Jesus' body
for burial [see Mark 15:43–46]).

The earliest grail romance is *Le Conte du Graal* ("The Story of the Grail"), which was composed by Chrétien de Troyes around 1190. It describes how, when a girl "entered holding the grail, so brilliant a light appeared that the candles lost their brightness like the stars or the moon when the sun rises. . . . The grail . . . was made of fine, pure gold, and in it were precious stones of many kinds." Two other grail stories, both written by Robert de Boron circa 1200, were *Joseph d'Arimathie* and *Merlin*. These gave the grail quest a new Christian focus, representing it as a spiritual rather than a chivalrous search. This epic constitutes the most important and best-known English version of the Arthurian and grail adventures (Barber 2004, 19; Cox 2004, 75–76).

Other legends represent the Holy Grail variously as a silver platter, a salver bearing a man's severed head (like that of John the Baptist in Matthew 14:3–12), or a crystal vase filled with blood. Over time the grail has also been represented as a reliquary (containing the Sacred Host or holy blood), a secret book, an effigy of Jesus, the philosopher's stone, and many other portrayals.

It was sometimes held to be supernatural—being in one embodiment a miraculous dish of plenty that could feed a multitude bread and wine. Around 1205, in a Bavarian poem titled *Parzival*, it was described as a magical luminous stone, more specifically as an emerald from Lucifer's crown that had fallen to earth during the struggle in heaven. The term *Holy Grail* now popularly refers to any object of a quest, usually an unattainable one (Nickell 2007, 50–53).

THE HISTORICAL EVIDENCE

Unfortunately, there is no story about Joseph of Arimathea and the Holy Grail in any text until the close of the twelfth century, when Robert de Boron penned his romance. Notably, the Gospel accounts of Jesus' death do not suggest that Joseph or anyone obtained a dish or other vessel from the Last Supper and used it or any other receptacle to preserve Jesus' blood. Records of the Holy Blood—the reputed contents of the cup Joseph possessed— are also of late vintage, perhaps the earliest coming from Mantra, Italy, in 804 (Nickell 2007, 53–56).

Nevertheless, several vessels lay claim to being the true Holy Grail—

some twenty of which had surfaced by the sixteenth century. John Calvin ([1543] 2009, 62, 63) reported on several of the rival claimants for the title of "the cup in which Christ gave the sacrament of his blood to the apostles" (at the Last Supper). Calvin mentioned one at Notre Dame de l'Isle, near Lyons; another was in a monastery in the Albigéois; still another could be found at Genoa. This was "a vessel or cup of emerald" so "costly," says Calvin sarcastically, that "our Lord must have had a splendid service on that occasion" (see also my introduction to Calvin [1543] 2009, 32–33).

THE EMERALD BOWL

Calvin is clearly referring to *Il Sacro Catino*, "The Holy Basin." Most sources allege that this vessel—actually an emerald-green, hexagonal bowl—was brought to Genoa by Guglielmo Embriaco, following the conquest of Caesarea in 1101.[2] A fresco on the main façade of the Palazzo San Giorgio (figure 22.2) depicts crusader Guglielmo ("William" in English) holding as war booty the distinctive catino. Twelfth-century writers acknowledged the purported intrinsic value of the bowl. For example, William of Tyre noted circa 1170 that it was "a vase of brilliant green shaped like a bowl" and that "the Genoese, believing that it was of emerald, took it in lieu of a large sum of money and thus acquired a splendid ornament for their church." He adds, "They still show this vase as a marvel to people of distinction who pass through their city, and persuade them to believe it is truly an emerald as its color indicates" (quoted in Barber 2004, 168).

Others have seemed even more skeptical. States George Frederick Kunz in his *The Curious Lore of Precious Stones* ([1913] 1971, 259):

A queer story has been told regarding the Genoese emerald. At one time when the government was hard pressed for money, the Sacro Catino was offered to a rich Jew of Metz as pledge for a loan of 100,000 crowns. He was loath to take it, as he probably recognized its spurious character, and when Christian clients forced him to accept it under threats of dire vengeance in case of refusal, he protested that they were taking a base advantage of the unpopularity of his faith, since they could not find a Christian who would make the loan. However, when some years later the Genoese were ready to redeem this precious relic, they were much puzzled to learn that a half-dozen different persons claimed to have it in their possession, the fact being that the Jew had fabricated a number of copies which he had succeeded in pawning for large sums, assuring the lender in each case that the redemption of the pledge was certain.

Be this anti-Semitic folktale as it may, the catino was indeed pawned in 1319 and redeemed in 1327 (Marica 2007, 7; Lottero 2010). It is still owned by the municipality of Genoa (Marica 2007, 12).

In any event, the catino is not made of emerald—no matter how much its color and hexagonal shape give it the appearance of a faceted gemstone. At about fifteen inches in diameter, it would have been an immense emerald indeed! Actually, according to the museum's guidebook (Marica 2007, 12), it is simply of "mould-blown green glass." Its manufacture is said to be Egyptian (Barber 2004, 168) or ninth-century Islamic (Marica 2007, 12), or possibly later.

Its glass composition was revealed when it became broken (figure 22.3). According to the 1910 *Encyclopedia Britannica* (s.v. "Genoa"), the catino "was long regarded as an emerald of matchless value, but was found when broken at Paris, whither it had been carried by Napoleon I., to be only a remarkable piece of ancient glass." (Another view is that it was broken on its return to Genoa [Marica 2007, 7], and a 1914 *New York Times* story claimed—possibly because of erroneous translation—that it had just been "accidentally broken" and was "beyond the possibility of repair" ["'Holy Grail' Shattered" 1914].) In any case, the bowl was restored in 1908 and again, finally, in 1951, when it received the metal armature that holds the pieces together Lottero 2010; Marica 2007, 7). (A rumor claims that the missing piece—again see figure 22.3—was kept in Paris in the Louvre [Lottero 2010].)

UNHOLY GRAIL

When the belief that the catino was made of emerald was broken to pieces, so was the claim that it was the Holy Grail. Its alleged Christological link was asserted long after the bowl arrived in Genoa, and *it was predicated on the basis of its supposed emerald composition.* This leap of faith was made by Jacopo da Voragine, archbishop of Genoa and author of *Legenda Aurea* (*Golden Legend*).

In a chronicle of Genoa written at the close of the thirteenth century, Jacopo, believing the vessel was indeed made of emerald, linked it to one of

the grail traditions. He cited certain English texts that claimed that Nicodemus had used an emerald vessel to collect Jesus' blood when his body was
placed in his tomb and that these texts called it "Sangraal"—that is, "Holy
Grail" (Marica 2007, 7; Barber 2004, 168).

Alas, there is nothing to credibly connect the Sacro Catino to a first-
century grail, and the same may be said of other supposed grail vessels.
Indeed, observes Barber (2004, 170), "there is little or no evidence that anyone
claimed in the thirteenth century to possess the Grail." Certainly, claims for all
such vessels date from after the period when most of the grail romances were
penned: between 1190 and 1240 (Nickell 2007, 60). This realization should put
an end to fanciful grail quests, but it probably will not: witness the popularity of
such books as *The Da Vinci Code* (Brown 2003) and the book on which its author
drew heavily, *Holy Blood, Holy Grail* (Baigent et al. 1996)—silliness all.

Figure 22.1. In Genoa, the author poses with Il Sacro Catino ("The Holy
Basin"), long believed to be the Holy Grail. (Author's photo)

Figure 22.2. A Genoese palace fresco depicts Guglielmo Embriaco, merchant and military leader, with the catino as war booty. (Photo by Joe Nickell)

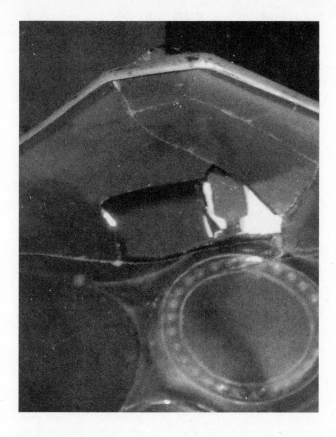

Figure 22.3. Supposedly made of emerald, the catino was broken in the early nineteenth century, disproving the claim. (Photo by Joe Nickell)

CHAPTER 23

ST. JAMES'S
MIRACULOUS RELICS

For centuries the site of the Cathedral of Santiago de Compostela in northwestern Spain has been a place of reputed miracles, including revelations and healings. Today, among its visitors are New Agers who consider the cathedral "a reservoir of powerful positive psychic energy," some even claiming to see apparitions of earlier pilgrims (Hauck 2000).

On September 6, 1997, I made my own "pilgrimage" to the historic cathedral. I had been attending the Ninth EuroSkeptics Conference in the nearby seaport city of La Coruña ("The Crown"), and the cathedral was the focus of a Saturday's scheduled sightseeing trip—a secular pilgrimage in the company of scientists and other skeptics, including CSICOP's chairman, Paul Kurtz, and Executive Director Barry Karr. Not only did I appreciate the cathedral's Romanesque architecture, but I also began to delve into its history, steeped in centuries-old myths and pious legends.

LEGENDS OF ST. JAMES

The cathedral marks the site of the allegedly miraculous discovery of the remains of St. James the Greater, so named to distinguish him from the other apostle of that name. (There were also various other Jameses in the Christian Gospels, including one of Jesus' brothers [Mark 6:3; Matthew 13:55].) James the Greater was a son of Zebedee. Jesus found him and his brother John mending nets by Lake Genesareth also known as the "Sea of Galilee") and

157

called them to his ministry. (This was just after he had similarly invited Simon and Andrew, promising to make them "fishers of men" [Mark 1:16–20].) In the early history of the church, James was the first disciple to be martyred (Acts 12:1–2). He was executed by King Herod Agrippa I in 44 CE. According to one legend, his accuser repented as the execution was about to occur and was beheaded with him (Jones 1994).

By the seventh century, another pious legend claimed that James had taken the Gospel to Spain. Subsequently, still another legend told how Herod had forbidden the burial of James's beheaded body, whereupon that night several Christians secretly carried his remains to a ship. "Angels" then conducted the vessel "miraculously" to Spain, and the body was transported to the site of the present-day cathedral.

The apostle's body lay undiscovered until the early ninth century (about 813 CE). Then, according to still another miracle tale, a pious friar was led to the site by a "star," in much the same manner as the wise men were supposedly guided to the birthplace of Jesus in the New Testament (Matthew 2:1–12). The supernatural light revealed the burial place. The local bishop accepted the validity of the friar's discovery and had a small basilica built over the supposed saint's sepulcher. It was destroyed a century later in a Muslim raid, but in 1078 work was begun on the present cathedral. It was mostly complete by 1128 (McBirnie 1973; Coulson 1958; *El Camino* 1990, 2–3, 36–37).

The alleged discovery came at an opportune time. After the Moors conquered Spain, only its northwest corner remained independent, and it was from there that the drive to reconquer the country for Christendom was launched ("Santiago de Compostela" 1960). The supposedly divine revelation of the relics seemed to endorse the quest, and St. James (Santiago) "became the rallying figure for Christian opposition to the Moors" (Jones 1994). Miracles began to occur at the site, resulting in "an extensive collection of stories" that were "designed to give courage to the warriors" fighting against the Moors. There were even stories of the saint appearing on the battlefield at crucial moments, and he was sometimes known as Santiago Matamoros, that is, "St. James the Moorslayer." The tales also bolstered the pilgrims who began to wend their way to Compostela (*El Camino* 1990, 3, 36–37; Cavendish 1989).

MAGICAL RELICS

Medieval pilgrims were attracted to holy places, including churches that hosted powerful relics. In Catholicism a relic is an object associated with a saint or martyr (such as a bone or piece of clothing). According to Kenneth L. Woodward's *Making Saints* (1990), "Just as the soul was totally present in every part of the body, so, it was popularly believed, the spirit of the saint was powerfully present in each relic. Thus, detached from the whole body and separated from the tomb, relics took on magical power of their own." As well, mere proximity could be enough: "the medieval pilgrim was satisfied if he could but gaze on the tomb of his cult-object" (Pick 1929).

At the Cathedral of Santiago de Compostela, the relics of St. James now began to work wonders, and various "prodigies, miracles and visions" multiplied there (*El Camino* 1990, 3). Many made the pilgrimage to Santiago to be healed of an affliction (Gitlitz and Davidson 2000), but perhaps most did so for the experience itself and to be compensated by "indulgences," remissions of punishment due a sinner (*El Camino* 1990, 4). "In the Middle Ages," notes one reference work (Kennedy 1984), "it was possible for the faithful to buy such pardon for their sins, and unscrupulous priests saw the selling of indulgences as an easy way of raising money." (Abuse of indulgences was among the criticisms that led to the Protestant Reformation.)

PILGRIMAGES

There were many roads to Compostela, but one of three major medieval pilgrimage routes remains popular today, inviting not only religious supplicants but also historians, art lovers, adventurers, and others. It is a nearly five-hundred-mile trek called the Santiago de Compostela Camino— or just "Camino" for short (meaning the road or way). Beginning in France, it winds across the Pyrénées, and then traverses northern Spain westward to Santiago (Gitlitz and Davidson 2000; MacLaine 2000).

Among those who made pilgrimages to Compostela were such historic notables as St. Francis of Assisi and the Spanish monarchs Ferdinand and Isabella. More recently there was Shirley MacLaine. The acclaimed actress—sometimes disparaged as "the archetypal New Age nut case" for her belief in past lives, alternative medicine, and other fringe topics (Neville 2000)—wrote about her experiences along the pilgrims' way in *The Camino: A Journey of the Spirit*. Although the book was published in 2000, she actually made the trek in 1994, as shown by her *compostelana* (pilgrim certificate of Santiago de Compostela) reproduced inside the book's covers.

The Camino is more than merely a record of MacLaine's inward and outward journeys; it is a veritable catalog of her mystical notions and fantasy experiences. Never religious, she says, she adopts a New Age mantra of "opting instead to seek spirituality."

On her trip she soon feels that she is "visited by an angel named Ariel," who, she writes, "began to talk to me in my head." Ariel told her to "learn to have pleasure as you experience it." She reflects on some of her alleged past-life memories or "revisitations" (her past lives included one as a geisha in Japan and others as inhabitants of India and Russia). When she is "not really dreaming" she has an "intensely real" experience in which a monk appears to her, announcing, "I am John the Scot." She is able to converse with him about the "science" of astrology and about "karma" (supposedly the consequences of a person's deeds that carry over and help shape his or her next reincarnation). They also discuss "ley lines" (imaginary connections between supposed sites of power, such as megaliths, ancient monuments, holy wells, temples, and so on) (Guiley 1991).

Occasionally, reality intrudes. Once, seeking to relieve herself, she squats over an anthill! Sometimes she is admirably observant:

> In every village I was awed by the opulent richness of the churches, while the poor people who attended them gave every last penny they had to the collection plate. One priest sold holy candles to the peasants, which they lit, placed on the altar, and prayed over. When they left, the priest put them up for sale again. They had paid for the privilege of praying.

Midway through her narrative MacLaine pauses to decide "whether to include the ensuing events" that promise to take the reader "off the Camino path and to the edge of reason." Then she launches into another of her "dream-visions" in which John the Scott guides her on an odyssey to the legendary lost continents of Lemuria and Atlantis. There she learns that the latter was "an advanced colony of Lemurians" and that they in turn had received input from extraterrestrials who have surveyed Earth for millennia (MacLaine 2000, 187, 213).

Eventually, she arrives at the cathedral to pay her respects to Santiago de Compostela—Saint James—or, as she describes him, "the saint with no head," adding, "I felt the same way" (MacLaine 2000, 294). There, in a practice familiar to countless visitors, she climbs the stairs that lead behind a Romanesque painted-stone statue of the seated apostle and, as directed by custom since the seventeenth century (Gitlitz and Davidson 2000, 344), she hugs the effigy (see figure 23.1). She does not mention whether she then descended to the crypt to view the reliquary that supposedly contains the saint's bones, but—after a priest ritualistically bathes her feet—she is soon out of the cathedral and on a flight to Madrid. She reflects on her odyssey of imagination and reality: "Perhaps all of it is simple. We came from the Divine; we create with that imaginative energy until we return to it. Lifetime after lifetime" (MacLaine 2000, 306).

Although the Camino pilgrimage has declined over the past few centuries, one reviewer predicts MacLaine's book "will change that" (Neville 2000). But even before her visit, pilgrims had begun to multiply, and now, according to *The International Directory of Haunted Places* (Hauck 2000), New Age visitors to the cathedral consider it "a reservoir of powerful positive psychic energy." Indeed, "they sense the spiritual energy and devotion to the divine that tens of thousands of pilgrims brought to this site, and sometimes they even report seeing the apparitions of those dedicated souls making their way through the city to the holy shrine."

INVESTIGATION

But are the relics of St. James—the central focus of the shrine and indeed its very *raison d'être*—genuine? And if they are not, what does that say about all of the reputed miracles there—the alleged revelations, healings, apparitions, and other supernatural and paranormal phenomena?

Few contemporary historians believe St. James ever visited Spain. According to one guidebook, *Roads to Santiago* (Nooteboom 1997, 201), "The fiery resplendence of Santiago and all it inspired came about because people *believed* they had found the grave of the apostle James in that town, events therefore that were set in motion by something that perhaps never took place at all." One dictionary of saints (Coulson 1958) explains some of the reasons for skepticism:

> Tradition asserts that James brought the gospel to Spain, but because of the early date of his death, this claim is quite untenable. In the Acts of the Apostles it is Paul who is depicted as the pioneer missionary, and James was dead before Paul's activity began.... In fact, the tradition only appears in written form for the first time in the seventh century, arising from a Greek source of doubtful historical credentials, but it was a century later, when a star miraculously revealed what was claimed to be the tomb of James, that popular belief spread. This shrine at Compostella (probably derived from Campus stellae: the field of the star) rivalled Rome as a center of pilgrimage.

But did the legend of the star give rise to the name Compostela, or was it the other way around? According to an official Spanish government guidebook (*El Camino de Santiago* 1990, 2), the place chosen to deposit St. James's sarcophagus was "at exactly the spot where a former *compostum* (cemetery) lay, which in the course of time became Compostela."[1] In fact, excavations beneath the cathedral have yielded "remnants of a pre-Roman necropolis" as well as "remains of a Roman cemetery," together with "an altar dedicated to Jupiter" (Gitlitz and Davidson 2000, 346, 351). In this light, it seems plausible that Compostela might have derived not from *Campus stellae* ("star field") but from *Campus stelae* (a *stele* being an inscribed stone), which is to say, "field of monuments" or "gravestone field." Another possibility is that it is a combined form of *compositus* ("orderly arrangement") and *stelae* ("tombstones"). Even more likely (according to Kevin Christopher, CSICOP's publicity director, who has degrees in classics and linguistics) is the possibility that *compostela* is simply a diminutive form of *compostum*.

If any of these alternate interpretations is correct, it would suggest that a name that originally meant "graveyard" was mistranslated as "star field," which in turn prompted the little tale purporting to "explain" the name.

This process—by which a folk etymology apparently leads to the creation of a legend—is well known. One example is the name of a British tribe (Trinovantes), which seems to have been corrupted to *Troynovant*, or "New Troy," prompting a legend that remnant Trojans had settled a then-uninhabited Britain (Howatson 1989). Again, the name of a class of "miraculous" Christ portraits, *vera iconica*, or "true images," became known as "veronicas"—hence apparently inspiring the legend that a pious woman of that name gave her veil to Jesus to wipe his face as he struggled to his crucifixion (Nickell 1998).

As we have seen, there were numerous other legends about St. James, as of course there were about other religious figures and subjects. Many factors contributed to the manufacture of saints' legends. For example, speaking specifically of Santiago, one source observes that "many of the great romances of the middle ages developed from the tales told by the pilgrims to while away the tedium of the long journey to this remote corner of Spain" ("Santiago de Compostela" 1960). A more sinister view of the entire affair regarding St. James and his legends is given by Hauck (2000):

> The discovery of his relics was apparently a hoax perpetrated by the Church to attract pilgrims and take the region back from Arabian settlers [the Moors]. It is known that the Cathedral of Santiago sent hired "storytellers" to spread the news of miracles associated with the relics, and their tactics seem to have worked, for by the twelfth century, this was the most popular pilgrimage site in Europe.

Of course, discrediting the legend of the relics' miraculous discovery, and even debunking the alleged missionary work of St. James in Spain, "does not dispose of the claim that the relics at Compostela are his" (Coulson 1958). Yet how likely is it that the apostle's remains would have been arduously transported to northern Spain in the first place, and then have remained unknown until they were allegedly revealed nearly eight centuries later?

There are additional doubts stemming from the fact that the discovered remains of St. James were accompanied by the skeletons of two others. While that would not be surprising at the site of an ancient cemetery, how would the pious legend makers explain the two extra bodies buried with the apostle? They simply declared them to be the relics of "two of his disciples" (McBirnie 1973, 94).

Further suspicion about the authenticity of the relics comes from the climate of relic mongering that was prevalent in the Middle Ages.

As demand for relics intensified, "a wholesale business in fakes" grew in response (Pick 1929). Alleged relics included the fingers of St. Paul, John the Baptist, and the doubting Thomas. Most prolific were "relics" associated with Jesus himself. No fewer than six churches preserved his foreskin. Other relics included hay from his manger, gifts from the wise men, and vials of Mary's breast milk. From the crucifixion various churches had thorns from the crown of thorns, while the Sainte Chapelle in Paris possessed the entire crown. There were some forty "true" shrouds, including the notorious Shroud of Turin, which appeared in the middle of the fourteenth century as part of a faith-healing scheme (Nickell 1998).

In the case of St. James, there is even a question about the exact nature of the relics. McBirnie (1973, 106–107), in his *The Search for the Twelve Apostles*, declares as a certainty that James's body was buried in Jerusalem. However, he believes it possible that later "some of the bones of the Apostle, perhaps the body" might have been removed to Spain with the head remaining in Jerusalem. On the other hand, there were alleged portions of the body elsewhere. For example, at Constantinople was enshrined "a silver arm encompassing a relic of St. James the Greater," which was later (after the capture of Constantinople in 1204) taken to Troyes, France (Gies and Gies 1969). Another relic, the saint's hand, is supposedly preserved at the abbey in Reading, England (Jones 1994). Still another relic is claimed by an Italian cathedral (McBirnie 1973, 96).

Of course, the relics could have been subdivided, a common medieval practice (McBirnie 1973, 107), but even the presumed link between the relics that were supposedly revealed miraculously in the early ninth century and those enshrined at Compostela today is questionable. Reports Gitlitz and Davidson (2000):

Actually, Santiago's bones were hidden several times in successive centuries to keep them out of the hands of various threatening parties, such as Drake, who wanted them for England, and various Spanish monarchs, who coveted them for the Escorial. Eventually their exact location was forgotten altogether, although pilgrims continued to venerate an urn on the altar that they believed held the bones. Excavations in 1878–9 unearthed some bones that—when the discoverer went temporarily blind—were held to be those of the Apostle. Six years later Pope Leo XIII issued a bull verifying the validity of the relics, thus—at least officially—ending all controversy.

In short, there are some bones at Compostela whose provenance cannot credibly be traced to James the Greater. As *The Penguin Dictionary of Saints* concludes, there is "no evidence whatever as to the identity of the relics discovered in Galicia early in the ninth century and claimed to be those of St. James" (Attwater 1983). But if the relics are bogus, as the evidence strongly indicates, how can we explain the reported supernatural and paranormal events there? Can they actually have naturalistic explanations? Indeed they can. For example, supposedly divine cures may simply be due to the body's own healing ability eventually proving effective, or to an abatement of the illness (known as "spontaneous remission"), or to the effects of suggestion (the well-known placebo effect). A reduction in pain—caused by suggestion or by the physiological effects of excitement—may also give the illusion that a miracle "cure" has taken place (Nickell 1998). (See part 3 of this book.)

Visionary experiences, like those of Shirley MacLaine, can also have prosaic explanations. They may be due to pilgrims' heightened expectations and other factors, including the propensity of certain individuals to fantasize. MacLaine exhibits several traits associated with a "fantasy-prone" personality. Such persons may have rich fantasy lives, believe they have psychic powers, supposedly receive special messages from higher beings, report vivid dreams and apparitional experiences, and so forth (Wilson and Barber 1983; Baker and Nickell 1992) (see part 4).

MacLaine's "dream-visions" that occurred when she rested along the Camino, having an experience that "seemed more than a dream" (MacLaine 2000, 79, 105), may have been what is termed "lucid dreaming." A lucid dream is one in which the dreamer is able to *direct* the dreaming, "something like waking up in your dreams" (Blackmore 1991). In fact, MacLaine (2000, 59) says she "realized that on some level I must be controlling in some manner what I dreamed." That she had her dream-visions while hiking nearly five hundred miles at a rate of up to twenty miles a day is interesting, since it is known that lucid dreaming tends to occur following "high levels of physical (and emotional) activity" (Blackmore 1991, 365).

Similar explanations may apply to the apparitions reported by some "New Age visitors" to Santiago de Compostela—ghostly pilgrims seen "making their way through the city to the holy shrine" (Hauck 2000). Such apparitions may be nothing more than mental images that are superimposed upon the visual scene—especially if the experiencer is daydreaming or performing some routine activity (Nickell 2000), conditions consistent with walking on a long journey.

As to any protective powers supposedly obtained by hugging the saint's statue, my own experience belied any such notion. After performing the charming ritual myself, I stepped up onto a narrow ledge of the small chamber to attempt a better view for some snapshots. While I survived that precarious act, later in the afternoon I slipped on steps outside my hotel in La Coruña and broke my leg very badly. (Picture me lying in agony surrounded by skeptics who suggest that I may only have a sprain and invite me to see if I can wiggle my toes. But when I lift my leg and they observe the bizarre angle of the foot, their doubts are silenced!)

If the Cathedral of Santiago de Compostela does not house a saint's relics that exude supernatural power, it nevertheless is a monument to the persistence of magical thinking. Built apparently on the site of a Roman shrine to Jupiter (with accompanying necropolis), it became a focal point for Christian pilgrims, yet it is now seemingly undergoing further transition as New Agers adapt it to their occultish superstitions. They see it as a site of powerful "psychic energy" and the pilgrimage route as a tracing of mystical "ley lines" (Hauck 2000; MacLaine 2000, 4–5). Although specific beliefs change, what philosopher Paul Kurtz (1991) terms "the quest for transcendence" seems perpetual.

Figures 23.1–23.3. In Spain's Cathedral of Santiago de Compostela, pilgrims climb stairs to an alcove behind the statue of Santiago (St. James), which they embrace in a centuries-old tradition. (Photos by Joe Nickell)

CHAPTER 24

"INCORRUPTIBLE" CORPSES

Growing up in Morgan County, Kentucky, in the Appalachian foothills, I heard a colorful legend of a remarkably preserved corpse that had been discovered in the nineteenth century when a cemetery was being relocated. I would later learn of certain "incorruptible" bodies—many of them saints of the Roman Catholic Church—found worldwide. Such cases are often held to contravene science, but is there more to the phenomenon than meets the eye?

"PETRIFIED GIRL"

Extensive research I conducted on the Kentucky case in the early 1990s revealed that the unmarked grave in question had been that of a seventeen-year-old girl named Nancy A. "Nannie" Wheeler, who had died October 1, 1885. When she was exhumed, the fact that her coffin proved too heavy to lift and that her body was remarkably preserved led people to conclude she was "petrified," and so a folktale was launched that grew in the retelling (Nickell 1994).

In fact, petrifaction in the case of a coffin burial is exceedingly rare. Several "petrified" people have been outright hoaxes, including the Forest City man, shown at the World's Columbian Exposition in Chicago in 1893, the "Pine River Man" (made of water lime, sand, and gravel) "discovered" in 1876, the "Colorado Man" (faked for P. T. Barnum at a cost of $2,000), and others, including the notorious Cardiff Giant (unearthed at Cardiff,

169

New York, in 1869) (MacDougall 1958, 23–24; Stein 1993, 123–24, 145).

Many times bodies are said to be petrified when observers are simply astonished to find them in a surprising state of preservation. The excessive weight in the case of Miss Wheeler's coffin was coincident with its having been waterlogged, necessitating the drilling of holes to drain the water.

As to the remarkable preservation, it was unlikely that the body had been embalmed even though it had remained relatively free of decomposition for almost thirty months. However, as is well known to forensic pathologists, a body long submerged in water—as apparently occurred in this instance—can form a whitish, soap-like substance called adipocere (or "grave wax") that may develop in the outer layer of fat after a few months. (Spitz 1993, 38). This condition is estimated to become "complete in adult bodies" after about eighteen months (Gonzales et al. 1954, 68). Depending on subsequent conditions, the body may eventually take on the leathery effect of mummification, or it may eventually decompose completely (Ubelaker and Scammell 1992, 150–51; Geberth 1993, 571–72).

Whatever the actual facts regarding Nannie Wheeler, she does appear to have been well preserved—some say as beautiful as she had been in life, with her hands still clutching her hat. However, the time between burial and disinterment had been less than two and a half years, and there have been instances of excellent preservation over much longer periods—also without apparent embalming.

THE "INCORRUPTIBLES"

Among the remarkable cases of preservation are the corpses of several Catholic saints, such as St. Charles Borromeo (1538–1584) and St. Philip Neri (1515–1595), who are said to be "incorruptible" and "undoubtedly miraculous" (figure 24.1). Yet in these and many other such cases it turns out that the viscera were removed and the bodies embalmed.

In other cases the bodies are in reality mummified—that is, desiccated—which can occur naturally under favorable conditions, such as the body being kept in sandy soil or a dry tomb or catacombs; it can also be induced by embalming. Several "incorruptible" saints' bodies are revealingly described as "dry," "darkened," "wrinkled," or the like, consistent with mummification (Cruz 1977; Nickell 2001, 7).

Often, in such instances, clothing and wax face masks are used to minimize the emaciated appearance and make the bodies presentable for viewing (usually in glass cases in European churches). These skillfully made wax faces explain the lifelike appearance of such saints' corpses when they appear in close-up photographs, like that of Saint Bernadette of Lourdes (Nickell 1993, 92). (Again, see figure 24.1)

Again, as with the "petrified girl," the opposite conditions to those of mummification may have been involved in some cases of supposedly saintly incorruptibility. For instance, long after the death of St. Catherine Labouré, "her body was found perfectly white and natural looking, even though her triple coffin had been affected in various ways by excessive moisture." That extended even to her winding sheet (Cruz 1977, 35).

For a discussion of many specific instances of saints' "incorruptibility" and revealing facts concerning them, please see "The Incorruptibles" in my earlier book *Looking for a Miracle: Weeping Icons, Relics, Stigmata, Visions and Healing Cures* (1993, 85–100).

"VAMPIRES"

While amazingly preserved corpses are found in various parts of the world, those discovered in certain Slavic countries may provoke a bizarre response. There, local people often believe that such preservation means the person is one of the "undead," and so they drive a wooden stake through the heart and then burn the body to end the imagined ghoulish activities of the "vampire."

Wilson and Wilson (1992, 374–76) cite the story of an eighteenth-century Serbian man, Peter Plogojowitz, whose body was exhumed and, except for a somewhat sunken nose, "was completely fresh" and even had "some fresh blood in his mouth." However, just such characteristics are frequently said to describe the "incorruptible" bodies of saints, for example, that of St. Sperandia (1216–1276), which was found intact well after her burial, exuding a "blood-fluid" (Cruz 1977, 48). Roman Catholics would not appreciate the suggestion that their saints were actually vampires! In contrast to the corpse of St. Sperandia, which was exhumed two years after her death, that of Plogojowitz had been interred little more than ten weeks. (For more on Plogojowitz, as well as explanations for the phenomena that give rise to a belief in vampires, see my *Tracking the Man-Beasts*, 2011, 121–29.)

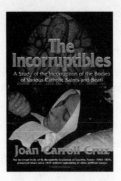

Figure 24.1. Joan Carroll Cruz's *The Incorruptibles* suggests that remarkable preservations of corpses are miracles.

PART 3
MIRACLE HEALINGS

CHAPTER 25

JESUS' HEALINGS

A mong the ancients, the belief that illness could be cured by divine intervention was widespread.

ANCIENT HEALING

The Egyptians worshipped various gods—notably the ibis-headed Thoth, who could be appealed to for healing. (Typically, priests played the role of intermediaries.) In Mesopotamia, where angry deities supposedly caused afflictions, a sufferer could appeal to the god or goddess—if he or she knew just which of the many had been offended! The ancient Greeks also appealed to their deities, especially Aesculapius, the god of medicine.

The ancient Jews recognized Yahweh (Jehovah) as the universal source of both illness and healing, although folk medicine might also be applied. (For instance, King Hezekiah was cured of an ulcerous boil by means of prayer and a fig poultice [2 Kings 20:1–11].)

According to legends in the New Testament, Jesus, the central figure of Christianity, launched a healing ministry and effected seemingly miraculous cures of body and mind wherever he went. The Gospels record more than forty healing acts (not counting duplicate or parallel accounts)—either of individuals or groups.

Jesus also gave his disciples the power of healing, saying that "they shall lay hands on the sick, and they shall recover" (Mark 16:15–18). (This practice continued in the Roman Catholic and Eastern Orthodox churches, but Protestant reformers like Luther and Calvin held that the age of faith heal-

175

ings ended with the death of the apostles. Later, certain Protestants—particularly Pentecostals—revived the practice.)

THE CURATIVE PROCESS

It is crucial to realize that the body has natural healing mechanisms. Routinely, wounds mend, broken bones knit, infections respond to the body's immune system, and so on. According to one estimate, up to 75 percent of patients would get better even without medical treatment (Hines 1988, 239). What may pass for miraculous healing may actually be the result of one of the following.

Misdiagnosis or misreporting. Illnesses may not be as believed or represented. For instance, one girl's "inoperable, malignant brain-stem tumor" was supposedly confirmed by two CT scans and attested by doctors at Johns Hopkins University. Actually, a medical investigator discovered that the "dark mass" in the CT scan was merely an imperfection of the scanning process, that the girl's physicians had not suspected a tumor at all, and that subsequently the "miracle" was an invented one (Randi 1987, 291–92).

Spontaneous remission. Some serious ailments, certain types of cancer for example, may undergo what is termed "spontaneous remission." They may either go away entirely or, as sometimes occurs, for instance with multiple sclerosis, they may abate for periods ranging from a few months to several years. Although the nature of such remissions is still not fully understood by medical science, the fact of their unpredictable occurrence is well documented. If a remission or regression should occur any time after a "healer" has performed his ritual, remission may be incorrectly attributed to his intervention (Hines 1988, 239; Larue 1990, 139).

Psychosomatic illnesses. Certain illnesses demonstrate how interrelated are mind (*psyche*) and body (*soma*), being most amenable to "miracle" cures. A striking variety of psychosomatic conditions, ranging from back pains to hysterical blindness, are proven to be responsive to suggestion, whether in the form of faith healing, so-called hypnosis, "alternative" medical treatments (such as acupuncture or chiropractic), or placebo medications. The main requisite for curative effects is the patient's belief in the practitioner and his or her methods (Hines 1988, 238–39; Larue 1990, 139–43).

Even illnesses with a distinct physical cause may respond partially to techniques of "mental medicine" such as meditation and "visualization" (in which the sufferer is encouraged to focus on his or her condition and envision a cure (for example, that a tumor is disappearing). Such approaches have been used together with traditional medicine in treating conditions like arthritis, high blood pressure, gastrointestinal disorders, and cancer (Baker 1990, 282–83). Pain is particularly responsive to suggestion. According to one authority, "The placebo effect and the temporal variability of pain in any painful disease work together to produce a powerful illusion that a faith healer or a quack has effected a 'cure'" (Hines 1988, 238–39).

JESUS' "MIRACULOUS" CURES

Whether or not the healings supposedly performed by Jesus actually occurred, they no doubt reflect similar afflictions and attitudes of the time, and explanations may be given accordingly. For example, the biblical word *leprosy* does not refer to the disease now called leprosy (Hansen's disease) but was loosely applied to a variety of skin disorders such as eczema, contagious ringworm, psoriasis, and the like. The woman who had a flow of blood for twelve years, who "had suffered many things of many physicians, and had spent all that she had" (Mark 5:25–34) may have suffered from a chronic and painful menstruation of a nervous variety (United Church 1967). So, too, the man with "an infirmity" who waited for thirty-eight years beside the supposedly curative pool of Bethesda (John 5:2–9) could have suffered from a profound neurosis (United Church 1967). (Of the "multitude of invalids"—"blind, halt, withered"—lying in the porticoes, he was the only one selected for healing [see figure 25.1].)

The various cases of demonic possession referred to in the Gospels are now seen as examples of psychiatric disorder (United Church 1967). Any of the illnesses cited above could prove responsive to charismatic healing, just as they were in the centuries after Jesus and have been to the present day. (Unfortunately, many of those so "cured" may receive only temporary relief before regressing to their former state and worse.)

Restoration of sight to the blind would be an amazing act, seemingly magical however accomplished. Yet apart from charismatic healings of the hysterically blind, which ancient healers probably performed, there was another class of blindness cures: for the Essenes (members of a sect of

Jesus' contemporaries) used "empirical medical procedures to restore the sight of those afflicted with cataracts" (Craveri 1970, 71). Now Mark says Jesus healed the blind man by applying spittle (Pliny's *Natural History* suggests it as an eye ointment for curing opthalmia [Allegro 1970, 56]); Matthew claims he healed two blind men by a touch; Luke makes no reference to the blind man; while John says he used clay made from spittle to anoint the man's eyes. In the latter, more detailed account we see the application of an abrasive, following which the man was told to go wash. From the Book of Tobit in Catholic Bibles is a comparable account of Tobias treating his father, Tobit. He sprinkled gall upon his father's eyes, and when Tobit's eyes began to smart he rubbed them, whereupon the white films were removed (Tobit 11:11–13). Then Tobit saw his son and embraced him. Perhaps at the root of such accounts is some attempt to employ a "medical"—rather than magical—treatment. Whatever was done, we are told, was successful. It was seemingly miraculous.

RAISING THE DEAD

Resurrection of the dead is a magico-religious concept deriving from the ancient Egyptians. They thought that the actual physical body participated with the immortal soul in the afterlife—hence the emphasis on embalming "to insure that the remains of their loved one, bound for the underworld and its final judgment before the gods, would make the trip intact" (Carroll 1975, 77–78). Their art thus portrayed the winged soul hovering over the dead body (Budge 1901, 113), and chapter 158 of the Book of the Dead describes one embalmed figure rising from his swathings (Budge 1901, 49).

The concept may have been prompted by some first-hand observation: "In the ancient world there were many cases of the hasty burial of an apparently dead person, who, as a subsequent opening of the grave revealed, had awakened from his coma to a living death" (Enslin 1968, 151). (However, after Egyptian mummification, this was not possible, for the corpse was eviscerated—the brain removed by a hook inserted through the nostrils—and the organs were preserved in jars to be entombed with the dead person [Carroll 1975, 78–80]. Quite some magic would be required to revive such a one!)

At some point, empirical attempts to resuscitate the comatose developed. Among the medical procedures employed by the pre-Christian

Essenes were "mouth-to-mouth breathing techniques to revive the unconscious" (Craveri 1970, 71). Such procedures, commonplace today, may
extend backward from the Qumran sect many centuries. The wonderworking prophet Elisha—as did Elijah before him—revived a small boy
who was "not awake" (2 Kings 4:34–35): "And he went up and lay upon the
child, and put his mouth upon his mouth, and his eyes upon his eyes, and his
hands upon his hands: and he stretched himself upon the child; and the flesh
of the child waxed warm. Then he returned, and walked in the house to and
fro; and went up, and stretched himself upon him: and the child sneezed
seven times, and the child opened his eyes."

The synoptic writers credit Jesus with similar feats, one the Raising
of Jairus's Daughter (Mark 5:22–43). In the story, Jairus, one of the rulers
of the synagogue, entreats Jesus to come with him, for he says, "My little
daughter lieth at the point of death." On the way others bring news that the
child has died. But when Jesus arrives he pronounces that "the damsel is not
dead but sleepeth." Taking the child by the hand, as the story goes, Jesus
says, "Damsel, I say unto you, arise." And immediately she did so. Christians have interpreted Jesus' statement that the child was only sleeping to
be figurative (Dummelow 1951, 658–59) despite the fact he says she was
"not dead." Perhaps in such a case a practiced eye had seen the truth of the
matter, for—like a physician—Jesus afterwards reportedly instructed she be
given something to eat.

A similar story—with equally shrewd observation—is told of Krishna
(Chrishna) in the Hindu *Hari-Purana*. "'Why do you weep?' replied Chrishna,
in a gentle voice. 'Do you not see that she is sleeping? See she moves. Kala-
vatti! [the girl's name] Rise and walk!'" Agreed, these tales of Chrishna and
Christ (virtually identical, as are the names of the wonder workers) are
intended by their storytellers to be understood as miraculous resurrections;
yet details in the accounts themselves—assuming them factual—suggest
the "dead" were possibly only unconscious.

That bystanders—especially among the Hebrews—might fail to
approach a supposedly dead person close enough to perceive the vital signs
would not be surprising. Superstition could play a part in this; and, to the
Hebrews, touching the dead meant one would become "unclean" and would
be denied the sacraments until the uncleanness was removed (Asimov 1968,
156–57).

STORY OF LAZARUS

Jesus' Raising of Lazarus is told only by John (11:1–2): "Now a certain man was sick, named Lazarus of Bethany, the town of Mary and her sister Martha. (It was that Mary who anointed the Lord with ointment, and wiped his feet with her hair, whose brother Lazarus was sick.)" In what is clearly a storytelling element, Jesus deliberately tarries, allowing Lazarus to die so that—as he tells his disciples—"ye may believe." He says, "I go that I may awake him out of sleep"; but John has him add: "Lazarus is dead." When Jesus comes to the tomb, a cave, it is covered by a stone.

Jesus asks that the stone be taken away, but Martha pleads, "By this time he stinketh: for he hath been dead four days" [that is, after three days]. Jesus admonishes her to have faith then gives a brief prayer, that "the people which stand by . . . may believe that thou hast sent me." John continues (11:43–44): "And when he thus had spoken, he cried with a loud voice, 'Lazarus, come forth.' And he that was dead came forth bound hand and foot with graveclothes, and his face was bound about with a napkin. Jesus saith to them, 'Loose him, and let him go.'" (See figure 25.2.)

Although only John's Gospel contains the miracle, he did not invent the story. It is, first of all, found in somewhat dislocated fashion in Luke—who relates the raising of an unnamed man and also gives the Parable of Lazarus the Beggar. The anonymous man is the only son of a widow whom Jesus tells, "Weep not." Luke continues (7:14–15): "And he came and touched the bier: and they that bare him stood still. And he said, 'Young man, I say unto thee, Arise.' And he that was dead sat up, and began to speak."

The parable also touches upon resurrection (Luke 16:19–31). The beggar named Lazarus, "full of sores," has died and gone to heaven. A rich man, who had shown little compassion, is in hell. The latter asks that Lazarus be returned to life so that he might warn the rich man's brothers of the fate awaiting them. But, from heaven, Abraham replies, "If they hear not Moses and the prophets, neither will they be persuaded though one rose from the dead."

Did John put together these two elements—the raising of the unnamed man and the parable of Lazarus—to create a single story? Or did both Luke and John tap an earlier source? In any case, as one scholar says of the Lazarus narrative, "it is only a preview of Jesus' own miraculous resurrection; therefore the two are one" (Graham 1975, 337).

Figure 25.1. Jesus heals the sick (mid-nineteenth-century illustration by Julius Schnorr von Carolsfeld).

Figure 25.2. Jesus raises Lazarus from the dead (mid-nineteenth-century illustration by Julius Schnorr von Carolsfeld).

CHAPTER 26

LOURDES AND OTHER HEALING WATERS

Around the world are various alleged "miracle" springs, many promoted by Roman Catholics, the most famous of which is Lourdes in southern France.

BACKGROUND

There, in 1858, a fourteen-year-old girl, Bernadette Soubirous (1844–1879), claimed to see apparitions of the Virgin Mary that directed her to the spring at the back of a grotto (figure 26.1). Soon, rumors of miraculous healings surfaced, along with tales of miracles in Bernadette's youth, and in 1933 the late visionary was canonized a saint (Jones 1994).

Meanwhile, in 1884, the Lourdes Medical Bureau was founded and has since recognized sixty-six miracle cures at the site. Moreover, some 6,800 cases that were said to be "medically inexplicable" did not meet the church's criteria to be declared miraculous. (The existence of a disease must not only be proven in a case but the cure must be "instantaneous" as well as "complete and permanent.") (Nickell 1998; Morris 2004)

MIRACULOUS? REALLY?

However, *miracle* is not a scientific term or concept. Since the Lourdes miracle, claims are derived from those cases that are held to be "medically inexplicable," Claimants are engaging in a logical fallacy called arguing from ignorance. That is, one cannot draw a conclusion from a lack of knowledge. Moreover, some cases appear to be nothing more than the result of poor investigation. For instance, doctors who examined one 1976 certification pronounced it "vague" and "obtuse," labeling the documents as "a lot of mumbo jumbo" and as "unscientific and totally unconvincing" (Nickell 1998, 150–51).

There are additional indicators that Lourdes lacks any true healing properties. One is that cases do have alternate explanations. For example, some concern illnesses—such as multiple sclerosis—that are known to show spontaneous remission. Other "cures" may be attributable to misdiagnosis, psychosomatic conditions, prior medical treatment, the body's own healing power, and other effects.

As well, some types of potential miracle healings never occur at Lourdes, as indicated by the comment of French writer Anatole France. On visiting the shrine and seeing the discarded crutches and canes, he exclaimed, "What, what, no wooden legs???" (Nickell 1998, 150–51).

Still another reason for skepticism is that those who seem eminently to deserve healing may receive no benefits at all. For example, Bernadette herself failed to be aided by the spring's touted curative powers. Having been sickly as a child, she was bedridden for the last years of her life and died young, at the age of only thirty-five (Nickell 1998, 149; Jones 1994).

And then there is the case of ailing Pope John Paul II, who visited Lourdes in August 2004. The eighty-four-year-old pontiff—who had Parkinson's disease and knee and hip debilities—struggled through Mass, gasping and trembling. In a rare reference to his own condition, he assured other ill pilgrims that he shared their suffering. Poignant as was that statement, it nevertheless underscored the fact that the claimed healing powers of Lourdes were ineffective even for the head of the church that promotes the claims of miracles there. He died the following year.

REFORM

As the evidence indicates, Lourdes offers pilgrims only the illusion of miracles. The overwhelming millions of visitors to the shrine receive no benefits, unless false hope is considered one. They are instead drained of money.

Now, Dr. Patrick Theiller, the secretary of the International Medical Committee of Lourdes, has announced that the Lourdes medical panel will no longer be in the "miracle" business. "It's a sort of rebellion, if you will, against laws that don't concern us—and shouldn't," Theiller told the Associated Press' Jamey Keaton (for an article published December 2, 2008). He added, "The medical corps must be independent of the ecclesiastic power." The bishop of the local diocese did acknowledge: "It seems 'miracle' may not be the right word to use anymore. It's no longer a black-and-white question."

Appropriately, it is now the church that will be left to decide on so-called miracles; the panel will only indicate whether cases are "remarkable." And remarkable healings can happen to anyone, independent of religious shrines and supposedly magical water. The $400 million that enrich Lourdes annually could be better spent on medical science than on superstitious beliefs from an earlier time.

OTHER SHRINES

Attributable in part to the success of Lourdes, other "curative" waters are (so to speak) springing up elsewhere. One is at Tlacote, Mexico, where a ranch owner claimed his well water could cure any disease, including AIDS. Scientists said the well yielded only ordinary water but noted that it was safe to drink.

A different verdict was rendered in the case of water on the Rockdale County, Georgia, property of Nancy Fowler, a woman who claimed to see scheduled apparitions of the Virgin Mary. Mrs. Fowler stated that her well water was blessed when Jesus Christ himself appeared to her. However, a sample of the water was found to be contaminated with coliform bacteria and therefore unsuitable for drinking. The Rockdale County Health Department asked the visionary to post a sign at the well to warn people of the possible danger (Nickell 1998, 153). (I later drank the water after it had been treated, and I suffered no ill effects.)

Then there is the "Lourdes of the Bronx," as the *New York Times* dubbed it, where curative water flows from a rocky replica of the French grotto. The fake spring is only piped city water, but the parish priest blesses the water annually in a special rite. The parish business manager says of some people's claims of miracles at the local shrine, "I can't prove anything but the faith they had in the Lord and themselves. I do know there is something here you can't touch, see or feel. But there is something here" (Gonzalez 1992).

That "something" is the aura of the miraculous attending ordinary water that is set in a religious context and offered to the credulous—especially those who are desperate for help.

Figure 26.1. An old print from the "miracle" spring at Lourdes, France, features a statue depicting the Virgin Mary as she supposedly appeared to a visionary in 1858. (Author's collection)

CHAPTER 27

THE BELGIAN LOURDES

I have twice visited the Shrine of Our Lady of Lourdes (named after the famous healing-spring grotto in the French Pyrenees) at Oostakker, Belgium. The shrine's most celebrated miracle is the healing of a laborer named Pierre De Rudder, whose lower left leg was broken by a felled tree in 1867. Reportedly, De Rudder refused amputation and for eight years suffered constant pain from his open and festering wound. Then, in April 1875, he visited the Oostakker shrine where, allegedly, he was instantaneously healed, after which he "walked normally until his death in 1898" at age seventy-six (Neiman 1995, 100–101). On July 25, 1908, the Holy See of Bruges declared the healing supernatural.

Over time, a number of legends grew up about the case, including a claim that De Rudder had been treated by Professor Thiriar, physician to King Léopold II (a claim dropped by the miraculists after a denial by Thiriar himself). More significantly, it was claimed that prior to 1875 De Rudder's unmended leg could be twisted at the fracture point to the extent of revolving the foot half a turn (i.e., putting the heel in front). Then, when De Rudder was allegedly cured in 1875, the mending was "instantaneous." Unfortunately, most of the important testimony in the case went unrecorded for eighteen years, and memories of this age are subject to error (Delcour 1987).

A NEW TWIST

For example, Dr. Van Hoestenberghe claimed that he had performed the twisting movement on De Rudder's leg, when in fact the physician's recollection was a false memory. A letter he had written on May 12, 1875 (which had become lost by the time of a canonical inquiry in 1893 but was rediscovered by 1957) revealed that he had not performed the twist, nor even seen it, but had only heard persons talk about it.

Moreover, the twist was apparently not demonstrated at the point of the fracture by showing the naked leg. Instead, it was done with the leg clothed, so the observers could not know where the twist actually occurred. This is a crucial point because certain supple persons can turn their feet almost completely around, like De Rudder, without benefit of any abnormal mobility.[1] Although some claimed the leg was uncovered when they saw De Rudder twist it, two men who were present for his demonstrations "well over a hundred times" stated the leg was never naked on those occasions (Delcour 1987). De Rudder's eagerness to demonstrate the effect at every opportunity suggests not a suffering man happy to suffer more but someone performing a stunt with a purpose—one that will soon become clear.

INSTANTANEOUS

As to the supposed instantaneous nature of the healing, that claim depends on the dubious testimony of just three persons: an illiterate woman who was apparently represented by hearsay and a father and son who seemed eager to help certify a miracle. (Their story even improved over the years.)

In contrast is the evidence that De Rudder had actually undergone "a certain improvement" about fourteen months after the accident. We know that the viscount who employed De Rudder at the time of the accident gave the invalid worker a pension, characterized as a "nice salary." It was rumored about the village that De Rudder was malingering in order to effect a life of ease.

After the viscount died on July 26, 1874, his heir stopped the pension, whereupon De Rudder's wife and daughter had to begin working. Some eight months later, De Rudder may have hit on a clever plan that would allow him to abruptly end his pretended disability so he could, necessarily, return to work: he went to Oostakker and claimed a miraculous cure. However, he returned home with a scar that, reported by Dr. Van Hoestenberghe, was "such as one finds a long time after a healing" (quoted in Delcour 1987).

Other medical evidence likewise supports the view that De Rudder's healing was less than miraculous. A broken leg such as he suffered could—with immobility and good hygiene—have healed without amputation. Besides, the bones (see figure 27.1) grew together obliquely in a fashion a surgeon would not have been proud of. Also, that which would have indeed been beyond nature—the reconstitution of De Rudder's dead tendon—did not occur (De Meester 1957, 106). One touted proof that the cure was instantaneous comes from the absence of thickening of the bone callus at the mending site, but this thickening could have been reabsorbed by the body in several months or a few years (*Encyclopedia Britannica* 2009, s.v. "callus"). Adrien Delcour (1987) concludes that the physicians who consider the De Rudder case miraculous almost unanimously do so on the basis that the cure was instantaneous, and that, as we have seen, is dependent on dubious testimony. Indeed, there is evidence to the contrary.

IN SUM

The De Rudder case gives one pause regarding other claims of miraculous healing at Oostakker, Lourdes, and elsewhere. Such certifications are often vague and unscientific. *Miracle* is not a scientific concept, and miracle claims are typically only those found to be "medically inexplicable." Thus, claimants are engaging in a logical fallacy called "arguing from ignorance"— that is, drawing a conclusion based on a lack of knowledge (Nickell 2007, 202–205). The De Rudder case is even worse, since there is evidence that an injury, healed long before, was passed off as instantaneous—a miracle that wasn't.

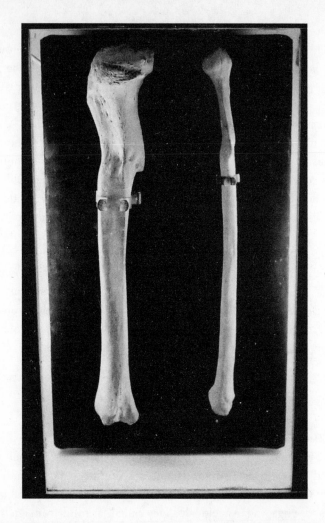

Figure 27.1. The lower left leg bones of Pierre De Rudder, allegedly healed by a miracle in 1875. (Copy photo from Shrine of Oostakker, Belgium, by Joe Nickell)

CHAPTER 28

MIRACLE DIRT OF CHIMAYÓ

C alled "the Lourdes of America" (after the famous French healing shrine), El Santuariò de Chimayó is a place of pilgrimages (figure 28.1). Scores visit the little adobe church daily, while thousands walk miles to worship there on Good Friday. Some carry heavy crosses, while others approach on their knees. Many come seeking a cure for their afflictions, scooping from a small pit in the church floor a reddish soil that they rub on afflicted areas of their bodies or even sprinkle on their food or brew in tea (Eckholm 2008).

THE LEGEND

The Hispanized word *Chimayó* derives from hot springs that were sacred to the Tewa Indians (a linguistic group of Pueblos) who called the springs *Tsimajopokwi* (*pokwì* in Tewa means "pool of water"). After the springs dried up the name was shortened to *Tsimayo* (Nealson 2001, 62). According to a pious legend (of which there are many versions), brethren from the secret Penitente Brotherhood were engaging in rites on a nearby hill on a dark Good Friday in 1810 when one saw a mysterious light coming from the valley. Investigating, and finding a half-buried crucifix, the men sent for a priest, the nearest church being ten miles away in Santa Cruz. The priest had the wooden crucifix carried in a procession to his church, but by the next morning it had disappeared—having been miraculously returned to its original site! This removal and return occurred two more times before people understood the message: the crucifix was to remain on the spot that had reportedly been a sacred area for the Pueblo Indians (Eckholm 2008).

This grafting of a Roman Catholic element onto a native one—a process called *syncretism*—was common. It was often similarly accomplished by the shrewd use of a "miracle." (For example, a "miraculous," actually tempera-painted, image of the Virgin of Guadalupe appeared in Mexico City in 1531 to prompt the building of a Catholic shrine—on a hill where the conquered Aztecs had had a temple to *their* virgin goddess, Tonantzin [Nickell 1998; 2004].)

One of the Penitente brothers, Don Bernardo Abeyta, built a small *hermita* (shelter) onto his house to enshrine the miracle crucifix. The hermita also allegedly "covered a hole from which came a blessed dirt that cured all ailments" (Kay 1987, 35). Abeyta himself was "instantly healed" of an undisclosed illness (Kutz 1988, 46–47). Alternately, Indian stories from the twentieth century suggested that a Tewa pueblo had once stood on the spot next to a pool whose mud had healing properties (Harrington 1916, 342). Revealingly, the chapel's full name (El Santuariò de Chimayó de Nuestro Señor de Esquipulas) evokes a shrine in Guatemala that had long been venerated for its miraculous healing crucifix and surrounding earth with curative powers. As well, there are much-touted healing mud baths at Chilca, Peru (which I visited with a guide in 2006). In any event, in 1816 a chapel was completed on the Chimayó site by Father Francisco de Otocio, who was in charge of all New Mexico missions (Kay 1987, 29–37; Eckholm 2008).

THE NITTY GRITTY ON THE DIRT

Today, pilgrims visiting El Santuariò de Chimayó stoop to enter a small, single-windowed room that is said to be Abeyta's original hermita. The central hole, *El Posito* ("little well"), measures some 16 to 18 inches wide and less than half as deep. Considering the great amount of earth that must have been scooped from it during its almost two centuries of history, however, this is a small hole indeed! Hence, there grew a pious legend "that the pit was refilled by divine intervention" (Eckholm 2008). (This was similar to the claim that regardless of how many pieces were taken from the True Cross, the alleged holy relic of Jesus' crucifixion, it never diminished in size [Nickell 2007, 91–92].)

But even though "legend still maintains that the hole miraculously replenishes itself," in fact "priests periodically refill the hole with dirt from outside the church" (Kay 1987, 77). Indeed, previously tipped off to this fact by a TV cameraman (Del Monte 2000), we searched for and found the storage area where five-gallon containers of the reddish soil are stored (figure 28.2). In recent years, priests at El Santuario de Chimayó have increasingly taken pains to point out the shed where the trucked-in soil is stored, with one complaining, "I even have to buy clean dirt!" (Eckholm 2008).

In fact, the holy dirt is nothing very special. An analysis conducted for *The Miracle Detectives* television series identified the presence of carbonates that might have a beneficial effect on heartburn by neutralizing excess acid. "Beyond that," stated series costar Indre Vìscontas, the show's skeptic, "there doesn't seem to be anything out of the ordinary" ("Holy Dirt of Chimayó" 2011).

I agree. I had collected my own samples for testing in a visit to Chimayó in 2003 with investigator Vaughn Rees. In the guise of a pilgrim needing healing (figure 1), I purchased a small, empty plastic container from the gift shop, labeled "Blessed Dirt." My examination, in my little lab at CSI headquarters, showed that the "dirt" contains no appreciable humus but is largely sand, consisting of tiny grains of minerals and small bits of rock. (Application of hydrochloric acid yielded a strong effervescence that confirmed the presence of carbonates. The addition of potassium ferrocyanide reagent produced a Prussian-blue reaction that identified a significant amount of iron, consistent with its color of red ocher, an earthy iron oxide. Stereomicroscopic examination showed grains of such common minerals as crystalline quartz and mica as well as small lumps of sandstone and occasional bits of organic material, including tiny fragments of bone and fine root stems.[1])

Chimayó priest Father Jim Suntum concedes that the dirt itself has no miraculous power ("Holy Dirt of Chimayó" 2011). In fact, the local dirt has actually acted in a very antimiraculous way: it has posed a threat to the church's artworks. As conservators found in 2003–2004, they "had to deal with the dirt." Indeed, "it had drifted down from the ceiling and walls in the almost 200 years the church had existed, covering the paintings on the five altar screens, the crucifix and the carved *bultos* [sculptures] with a fine dust that needed cleaning. Dirt also had fallen behind the main altar screen to push it out of joint and threaten its very existence." Still, a writer would claim that the preservation process itself, at least, was "almost a miracle" (Russell 2004, 36, 40).

THE HEALING "MIRACLES"

Nevertheless, while Father Suntum concedes it is not the holy dirt that heals but rather one's "relationship with God," he insists, "Something happens in this place." However, he admits, "We can't quantify it. We can't document it. We do ask people to tell their story ("Holy Dirt of Chimayó" 2011). In fact, "officially, the Church has never investigated any of the claims" (*El Santuarió . . .* 1994, 26).

The complete lack of records regarding alleged miraculous experiences means that claims are entirely dependent on anecdotal evidence, such as the unverifiable stories told by an aging priest at the site. For example, in the mid-1950s, he recalled, a man carried his frail, ill mother into the church. "A few minutes later," said the priest, "he called me, something has happened. She was kneeling in front of the altar. She was talking and full of health" (Hamm 2006, 42, 45). Yet we do not need to invoke the miraculous to explain what may have been only a simple rejuvenation of the woman's spirits.

Or consider the tale about a girl from Texas whose family "was told she had little time to live" and that even an operation might not save her. Following their visit to Chimayó the child was well and no operation was necessary. "Two days later," recalls the old priest, "they came back to thank God for the cure" (quoted in Hamm 2006, 45). Now, we cannot prove this story is untrue, but fortunately we do not have to. The tellers of such unverifiable tales have the entire burden of proof.

However, when such cases can be investigated, they are invariably illuminating. For instance, *The Miracle Detectives* examined the case of a Colorado woman, Deseree "Dese" Martinez, who claims the dirt of Chimayó helped her cancer go into remission. Diagnosed at the age of fifteen with aggressive bone cancer in numerous sites in her body, she visited Chimayó, where she mixed the holy dirt with spit and applied it to a sore spot on her leg. The pain was gone by the next morning, and scans the following week showed the area healed. Inexplicably, she did not then rub dirt on the other lesion spots, but they soon disappeared, too.

However, the woman's doctor, Brian Greffe, at the children's hospital in Denver, observed that with such non-Hodgkin's lymphoma in pediatric cases, the hospital's "cure rates are quite high." He attributed Ms. Martinez's success to the chemo treatments that had worked "within days" of their beginning. Obviously, there is no evidence that the interim application of holy dirt to a single site had any effect, although Dr. Greffe did say Martinez's positive outlook and the support of her family were helpful ("Holy Dirt of Chimayó" 2011).

As invariably shown by the evidence, so-called miraculous healings are never scientifically verified. Such claims, like those at Lourdes, the most famous "miracle" shrine, are derived from cases that are supposedly "medically inexplicable"; therefore, they are really examples of a logical fallacy called "arguing from ignorance"—that is, drawing a conclusion from a lack of knowledge. Besides, some illnesses are known to exhibit spontaneous remission, and other reputed cures may be attributable to a host of other factors: misdiagnosis, psychosomatic conditions, the body's own healing mechanisms, and the like, including—as in the case of Ms. Martinez—prior medical treatment (Nickell 2008).

While the church displays crutches and canes—ostensibly cast off after previous cures—they may well have been discarded prematurely. Persons may feel better temporarily after experiencing the hope and excitement of a pilgrimage. Writer Anatole France, on visiting Lourdes and seeing the abandoned canes and crutches there, sagely remarked, "What, what, no wooden legs???" (quoted in Hines 1988, 250).

CONCLUSIONS

As the evidence shows, therefore, claims made for holy dirt at Chimayó are unwarranted. Despite borrowed and contrived legends that the site is miraculous, the soil is actually an ordinary variety trucked in from elsewhere and merely blessed. Priests admit that the "something" that happens at the site cannot be quantified or documented—and indeed a major healing claim fell apart on investigation.

One suspects that the "something" is merely what is termed confirmation bias—the willingness to credit any supposed benefits while ignoring countless failures. One writer offers the apologetic, "It is a mystery why certain people and situations are granted a miracle and others are not" (Hamm 2006). But it is only a "mystery" if one chooses to be blind to the evidence.

Figure 28.1. The author, in the persona of a pilgrim, visits the famous "Lourdes of America," where holy dirt supposedly effects miracle cures. (Author's photo by Vaughn Rees)

Figure 28.2. Despite a legend that the dirt, scooped from a small hole in the church floor, replenishes itself, it is actually purchased from outside and kept in a storeroom until it is time to refill the hole. (Author's photo)

CHAPTER 29

PETER POPOFF'S "GIFT OF KNOWLEDGE"

In case you haven't heard, God is still talking to Peter Popoff. But the "word of knowledge" seemingly whispered into the TV evangelist's ear is no longer secretly broadcast by Mrs. Popoff.

I had wondered what the good reverend was doing since his 1986 exposé, so, when he brought his act to Toronto on Sunday, June 2, 2002 (figure 29.1), I determined to be there. I decided to adopt the character of a working man who was obviously afflicted with a bad back.

OUT WITH THE OLD

Peter Popoff is director of a religious empire in Upland, California, that once raked in an estimated ten to twenty million tax-free dollars annually. A Pentecostal, he claims that as a child he witnessed his father transform water into wine for a wartime communion service in Berlin.

An "Anointed Minister of God," the evangelist supposedly exhibits several of the "gifts of the spirit" that are central to Pentecostalism. Christians believe that between Jesus' resurrection and ascension to heaven, he promised his disciples they would be "baptised with the Holy Ghost" (Acts 1:5). This occurred when the apostles gathered for Pentecost and were struck with religious ecstasy (Asimov 1969).

The apostle Paul (1 Corinthians 12:7–11) enumerated nine gifts that are manifestations of the Holy Spirit: (1) the word of wisdom, (2) the word of knowledge, (3) faith, (4) healing, (5) the working of miracles, (6) prophecy,

(7) discernment of spirits, (8) speaking in unknown tongues, and (9) the ability to interpret tongues. Pentecostals place a special emphasis on such gifts, while many other fundamentalists believe they were intended only for those early disciples who were specifically anointed by Jesus (Nickell 1993, 101–102).

Peter Popoff combines his gift of healing with that of the word of knowledge. The latter consists, Pentecostals believe, of one receiving supernatural revelation. According to *Christian Online Magazine* (Kazenske 2003), this is "the God-given ability to receive from God, by revelation, the facts concerning something that is humanly impossible for us to know anything about"—a sort of holy clairvoyance.

Popoff's gift was openly demonstrated, taking the form of "calling out" audience members for healing and telling them their diseases, stating their addresses, and providing similar information, including occasionally the names of their doctors—all promptly verified by the astonished individuals concerned. For example, at a service in Anaheim, California, on March 16, 1986, Popoff called out, "Virgil. Is it Jorgenson? Who is Virgil?"—whereupon a man in the audience identified himself as that person. Then Popoff continued, "Are you ready for God to overhaul those knees?" As Jorgenson reacted to Popoff's amazing knowledge about him, the evangelist continued, "Oh, glory to God. I'll tell you, God's going to touch that sister of yours all the way over in Sweden." Popoff then took the "healed" man's cane. Breaking it over his knee, Popoff stood by as the man walked about unaided, giving praise to both Popoff and God (Steiner 1989).

Soon, however, Popoff's apparent gift was exposed as blatant trickery. Famed magician and paranormal investigator James Randi—wondering at the alleged healer's wearing of an apparent hearing aid—began to suspect that the device might actually be a tiny radio receiver and that someone was secretly broadcasting the information that was alleged to come from God. In fact, what would become a classic in the history of paranormal investigation, Randi smuggled in an electronics expert with computerized scanning equipment and so discovered that the words of knowledge came not from heaven but from much closer: from the ministry's TV trailer parked just outside.

The evangelist's wife, Elizabeth, was obtaining the relevant information from so-called prayer cards that attendees filled out before the service. She then broadcast the information to Popoff's "hearing aid." The first message at the service was a test: "Hello, Petey. I love you. I'm talking to you. Can you hear me? If you can't you're in trouble." (Steiner 1986; Steiner 1989; Randi 1987, 141–49). The session with the ailing Mr. Jorgenson—actually investigator Don Henvick!—sounded like this when Mrs. Popoff's secret broadcasts were also heard (Steiner 1989, 126):

> Elizabeth Popoff transmits to Peter Popoff: "Virgil Jorgenson. Virgil."
> Peter Popoff calls out "Virgil."
> Elizabeth: "Jorgenson."
> Peter (inquiringly): "Is it Jorgenson?"
> Elizabeth: "Way back in the back somewhere. Arthritis in knees. He's got a cane."
> Peter: "Who is Virgil?"
> Elizabeth: "He's got a cane."
> Peter: "Are you ready for God to overhaul those knees?"
> Elizabeth: "He's got arthritis. He's praying for his sister in Sweden, too."
> Peter: "Oh, glory to God. I'll tell you, God's going to touch that sister of yours all the way over in Sweden."

Subsequently, on Johnny Carson's *The Tonight Show*, Randi played a videotape of one of several recorded "calling out" sessions that had been intercepted. Randi presented it in before-and-after fashion so viewers could appreciate the original effect of Popoff's apparent gift of knowledge then see the true situation involving the secret broadcast. Popoff reacted first by denying everything; his ministry later charged that the videotapes had been "doctored" by NBC. Finally, Popoff admitted to use of the "communicator" device (the radio receiver), but he attempted to deny any intention to deceive. In fact, however, Randi had videotaped documentation to the contrary (Randi 1987, 149–50, 291; Garrison 1991).

The callousness of Popoff and his organization was deep. A former aide told how, when Popoff was sending out "personal" special-appeal letters to top donors, he had the aide sign a majority of them for him. Popoff promised those who sent him letters (with expected donations enclosed) that he would pray over them, but, says the aide, "he never prayed over them." Instead, "they'd sit there in a big pile for a month, then they'd be shredded" (quoted in Randi 1987, 158).

Like some donor-fleecing religious (or secular not-for-profit) organizations, Popoff made special appeals for projects that sometimes did not really even exist. Donors would send in money but, according to a former Peter Popoff Evangelical Association controller, "the money would just go into the daily deposit." Also, Elizabeth Popoff (who, unbeknownst to the faithful, was not even a Pentecostalist but a Roman Catholic) "laughed and joked at the 'boobs' and 'big butts' of terminally ill women who were there, giving their money and their confidence to the Popoffs" (Randi 1987, 152, 158, 298).

Nevertheless, Randi's effective exposé of Popoff, carried by the national media, dealt the evangelist a body blow. In just four months he became unable to draw the large crowds he was accustomed to. Worse, public outrage and diminishing donations eventually forced him off television entirely (Alexander 1987). He even changed the organization's name from The Peter Popoff Evangelical Association to People United for Christ, and he relocated it to a shopping-center storefront (Randi 1987, 156).

RESURRECTING THE WORD OF KNOWLEDGE

Despite all this, Popoff managed to rebound, eventually returning to the airways—and his old ways—albeit without his "hearing aid" (Stein 1993). Now he depends on other means to seemingly receive words of knowledge.

One method is the old generalization technique that is a mainstay of fortunetellers and Spiritualists. Consider this letter of July 26, 2001, written by Popoff—or one of the professional letter writers he is known to have employed (Randi 1987, 140). In any case, Popoff sent it to me, personally (and no doubt to thousands upon thousands of others):

Dear Joe,

In prayer for you this morning . . . God showed me that I must come to Toronto, Ontario. We are in the 7th month of the year and still you are feeling crushed by an onslaught of excessive worry in and around your home. During this time of prayer . . . I felt an unusual "BONDING" between us. I feel now as if I am speaking to you face to face.

There is something I just can't quite put my finger on . . . it has been troubling you, and it seems it keeps interfering with your day to day life.

GOD DID SHOW ME . . . that you need Him to move in the lives of your loved ones. I SEE through the eyes of the spirit . . . you also need a touch in your life, your finances are not the way you want them. . . . If it seems I'm reading you like a book . . . I sense it's happening because of this "BONDING" between us in the spirit.

Now, if this isn't holy clairvoyance—a true word of knowledge—I don't know what is.

A second technique for appearing to receive a word of knowledge, before an audience of believers, is a version of the "shotgun" technique. As typically practiced by evangelists like Pat Robertson and Benny Hinn, this involves mentioning that certain healings are taking place, without specifying just who is being favored (Randi 1987, 228–29; Nickell 2002). Popoff also uses it as a means of "calling out" someone for a healing. For example, on one television "Miracle Crusade," Popoff (2002c) seemed to hear a word of knowledge that someone was afflicted with a ringing in the ears; a woman with that condition then identified herself and came forward.

Popoff does not limit the shotgun technique to illnesses. He applies it to other problems people might experience. On television, he can even direct the method to the home audience. "I feel there's a mother out there," he says, without fear of contradiction, "whose son is in jail. . . ." (Popoff 2003). In this way many may be led to believe Popoff is speaking individually to them.

In his live crusades, Popoff uses the shotgun technique extensively. At the service I attended—after Popoff (2002a) had written me, saying, "Joe, you are going to see some awesome things happen in your life"—many vied to be the person to fit a certain illness that Popoff mentioned. A woman in front of me seemed to have several conditions—or perhaps was anxious to be videotaped by the ministry's TV crew and so achieve her moment of fame.

PETER POPOFF PACKS A PUNCH OF "PENTECOSTAL POWER"

One woman, who was called to come forward to receive Popoff's "laying on of hands," started to come without her cane (indicating clearly that she could walk without it). Popoff had her fetch it and made a big production of tossing it away (up onto the stage). She and others were treated to Popoff's touch—actually more of a push—and reacted accordingly. A few merely staggered or trembled, while others promptly fell into the arms of one of Popoff's catchers who had moved into position behind them. They collapsed in a variety of styles: some slumping, others reeling, still others stiffening and falling straight back. Once down, many seemed knocked out, while others writhed as if possessed.

In short, they experienced "going under the power," as it is usually called. In the caption to a publicity photo showing a woman wildly falling backward at his touch, Popoff (2002a) terms this "Pentecostal Power." Pentecostals and others of the charismatic movement (after the Greek *charisma*, "gift"), refer to the effect as being "slain in the Spirit."

Even many Christians regard the phenomenon skeptically, suspecting—correctly—that the persons involved are merely engaging in role playing as a result of suggestion, that they are "predisposed to fall" ("Benny Hinn" 2002; Nickell 2002).

I did not get to experience Popoff's powerful touch. Only a few of the audience of perhaps fifteen hundred (half or more of whom were African Canadians) could be singled out for the "power" treatment. I almost got lucky when he called out a woman with back trouble and then said there was also a man so afflicted. I stood up, but, since I was a distance away, Popoff gestured for me to stay there, saying that when the woman received her anointing I would receive mine, too. Apparently his gift of the word of knowledge failed to tell him I was malingering—just as it often did during Randi's extensive investigation.

I had two more opportunities to be healed, though not by touch. After many individual callings out, Popoff tried a group approach. Having been given packets of anointing oil, people were told to place them on their afflicted spot (or alternately on their forehead) while the evangelist beseeched, entreated, gesticulated, and—as at other times during the service—spoke in tongues. (Known as *glossolalia*, this is the babbling of nonsense syllables that passes as an unknown language but is actually pseudolanguage [Nickell 1993].) Finally, Popoff prayed over several people (including me) who had gathered while his helpers were collecting wastebaskets full of envelopes bearing offerings (figure 29.1).

People were to exchange their offering envelopes for some sort of mystico-magico wristband, but they ran out of those and later substituted small packets of "Miracle Spring Water," which a helper tossed out by the handful. (I keep mine with all the reverence I'm sure it's due.) Great efforts were made to collect every offering, and one helper—ending up with a handful of stragglers' envelopes but with no wastebasket to deposit them in—simply stuffed them in his inside coat pocket.

Many were supposedly healed at the service. One attention-seeking woman put on a big show of running around the congregation, although there was no reason to think she had previously been unable to do that. Several gave testimonials, a common response to a healing session. Due to the power of suggestion and the excitement of the event, which can release endorphins that reduce pain temporarily, people believe themselves healed and so convince others. According to psychologist Terence Hines, "One can find testimonials attesting to the effectiveness of almost anything." Regarding faith-healing testimonials, like those Popoff touts, Hines states, "It is safe to say that if testimonials play a major part in the 'come on' for a cure or therapy, the cure or therapy is almost certainly worthless. If the promoters of the therapy had actual evidence for its effectiveness, they would cite it and not have to rely on testimonials" (Hines 1988, 236–37).

Like the touted successes of Benny Hinn and other faith healers, those of Peter Popoff do not withstand scrutiny. In one case, for example, a girl's "inoperable, malignant brain-stem tumor" was supposedly confirmed by two computerized tomography (CT) scans and attested by doctors at Johns Hopkins University. In fact, medical investigator and CSICOP consultant Dr. Gary P. Posner discovered that the "dark mass" in the CT scan was only an imperfection in the scanning process and that the girl's physicians had not suspected a tumor at all. The "miracle" was an invented one and the girl continued to suffer from the migraine headaches that had prompted the CT scan (Randi 1987, 291–92).

While many may have left Popoff's "Miracle Crusade" falsely believing themselves healed, some knew better. One was a woman I photographed exiting the service in the wheelchair she had arrived in. James Randi (1987, 305) calls attention to an appropriate passage—yea, a word of knowledge—in Matthew (7:15–16):

Beware of false prophets, which come to you in sheep's clothing, but inwardly they are ravening wolves.

Ye shall know them by their fruits.

Figure 29.1. Peter Popoff works the crowd at a performance in Toronto, Ontario, Canada. (Photo by Joe Nickell)

CHAPTER 30

BENNY HINN'S MIRACLE CRUSADES

B enny Hinn tours the world with his "Miracle Crusade," drawing thousands to each service, with many hoping for a healing of body, mind, or spirit. A significant number seem rewarded and are brought onstage to pour out tearful testimonials. Then, seemingly by the Holy Spirit, they are knocked down at a mere touch or gesture from the charismatic evangelist. Although I had seen clips of Hinn's services on television, I decided to attend and witness his performance live when his crusade came to Buffalo, New York, June 28–29, 2001. Donning a suitable garb and sporting a cane (left over from a 1997 accident in Spain), I limped into my seat at the HSBC Arena in downtown Buffalo.

LEARNING THE ROPES

Benny Hinn was born in 1953, the son of an Armenian mother and Greek father. He grew up in Jaffa, Israel, "in a Greek Orthodox home" but was "taught by nuns at a Catholic school" (Hinn 1999, 8). Following the Six-Day War in 1967, he emigrated to Canada with his family. When he was nineteen he became a born-again Christian. Nearly two years later, in December 1973, he traveled by charter bus from Toronto to Pittsburgh to attend a "miracle service" by Pentecostal faith-healing evangelist Kathryn Kuhlman (1907–1976). At that service he had a profound religious experience, and that very night he was pulled from bed and "began to shake and vibrate all over" with the Holy Spirit (Hinn 1999, 8–14). (See figure 30.1.)

Before long Hinn began to conduct services sponsored by the Kathryn Kuhlman Foundation. Kuhlman died before Hinn could meet her personally, but her influence on him was profound, as he acknowledged in a book *Kathryn Kuhlman: Her Spiritual Legacy and Its Impact on My Life* (Hinn 1999). Eventually he began preaching elsewhere, including the Full Gospel Tabernacle in Orchard Park, New York (near Buffalo) and later at a church in Orlando, Florida. By 1990 he was receiving national prominence from his book *Good Morning, Holy Spirit*, and in 1999 he moved his ministry headquarters to Dallas.

Lacking any biblical or other theological training, Hinn was soon criticized by other Christian ministries. One, Personal Freedom Outreach, labeled his teachings a "theological quagmire emanating from biblical misinterpretation and extra-biblical 'revelation knowledge.'" He admitted to *Christianity Today* magazine that he had erred theologically and vowed to make changes (Frame 1991), but he has continued to remain controversial. Nevertheless, according to a minister friend, "Outside of the Billy Graham crusade, he probably draws the largest crowd of any evangelist in America today" (Condren 2001).

Hinn's mentor, Kathryn Kuhlman, who performed in flowing white garments trimmed with gold (Spraggett 1971, 16), was apparently the inspiration for Hinn's trademark white suits and gold jewelry. From her he obviously learned the clever "shotgun" technique of faith healing (also practiced by Pat Robertson and others). This involves announcing to an audience that certain healings are taking place without specifying just who is being favored (Randi 1987, 228–29).

SELECTION PROCESS

In employing this technique, Hinn first sets the stage with mood music, leading the audience (as did Kuhlman) in a gentle rendering of "He Touched Me," the well-known gospel song written by Bill Gaither in 1963 and later recorded by Elvis Presley. Spraggett (1971, 17) says that with Kuhlman, as the lyrics were sung over and over, it would "a chant, an incantation, hypnotic in its effect," and the same is true of Hinn's approach.

In time, the evangelist announces that miracles are taking place. At the service I attended, he declared that someone was being "healed of witchcraft"; others were having the "demon of suicide" driven out; still others were being cured of cancer. He named various diseases and conditions that were supposedly being alleviated and mentioned different areas of the anatomy—a back, a leg, and so on—that he claimed were being healed. He even stated that he need not name every disease or body part, that God's power was effecting a multitude of cures all over the arena.

Thus, instead of the afflicted being invited up to be healed (with no guarantee of success), the "shotgun" method encourages receptive, emotional individuals to believe they are healed. Only that self-selected group is invited to come forward and testify to their supposedly miraculous transformation. While I remained seated (seeing no investigative purpose to making a false testimonial), others were more tragically left behind. At one Hinn service a woman—hearing the evangelist's anonymously directed command to "stand up out of that wheelchair!"—struggled to do so for almost half an hour before finally sinking back, exhausted (Thomas 2001).

There is even a further step in the selection process: of those who do make it down the aisles, only a very few will actually be invited on stage. They must first undergo what amounts to an audition for the privilege. Those who tell the most interesting stories and show the greatest enthusiasm are the ones likely to be chosen (Underdown 2001).

This selection process is—perhaps not surprisingly—virtually identical to that employed by professional stage hypnotists. According to Robert A. Baker, in his definitive book *They Call It Hypnosis* (1990, 138–39):

> Stage hypnotists, like successful trial lawyers, have long known their most important task is to carefully pick their subjects—for the stage as for a jury—if they expect to win. Compliance is highly desirable, and to determine this ahead of time, the stage magician will usually give several test suggestions to those who volunteer to come up on the stage. Typically, he may ask the volunteers to clasp their hands together tightly and then suggest that the hands are stuck together so that they can't pull them apart. The stage hypnotist selects the candidates who go along with the suggestion and cannot get their hands apart until he tells them, "Now, it's okay to relax and separate them." If he has too many candidates from the first test, he may then give them a second test by suggesting they cannot open their mouths, move a limb, or open their eyes after closing them. Those volunteers who fail one or more of the tests are sent back to their seats, and those who pass all the tests are kept for the demonstration. Need-

less to say, not only are they compliant, cooperative, and suggestible, but most have already made up their minds in volunteering to help out and do exactly as they are told.

ROLE-PLAYING

Once on stage, one of Hinn's screeners announces each "healed" person in turn, giving a quick summary of the alleged miracle. At the service I attended, one woman put on a show of jumping up and down to demonstrate that she was free of pain following knee surgery three weeks before. Another was cured of "depression" caused by "the demon," said a screener, that resulted from "an abusive relationship with her husband." Still another (who admitted to being "an emotional person") said that her sister-in-law sitting beside her had begun to "speak in tongues" and that she herself felt she was healed of various ailments, including high blood pressure and marital trouble. At her mention of her brother, Hinn brought him up and learned that he had been healed of "sixteen demons" two years previously and that he expected to be cured of diabetes; Hinn prayed for God to "set him free" of the disease. Another was supposedly cured of being "afraid of the Lord" (although he was carrying the Bible of a friend who had died of AIDS), and one woman stated that she believed she had just been cured of ovarian cancer.

In each instance—after the person has given a little performance (running about, offering a sobbing testimonial, and so on) and Hinn has responded with some miniature sermon, prayer, or other reaction—the next step in the role-playing is acted out. As one of his official catchers moves into place behind the person, Hinn gives a gesture, touch, or other signal. Most often, while squeezing the person's face between thumb and finger, he gives a little push, and down the compliant individual goes. Some slump; some stiffen and fall backward; a few reel. Once down, many lie as if entranced, while others writhe and seem almost possessed.

Along with speaking or praying in tongues (glossolalia) and other emotional expressions, this phenomenon of "going under the power" is a characteristic of the modern charismatic movement (after the Greek *charisma*, "gift"). Also known as being "slain in the Spirit," it is often regarded skeptically even by other Christians who suspect—correctly—that the individuals involved are merely "predisposed to fall" ("Benny Hinn" 2002). That is, they merely engage in a form of role-playing that is prompted by their strong desire to receive divine power as well as by the influence of suggestion that they do so. Even the less emotionally suggestible people will be unwilling not to comply when those around them expect it.

In short, they behave just as if "hypnotized." Although popularly believed to involve a mystical "trance" state, hypnosis is in fact just compliant behavior in response to suggestions (Baker 1990, 286). One professional hypnotist said of Hinn's performance, "This is something we do every day and Mr. Hinn is a real professional" (Thomas 2001).

CURES?

But what about the healings? Do faith healers like Benny Hinn really help nudge God to work miracle cures? In fact, such claims are invariably based on negative evidence—"we don't know what caused the illness to abate, so it must have been supernatural"—and so represent the logical fallacy called "arguing from ignorance." In fact, as I explained to a reporter from the *Buffalo News* following a Benny Hinn service, people may feel they are healed due to several factors. In addition to the body's own natural healing mechanisms, there is the fact that some serious ailments, including certain types of cancer, are unpredictable and may undergo "spontaneous remission"—that is, may abate for a time or go away entirely. Other factors include misdiagnosis (such as that of a supposedly "inoperable, malignant brain-stem tumor" that was actually due to a faulty CT scan [Randi 1987, 291–92]).

And then there are the powerful effects of suggestion. Not only psychosomatic illnesses (of which there is an impressive variety) but also those with distinct physical causes may respond to a greater or lesser degree to "mental medicine." Pain is especially responsive to suggestion. In the excitement of an evangelical revival, the reduction of pain due to the release of endorphins (painkilling substances produced by the body) often causes people to believe and act as if they have been miraculously healed (Condren 2001; Nickell 1993; Nolen 1974).

Critical studies are illuminating. Dr. William A. Nolen, in his book *Healing: A Doctor in Search of a Miracle* (1974), followed up on several reported cases of healing from a Kathryn Kuhlman service but found no miracles— only remissions, psychosomatic diseases, and other explanations, including the power of suggestion.

More recently a study was conducted following a Benny Hinn crusade in Portland, Oregon, where seventy-six miracles were alleged. For an HBO television special, *A Question of Miracles* (Thomas 2001), Benny Hinn Ministries was asked to supply the names of as many of these as possible for investigation. After thirteen weeks, just five names were provided. Each case was followed for one year.

The first involved a grandmother who stated she had had "seven broken vertebras" but that the Lord had healed her at the evening service in Portland. In fact, X-rays afterward revealed otherwise, although the woman felt her pain had lessened.

The second case was that of a man who had suffered a logging accident ten years previously. He demonstrated improved mobility at the crusade, but his condition afterward deteriorated and "movement became so painful he could no longer dress himself." Yet he remained convinced he was healed and refused the medication and surgery his doctors insisted was necessary.

The next individual was a lady who, for fifty years, had only "thirty percent of her hearing," as claimed at the Portland crusade. However, her physician stated, "I do not think this was a miracle in any sense." He reported that the woman had had only a "very mild hearing loss" just two years before and that she had made "a normal recovery."

The fourth case was that of a girl who had not been "getting enough oxygen" but who claimed to have been healed at Hinn's service. In fact, since the crusade she "continued to suffer breathlessness," yet her mother was so convinced that a miracle had occurred that she did not continue to have her daughter seek medical care.

Finally, there was what the crusade billed as "a walking dead woman." She had had cancer throughout both lungs, but her doctors were now "overwhelmed" that she was "still alive and still breathing." Actually, her oncologist rejected all such claims, saying the woman had an "unpredictable form of cancer that was stable at the time of the crusade." Tragically, her condition subsequently deteriorated and she died just nine months afterward.

WHAT HARM?

As these cases demonstrate, there is a danger that people who believe themselves cured will forsake medical assistance that could bring them relief or even save their lives. Dr. Nolen (1974, 97–99) relates the tragic case of Mrs. Helen Sullivan, who suffered from cancer that had spread to her vertebrae. Kathryn Kuhlman had her get out of her wheelchair, remove her back brace, and run across the stage repeatedly. The crowd applauded what they thought was a miracle, but the antics cost Mrs. Sullivan a collapsed vertebra. Four months after her "cure," she died.

Nolen (1974, 101) stated that he did not think Miss Kuhlman was a deliberate charlatan. She was, he said, ignorant of diseases and the effects of suggestion. But he suspected she had "trained herself to deny, emotionally and intellectually, anything that might threaten the validity of her ministry." The same may apply to Benny Hinn. Expert opinion suggests people like Hinn have fantasy-prone personalities (Thomas 2001). Indeed, the backgrounds of both Kuhlman and Hinn reveal many traits associated with fantasy-proneness, but it must be noted that being fantasy prone does not preclude also being deceptive and manipulative.

Hinn notes that only rarely does he lay hands on someone for healing, but he made an exception for one child whose case was being filmed for the HBO documentary. The boy was blind and dying from a brain tumor. "The Lord's going to touch you," Hinn promised. The child's parents believed and, although not wealthy, pledged $100 per month to the Benny Hinn Ministries. Subsequently, however, the child died.

Critics, like Reverend Joseph C. Hough, president of New York's Union Theological Seminary, say of the desperately hopeful: "It breaks your heart to know that they are being deceived, because they genuinely are hoping and believing. And they'll leave there thinking that if they didn't get a miracle it's because they didn't believe." More pointedly, Rabbi Harold S. Kushner stated on *A Question of Miracles* (Thomas 2001):

> I hope there is a special place in Hell for people who try and enrich themselves on the suffering of others. To tantalize the blind, the lame, the dying, the afflicted, the terminally ill, to dangle hope before parents of a severely afflicted child, is an indescribably cruel thing to do, and to do it in the name of God, to do it in the name of religion, I think, is unforgivable.

Amen.

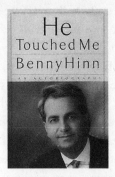

Figure 30.1. Benny Hinn not only allegedly works miracles; he also writes books like this one, his autobiography.

CHAPTER 31

SPIRITIST HEALER: "JOHN OF GOD"

Known as "John of God," a Brazilian faith healer claims spirits take control of his body to enable him to perform surgeries (without anesthesia) and other healing procedures. The spiritual center he founded, located in the little town of Abadiania in Brazil's remote central highlands, has been dubbed "the Lourdes of South America" ("Controversial Faith-Healer" 2006), while he himself has been called a charlatan and worse ("Is 'John of God' a Healer or Charlatan" 2005).

First alerted by a CNN producer to a John of God healing service in Atlanta, I determined to go undercover to get a close look at what was transpiring. I worked with National Geographic Television and Film on a segment for their *Is It Real?* program titled "Miracle Cures," which included an analysis of the John of God phenomenon.

JOHN OF GOD

Known in his native Portuguese as *João de Deus*—"John of God"—João Teixeira de Faria was born in 1942 to poor parents. He grew up unable to stay in school or hold a job. At sixteen, he reportedly discovered his miraculous ability when, in a vision, a woman directed him to a nearby church. There, although he maintains he does not remember what happened, having been entranced, he allegedly performed a miraculous healing.

He thus began a career that impresses the credulous. Claiming to be a medium (one who communicates with spirits of the dead), he insists he is guided by more than thirty entities—although, curiously, João speaks only Portuguese, regardless of which entity is possessing him at a given time. King Solomon was his first entity. Others followed, including Ignatius Loyola, the Spanish noble who founded the Jesuit order in 1540. João's center is named for him: Casa de Dom Inácio de Loyola. Oswaldo Cruz, a physician who helped eradicate yellow fever, is another alleged entity, along with other past healers, in a sort of spiritist pantheon ("Controversial Faith-Healer" 2006; "Is 'John of God' a Healer or Charlatan" 2005).

Spiritism is essentially spiritualism, a belief that one can communicate with spirits, but with the added conviction that spirits repeatedly reincarnate in a progression toward enlightenment. In Brazil, which is steeped in superstition and has a climate of belief in African spirits, spiritism has become a powerful religious movement, overlaid onto Catholicism. It may involve mediumistic searches for past lives and even so-called "psychic surgery" (Bragdon 2002, 14–20; Guiley 2000, 360–62).

Supposedly, psychic surgeons open the body paranormally—without surgical instruments or anesthetic—and heal diseases by manipulating vital organs. Typically, they have involved fraudulent practices including sleight of hand. For instance, "tumors" have proved to be pieces of chicken intestines and blood that of a cow (Nickell 1998, 159–62).

John of God, however—styled "João-in-Entity" when supposedly possessed—has a different style. He performs dubious "surgeries" that are either "visible" or "invisible." The former may involve twisting forceps up a person's nostrils or using a knife to scrape an eyeball or slice open a fleshy abdomen—all without anesthesia. According to a pro-João book, "In over thirty-five years of the Entity's surgery, it has been extremely rare for there to be any infections" (Bragdon 2002, 11).

With "invisible surgery," the entity du jour gives a prayer, after which thousands of "healing entities" busy themselves, allegedly, by operating on an organ, revitalizing a muscle, or otherwise "simultaneously attending to the problems of the people in the room" (Bragdon 2002, 11). Augmenting the sessions are encouragements to meditate, drink water blessed by the entities, and take prescribed herbal remedies.

INVESTIGATION

I had already obtained a ticket to the John of God event in Atlanta when I was contacted by National Geographic Television. We then worked together on an investigation that shed new light on the Brazilian's claims.

Shrewdly, João's entities avoided performing "visible surgeries" in Atlanta, where he might have been arrested. I was chosen for an "invisible" procedure as I hobbled by with a cane, wearing the requisite white outfit that, I was told, "helps maintain a higher vibrational frequency" ("John of God in Atlanta" 2006a; 2006b). I also wore a minor disguise, since frequent media appearances have made me more recognizable (see figures 31.1 and 31.2).

As I would discover, João is an unlikely miracle worker. A grade-school dropout, he was, reports an admirer, "forced to live as a wanderer, traveling from city to city healing the sick and living from their donations of food" (Pellegrino-Estrich 1995). Because, in Brazil, it is illegal to practice medicine without a license, he has been charged and fined—even jailed briefly. A district attorney who investigated him has reported that João sent her—indirectly, through a relative—death threats. John of God denies that, along with an accusation that he took advantage of one woman who had come to him for healing. "There is a lot of jealousy. People talk," he says defensively. "What dictates is the conscience toward God." Noting his apparent wealth, some critics say his "healings" are merely a front to make him a rich man ("Is 'John of God' a Healer or Charlatan" 2005).

Certainly, his procedures are a sham. The twisting of forceps up a pilgrim's nose is an old circus and carnival sideshow stunt, explained in my book *Secrets of the Sideshows* (Nickell 2005, 238–41). Looking far more tortuous than it is, the feat depends on the fact that, unknown to many people, there is a sinus cavity that extends horizontally from the nostrils over the roof of the mouth to a surprising distance—enough to accommodate a spike, ice pick, or other implement used in the "Human Blockhead" act.

At my instigation, National Geographic filmed a performance of such an act at the Washington, DC, show bar Palace of Wonders, operated by carny impresario (and friend) James Taylor. Our blockhead was "Swami Yomahmi," also known as Stephon Walker, whom I introduced with my best carny-sideshow spiel. Walker even cranked a rotating drill bit into his nose. He also used a blunt knife to scrape the white part of his eyeball and acknowledged that such stunts look more risky than they are.

A surgeon who commented on John of God's incisions stated that they were superficial (little more than skin deep, apparently) and would not be expected either to bleed very much or even to cause much initial pain. The same is true of scraping the white of the eye or inserting something into the nasal cavity ("Controversial Faith-Healer" 2006). Physicians affiliated with the *Skeptical Inquirer* voiced similar opinions. The brief nasal procedure occasionally leaves someone's nose bleeding, but his or her body's own healing mechanisms will no doubt repair the minor injury. The bottom line regarding the procedures is that they are pseudosurgeries that have no objective medical benefit other than the well-known placebo effect.

Furthermore, the "holy water" that "João-in-Entity" blesses, and that supposedly helps effect cures, is ordinary water. I provided a specially labeled bottle I had purchased in Atlanta, and National Geographic had it tested at a major DC-area facility, the Washington Suburban Sanitation Commission. It was found to have no unusual properties and to be entirely unremarkable ("Miracle Cures" 2006).[1]

As to João-in-Entity's herbal remedies, actually only a single herb is prescribed, but those seeking aid are told that the entities are able to use it to help cure a wide variety of ailments ("Miracle Cures" 2006). The herb is one of the many varieties of *passionflower*, a mystical plant associated with Jesus' crucifixion, and it has been used since ancient times as a "sedative, nervine and antispasmodic." Herbalists say it soothes the nervous system and produces restful sleep that brightens one's outlook (Lucas 1972, 128–29). Small wonder it would be the drug of choice for a "healing" center to distribute widely.

Many people offer testimonials as to the beneficial effects they have supposedly received at the hands of John of God. In fact, however, the successes attributed to the entities may be nothing more than what occurs at other alleged miracle sites, like Lourdes, where the vast majority of supplicants remain uncured. Since such "healings" are typically held to be miraculous because they are "medically inexplicable," claimants are engaging in the logical fallacy of "arguing from ignorance"—that is, drawing a conclusion from a lack of knowledge. Touted healings may actually be attributable to such factors as misdiagnosis, spontaneous remission, psychosomatic conditions, prior medical treatment, the body's own healing power, and other effects (Nickell 1998, 133–37).

Consider, for example, the case of Matthew Ireland, a pilgrim from Guilford, Vermont, whose doctor told him he had a type of brain tumor that was fast growing and inoperable. After two years of radiation treatments and chemotherapy, Ireland made three visits to John of God. Subsequent MRI testing did show that the tumor mass had shrunk by 50 percent, but it was not gone as the entity had claimed. Ireland's former oncologist attributes the partial success to the aggressive radiation treatment and concedes it is possible that the specific type of tumor may have been misdiagnosed ("Miracle Cures" 2006; "Is 'John of God' a Healer or Charlatan" 2005).

Often, at healing services like those of John of God in Brazil, pilgrims' emotions may trigger the release of endorphins, brain-produced substances that reduce sensitivity to pain. They may thus believe and act as if they have been miraculously healed—even throwing away their crutches—whereas later investigation reveals their situation to be as bad, or worse, than before (Nickell 1998, 136). However, I did note that, at the Atlanta John of God event, those who came with walkers, crutches, and wheelchairs *left with them.* Sadly, the entities had not taken away their afflictions, only their money.

Figure 31.1. The author, adopting the persona of a pilgrim seeking a miracle cure, attends a "John of God" healing service. Dressing in white was a requisite of the event. (Photos from the author's file)

Figure 31.2. "John of God" (*right*)—supposedly possessed by a spirit entity—directs treatments for the afflicted. Seated in the background is the author, ready to undergo an "invisible surgery."

CHAPTER 32

HEALINGS BY A "VICTIM SOUL"

A milestone in supernatural claims has been reached: Audrey Santo—the brain-damaged girl in Worcester, Massachusetts, who, supposedly, exhibited stigmata, prompted effigies to drip oil and Communion wafers to bleed, and miraculously sparked healings of the sick—died on April 14, 2007. She was twenty-three.

Known as "Little Audrey," she had been in a coma-like state since August 9, 1987, when, at the age of three, she suffered a near drowning. Controversy began a year after the accident, when her mother, Linda, spent $8,000 to take her to the shrine at Medjugorje, Yugoslavia, in hopes of a miracle. Instead, Audrey suffered a sudden cardiac arrest. Although she survived, the air ambulance that was needed to rush her home cost $25,000—a sum her grandmother had to mortgage her home to pay. Linda Santo's response to the near-fatal incident was to blame it on the proximity of a Yugoslavian abortion clinic (Harrison 1998; Sherr 1998).

"VICTIM SOUL"

Soon, Audrey was being promoted as a "victim soul." However, Catholic theologians, observing that that term was not an official one within the church, questioned whether Audrey demonstrated the capacity—at the age of three or later—to make a free choice to suffer on behalf of others.

After Audrey was exhibited at a stadium with some ten thousand in attendance and a window was added to her bedroom so that pilgrims could file by and pray for her to intercede with God on their behalf, the local bishop ordered that such practices be discontinued. Also curbed was the practice of offering oil-soaked cotton swabs as healing talismans. These restrictions may have diminished revenues, but the Santo family's situation was perhaps less financially desperate than many imagined, since Audrey received round-the-clock nursing care from the Massachusetts Commission for the Blind (Weingarten 1998).

I began to follow the Audrey Santo case as "miracle" claims about her proliferated. When an investigating commission appointed by the Worcester bishop issued a preliminary report on January 21, 1999, I appeared that evening on the *NBC Nightly News with Tom Brokaw* to offer a brief skeptical view of the case.

SUSPICIOUS PHENOMENA

For a later ABC *20/20* segment, a producer called and discussed with me the phenomenon of weeping icons in the Santo home. We considered monitoring the effigies with surveillance cameras, but I pointed out that, if trickery were involved, it was unlikely that such an investigative technique would be allowed. As Lynn Sherr subsequently reported on the program, "We wanted to do our own test with a surveillance camera in the [home] chapel, but the family prefers to let the commission finish its work first" (Sherr 1998).

On an episode of CBS's *48 Hours* titled "Desperate Measures" (1999), a reporter asked Linda Santo how one would know whether someone in the household was simply applying the oil "in the middle of the night." She replied, "You don't know." Samples of oil were independently tested on a few occasions. One analysis by a Pittsburgh laboratory revealed the substance to consist of 80 percent vegetable oil and 20 percent chicken fat, according to the *Washington Post*, which ordered the test (Weingarten 1998). The presence of chicken fat—which, along with common vegetable oil, is readily available in a home kitchen (consistent with chicken having been deep-fried)—seems particularly revealing. So does one volunteer's observation that there tended to be an increase in oil on effigies on the days pilgrims were expected ("Desperate Measures" 1999).

Much later, when I was involved with a television documentary on the case, the producer tried to arrange for me to visit the Santo home. Linda Santo, I was told, was tentatively agreeable, but, after she consulted a priest who was a behind-the-scenes promoter of alleged phenomena there, she refused. I had clearly become persona non grata, no doubt because of my repeatedly voiced suspicions about the circumstances under which the icons and figurines dripped oil and the hosts (Communion wafers) supposedly bled. (I have observed that when I have unrestricted possession of a "miraculous" object it either ceases to perform or I explain the phenomenon [Nickell 2006]). (For more on this phenomenon, see chapter 9, "Animated Images.")

MIRACULOUS CURES

Miracle healings attributed to Audrey's intercession were also unconvincing. For example, a woman was supposedly healed of liver cancer, but the patient's oncologist pointed out that she had already begun a new cancer treatment and that it had clearly begun to work even before she had gone to see Audrey. The woman continued to regard the remission as a miracle even when the cancer returned, spreading to her brain ("Desperate Measures" 1999). Again, there was the case of a young man injured in a motorcycle accident whose doctors reportedly said he would never walk again; yet, after his mother went to see Audrey, he was able to walk without his crutches. Actually, his personal physician noted that there had been a 75 percent chance that he would indeed walk (Sherr 1998).

Audrey's reputed stigmata was especially troubling. If faked, it indicated outright abuse. Therefore, not surprisingly, in 1999, the Santo case—perhaps unknown to most viewers—provided the impetus for an episode of the CBS television dramatic series *Judging Amy*. As a researcher wrote CSI executive director Barry Karr, the show was to be "similar to the Audrey Santo story that Joe Nickell has been involved with" (Yeuell 1999). I subsequently discussed the case with the researcher and made some suggestions. Called "Victim Soul," the episode (which first aired on October 5, 1999) featured Judge Amy Madison Gray being challenged to "determine if a comatose boy who is believed to have healing powers is being abused by his grandmother" ("Victim Soul" 1999).

I took no pleasure in my adversarial role as the arch skeptic in the

Santo case. Indeed, I was deeply saddened by the family's plight: Far from receiving the miracle they prayed for, Audrey almost died from a trip to a healing shrine, lingered in a persistent vegetative state for two decades, unknowingly suffered indignities and controversy, and finally died. Supposed to heal others, she was bereft of powers.

Her sad story has now ended. Although many have tried to find meaning in the tragedy, even Linda Santo wondered aloud: if there had not been phenomena like the "bleeding" Communion wafers, she asked, "if there was just this child in bed, would anyone pay attention to this?" (Weingarten 1998).

PART 4
VISIONARY EXPERIENCES

CHAPTER 33

JESUS' RESURRECTION APPARITIONS

C entral to Christianity is the belief that Jesus rose from the dead and (at least according to fundamentalists) that he rose bodily into heaven. But were the biblical narratives of Jesus' resurrection really only ghost stories of their day—belief tales intended to convince the credulous that his death was not an ending?

BACKGROUND

As discussed in chapter 25, resurrection of the dead is a supernatural concept deriving from certain ancient religions. The concept may have been prompted by first-hand observation of hasty burials of apparently dead people who were not in fact dead, and later returned to the living.

Such cases may well have inspired ancient stories of resurrection, such as the account of the prophet Elijah (1 Kings 17:17–24) and again that of Elisha (2 Kings 4:34–35).

The Gospel of John (11:1–12:11) credits Jesus with a similar feat, raising Lazarus from the dead. But many scholars would agree with Lloyd Graham (1975, 337) that the story is merely a foreshadowing of the resurrection of Jesus.

At the time of Jesus, the doctrine of the resurrection of the dead was a principal article of faith among many Jews, especially the Pharisees; however, the Sadducees believed the soul perished with the body (Stravinskas 2002, 677; Riley 1995, 20–21). Specifically, the Hebrews believed that for three days "the soul hovered round, fain to re-enter and re-animate its fleshly tenement" (Dummelow 1951, 793–94), so for three days the mourners used to visit the grave. They believed that on the fourth day the soul left and decomposition began. Such a three-day vigil could do no harm, especially since—as we know—one who was apparently dead might revive.

THE RESURRECTION ACCOUNTS

The Gospels say that after his crucifixion Jesus' body (like that of Lazarus) was wrapped in linen and laid in a tomb hewn from rock; then a great stone was rolled over the entrance. *Only Matthew* adds that the tomb was "sealed" and that a guard was placed. But only Matthew confronts the allegation of scandal—that the disciples came by night while the guards slept and stole away the corpse; he says the chief priests bribed the guards to spread the rumor. In any case, the stone was rolled back by an angel during an earthquake. Or so Matthew—and only he—claims (figure 33.1).

It is at this point that the four Gospels diverge. The earliest source, Mark, says that "Mary Magdalene, and Mary the mother of James, and Salome" approached the tomb bringing spices and wondering who would roll the stone away for them. However, they found the tomb open and inside "saw a young man sitting on the right side, dressed in a white robe." He tells them that Jesus has risen and has gone on before the disciples to Galilee. At this the three women are frightened:

> Mark 16:8. *And they went out and fled from the tomb; for trembling and astonishment had come upon them; and they said nothing to any one, for they were afraid.*

Only in a subsequent passage (Mark 16:9–20)—one believed to be a spurious addition to Mark's Gospel (Fuller 1971, 2; Price 2003, 22)—does Jesus appear, and then only to Mary Magdalene and "in another form" to two others.

In Matthew the "young man" becomes the "angel" who rolled away the stone. Matthew drops Salome from the group of women, leaving only the two Marys. In their rush to tell the disciples what they had seen and heard, they actually encountered Jesus "and took hold of his feet and worshipped him" (Matthew 28:2–9).

Luke relates that the two Marys, Joanna, and "the other women with them" went to the tomb, finding the stone rolled away. And "behold, two men stood by them in dazzling apparel," telling them Jesus had risen. Although the disciples suspect these are only "idle tales," Jesus later appears to others, although he is not at first recognized (Luke 24:1–37). Upon the return of two disciples from Emmaus, Jesus appears once again in the midst of the twelve.

In John's account (20:1–15), only Mary Magdalene goes and finds the stone removed. Fetching Peter and another (the so-called Beloved Disciple), she returns with them to the tomb and the two disciples enter, finding the grave cloths. After they depart, Mary Magdalene sees "two angels in white" sitting where Jesus' body had lain. Then suddenly she turns around and sees Jesus standing there, although she supposes him to be "the gardener." In other words, she sees Jesus emerge from his tomb much as the Old Testament Saul saw the ghost of Samuel conjured from his grave by the witch (or medium) of Endor (1 Sam. 28:7–20). More on this presently.

THE JESUS APPARITIONS

The Gospels relate several sightings of Jesus after his death. Because the narratives have surely been corrupted in transmission (Price 2003, 9–23), I will not spend much time parsing the text. I will instead treat the tales as a group having certain identifiable characteristics. The accounts are important in part because, as Reginald H. Fuller (1971, 16) observes, "Never in the New Testament is there any actual narrative of the resurrection as such, only of its accompanying phenomena: the empty tomb and the appearances." This, in itself, suggests we are dealing with the familiar genre of ghost sightings.

In some of the stories Jesus is seen quite clearly, although he is not at first recognized (for example, Luke 24:15–16). Again, he materializes inside a building with shut doors (John 20:19) (figure 33.2). In one instance he forbids being touched (John 20:17), while in another (involving doubting Thomas) he invites contact (John 20:27) (figure 33.2). This is after the disciples "supposed that they saw a spirit," whereupon Jesus says that "a spirit has not flesh and bones as you see that I have" (Luke 24:37–39).[1]

In addition to the Gospel accounts of Jesus' resurrection apparitions, there were others, including his appearance to John the Seer (Revelation 1:10, 12–20), to Saul (Paul) on the road to Damascus (Acts 9:1–9), "to James, then to all the apostles" (as reported by Paul), and even "to more than five hundred brethren at one time" (1 Corinthians 15:6–7). As well, there have been "visions" of the glorified Christ among Christians in succeeding years and centuries. While these are usually distinguished from resurrection appearances on theological grounds (Fuller 1971, 42–43), to the modern paranormal investigator this seems a distinction without a difference.

Clearly, the narratives are what folklorists call "belief tales," those intended "to give credence to folk beliefs." Ghost legends, for instance, are typically not mere scary tales but instead feature ghosts that appear lifelike and have returned from the dead to complete some task (Brunvand 1978, 108–109). Ghostlore may contain contradictory elements. For instance, the ghost may be nonphysical and so walk through walls, yet have some effect on the physical world due to the requirements of the genre: the teller is often at pains to convince his audience both that a ghost is involved and that it is not the result of mere imagination or hallucination.

In one account, Jesus works a miracle, the draught of fishes (John 21:6), and it is tempting to see at least two other miracles as being misplaced resurrection (ghost) tales. One is the story of Jesus' nighttime stroll upon the water of Lake Gennesaret (also known as the Sea of Galilee), at which his disciples "thought it was a ghost, and cried out" (Mark 6:49).[2] The other is the account of Jesus' Transfiguration, in which Peter and those with him awakened to have a "vision" of Jesus "transfigured": "the appearance of his countenance was altered, and his raiment became dazzling white"; he was seen *conversing with the spirits* of Moses and Elijah (Matthew 17:1–9; Luke 9:28–36).[3] Both of these miracle stories are consistent with resurrection tales that have been misunderstood as such and so wrongly inserted into the life story of Jesus.

EXPLAINING APPARITIONS

Indeed, the Transfiguration story, occurring as a reported "vision" seen upon waking, may explain how some of the sightings of the resurrected Jesus took place. There is a common experience, called a "waking dream," that occurs in the twilight between wakefulness and sleep. It has been responsible for countless "ghost" sightings (Nickell 2001, 215–16) as well as bedside visitations of demons, extraterrestrials, and other entities. (Joseph Smith, founder of the Mormon religion, encountered the angel Moroni under conditions highly indicative of a waking dream [Nickell 2004, 300].)

Those most likely to have apparitional experiences (apart from the psychotic) are those termed fantasy prone—that is, otherwise normal people who have an exceptional ability to fantasize. In their classic study of fantasy proneness, Wilson and Barber (1983) found several identifying characteristics of the fantasy-prone personality, including susceptibility to hypnosis, having imaginary playmates in childhood, believing one has psychic powers, having vivid sensory experiences, receiving messages from higher entities, and others, including experiencing vivid dreams (as discussed above). Many reputed mediums, psychics, visionaries, and the like throughout history have exhibited fantasy proneness (Wilson and Barber 1983; Nickell 2001, 215).

As well, ghosts are perceived under other conditions, such as when the percipient is tired or in a daydreaming state. The evidence that many ghostly perceptions derive from reverie and other dissociative states is well established (Nickell 2001, 216). The relationship between apparitional states and a dream-like state was observed, for example, by G. N. M. Tyrrell (1973). He noted that, as apparitions, people appear fully clothed and are often accompanied by objects, just as they are in dreams, because the clothes and objects are required by the apparitional drama.

Some would place Mary Magdalene among such visionaries. It would seem that she was the source of the "vision of angels" in Luke (24:23) and possibly the first to "see" the apparitional Jesus. This was the same Mary Magdalene from whom Jesus had exorcised "seven demons" (Mark 16:9). According to Marcello Craveri, in his *The Life of Jesus* (1967, 424), "Ancient and modern students of Christianity agree that the belief in the Resurrection is founded on the hallucinations of a female visionary, Mary Magdalene or on a collective hallucination."

Actually, the other reported sightings were probably prompted by psychological contagion—the spreading of an idea, behavior, or belief from person to person by means of suggestion (examples being the Salem witch hysteria of 1692–1693 and the Spiritualist craze of the nineteenth century) (Nickell 2004, 226). During the contagion, many who, like Paul, had not known Jesus but wished they had, were able to "see" him through individual dreams, waking dreams, other types of "visions," and even at second hand through the claimed experiences of others.

Viewed from our modern perspective, Jesus' appearances to the twelve apostles may have been just a series of personal imaginative experiences—not unlike those associated with a typical "haunting" or even Elvis Presley sightings, which "can be seen as similar to spiritual visions" (Southwell and Twist 2004, 20). And the appearance to the five hundred may have been only an incident in which a group experienced a contagious outbreak of evangelical fervor, such as expressed perhaps by speaking in tongues (see Fuller 1971, 36).

In any event, whether Jesus' resurrection apparitions are the product of experiences conveyed through oral tradition, or are even literary invention, or both, they are consistent with other alleged apparitional experiences. As such, they are therefore evidence, not of another world, but of this one.

Figure 33.1. Jesus is resurrected (mid-nineteenth-century illustration by Julius Schnorr von Carolsfeld).

Figure 33.2. The resurrected Jesus appears to his disciples (mid-nineteenth-century illustration by Julius Schnorr von Carolsfeld).

CHAPTER 34

"VISIONS" BEHIND
THE PASSION

The controversy over Mel Gibson's *The Passion of the Christ* has largely ignored an essential fact. While some Christians have praised its "biblical authenticity" and others have criticized its "brutal violence and portrayal of ancient Jews" (Tokasz 2004), a major source for much of the movie has received comparatively little attention.

PLAYBOOK

Reportedly, Mel Gibson "accidentally stumbled upon" a book—*The Dolorous Passion of Our Lord Jesus Christ*, first published in 1833, which "planted a seed in his mind and finally played a large role in motivating him to make the film" ("Book That Inspired . . ." 2004). In fact, Gibson (2004) termed the book "great background and foundation material."

Unfortunately, the book consists of the "visions" of a German nun, Anne Catherine Emmerich (1774–1824). As a child she had an invisible "guardian angel"; experienced apparitional encounters with Jesus, Mary, and various saints; and displayed a special sensitivity to anything held sacred (Brentano, 1833). In short, she exhibited many of the traits indicative of a "fantasy-prone" personality (Wilson and Barber 1983), not only the personality type of numerous religious visionaries, but also of countless Spiritualist mediums, alien abductees, and other fantasizers. They typically believe they have special powers, often including the ability to communicate with higher entities—a sort of adult version of a child's imaginary playmate.

233

A mystic, Emmerich may also have been a pious fraud. She made a show of being Christ like, even sleeping on planks placed on the ground in the shape of a cross, and from the age of about twenty-four she claimed to receive the pain of Jesus' crown of thorns. Soon, blood was flowing down her face. After she was accepted into an Augustinian convent, she supposedly received "a mark like a cross upon her bosom" and still later exhibited a full array of stigmata (that is, the wounds of Christ's crucifixion).

She was subjected to a three-week medical examination in 1819, but "this examination appears to have produced no particular effects in any way" (Brentano 1833). Neither science nor the Catholic Church has ever authenticated a single instance of stigmata. Indeed, many stigmatics have been proven fraudulent (Nickell 2000; Nickell 2004).

Still later, Emmerich claimed to practice inedia, the alleged ability to forgo nourishment by suspending all eating and, sometimes, drinking (Nickell 1993, 225–29). Emmerich supposedly subsisted only on wine, and eventually "only pure water" (Brentano 1833). She was never properly investigated, but some inedics who *were* were exposed as frauds.

VISIONS

Anne Catherine Emmerich's purported visions—which provide far more elaborate and intimate details of Jesus' final hours than do the Gospels— are also suspect. According to Catholic writer Ian Wilson (1988, 76):

> In these we follow the elaborate preparations and ceremonial for the Last Supper. We are accorded flowing descriptions of the judgment hall of Caiaphas and the palace of Pilate. Not a blow seems to be omitted from Jesus's savage scourging by six drunken and blood-thirsty sadists. We are told of housewife Veronica wiping Jesus's face with her veil. We learn how special holes had to be dug for the three crosses. And we grieve with the holy women as they wash Jesus's lifeless body and lavish it with unguents in preparation for his burial.

Wilson continues:

But it is precisely this welter of detail that gives rise to most disquiet. Just how satisfied can we be that her account of the Last Supper is authentic? Should we really believe her assertion that the Last Supper chalice once belonged to Abraham? Does her description of Caiaphas's mansion accord with modern excavations of the city's first century priestly dwellings? Is it not a little suspicious that the Veronica story as she describes it owes nothing to any original gospel and everything to medieval legend? Does her assertion that Adam was buried at Golgotha owe more to symbol-seeking tradition than accurate reportage? How sure can we be that Jesus's body was washed and anointed before burial? The gospels do not specifically say so, and according to some, when a Jew died a bloody death the religious requirement was that he should not be washed in order that his life's blood should be buried with him.

Interestingly, Emmerich (1904, 137–38) envisioned Jesus' mother, Mary, and others wiping up the "sacred blood" from Jesus' flagellation, presumably to preserve it. In this imagined anecdote—repeated in Mel Gibson's *The Passion of the Christ*—the linen towels were provided by the wife of the Roman prefect, Pilate. Gibson even goes further: whereas Emmerich only claimed to see Pilate's wife "send" the cloths, Gibson has her deliver them in person.

Ian Wilson concludes:

> One could go into detail on the way Catharine [*sic*] was anachronistic or just plain wrong on point after point. . . . But perhaps more telling is the absence in her visions of any convincing "period" feel, and the inclusion of many stories, like that of Veronica, difficult to accept as anything other than apocrypha.

Emmerich's handling of Veronica's tale is instructive. Representing one of the stations of the cross in Catholic ritual, the medieval story derives from earlier legends (dating back to the fourth century) concerning certain miraculous self-portraits of Jesus. Over the centuries, one type of these came to be known as "Veronica's Veil." According to a pious legend, Veronica was a Jerusalem woman who took pity on Jesus as he struggled with his cross on the way to Golgotha. In some versions of the tale, she gave her kerchief or veil to Jesus so he could wipe the blood and sweat from his face, and—in return for her generosity—he miraculously imprinted the cloth with his holy visage.

There were numerous such portrait veils, known, not surprisingly, as "Veronicas." However, the term is believed to be a corruption of *vera iconica*, that is, "true image," the corruption probably inspiring the Veronica tale. (Although the "Veronicas" were supposedly miraculously bestowed, they were actually painted. To explain how there could be many of the "original," another story was invented telling of how the holy image could supernaturally duplicate itself [Nickell 1993, 19–22].)

Anne Catherine Emmerich, who was steeped in Catholic traditions, knew that Veronica was a made-up name, deriving from "*vera icon*" [*sic*], but she claimed it was used to "commemorate" the woman's brave act. Emmerich somehow divined that Veronica's real name was Seraphia, and she added other unlikely details.

ANTI-SEMITISM? GRATUITOUS VIOLENCE?

Much of what critics have objected to in *The Passion*—namely the portrayals of Pilate and the Jewish high priest, Caiaphas, as well as what many have viewed as anti-Semitism and gratuitous violence—appears to derive largely from Emmerich.

The movie's depiction of Pilate as vacillating and as eventually succumbing to Caiaphas's desire that Jesus be crucified (Tokasz 2004) seems to come straight out of Emmerich. She refers to "the undecided, weak conduct of Pilate" who was "that most weak and undecided of all judges." In contrast, Caiaphas, she says, "even went so far as to endeavor to exclude from the Council all those members who were in the slightest degree favorable to Jesus." According to her, Caiaphas made no effort to conceal his hatred of Jesus (Emmerich 1904, 108, 132, 147).

Although at times Emmerich simply speaks of Jesus' "malicious and cruel enemies" (122), at other times, whether intentionally or not, she appears to malign an entire people. She refers to "the wicked Jews," "the hard hearted Jews," "the cruel Jews" (101, 106, 115), and other disparagements, reflected in Gibson's *The Passion* in the sinister countenances and actions of Caiaphas's followers.

Regarding the film's extreme violence, while acknowledging that *The Passion* offers a "meticulous evocation of its time and setting," *Entertainment Weekly* added (Jensen 2004):

It's also, apparently, the Most Violent Story Ever Told. The scourging of Christ—for some, *The Passion*'s most gruesome sequence—sounds like a textbook lesson in torture, with Gibson's camera doting on the instruments used and the flesh-rendering damage they can inflict.

And the textbook that obviously provided the lesson is, again, Emmerich's *The Dolorous Passion.*

According to Emmerich's visions (134):

They then dragged his arms to such a height that his feet, which were tightly bound to the base of the pillar, scarcely touched the ground. Thus was the Holy of Holies violently stretched, without a particle of clothing, on a pillar used for the punishment of the greatest criminals; and then did two furious ruffians who were thirsting for his blood begin in the most barbarous manner to scourge his sacred body from head to foot. The whips of scourges which they first made use of appeared to me to be made of a species of flexible white wood, but perhaps they were composed of the sinews of the ox, or of strips of leather.

She further envisioned:

Our loving Lord, the Son of God, true God and true Man, writhed as a worm under the blows of these barbarians; his mild but deep groans might be heard from afar; they resounded through the air, as a kind of touching accompaniment to the hissing of the instruments of torture. These groans resembled rather a cry of prayer and supplication, than moans of anguish....

The Jewish mob was gathered together at some distance from the pillar at which the dreadful punishment was taking place.... I saw groups of infamous, bold-looking young men, who were for the most part busying themselves near the watch-house in preparing fresh scourges, while others went to seek branches of thorns.

And so on, in this extreme detailing of violence.

The scope of Emmerich's *The Dolorous Passion* is essentially that chosen by Gibson for *The Passion*. Although an article in *Christianity Today* magazine noted that Gibson did not follow Emmerich slavishly, it did concede the debt, acknowledging, "Many of the details needed to fill out the Gospel accounts he drew from her book" (Neff 2004).

A "CATHOLIC" FILM?

And that is the point many seem to have missed. Conservative Catholic commentator Cal Thomas (2004) stated that the Veronica incident was the only "doctrinally Catholic" element he could see in *The Passion*, thus ignoring the heavy reliance on a Catholic "visionary" for much of the film's content.

The emphasis on Mary is another strongly Catholic element. The film does stop short of making Mary a major object of veneration (creating what some refer to as "Marianity" [Craveri 1967, 32] or, especially when expressed before statues and other images, "Mariolatry" [Ashton 1991]). Yet Gibson, who has been struck by the positive evangelical response to *The Passion*, admits that it is all the more amazing, since "the film is so Marian" (quoted in Neff 2004, 35).

The focus should not be surprising. After all, Mel Gibson is a devout Catholic. Moreover, the film's Jesus, Jim Caviezel, insisted each day's filming begin with the celebration of Mass (Neff 2004, 30).

The result is a film that offers neither a historical nor a fundamentalist view. Of course, historically, apart from later Christian sources, there is virtually no evidence for Jesus' crucifixion—or even his very existence. There are merely a few texts that many critics hold to be "too uncertain or too late to provide any support for the Gospel story, with the only substantial piece of it [allegedly by the Jewish historian Josephus] easily discreditable as a total Christian forgery" (Doherty 2001, 47; see also Price 2003).

As to the accounts of the Passion in the Gospels, they are very brief, and scholarly analysis demonstrates that they are also untrustworthy. For example, as Jesus Seminar scholar Robert Price (2003, 321) observes, "The crucifixion account of Mark, the basis for all the others, is simply a tacit rewrite of Psalm 22, with a few other texts thrown in." Jesus' exclamation—

"My God, my God, why hast thou forsaken me?"—comes verbatim from Psalm 22; also from that psalm are the piercing of the hands and the feet, the casting of lots for the garments, and other story motifs.

Small wonder that a filmmaker would look elsewhere for details to fill in an otherwise sketchy outline. But Mel Gibson's heavy reliance on a dubious "visionary" is unfortunate, producing not a praiseworthy cinematic account of a story essential to Christianity, but merely another technically impressive yet pseudohistorical Hollywood shockumentary.

CHAPTER 35

EUCHARISTIC SIGNS

Did an incident that reportedly occurred in Turin, Italy, in 1453 (unrelated to the famous "shroud" later enshrined there) offer unimpeachable evidence of the supernatural? How else can one explain the wonderful story of "the Miracle of Turin" and other Eucharistic miracle claims?[1]

INTRODUCTION

In her book *Eucharistic Miracles*, Joan Carroll Cruz (1987, xi) states, "The greatest treasure in the Catholic Church is, without question, the Holy Eucharist—in which Jesus Christ humbly assumes the appearance of bread." In Catholicism, the Eucharist is the sacrament in which the bread and wine consumed at Communion in remembrance of Jesus' Last Supper are, by the miracle of "transubstantiation," changed into the actual body and blood of Christ, whence they are known as the Blessed Sacrament (Stravinskas 2002, 139, 302, 734). In other words, Catholics take literally Jesus' statement regarding the bread: "Take, eat: this is my body," and regarding the wine, "Drink ye all of it; for this is my blood of the new testament, which is shed for many for the remission of sins" (Matt. 26:26–28).

In contrast, Protestants understand the story (given in various other versions: Mark 14:22–25; Luke 22:19, 20; John 6:48–58; and 1 Corinthians 11:23–26)[2] as symbolic of Jesus' dying for mankind. Indeed, it is an evolved form of the Jewish Passover ritual (Dummelow 1951, 710). Religious writers Marcus J. Borg and John Dominic Crossan (2006, 192–94) consider the story, together with the entire Easter narrative, as a parable (a simple story with a moral, whether factually true or not).

EUCHARISTIC MIRACLES

Nevertheless, transubstantiation is a dogma of Catholicism and, from at least the eighth century, numerous "Eucharistic miracles" that seem to verify its reality have been reported. In addition to a few dozen accounts in Cruz (1987), many more are related in *Legends of the Blessed Sacrament* (Shapcote 1877), and no fewer than 142 are featured in a Vatican international traveling exhibition titled the "Eucharistic Miracles of the World," which I was able to view in Lackawanna, New York, on September 20, 2007. (The exhibition consists of display panels, otherwise available online ["Eucharistic Miracles of the World" 2007].)

Some Eucharistic miracle tales (Cruz 1987, 187–88, 191–92, 208–209) seem to be little more than derivations of biblical stories. For example, the account of a boy having eaten Communion bread that keeps him from harm inside a fiery furnace evokes the story of Shadrach, Meshach, and Abednego in Daniel (3:10–30); the Holy Sacrament's curing of a demoniac recalls Jesus' similar feat in Mark (5:1–16); and the multiplication of some twenty consecrated wafers—or Hosts—into enough to serve almost six hundred people obviously recalls Jesus' miraculous feeding of the multitude of five thousand with only "five loaves, and two fishes" (Matthew 14:15–21). (Interestingly, the multiplying Hosts was accomplished by St. John Bosco, 1815–1888, who, in his youth, had been a magician [Cruz 1987, 208]!)

Many of the Eucharistic miracle stories have a suspiciously similar plot, which suggests derivation. For example, at least three stories—from Lanciano, Italy, eighth century; Regensburg, Germany, 1257; and Bolsena, Italy, 1263—concern a priest who had doubts about the reality of transubstantiation. When he spoke the words of consecration, the Host was suddenly transformed into flesh and/or the wine became visible blood (Cruz 1987, 3–7; 59–62).

As another example, several tales—from Alatri, Italy, 1228; Santarem, Portugal, early thirteenth century; and Offida, Italy, 1280—feature a woman who kept the Host in her mouth so she could make off with it and, as instructed by some occultist, transform it into a love potion. Subsequently, the Host was turned into flesh (Cruz 1987, 30–37; 70–83), and in one instance it also issued a mysterious light (Cruz 1987, 38–46).

At least two anti-Semitic tales—one from Paris, France, 1290; and one from Brussels, Belgium, 1370—involve a Jew or Jews illicitly acquiring a consecrated wafer and stabbing it with a knife, whereupon blood spurted forth in triumph over their mocking disbelief (Cruz 1987, 63–65; 112–22).[3] In the latter tale there are even conflicting accounts of the Jews' fate: one says they were burned at the stake, the other that they were banished from the area. Such *variants*—as folklorists call them—are a "defining character-istic of folklore," since oral transmission naturally produces differing ver-sions of the same tale (Brunvand 1978, 7).

TURIN "MIRACLE"

The story of "the miracle of Turin" begins just before the middle of the year 1453 at a church in Exilles (then in the French Dauphinate), according to a parchment that I personally examined at the Turin city archives (Valle n. d.). Reportedly, some men (two soldiers, in popular legend [Cruz 1987, 145]) had come from a war between the French Savoys and the Piedmontese, pillaged a church, and then loaded a sack full of plunder—including a silver reliquary with a sacred Host—upon a mule. They made their way via Susa, Avigliana, and Rivoli to Turin, but after the beast passed through the city gate, it halted in front of the church of San Silvestro and fell to the ground. Out of the pack tumbled the Host—"the true body of Christ"— and it miraculously ascended into the air, shining "like the sun." The bishop, Ludovico Romagno, was summoned along with the clergy, whereupon they discovered the reliquary on the ground and "the body of the Lord in the air with great Radiant splendor." The bishop knelt and brought out a chalice into which the Host descended, thence being transported to "the doorway of the Cathedral."

The parchment, signed only by a ducal official, nevertheless lists the names of several witnesses and notes that "after completion of the new cathedral" the Host is to rest therein and to be the subject of an annual octave (an eight-day event) in commemoration of the "miracle" (Valle n. d.).

Unfortunately, there are problems with the document, although it is certainly consistent with a parchment of the fifteenth or early sixteenth century.[4] Significantly, it is undated and merely bears in the heading the date of the reported event: "in the year 1453 on the 6 of June, a Thursday."

Actually, the sixth was a Wednesday, only one of several indications that something is amiss. Another problem is the reference to the anticipated completion of the "new cathedral," presumably that of St. John the Baptist, which was not built until 1491–98 ("Turin Cathedral" 2007).

Everything about the document indicates that it is not original, including the fact that another undated one—with a similar text (including the erroneous "Thursday")—is known. Indeed, it is the latter whose text is reproduced in the official booklet published with the imprimatur of the Metropolitan Curia of Turin. However, this document is noted as "presently missing," and—lest it be thought to have been the original—it is described as a "sixteenth-century text" (*Il Miracolo di Torino* 1997, 55). Moreover, although the two documents include many similarities, there are differences in wording and detail. For instance, the published document specifically mentions the Cathedral of St. John the Baptist by name, and the respective lists of witnesses' names show evidence of garbling. (For example, "Michaele Burry" is given in the parchment versus "Michel Muri" in the published document; only one of the eleven names is exactly the same, and the published document omits a name. The list in Cruz [1987] is different still.)

Despite the late, differing versions and the apparent lack of a true original—all of which inspires skepticism—the copies themselves nevertheless indicate there was, at least at some point, a narrative and a list of names of alleged eyewitnesses to some occurrence. But what was it?

AN EXPLANATION

The texts suggest that it may well have been some celestial event, the supposed Host being described as "in the air with great Radiant splendor" and "shining like the sun" (see figure 35.1). The accounts say the event occurred "at hour 20" (Valle n. d.; *Il Miracolo di Torino* 1997, 55), but the printed text has an editorial insertion clarifying that it was "between the hours 16 and 17"—that is, between four and five o'clock in the afternoon (*Il Miracolo di Torino* 1997, 55). Therefore, the duration was apparently less than one hour. On the other hand, the event obviously lasted long enough for residents to fetch the bishop and clergy, so it was too long for, say, a meteor.

That it was described as "shining like the sun" suggests to me that it could have been a phenomenon known as a "mock sun" (or "sun dog"), that is, a parhelion. Parhelia can appear as very bright patches in the sky. They are among the various ice-crystal refraction effects that include halos, arcs, solar pillars, and other atmospheric phenomena (Greenler 1999, 23–64).

I posed the question of the mystery occurrence to Major James McGaha (USAF, retired), who is not only an experienced pilot and noted UFO expert but also director of the Grasslands Observatory in Tucson, Arizona. He conducted a computer search of the sky for the place, date, and time of the occurrence. He found nothing of an astronomical nature that might have caused such an effect. (For example, there was no conjunction of planets, and the moon—a new moon—would have been invisible [McGaha 2008].)

He agreed with my suggestion that a parhelion-type phenomenon could be consistent with the "miracle of Turin." That is especially likely in light of the celestial object being reported as "over the surrounding houses" and "shining, as a second sun" ("Eucharistic Miracles of the World" 2007)—an apt description if the phenomenon were indeed a mock sun. A parhelion could well last for the duration reported, and it would be most likely to appear when the sun was relatively low in the sky, observed McGaha (2008).

He considered one other possibility, given that there was a question of the date. If the event did occur on June 6 but three years later, in 1456, the celestial object could convincingly be identified as Halley's Comet.

In any event, what might have happened is that the witnessing of a genuine, sensational occurrence was seen as miraculous—a "sign"—by superstitious folk and clergy, the latter interpreting it as the radiant body of Christ in the sky. This could have prompted the bishop to hold aloft not only a chalice but also a Host, and as the phenomenon soon ceased to be visible, the belief was that the celestial light was absorbed by the wafer. According to this scenario, it was this "miraculous" Host that was displayed. (It was thus kept until 1584 when the Holy See ordered it consumed so as "not to oblige God to maintain an eternal miracle by keeping the Host always perfect and pure" (quoted in Cruz 1987, 147).

This celestial incident, witnessed by various persons, might then have been grafted by the process of folklore onto a somewhat similar tale, like one set in Paris in 1274 (Cruz 1987, 63). Or it could have been confabulated—in the manner of the Roswell UFO crash myth (McAndrew 1997)—and enhanced by faulty perceptions and memories, together with the impulse to create a pious legend.

Such religious legends are often called *belief tales* because they are intentionally grafted "to give credence to folk beliefs" (Brunvand 1978, 106–108). Indeed, Cruz (1987, 145) states revealingly that "at the time of the miracle of Turin, the faith of the people had grown feeble, and it is thought God wanted to give a sign to arouse them from their apathy." The miracle, she states, "effected the desired change."

Arguing in favor of this hypothesis, I think, is the allegorical nature of the Turin narrative—a dramatic tale in its own right, and an even more profoundly Christian one if seen as allegory of the life, death, and resurrection of Jesus. Consider, for example that similar to Jesus' emerging from exile (Matthew 2:13–15), in the Turin-miracle narrative the *Corpus Domini* ("Body of Christ") is placed on a mule and led from Exilles into Turin (which would become known as "the city of the Holy sacrament" [*Il Miracolo di Torino* 1997, 32]). Jesus' Last Supper (Matthew 26:17–30) is evoked by the wafer of Communion bread, which has been spilled.

This (tradition says) happened between two robbers, like Jesus' crucifixion, which occurred between two thieves (Matthew 27:38). And just as Jesus bodily arose from his tomb (Matthew 28:1–7) and was "carried up into heaven" (Mark 24:51), the "Body of Christ" emerged from its reliquary (a container for holy remains) and ascended into the sky, radiant like the sun, as Jesus came to be (says John 9:5) "the light of the world." The subsequent descent of the Holy Host into the chalice obviously symbolizes the gift of the Eucharist to Christianity—a theme common to all of the Eucharistic "miracle" tales.

Figure 35.1. Painting depicting the "Miracle of Turin" by Bartolomeo Garavaglia in the Church of Corpus Domini, Turin, Italy. (Photo by Joe Nickell)

CHAPTER 36

THE SECRETS OF FATIMA

Among the intriguing mysteries of modern Catholicism are the "miracles" and "secrets" supposedly imparted by the Virgin Mary at Fatima, Portugal, in 1917 (Oliveira 1999). In addition to an allegedly miraculous "dance of the sun," there were three major secrets, two of which were revealed at the time. The third and final one—kept in an envelope by the Vatican—was not made public until mid-2000, provoking much interest and controversy. I was involved in the media debate over the release of the third secret, appearing on a documentary for the History Channel series *History's Mysteries* titled "Fatima: Secrets Unveiled" (which aired January 4, 2001) as well as being interviewed for newspaper articles (for example, Valpy 2000; Barss 2000). Here is my investigative take on the entire Fatima phenomenon.

THE LADY APPEARS

The reported visits of the Virgin Mary to Fatima occurred in a time of trouble. After the fall of the Portuguese monarchy in 1910, there came a wave of anticlerical sentiment and persecution, followed by various revolutionary conflicts and Portugal's involvement in World War I.

On May 13, 1917, three shepherd children were tending their flock about two miles west of Fatima in a town near Ourém. The children were Lucia Santos, age ten, and her two cousins, nine-year-old Francisco Marto and his seven-year-old sister, Jacinta. A sudden flash of lightning sent the children fleeing down a slope, whereupon the two girls beheld the dazzling apparition of a beautiful lady, radiant in white light, standing among the holly-like leaves of a small holm oak.

Lucia was the only one who talked with the figure, who promised to identify herself at the end of a six-month period, during which time the children were to return to the site on the thirteenth day of each month. The woman said that all three of them would go to heaven but that Francisco, who could not see her, would have to recite many rosaries. When she instructed Lucia to have Francisco say the rosary, the boy became able to see the apparition, but he was still unable to hear her speak. After she instructed the children to pray for an end to the war, the lady vanished into the sky.

Even though the children had agreed that they should keep the event secret, once home, little Jacinta blurted out to her parents that she had shared in a vision of the Virgin Mary. News quickly spread throughout the town, and when the children revisited the site on June 13, they were accompanied by some fifty devout villagers. Kneeling in prayer at the oak, the children saw the woman glide down from heaven and take a position amid the oak's foliage (Arvey 1990, 66; Rogo 1982, 221–23).

Thus began a pattern that was repeated each month during the specified period, although the children were absent on August 13 (having been detained by secular authorities who disbelieved their tale and held them briefly for questioning in the public jail at Ourém). On July 13, the children claimed to have received a special revelation that the lady forbade them to disclose. The apparition remained invisible to the onlookers, but some reported seeing a little cloud rise from (or from behind) the tree, together with a movement of the tree's branches "as if in going away the Lady's dress had trailed over them" (Dacruz n. d.).

When the period ended on a stormy October 13, as many as seventy thousand people were gathered at the site anticipating the Virgin's final visit, many anticipating a great miracle. Again, the figure appeared only to the children. Identifying herself as "the Lady of the Rosary," she urged people to repent and to build a chapel at the site. After predicting an end to the war and giving the children certain undisclosed visions, the lady lifted her hands to the sky. Thereupon Lucia exclaimed, "The sun!" As everyone gazed upward to see that a silvery disc had emerged from behind the clouds, they experienced what is known in the terminology of Marian apparitions as a "sun miracle" (Arvey 1990, 69–71).

MIRACLE OF THE SUN

This Fatima "miracle" has been described in many very different ways. Some claimed that the sun spun pinwheel-like with colored streamers, while others maintained that it danced. One reported, "I saw clearly and distinctly a globe of light advancing from east to west, gliding slowly and majestically through the air." To some, the sun seemed to be falling toward the spectators. Still others, before the "dance of the sun" occurred, saw white petals shower down and disintegrate before reaching the earth (Larue 1990, 195–96; Arvey 1990, 70–71; Rogo 1982, 227, 230–32).

Precisely what happened at Fatima has been the subject of much controversy. Church authorities made inquiries, collected eyewitness testimony, and declared the events worthy of belief as a miracle (Zimdars-Swartz 1991, 90). However, people elsewhere in the world, viewing the very same sun, did not see the alleged gyrations; neither did astronomical observatories detect the sun deviating from the norm (which would have had a devastating effect on Earth!). Therefore, more tenable explanations for the reports include mass hysteria and local meteorological phenomena such as a sundog (a parhelion or "mock sun").

On the other hand, several eyewitnesses of the October 13, 1917, gathering at Fatima specifically stated they were looking "fixedly at the sun" or "tried to look straight at it" or otherwise made clear they were gazing directly at the actual sun (quoted in Rogo 1982, 230, 231). If this is so, the "dancing sun" and other solar phenomena may have been due to optical effects resulting from temporary retinal distortion caused by staring at such an intense light or to the effect of darting the eyes to and fro to avoid fixed gazing (thus combining image, afterimage, and movement).

Most likely, there was a combination of factors, including optical effects and meteorological phenomena, such as the sun being seen through thin clouds, causing it to appear as a silver disc. Other possibilities include an alteration in the density of the passing clouds, causing the sun's image to alternately brighten and dim and so seem to advance and recede, and dust or moisture droplets in the atmosphere refracting the sunlight and thus imparting a variety of colors. The effects of suggestion were also likely involved, since devout spectators had come to the site fully expecting some miraculous event, had their gaze dramatically directed at the sun by the charismatic Lucia, and excitedly discussed and compared their perceptions in a way almost certain to foster psychological contagion (Nickell 1993, 176–81).

Not surprisingly, perhaps, sun miracles have been reported at other Marian sites—at Lubbock, Texas, in 1989; Mother Cabrini Shrine near Denver, Colorado, in 1992; Conyers, Georgia, in the early to mid-1990s; and elsewhere, including Thiruvananthapuram, India, in 2008. Tragically, at the Colorado and India sites, many people suffered eye damage (solar retinopathy)—in some instances, possibly permanent damage (Nickell 1993, 196–200; Sebastian 2008).

At the Conyers site, the Georgia Skeptics set up a telescope outfitted with a vision-protecting Mylar solar filter, and on one occasion I participated in the experiment. Becky Long, president of the organization, stated that more than two hundred people had viewed the sun through one of the solar filters and not a single person saw anything unusual (Long 1992, 3).

THE SECRETS

Those who believe in the Fatima "miracle" also cite certain predictions the apparition allegedly made to Lucia, one being that Jacinta and Francisco would soon die. Both did soon succumb to influenza: Francisco in 1919 and Jacinta the following year. However, Zimdars-Swartz observes that "much of what devotees today accept as the content of the apparition comes from four memoirs written by Lucia in the convent [where she later resided] between 1935 and 1941, many years after the series of experiences that constitute the apparition event" (Zimdars-Swartz 1991, 68). Indeed, Lucia recorded her first "prediction" of the children's deaths in 1927—several years after the fact!

As to the other predictions, they were supposedly part of three secrets that had been delivered to Lucia by the apparition on July 13, 1917 (Alban 1997, 290–91). Lucia's *Third Memoir* gave the first secret as a vision of hell. The second was a statement that World War I would end, "but if people do not cease offending God, a worse one will break out during the pontificate of Pius XI" (who was pope from 1922 to 1939). However, since the *Third Memoir* was penned in August 1941, the so-called predictions were actually written after the fact (Zimdars-Swartz 1991, 198–99).

Before considering the important third secret of Fatima, and to fully comprehend the entire Fatima experience, we must look more closely at its central figure—not the Virgin Mary but Lucia de Jesus Santos. Born on March 22, 1907, to Antonio and Maria Rosa Santos, Lucia was the youngest of seven children. Five years younger than her next-oldest sibling, Lucia was a petted and spoiled child. Her sisters fostered in her a desire to be the center of attention by teaching her to dance and sing. At festivals, Lucia would stand on a crate to entertain an adoring crowd. Among her other talents was a gift for telling stories—fairy tales, biblical narratives, and saints' legends—which made her popular with village children, and an ability to persuade others to do her bidding.

Two years before the famous series of apparitions occurred at Fatima, eight-year-old Lucia and three girlfriends claimed to have seen apparitions of a snow-white figure on three occasions. Lucia's mother called the experiences "childish nonsense." The following year, Lucia, Francisco, and Jacinta were thrice visited by an "angel."

Lucia's background is revealing. The seeds of her later visionary encounters were clearly contained in her childhood experiences and in her obviously fantasy-prone personality.[1] Her charismatic ability to influence others drew little Francisco and Jacinta into the Fatima fantasy. As Zimdars-Swartz says of Lucia:

> It is clear that she played the leading role in the scenario of the apparition itself. All accounts agree that she was the only one of the three seers to interact with both her vision and with the crowd, carrying on conversations with both while her two çousins stood by silently. She has said, moreover, and probably not incorrectly, that Francisco and Jacinta had been accustomed to follow her directives before the apparition began, that they turned to her for guidance afterwards, and that it was she who convinced them that they had to be very careful in their experiences. (Zimdars-Swartz 1991, 68)

Further evidence that Lucia orchestrated the fantasy and manipulated the other children is provided by certain incidents. For example, when Jacinta first told the story, she stated that the Virgin had said many things that she was unable to recall but "which Lucia knows." Lucia's own mother was convinced that her precocious daughter was, in her words, "nothing but a fake who is leading half the world astray" (quoted in Zimdars-Swartz 1991, 71, 86).

THIRD SECRET REVEALED

But there was a third secret of Fatima, possessed by the Vatican since 1957 and the subject of endless interest and speculation (Alban 1997, 291). Certain Catholic notables have claimed to have the third secret, but their credibility is at issue because they seem to describe documents that were not first hand in their accounts. Nevertheless, they have hinted that the text predicted another world war and a great disaster of some kind (see Kramer 2006).

In mid-2000, the Catholic Church revealed the third secret that was supposedly imparted to Lucia in 1917, which she set down as text in a 1944 letter. It was forwarded in 1957 to the Secret Archives of the Vatican's Holy Office, where it had since reposed.

On Monday, June 26, 2000, Cardinal Joseph Ratzinger—then prefect of church doctrine, later Pope Benedict XVI—spoke in a nationally televised news conference at the Vatican. Scrawled with a thick-nibbed pen in Portuguese—in wording Ratzinger characterized as "symbolic and not easy to decipher" (Valpy 2000)—Lucia had described seeing (at no specific time in the future) "an angel with a flaming sword in his left hand; flashing, it gave out flames that looked as though they would set the world on fire; but they died out in contact with the splendor that Our Lady radiated towards him from her right hand: pointing to the earth with his right hand, the angel cried out in a loud voice: *'Penance, Penance, Penance!'*"

The visionary continued describing the appearance of a "bishop dressed in white" who was "afflicted with pain and sorrow" as he made his way through a ruined city. Moreover, "he prayed for the souls of the corpses he met on his way; having reached the top of the mountain, on his knees at the foot of the big Cross he was killed by a group of soldiers who fired bullets and arrows at him, and in the same way there died one after another, the other bishops, priests, men and women Religious."

Now, many of the faithful have seen the text as having forecast the attempted assassination of Pope John Paul II, who was shot and wounded by a Turk in 1981 (Fleishman 2000). However, nearly all aspects of the vision—if indeed it was supposed to predict the assassination attempt on John Paul—were in error. It described not a pope but a bishop, who was not killed, who was not shot by soldiers, certainly not by arrows (an implausibility attributable to a child's imagination); neither were all of the other bishops and priests killed.

The vision only seems accurate if one engages in "retrofitting"—after-the-fact matching that fits statements to facts once they are known. This is the same process used to claim that the prognostications of Nostradamus (1503–1566), the French seer, accurately described future events (see Nickell 1989, 45–47). In the case of the "third secret," the retrofitting involves counting the plausibly correct statements (for example, the pope is "*Bishop* of Rome," was dressed in white, and was struck by a would-be assassin's bullet) while ignoring—or rationalizing—the many erroneous facts. Nevertheless, the Vatican statement claimed all three secrets represented authentic prophecy: "No one could have imagined all this" (quoted in Valpy 2000).

In any event, many conspiracy-minded Catholics refuse to believe that the third secret has been fully revealed. They opine that it may be "an indictment of most of the changes in the Church since Vatican II" (held between 1962 and 1965) and would thus cause embarrassment to the current defenders of that council (Alban 2006, 42). Meanwhile, the visionary who started it all, Lucia Santos—who became a Carmelite nun, Sister Lúcia of Jesus, and died on February 13, 2005—has been placed on the track to sainthood ("Lúcia" 2008). Certainly, the story will continue.

CHAPTER 37

THE MEDJUGORJE PHENOMENON

On June 24, 1981, on a rocky hill overlooking the village of Medjugorje, six children (four girls, ages fifteen to seventeen, and two boys, ten and sixteen) claimed that at dusk they were suddenly startled by an extremely bright light, at the center of which was a beautiful woman wearing a gray dress with white mantle and veil. Events continued but were moved eventually to St. James Catholic Church, where the children would stand in a line facing one wall and begin reciting the Lord's Prayer. Suddenly they would kneel in unison and seemingly enter their visionary state wherein—their lips moving inaudibly—they allegedly communicated with the Virgin. In 1984 the Virgin began giving weekly messages to the parish and, in 1987, to the world.

Until war greatly reduced pilgrimages to the site by 1991, Medjugorje attracted crowds of up to fifty thousand on holy days, and an estimated nineteen million visited over the ten-year period. Villagers built additions onto their homes, and "apparition watch" gazebos and a pavilion of confessional booths sprang up. Incredible claims were attributed to the site. In addition to the daily visitations and messages, there were sun miracles (like those at Fatima), images of Jesus and Mary that sometimes appeared in the clouds, numerous healings, and other supposedly miraculous occurrences, such as rosary beads turning from silver to gold! (Nickell 1995, 168–72)

Medjugorje mania was not going unchallenged, however. Although the local bishop, Pavao Zanic, at first accepted the claims as genuine, he soon changed his view. One revelation occurred when a message allegedly from the Virgin took the side of the Franciscan friars against the bishop in a rather petty matter. Once his suspicions were aroused, Bishop Zanic found additional evidence that things were not as they seemed. For example, the children had changed their story about why they had gone to the hill on the day they first saw the apparition. In addition, some of the alleged messages from the Virgin became progressively elaborated—another indication that they may have been spurious. The bishop also found points of incompatibility with Catholic theology as well as other problems. Eventually, Bishop Zanic stated publicly:

> The majority of the pious public has naively fallen victim to the great propaganda, the talk of the apparitions and the feelings. These people themselves have become the greatest propaganda for the event. They do not even stop to think that the truth has been hidden by deliberate falsehood. They do not know that not one miraculous healing has occurred that could have been verified by competent experts. (quoted in Nickell 1995, 169)

In 1986 the Vatican became involved in the Medjugorje affair, taking the matter out of Bishop Zanic's hands and entrusting the question of authenticity to Yugoslavia's national bishops conference. The bishops issued a warning against any public worship that is directly linked to the alleged apparitions. However, until civil war came to the region, Medjugorje seemed unaffected by any such warnings (Sheler et al. 1990; Sudetic 1990).

In the meantime, however, apparition sites had begun to spring up across the United States, as pilgrims brought the "Medjugorje pox" home. The *Hartford Courant* (May 18, 1994) noted that "a 'copycat' effect may be at work similar to what happened all over France in 1858 after Bernadette of Lourdes said Mary was appearing to her in visions." The sites include the following (with dates they became public): Conyers, Georgia (1990); Mother Cabrini Shrine, near Denver, Colorado (1991); Marlboro Township, New Jersey (1992); Cold Spring, Kentucky (1992); and Falmouth, Kentucky (1993).

These have not fared well. The diocesan bishop said at the time of the initial Cold Spring event, at which the Virgin Mary was to appear at midnight, that "nothing of a miraculous nature" had occurred there (Prather 1992). At Marlboro Township, where Joseph Januszkiewicz began to see visions six months after visiting Medjugorje, a church commission dismissed the reported visions. And at the Mother Cabrini Shrine, where a laywoman, Theresa Antonia Lopez, said she had visions that began at Medjugorje, a commission's investigation prompted the archbishop to say that the visions were "devoid of any supernatural origin."

I have had the opportunity to visit and investigate three of the sites at the time the apparitions are said to appear (typically at a specified monthly date). These were Cold Spring (which I reported on for *Skeptical Inquirer* magazine), Conyers (which an Atlanta television station commissioned me to visit and which I did, accompanied by members of Georgia Skeptics), and Falmouth (which I investigated at the request of *Mysterious Forces Beyond*, a Learning Channel television program). In each case my main interest was in examining allegedly miraculous occurrences.

For example, the claim that rosaries change from silver to gold apparently began at Medjugorje, but it is now common at sites across the United States. Rosaries that I have been able to examine on site (using a Bausch & Lomb illuminated 10x magnifying loupe) have typically been those with a thin silver plating over a brassy metal base; as the plating is rubbed off, the yellowish metal shows through, giving the illusion that the metal is undergoing transmutation. Others report similar findings; in some instances (including rosaries from Conyers), the effect is simply due to tarnish. Apparently aware that the rosaries are not yielding real gold, in several instances claimants have been careful to use the term "gold color."

Other phenomena are treated elsewhere, including sun miracles (chapter 36), Golden Door photos (chapter 7), weeping statues (chapters 9–11), and effigies with heartbeats (chapter 9).

CHAPTER 38

GUARDIAN ANGEL ENCOUNTERS

Interest in angels waxes and wanes. In 1975 evangelist Billy Graham lamented in his book *Angels: God's Secret Agents* that "little had been written on the subject in this century" (ix). However, belief in angels went up from 50 percent in 1988 to 69 percent at the end of 1993, with 66 percent believing they were actually watched over by their "own personal guardian angel." Furthermore, between 1990 and 1993, Sophy Burnham's *A Book of Angels* sold over half a million copies in thirty printings (Woodward et al. 1993, 54), and many similar books were as successful.

A poll in September 2008 showed interest in the celestial beings reaching a new level. Conducted by the Baylor University Institute for Studies of Religion, the poll of 1,700 respondents yielded 55 percent answering in the affirmative to the statement, "I was protected from harm by a guardian angel" (Stark 2008, 57). Christopher Bader, director of the Baylor survey, which also covered a number of other religious issues, found that response "the big shocker" in the report. He explained, "If you ask whether people *believe* in guardian angels, a lot of people will say, 'sure.' But this is different. It's experiential. It means that lots of Americans are having these lived supernatural experiences" (quoted in Van Biema 2008).

But are these experiences really supernatural? Or are they only natural, the result of misperceptions and even misreporting? A look into the phenomenon of claimed guardian-angel encounters is illuminating.

ANGEL GUARDIANS

Perhaps the earliest depiction of an angelic being, or a precursor of angels, is a winged figure on an ancient Sumerian *stele*. The entity is pouring the water of life from a jar into the king's cup. Other precursors may be the giant, winged, supernatural beings—part animal, part human—that guarded the temples of ancient Assyria, thus perhaps serving as models for the concept that angels are protectors. The word *angel* derives from the Greek *angelos*, or "messenger"; however, in biblical accounts, the entities fulfilled not only the role of messengers (see, for example, Matthew 1:20) but also that of avengers (2 Samuel 24:16), protectors (Psalms 91:11), rescuers (Daniel 6:22), and more (Burnham 1990, 81–82; Larue 1990, 57–61; Guiley 1991, 20).

In modern times, angels have been seen primarily as guardians (figure 38.1). "Angels represent God's personal care for each one of us," observes Father Andrew Greeley, a priest turned sociologist and novelist (quoted in Woodward et al. 1993). This "new angelology"—the belief in personal guardian angels—is manifested not only in books, but also in angel focus groups and workshops as well as in angel bric-a-brac, posters, greeting cards, and so on. According to *Newsweek*, "It may be kitsch, but there's more to the current angel obsession than the Hallmarking of America. Like the search for extraterrestrials, the belief in angels implies that we are not alone in the universe—that someone up there likes me" (Woodward et al. 1993).

Personal encounters with angels—related as inspirational stories—fill the books on angels. One such account appears in Graham's book (1975, 2–3). It tells of a little girl who fetches a doctor to help her ailing mother. After caring for the woman, the doctor learns that her daughter died a month before. In the closet he finds the little girl's coat, reporting that "it was warm and dry and could not possibly have been out in the wintry night."

Investigating the account, I discovered that it is a very old tale, circulated in various forms and with conflicting details (Nickell 1995, 153–55). Noted folklorist Jan Brunvand (2000, 123–36) followed up on the tale (with some assistance from me) and demonstrated that it derived from a story told by S. Weir Mitchell (1829–1914), a physician and writer of prose fiction. Mitchell himself referred to it as "an early [illegible] ghost tale of [mine?]"—a seemingly tacit admission that the narrative was pure fiction (Nickell 2011).

ENCOUNTERS

Most of the currently popular angel stories are personal narratives. Among these are tales of "mysterious stranger angels," ordinary-looking people who "appear suddenly when they are needed, and disappear just as suddenly when their job is done" (Guiley 1993, 65).

This genre includes the "roadside rescue" story, which one source admits "happens so often that it is almost a cliché in angel lore." Essentially, "In the roadside rescue, the mysterious stranger arrives to help the motorist stranded on a lonely road at night, or who is injured in an accident in an isolated spot. Or, human beings arrive just in the nick of time" (Guiley 1993, 66). One such testimonial has come from Jane M. Howard, an "angel channeler and author." According to Guiley (1993, 66):

> One night, the gas pedal in Janie's car became stuck, and she ran off the freeway near Baltimore. She stopped the car by throwing the transmission into park. It would not restart, and she began to panic. It was ten p.m. and she was miles from the nearest exit. She prayed to the angels for help, and within minutes, a van pulled up, carrying a man and a woman.
>
> The woman rolled down her window and told Janie not to be frightened, for they were Christians. Even so, many people would have been wary of strangers at night. But the angels gave Janie assurances, and she accepted a ride to a gas station. She discovered that the couple lived in a town near hers, and knew her family. They pulled off to help Janie, they said, because they had a daughter, and they hoped that if their daughter ever was in distress, she, too, would be aided.

Notwithstanding such mundane occurrences, often the intervention is described so as to leave little doubt that it must have been a supernatural event. One such narrative tells of a woman's visit to an electronics store and a young man who helped her son with some technical knowledge. The woman stated (in Guiley 1993, 65):

> I was just dumbfounded. The young man wished us a nice day and left the store. A couple of seconds later, I rushed out the door to thank him, but he was gone. He literally disappeared. The store is in the middle of the

block, so you would still be able to see someone walking down the side-
walk. Obviously, this was not an ordinary human. I still get chills about it.

However, we must ask: Was it really only "a couple of seconds later" or
could it have been *several* seconds—long enough for the man to have entered
a waiting car or stepped into an adjacent store?

Then there are the bedside angelic encounters, such as a story told by a
Louisville woman in Burnham's *A Book of Angels* (1990, 275–76). One of the
woman's good friends had died but seemed to linger as a "presence." Moreover, she says,

> Twice I have awakened from sleep to see something mystical. I sat up in
> bed to convince myself I was not dreaming.
>
> To the right of me, hovering about five feet from the floor, was a
> bright mass of energy, a yellow and orange ball about six inches in diam-
> eter. I closed my eyes and reopened them. I even pinched myself to make
> sure I was really seeing what was before my eyes, and there it remained
> until I fell asleep again.
>
> I was frightened. About a year later, the same thing happened under
> the same circumstances. However, this time I asked questions subcon-
> sciously and they were answered. They were all in reference to my friend
> who had left this world. And the overall summation was, I was not to fear
> or worry, because I was being watched over. His protection, caring, and
> love were continuing, though his physical being was gone.

One immediately recognizes in this account the unmistakable characteristics
of a "waking dream"—a very realistic-seeming hallucination that occurs
in the state between full wakefulness and sleep. Waking dreams are
responsible for countless supposed visitations by angels, as well as by ghosts,
extraterrestrials, demons, and other otherworldly entities that lurk in the
subconscious mind (Nickell 1995, 41, 46, 117, 131, 157, 209, 214; Baker 1995,
278).

In still other cases the percipient may simply be a classic fantasizer
(Nickell 1995, 40–41, 57). Children are especially well known for engaging
in fantasies. Consider, for example, this anecdote related by Sophy Burnham
(1990, 4):

Once my mother saw an angel. She was five years old at the time, just a little girl in her nightie, getting ready for bed, when she looked up and saw an angel standing in the bedroom door.

"Auntie!" She pointed at the figure. "Look!" but her beloved auntie could not see.

"Go to sleep, child," she said. "There's nothing there." I don't know what her angel looked like. When I asked her, my mother's face took on a dreamy and exalted look, simultaneously nostalgic and alight. She used words like *brilliance* or *radiance*, and I have the impression of many colors. But I have no idea what she saw.

As indicated by the aunt's inability to see it, the angel obviously resulted from a child's imagination and is no more credible than an eyewitness account of Santa Claus, a leprechaun, or an elf.

Stress can even produce angels in crisis situations. As psychologist Robert A. Baker observes, there is a "well-known psychological fact that human beings, when subjected to extreme fear and stress, frequently hallucinate. These hallucinations, in many instances, take the form of helpers, aides, guides, assistants, et al., playing the role of Savior." Adds Baker, "If the hallucinator also has religious leanings it is easy to understand how such a 'helper' is converted into one of the heavenly host, i.e., a guardian angel" (quoted in Nickell 1995, 157–58).

Then there are stories that appear to fall into the category of urban legends. One of these features the Angel of Mons that supposedly came to the aid of British soldiers at that Belgian battlefield during World War I. Folklorist David Clarke, for his *The Angel of Mons: Phantom Soldiers and Ghostly Guardians*, exhaustively investigated the story, finding it had been inspired by a fictional tale "at a time when the British people were desperate for news of a miracle" (2004, 241). Appearing in the *London Evening News* of September 29, 1914, "The Bowmen," by Arthur Machen, dramatized the British routing of the Germans in symbolic terms of St. George and "his Agincourt bowmen." Many read the story as true, prompting rumors of eyewitness accounts. Concludes Clarke (2004, 246):

In 1914, Britain was an imperial nation with a long tradition of success in combat that was sustained by belief in divine intervention. At Mons, the cream of the British Army narrowly escaped defeat at the hands of the Germans during the first month of the war. Many believed it was a miracle, and Arthur Machen's story provided a perfect conduit for the creation and transmission of a reassuring modern legend that was based upon ancient precedents. His literary skills gave the story a resonance and power that would sustain it long beyond his lifetime. It was a legend that had an important and positive function during the war, sustaining hope, boosting patriotic optimism and shoring up faltering faith during the dark days of the Somme, Passchendaele and all the other disastrous battles that almost exterminated a generation of young men. Today the Angel of Mons remains one of the undying icons of that war and lives on as a symbol of the loss of innocence that was the legacy it left upon the British psyche. This legend re-emerged for a brief spell during the national crisis of 1940, at Dunkirk and during the Battle of Britain. Maybe one day the angels will be needed again.

The concept of guardian angels, notes one writer (Willin 2008, 37), "was given a huge impetus" by the publication of Machen's tale.

PHOTOGRAPHING ANGELS

Thus far we have considered personal accounts of angels acting as guardians; however, if such accounts represent only what serious researchers disparage as "anecdotal evidence," then what about photographic evidence—photos offered to support claims of angelic encounters? Unfortunately, the evidence is at best unconvincing, usually easily explainable. Many touted examples, for instance, are nothing more than simulacra, images perceived by the mind's tendency to "recognize" common shapes in random patterns, like seeing pictures in inkblots, clouds, wood-grain patterns, and the like (Nickell 2007, 18).

Such images may also be faked. Consider the "Cloud Angel" photo circulated by Betty Malz, author of *Angels Watching Over Me* and other books. The picture Malz (1993) was kind enough to send me was accompanied by a brief narrative telling how a honeymooning couple had taken the photo from the window of their airplane. They had undergone severe turbulence that provoked them to pray for safety, whereupon the turbulence soon subsided and later the angel-shaped cloud appeared in one of their photos. It turns out, however, that the same picture has a long history—touted variously as an image of Christ taken during Hurricane Hugo ("Experts Call "Hugo Christ' Photo Fake" 1990) and a "ghostly apparition" taken in 1971 by an "ordained spiritual minister" (Holzer 1993). Suspiciously, the cloud lacks the three-dimensional qualities of genuine cloud photographs, as determined by a computer-imaging expert (Nickell 2001, 200–203).

Much more recently, a few "angel" photos were included in the book *The Paranormal Caught on Film* by Melvyn Willin (2008, 36–37, 42–43, 46–47, 62–63). Alas, however, these range from the poorly documented to the suspiciously anonymous. They are attributable to a variety of photographic anomalies, including reflections, simulacra, and other factors, as well as outright fakery.

As these narrative and photograph examples demonstrate, to many people guardian angels offer comfort in difficult times, while to others they are confirmation of deeply held religious or New Age beliefs. However, the evidence for their existence appears to be as ethereal, elusive, and doubtful as the alleged entities themselves.

Figure 38.1. Guardian angel depicted in a late-nineteenth-century print. (Author's collection)

CHAPTER 39

HEAVEN'S STENOGRAPHER

She claims to receive communications not only from her guardian angel, "Daniel," but also from Jesus and even Yahweh himself, all of whom guide her hand to produce written messages. She has provoked both skepticism and credulity from Catholic laity and clergy, and her texts—an amalgam of Bible verses and Orthodox and Catholic teachings—have helped her attract an increasingly large following. Some claim to have witnessed supernatural experiences at her talks, although I did not when in 2004 I witnessed her first appearance in Western New York. I have since sought to learn just who Vassula Ryden is as well as more about the phenomenon behind that name (Ryden 1995; "Vassula Ryden" 2010; Tokasz 2004).

VASSULA

Born to Greek Orthodox parents in Heliopolis, Egypt, on January 18, 1942, Vassula Ryden emigrated to Europe when she was fifteen. She says that as a teenager she saw herself surrounded by souls of the dead, although she claims to have been indifferent to religion for a time. She claims that, following marriage, the birth of two sons, divorce, and remarriage, she began receiving messages from her own invisible "guardian angel," Daniel. "I almost freaked out," she said (Ryden 2004). That occurred in late 1985 while she was living in Bangladesh. Five years later, she "regularized" her marriage in the rites of the Greek Orthodox Church, to which she still belongs ("Vassula Ryden" 2010). Nevertheless, Ryden says that God revealed to her the Sacred Heart (a Catholic symbol of Christ's love for the human family) to show her the equality of all faiths (Ryden 2004).

269

In the mid-1990s, the Vatican's Congregation for the Doctrine of the Faith issued two notices of concern about Ryden. The first came in 1995, pointing out "several negative elements and errors." It requested that bishops refuse to give her the opportunity to spread her questionable ideas within their dioceses and asked them not to treat her writings or speeches as "supernatural." The following year, another notification encouraged priests to "exercise serious spiritual discernment" regarding Ryden's messages, declaring that they must be considered merely "private meditations" and not divine revelations. However, some of her Catholic supporters observe that the church does not completely discount her teachings, and the publications of her organization, the American Association for True Life in God, have obvious Catholic trappings ("Vassula Ryden" 2010; Tokasz 2004).

The Catholic Church is skittish about such freelancers—urging caution toward supposedly supernatural phenomena (such as stigmata or weeping effigies) and any reputed visions or messages. The church is all too aware of delusional persons and pious frauds. However, such matters are usually left to the local bishop, and investigations are typically less about science than about how a claim comports with Catholic teachings.

I determined to take an objective look at three aspects of Ryden's purported messages (within my own areas of expertise): first, the distinctive handwriting (I am author of textbooks on writing and forgery, including *Pen, Ink, and Evidence* [Nickell 1990]); second, the text (I have a PhD in English, experience in examining unusual texts, and membership, by invitation, in the International Association of Forensic Linguists) [Nickell 2008]; and third, whether Ryden might have a fantasy-prone personality (I have studied this trait for years, especially under the direction of the late psychologist Robert A. Baker [Nickell 1997]).

HANDWRITING

Ryden insists that the messages she receives and writes down are not the result of Spiritualistic phenomena such as channeling or automatic writing ("Vassula Ryden" 2010). However, neither phenomenon is defined as being limited to spirits of the dead; either may involve interaction with any type of alleged nonphysical beings, such as angels, deities, extraterrestrials, or the like (Guiley 2000, 25–26, 70–71). So, Ryden is by definition a channeler and an automatic writer.

Reportedly, the messages began in late November 1985 when Ryden was about to make a shopping list. Her hand suddenly began to move, seemingly without her control, to form words and drawings, initiating a phenomenon that continues to the present day. The self-styled visionary reportedly receives about four to six hours of guided-hand "dictation" each day (Carroll 1995, ix; "Vassula Ryden" 2010). From a scientific perspective (assuming it is not deliberately contrived), such a phenomenon is attributed to the ideomotor effect, in which a participant unconsciously produces a movement. The same psychological phenomenon is responsible for the motion of dowsing rods and pendulums, Ouija-board planchette movement, table tipping, and the like (Randi 1995, 169–70).

Ryden's messages supposedly "come through dictation by an audible voice within, then are written in a stately handwriting—distinct from her own—as she allows her hand to be guided supernaturally" ("About Vassula Ryden" 1995). Interestingly enough, the same "distinct" script that is used for messages from the angel "Daniel" is employed by "Jesus," "Mary," and "Yahweh," rather than each entity having his or her own individual handwriting.

Keeping in mind that Ryden is an artist ("About Vassula Ryden" 1995), it seems noteworthy that the "guided" handwriting has the characteristics of a script that is artistically drawn rather than naturally and freely written. It is a "mannered" or affected hand, rendered in a self-consciously nonslanted style—rather like the so-called "vertical writing" that was taught in American and Canadian schools from 1890 to 1900 but was deemed too time consuming to produce practically and subsequently abandoned (Nickell 1990, 124, 126; Osborn 1978, 140). Most mainstream scripts, intended for right-handed persons to render with some speed, slope in the forward direction, as does Ryden's ordinary handwriting. Interestingly, an alteration in slant is one of the most common ploys used for disguising handwriting (Hilton 1982, 169; Osborn 1978, 147, 149, 211). Use of this simple change can thus instantly impart a new look to an entire page. The "stately" hand also differs from Ryden's in size (being larger than hers), another common disguise ploy (Nickell 1996, 49).

Apart from the "stately" affectation, the supposedly supernatural handwriting is essentially a formal, copybook version of Ryden's own naturally jotted script that alternates with the "stately" hand in her notebooks.

The "stately" hand avoids some of her script's idiosyncrasies, yet it still has mostly printed capitals just like her own handwriting. On occasion, one of the copybook forms sneaks back into her natural script (replacing, for instance, her individualistic *f*, which has a backwardly made loop, with the standard copybook *f*) (see Ryden 1995, 171, 223).

Consistent with its neat, drawn appearance is the fact that the "guided" handwriting is done on lined paper, with the lines showing in some of the reproduced pages (Ryden 1995, for example, 232–33). This is consistent with the use of eye-hand coordination. One suspects that if Ryden were prevented from seeing what was being written, the entities supposedly guiding her hand would be unable to so faithfully follow the lines! I invite Ryden to accept my invitation to perform a scientific test to refute or confirm this suspicion.

TEXT

On January 25, 1987, Ryden wrote:

> Courage daughter, I, Jesus Christ have instructed you that the cross you bear is My Cross of Peace and Love, but to bear My precious Cross, daughter, you will have to do much self-sacrifice; be strong and bear my Cross with love; with Me you will share it and you will share My sufferings; I was pleased to hear your prayer of surrender; in surrendering to Me I will lift you to the heights and show you how I work; I will mould you, if you let Me, into a better person; you have given Me your consent to become My bride, so what [*sic*] more natural for a bride to follow her Spouse? I am glad you realize your worthlessness, do not fear, I love you anyway. (Ryden 1995, 233–34)

Is this really a message from Jesus guiding Ryden's hand? Not only is the handwriting the identical, mannered script that is also used for her "Daniel," "Yahweh," and "Mary," but the perpetual use of semicolons is another similarity from alleged speaker to alleged speaker. All—except, appropriately, Daniel—call her "daughter" (Ryden 1995, 153, 188, 225), and they refer to themselves with the same construction: "I, Jesus," "I, God," "I 'i Panayia'" (Greek for "Our Lady, most Holy") (Ryden 1995, 155, 231, 293).

Ryden's purported messages can be compared with other alleged communications from Jesus. One set of writings was "received from Jesus" by Lilian Bernas (1999), a purported stigmatic. (*Stigmata* are the supposedly supernaturally received wounds resembling those of Christ. However, Bernas's wounds—which I have seen up close—appear to be consistent with self-infliction [Nickell 2007, 59–66].) In one communication with Bernas, Jesus supposedly said (Bernas 1999, 23):

> My Suffering Soul—
> This is your Beloved. I have come as promised to embrace you
> with the spirit of peace. Take this time, and have respite from
> the wicked assaults of the evil one. My child, you have bent,
> but you have not broken. This pleases your Beloved. . . .
> My child—humble yourself now, and ascend the hill of your
> Beloved with your Beloved. . . .

Nancy Fowler, a homemaker in Conyers, Georgia, claimed for several years to be receiving messages from both Jesus and, more often, the Virgin Mary. (The latter appeared punctually on the thirteenth of each month, and I was able to attend a session [Nickell 1993, 196–97]). One message from "Jesus" instructed the faithful (Fowler 1993):

> Come through My Mother on your journey back to Me. From this very
> cross I give the world My perfect love. I give the world, I give everyone
> in the world, My dear, Holy Mother. Please, if you accept My Love, then
> how can you reject, ignore, not honor, not love My Mother. I come through
> My Mother and I want you, dear children, to come through My Mother
> on your journey back to Me.
>
> I choose the word "Come" intentionally, not past tense. I still come
> through My Mother. Graces are poured forth through My Mother, the
> Graces come from Me.

I am especially familiar with these two groups of writings, although they are supposedly received by clairaudience (trance hearing) rather than by automatic writing. (Therefore, errors of grammar and the like could be attributed to mistaken transcription by the percipient.)

Now, whereas Vassula Ryden's "Jesus" frequently identifies himself as "I, Jesus," Lilian Bernas's Jesus persona never does, nor does the one channeled by Nancy Fowler. There are many other differences among the three sets of texts; for example, the dominant themes of each: Fowler's is the near deification of the Virgin Mary (an emphasis sometimes disparagingly referred to as "Mariolatry"), Bernas's is the importance of suffering, and Ryden's is the need for divine love and guidance.

Style also differs from channeler to channeler. Ryden's "God" and "Jesus" (as well as "Daniel") speak similarly, often using convoluted diction (for example, "do not leave yourself be drifted away" [144], instead of "do not let yourself drift away"); wrong prepositions (for example, "irrespective to their deeds" [146], rather than "irrespective of"); missing prepositions (such as in "I, Yahweh will remind them in this call many events" [150], wherein "of" is missing after "call"); subject/verb agreement error (for example, "the reasons that makes" [44]); faulty auxiliary verbs (such as "I have restored you since the time you have accepted Me" [158], the second "have" being unnecessary); incorrect verb forms (for example, "I will progress you" [163], "I fragranced you" [34], and "Jesus flourished you" [42]); and so on.

Ryden's messages also have occasional misspellings: for example, "God" says, "work with Me writting [sic] down My messages" (231), and he also uses the misspellings "joyfull" (138) and "analising" (101, 105). If God deigns to use the English language, should we not expect it to be rendered accurately?

Before we become invested in imagining what a deity might or might not do, we should note that Ryden's own written text has similar faults—for example, using "sprung" when "sprang" would be correct, the misspelling "panick," faulty subject/verb agreement (for example, "Joy and Peace is"), and many others. At times the respective errors are eerily similar, as when "God" uses "do" for "make" (for example, "do not get discouraged when you do errors") just as Ryden does (for example, "I do so many mistakes") (see Ryden 1995, 22, 89, 93, 235).

FANTASY PRONENESS

From the evidence, it looks like Ryden's channeled automatic writings are merely emanations from a single source: her imagination. Indeed, she exhibits many traits of what is known as a "fantasy-prone" personality: sane and normal but with a propensity to fantasize, as described in a pioneering study by Sheryl C. Wilson and Theodore X. Barber (1983). Since childhood, Ryden has had various "mystical" experiences. She has encountered apparitions (such as the souls of "dead people"), had vivid or "waking" dreams (with paranormal imagery), experienced religious visions, interacted with invisible companions, received messages from higher entities, and had other experiences common to many fantasizers (Carroll 1995; Ryden 1995, xx–xxl).

Taken together, the contrived handwriting, the linguistic lapses, and the indications of fantasizing all suggest that Vassula Ryden is not in touch with supernatural entities but is simply engaging in self-deception that in turn deceives the credulous. Her automatic writings therefore are not works of revelation but simply of pious imagination.

CHAPTER 40

THE MORMON SEER

The "Mormon" church—that is, the Church of Jesus Christ of Latter-day Saints—was founded by a man who had allegedly been visited by an angel. His is an illuminating story.

BACKGROUND

Joseph Smith Jr. (1805–1844) was born in Sharon, Vermont, the third of nine children of Joseph and Lucy (Mack) Smith. A poor, unchurched, but religious family, the Smiths migrated in 1816 to Palmyra, New York. A contemporary recalled the young Joe as a disheveled boy, dressed in patched clothing, with homemade suspenders and a battered hat.

> He was a good talker, and would have made a fine stump speaker if he had had the training. He was known among the young men I associated with as a romancer of the first water. I never knew so ignorant a man as Joe was to have such a fertile imagination. He never could tell a common occurrence in his daily life without embellishing the story with his imagination; yet I remember that he was grieved one day when old Parson Reed told Joe that he was going to hell for his lying habits. (quoted in Taves 1984, 16)

At the age of fourteen, Smith later wrote, he became troubled by the various religious revivals in the area, and so he sought a wooded area where he hoped to commune directly with God.

277

It was the first time in my life that I had made such an attempt, for amidst all my anxieties I had never as yet made the attempt to pray vocally. . . . I kneeled down and began to offer up the desires of my heart to God. I had scarcely done so, when immediately I was seized upon by some power which entirely overcame me, and had such an astonishing influence over me as to bind my tongue so that I could not speak. Thick darkness gathered around me, and it seemed to me for a time as if I were doomed to sudden destruction. But, exerting all my powers to call upon God to deliver me out of the power of this enemy which had seized upon me, and at the very moment when I was ready to sink into despair and abandon myself to destruction—not to an imaginary ruin, but to the power of some actual being from the unseen world, who had such marvelous power as I had never before felt in any being—just at this moment of great alarm, I saw a pillar of light exactly over my head, above the brightness of the sun, which descended gradually until it fell upon me.

Smith continued:

It no sooner appeared than I found myself delivered from the enemy which held me bound. When the light rested upon me I saw two personages, whose brightness and glory defy all description, standing above me in the air. One of them spake unto me, calling me by name, and said—pointing to the other—"*This is my beloved Son, hear Him.*"

My object in going to inquire of the Lord was to know which of all the sects was right, that I might know which to join. No sooner, therefore, did I get possession of myself, so as to be able to speak, that I asked the personages who stood above me in the light, which of all sects was right—and which I should join. I was answered that I must join none of them, for they were all wrong, and the personage who addressed me said that all their creeds were an abomination in His sight: that those professors were all corrupt; that "they drawn near to me with their lips, but their hearts are far from me; they teach for doctrines the commandments of men: having a form of godliness, but they deny the power thereof." He again forbade me to join with any of them: and many other things did he say unto me, which I cannot write at this time. When I came to myself again, I found myself lying on my back, looking up into heaven. (quoted in Brodie 1993, 21–22)

Although Smith would give different versions of his visions (Persuitte 2000), his biographer Fawn M. Brodie notes that somewhat similar experiences "were common in the folklore of the area"—an indication that Joseph's experience was probably genuinely real to him. In fact, Smith's account suggests he probably dozed off and had a common hypnagogic hallucination (or waking dream). His reference to an entity having "held me bound" suggests the immobility that often accompanies such an experience. It is due to "sleep paralysis"—one's inability to move because the body is still in the sleep mode. The reported light and the fantastic beings are also common to such an occurrence, which combines features of both wakefulness and dreaming.

ENTER MORONI

A few years later, at the age of seventeen, Smith had another experience. Although again there are different versions, it is described in terms entirely consistent with an actual hypnagogic hallucination:

> A personage appeared at my bedside, standing in the air. . . . He had on a loose robe of most exquisite whiteness. . . . His whole person was glorious beyond description. I was afraid; but the fear soon left me. He called me by name, and said unto me that he was a messenger sent from the presence of God to me and that his name was Moroni; that God had a work for me to do; and that my name should be had for good and evil among all nations, kindreds and tongues. (quoted in Taves 1984, 277)

In 1823 Joseph Smith claimed that Moroni had revealed the existence of a new gospel—the Book of Mormon—which was engraved on gold plates hidden in a hill near Palmyra, New York. Smith "translated" the text (or, more likely, he imagined it, while borrowing from certain contemporary writings). His bride, Emma, was his first scribe, followed by an early convert named Martin Harris. To effect the translation, Smith sat on one side of the room staring into a special stone (in the type of reverie practiced by scryers; that is, crystal gazers), with Harris on the other side, writing at a table, while a blanket across a rope separated the two (Taves 1984, 35–40). After the translation, Smith claimed, he returned the gold plates to the angel, thus thwarting critics who wished to examine them. A follower of Smith, Martin Harris, was permitted to show a partial "transcript" of the writing to some experts, including Columbia University professor Charles Anthon. Anthon's opinion was that the language was bogus and the tale of the gold plates a hoax. But Smith persuaded the gullible Harris that because of the difficulty in engraving the plates the scribe had switched to a "shorthand" form of Egyptian writing unknown to the professor.

Like Edgar Cayce (1877–1945), known as the "sleeping prophet," Smith sometimes temporarily lost his gift of seeing—as notably happened after Harris managed to lose the first 116 pages of the manuscript, leaving the prophet inconsolable for a time. The same waning of power occurred with regard to Smith's ability to perform healings. Although he allegedly cast out a devil from one man and healed a woman of a "rheumatic" arm (Taves 1984, 63–69), on occasion he tried unsuccessfully to heal the sick and even, in one instance, to revive the dead (Taves 1984, 70).

FRAUD AND FANTASY

It should be mentioned that Smith had been engaged in "money-digging," searching for hidden treasure either by scrying or by dowsing (using a witch-hazel wand or mineral rod that was supposedly attracted by whatever was sought). Some have seen this as a form of fraud, but Taves (1984, 19) points out that the practice was an old one and that treasure-laden burial mounds dotted the area. Nevertheless, Joseph Smith Jr. was arrested on the complaint of a neighbor that he was "a disorderly person and an impostor." The dispensation of the case is unclear, but apparently Smith agreed to leave town (Persuitte 2000, 40–53; Taves 1984, 17–18).

Brodie describes the young treasure-seeker as having "an extraordinary capacity for fantasy," which, she says, "with proper training might even have turned him to novel-writing." She also says that "his imagination spilled over like a spring freshet. When he stared into his crystal and saw gold in every odd-shaped hill, he was escaping from the drudgery of farm labor into a glorious opulence." She adds, "Had he been able to continue his schooling, subjecting his plastic fancy and tremendous dramatic talent to discipline and molding, his life might never have taken the exotic turn it did" (Brodie 1993, 27).

In the past, attempts to understand the motivations of visionaries like Smith (including psychics, faith healers, and other mystics) often focused on a single, difficult question: Were they mentally ill, or were they instead charlatans? Increasingly, there is evidence that this is a false dichotomy, that many of the most celebrated mystics may in fact simply have possessed fantasy-prone personalities. Called "fantasizers," such individuals fall within the normal range and represent an estimated 4 percent of the population.

This personality type was characterized in 1983 in a pioneering study by Sheryl C. Wilson and Theodore X. Barber. Some thirteen shared traits were identified, several of which Joseph Smith exhibited:

1. frequently fantasizing as a child
2. easily undergoing self-hypnosis (as during his scrying and translating)
3. having imagined sensations that seemed real
4. believing he had divinatory powers
5. receiving special messages from on high
6. believing he had healing powers
7. encountering apparitions
8. experiencing waking dreams with classical imagery.

These eight characteristics—possibly among others—confirm Wilson and Barber's earlier diagnosis and thereby reveal Smith to be typical of religious visionaries who share the characteristics of fantasy proneness. As in previous studies (Nickell 1997), I consider the presence of six or more of these traits in an individual to be indicative of fantasy proneness. (Anyone may have a few of these traits, and only the very rare person would exhibit all of them.)

Wilson and Barber also found evidence suggesting that "individuals manifesting the fantasy-prone syndrome may have been overrepresented among famous mediums, psychics, and religious visionaries of the past" (1983, 371). These researchers further found that biographies could yield evidence that a subject was a fantasizer, and they reached such a determination in the cases of Mary Baker Eddy, founder of Christian Science; Joan of Arc, the Catholic saint; and Gladys Osborne Leonard, the British Spiritualist, among others. It should be noted that Wilson and Barber also included Theosophy founder Madame Helena P. Blavatsky, although her propensity for trickery during séances is well known. Deception and fantasy are obviously not mutually exclusive, as Smith's case well illustrates. Wilson and Barber specifically include him in their list of historical fantasizers (372).

LATER YEARS

The *Book of Mormon* was published in 1830. Shortly afterward, Joseph Smith and his associate, Oliver Crowdery, having been conferred priests by divine revelation to Smith, officially founded the Church of Christ at Fayette, New York. Eight years later the name was changed to the Church of Jesus Christ of Latter-day Saints (Hansen 1995, 365).

An invitation from Sidney Rigdon, onetime associate of revivalist Andrew Campbell, led Smith and his New York brethren to found a Mormon settlement at Kirtland, Ohio. There, Smith claimed to experience a further series of revelations (published in 1833 under the title *Book of Commandments*), which expanded his theological principles. The revelations directed the Saints to gather into communities in a patriarchal order and to erect a temple at the center of the community.

When Smith ran out of money after buying up land surrounding his Kirtland, Ohio, Mormon community, he decided to open his own bank. According to one source:

> There was just one problem: you had to have money to open a bank. Never a stickler for details, Smith went out and borrowed the money to open the Kirtland Safety Society Bank and have plates made up for printing the currency the bank would issue. To assure depositors that their money would be secure, he filled several strong boxes with sand, lead, old iron, and stones, then covered them with a single layer of bright fifty-cent silver coins. Prospective customers were brought into the vault and shown the heaping chests of silver. "The effect of those boxes was like magic," claimed one witness. "They created general confidence in the solidity of the bank, and that beautiful paper money went like hot cakes. For about a month it was the best money in the country." (Naifeh and Smith 1988, 25–26)

Eventually, of course, the bubble burst, the bank failed, and in 1838 Smith "declared bankruptcy with his feet," fleeing the community along with his followers.

Smith also founded communities in Missouri, but in 1839 he and his followers were driven ruthlessly from that state by anti-Mormon vigilantes. The Saints then gathered at a settlement called Nauvoo on the Mississippi River. By 1844, it was the most populous city in Illinois, and it was entirely under Mormon control (Hansen 1995, 365).

It was at Nauvoo that Joseph Smith met his end. He had increasingly acted on pretensions of grandeur that led him to become leader of the Mormon militia, bedecked in the uniform of a lieutenant general, and an announced candidate for the United States presidency. As before, anti-Mormon mobs plagued Smith and his followers, and when the latter destroyed an anti-Mormon press, Smith was jailed on a charge of riot. On June 27, 1844, a mob stormed the jail, killing Smith and his brother Hyrum (Hansen 1995, 365). Concludes Taves (1984, 213): "It was over. The gangly, ill-clad youth who had regaled his Palmyra neighbors with fanciful tales had come a long, long way before reaching the end of his road. Others would continue what he had started."

CHAPTER 41

VISITS FROM THE BEYOND

hose who suffer the loss of a loved one may experience such anguish and emptiness that they are unable to let go, and they may come to believe they have had some contact with the deceased. "It's commonly reported that the deceased person has communicated in some way," says Judith Skretny (2001), vice-president of the Life Transitions Center, "either by giving a sign or causing things to happen with no rational explanation." She adds, "It's equally common for people to wake in the middle of the night, lying in bed, or even to walk into a room and think they see their husband or child." These experiences are sometimes called "visitations" (Voell 2001), and they include deathbed visitations (Wills-Brandon 2000).

During over forty years of paranormal investigation, I have encountered countless claims of such direct contacts (as opposed to those supposedly made through Spiritualist mediums [Nickell 2001a; 2001b]). I have also occasionally been interviewed on the subject—sometimes in response to books promoting contact claims (Voell 2001). Here is a look at the evidence regarding purported signs, dream contacts, apparitions, and deathbed visions.

"SIGNS"

In her coauthored book *Childlight: How Children Reach out to Their Parents from the Beyond*, Donna Theisen relates a personal contact she believes she received from her only son, Michael, who had been killed in an auto accident a month before. She was browsing in a gift shop when she noticed a display of dollhouse furnishings. Nearby, on a small hutch, were a pair of tiny cups that were touching, one bearing the name "Michael," the other the words "I love you, Mom." Although at the time a "strange, warm feeling" came over her, she was later to wonder: "Was I merely finding what I so desperately wanted to see? Was I making mystical connections out of ordinary circumstances?"

On the other hand, the fact that the two cups were displayed together, out of dozens of others sold there, convinced Theisen that the incident "defied the odds." Soon she "began looking for more strange occurrences" so as to confirm that the cups incident was "a real sign." Her book chronicles them and the experiences of other grieving parents (forty of forty-one of them mothers). One, whose son was killed by a train, was wondering whether to give his friend some of his baseball equipment when she heard a train whistle blow and accepted it as an affirmation. Others received signs in the form of a rainbow, television and telephone glitches, the arrival and sudden departure of pigeons, a moved angel doll, and other occurrences (Theisen and Matera 2001).

To explain such "signs" or "meaningful coincidences" (conjunctions of events that seem imbued with mystical significance), psychologist Carl Jung (1960) theorized that—in addition to the usual cause-and-effect relationship of events—there is an "acausal connecting principle." He termed this *synchronicity*. However, in *The Psychology of Superstition*, Gustav Jahoda (1970) suggests that there may often be causal links of which we are simply unaware.

Even in instances where there may in fact be no latent causal connections, other factors could apply. One is the problem of overestimating how rare the occurrence really is. Nobel Prize–winning physicist Luis Alvarez (1965) told how, while reading a newspaper, he came across a phrase that triggered certain associations and left him thinking of a long-forgotten youthful acquaintance; just minutes afterward, he came across that person's obituary. On reflection, however, Alvarez assessed the factors involved, worked out a formula to determine the unlikeliness of such an event, and concluded that three thousand similar experiences could be expected each year in the United States, or approximately ten per day. Synchronous events involving family and friends would be proportionately more common.

A related problem is what psychologist Ruma Falk (1981–82) terms "a selection fallacy" that occurs with anecdotal events, as contrasted with scientifically selected ones. As he explains: "Instead of starting by drawing a random sample and then testing for the occurrence of a rare event, we select rare events that happened and find ourselves marveling at their non-randomness. This is like the archer who first shoots an arrow and then draws the target circle around it."

Some occurrences that are interpreted as signs probably have mundane explanations. Although unexplained, they are not unexplainable. For example, the mother of a severely handicapped little boy reported that on the morning of his funeral she awoke to see a small, glowing red light on the dresser where his baby monitor had been. It was in fact a tiny lantern on her keychain. "It had never been turned on before," she says. "In fact, I didn't even know it worked! The moment I touched the light, it went out." This happened for several subsequent mornings (Theisen and Matera 2001, 192). How do we explain such a mystery? One possibility is that the light was not turned on at all but only appeared so as sunlight reflected off its red cover; when it was picked up, the illusion was dispelled.

Photographic "signs," which are also becoming common, may be easily explained. I recall a Massachusetts woman approaching me after a lecture to show me some "ghost" photographs. I immediately recognized the white shapes in the pictures as resulting from the camera's flash bouncing off the stray wrist strap—a phenomenon I had previously investigated and replicated (Nickell 1996). In fact, in one snapshot, the strap's adjustment slide was even recognizable, silhouetted in white. But the lady would not hear my explanation, instead taking back the pictures and stating defiantly that her father had recently died and had been communicating with the family in a variety of strange ways.

In addition to numerous glitches caused by camera, film, and other factors, photos may also exhibit simulacra, random shapes that are interpreted, like inkblots, as recognizable figures (such as a profile of Jesus seen in the foliage of a vine-covered tree [Nickell 1993]). These can easily become visitation "signs," as in the case of a photo snapped from a moving vehicle at the site of a young man's auto death. "When this photo was developed," the victim's mother wrote, "the tree branches formed a startling figure that looked just like Greg wearing his hat. In addition, there appeared to be an angel looking out toward the road." She added, "We all viewed this photo as more evidence of Greg's ongoing existence" (Theisen and Matera 2001, 47).

DREAM CONTACTS

A significant number of after-death "contacts" come from dreams. They have been associated with the supernatural since very ancient times, and attempts to interpret them are recorded in a papyrus of 1350 BCE in the British Museum (Wortman and Loftus 1981). Now New Age writers like Theisen and Matera (2001) are increasingly chronicling instances of people having dreams about their departed loved ones.

It has been estimated that the average person will have approximately 150,000 dreams by age seventy. Although most are forgotten, the more dramatic and interesting ones are those that are remembered and talked about (Wortman and Loftus 1981). But people's reports of their dreams may be undependable due to the effects of memory distortion, ego, superstition, and other factors.

Even an ordinary dream can be especially powerful when it involves after-death content, and there are types of dreams that can be extremely vivid and seemingly real. They include "lucid dreams," in which the dreamer is able to direct the dreaming, "something like waking up in your dreams" (Blackmore 1991a).

A powerful source of "visitations" is the so-called waking dream (discussed in chapter 40), which occurs in the twilight between wakefulness and sleep and combines features of both. Actually a hallucination—called hypnagogic, if the subject is going to sleep, or hypnopompic, if he or she is awakened—it typically includes bizarre imagery such as apparitions of "ghosts," "angels," "aliens," or other imagined entities. The content, according to psychologist Robert A. Baker (1990), "may be related to the dreamer's current concerns."

For example, here is an account I obtained in 1998 from a Buffalo, New York, woman: "My father had passed away and I was taking care of my sick mother. I went to lay down to rest. I don't remember if I actually fell asleep or if I was awake, but I saw the upper part of my father and he said, 'Mary Ellen, you're doing a good job!' When I said 'Dad,' he went away."

To say, correctly, that this describes a rather common hypnagogic event, does not, however, do justice to the person who experienced it. For her, I think, it represented a final goodbye from her father—and therefore a form of closure—and provided a welcome reassurance during a period of difficulty.

Sometimes, a waking dream is accompanied by what is termed "sleep paralysis," an inability to move caused by the body remaining in the sleep mode. Consider this account (Wills-Brandon 2000, 228–29): "My sister said she was abruptly awakened from a very deep sleep. When she woke up, she said her body felt frozen and she couldn't open her eyes. Suddenly she felt a presence in the room and knew it was Mother. She felt her standing at the foot of the bed."

By their nature, waking dreams seem so real that the experiencer will typically insist that he or she was not dreaming. One woman, who "hardly slept" after her daughter's suicide, saw her, late at night, standing at the end of a long hallway, smiling sadly then walking away into a brilliant light. "At first I thought I was hallucinating," the mother said, "but after a new round of tears, I realized that I was wide awake and I had indeed seen Wendy" (Theisen and Matera 2001, 130). Another, describing a friend's "visitation" experience of her deceased mother-in-law, said, "At first my friend thought she was dreaming but quickly realized she was wide awake" (Wills-Brandon 2000, 60)—a confusion typical of a waking dream.

APPARITIONS

Some "visitations," however, are reported as being quite undreamlike, in the sense that they occur during normal daily activity. However, my own investigatory experience, as well as research data, demonstrates that apparitions are most apt to be perceived during daydreams or other altered states of consciousness. Many occur, for example, while the percipient is in a relaxed state or concentrating on some activity like reading, or is performing routine work. In some instances the person may simply be tired, as from a long day's work. Under such conditions, particularly in the case of imaginative individuals, a mental image might be superimposed upon the visual scene to create a "sighting" (Nickell 2001a, 291–92).

Also, as indicated earlier, faulty recall, bias, and other factors can betray even the most credible and sincere witness. Consider, for instance, an anecdotal case provided by Sir Edmund Hornby, a Shanghai jurist. He related how, years earlier, he was awakened one night by a newspaperman who had arrived belatedly to get the customary written judgment for the following day's edition. The man would not be put off, and—looking "deadly pale"—

sat on the jurist's bed. Eventually Judge Hornby provided a verbal summary, which the man took down in his pocket notebook. After he left, the judge related the incident to Lady Hornby. The following day the judge learned that the reporter had died during the night and—more importantly—that his wife and servants were certain he had not left the house; yet with his body was discovered the notebook, containing a summary of Hornby's judgment!

This apparent proof of a visitation was reported by psychical researchers. However, the tale soon succumbed to investigation. As it was discovered, the reporter did not die at the time reported (about 1:00 a.m.) but much later—between 8:00 and 9:00 in the morning. Furthermore, the judge could not have told his wife about the events at the time, since he was then between marriages. And, finally, although the story depends on a certain judgment that was to be delivered the following day, no such judgment was recorded (Hansel 1966).

When confronted with this evidence of error, Judge Hornby admitted, "My vision must have followed the death (some three months) instead of synchronizing with it." Bewildered by what had happened, he added, "If I had not believed, as I still believe, that every word of it [the story] was accurate, and that my memory was to be relied on, I should not have ever told it as a personal experience" (quoted in Hansel 1966, 188–89). No doubt many other accounts of alleged visitations involve such confabulation—a term psychologists use to refer to the confusing of fact with fiction; unable to retrieve something from memory, the person—perhaps inadvertently—manufactures something that is seemingly appropriate to replace it. "Thus," explain Wortman and Loftus (1981, 204), "the man asked to remember his sixth birthday combines his recollections of several childhood parties and invents the missing details."

Tales such as that related by Judge Hornby represent alleged "moment-of-death visitations" (Finucane 1984). In that story the reporter had allegedly died approximately the same time ("about twenty minutes past one") that he appeared as an apparition to Judge Hornby, although, as we have seen, the death actually occurred several hours later. This case should serve as a cautionary example to other such accounts, which are obviously intended to validate superstitious beliefs.

DEATHBED VISIONS

Another type of alleged visitation comes in the form of deathbed visions. According to Brad Steiger (real name Eugene E. Olson), who endlessly cranks out books promoting paranormal claims, "The phenomenon of deathbed visions is as old as humankind, and such visitations of angels, light beings, previously deceased personalities and holy figures manifesting to those about to cross over to the Other Side have been recorded throughout all of human history." Steiger (2000) goes on to praise writer and family grief counselor Carla Wills-Brandon for her "inspirational book," *One Last Hug before I Go: The Mystery and Meaning of Deathbed Visions* (2000).

Like others before her (for example, Kubler-Ross 1973), Wills-Brandon promotes deathbed visions (DBVs) largely through anecdotal accounts that, as we have seen, are untrustworthy. She asserts that "the scientific community" has great difficulty explaining a type of DBV in which the dying supposedly see people they believe are among the living but who have actually died. She cites an old case involving a Frenchman who died in Venezuela in 1894. His nephew—who had not been present—reported:

> Just before his death, and while surrounded by all of his family, he had a prolonged delirium, during which he called out the names of certain friends left in France....
>
> Although struck by this incident, nobody attached any extraordinary importance to these words at the time they were uttered, but they acquired later an exceptional importance when the family found, on their return to Paris, the funeral invitation cards of the persons named by my uncle before his death, and who had died before him.

Unfortunately, when we hear two other accounts of the reported events, we find there is less to this story than meets the ear. A version given by one of the man's two children says nothing of his being delirious, implying otherwise by stating that "he told us of having seen some persons in heaven and of having spoken to them at some length." But she had been quite young at the time and referred the inquirer to her brother. His account—the most trustworthy of the three, since it is a firsthand narrative by a mature informant—lacks the multiple names, the corresponding funeral cards, and other elements, indicating that the story has been much improved in the retellings. The son wrote:

> Concerning what you ask me with regard to the death of my father, which occurred a good many years ago, I recall that a few moments before his death my father called the name of one of his old companions—M. Etch-everry—with whom he had not kept up any connexion, even by correspondence, for a long time past, crying out, "Ah! You too," or some similar phrase. It was only on returning home to Paris that we found the funeral card of this gentleman.

He added, "Perhaps my father may have mentioned other names as well, but I do not remember."

It is hardly surprising that a man's thoughts should, at the close of life, turn to an old friend, or that—having long been out of touch with him—he should have thought him already dead. (The individual reporting the case conceded that there was no certainty the friend had even died before the vision occurred.) Since the most trustworthy account is the least elaborate, lacking even the vision-of-heaven motif, it seems not a corroboration of the nephew's hearsay accounts (Barrett 1926, 22–24) but rather evidence of confabulation at work.

In their book *The Afterlife,* Jenny Randles and Peter Hough (1993, 98–99) tell of a dying man who had lapsed into a coma:

> Then the patient became wonderfully alert, as some people do very near the end. He looked to one side, staring into vacant space. As time went by it was clear he could see someone there whom nobody else in the room could see. Suddenly, his face lit up like a beacon. He was staring and smiling at what was clearly a long-lost friend, his eyes so full of love and serenity that it was hard for those around him to not be overcome by tears.
>
> Sheila [his nurse] says: "There was no mistake. Someone had come for him at the last to show him the way."

But how did the nurse know it was "a long-lost friend" and not, say, Jesus or an angel? Indeed, how did she know he saw "someone" at all, rather than something—perhaps an entrancing view of heaven? The way the nurse makes such assertions—emphasized with words like "clearly" and "no mistake"—suggests she is speaking more of faith than of fact, and her belief is accepted and reported uncritically by Randles and Hough. In fact, the tale contains no evidence of a visitation at all.

Instead, it would appear to represent what is termed a near-death experience (NDE), in which a person typically "comes back" from a state close to death with a story of an otherworldly visit, perhaps involving an out-of-body experience, travel down a dark tunnel, and an encounter with beings of light who help him or her decide whether or not to cross over (figure 41.1).

Susan Blackmore (1991b) describes the NDE as "an essentially physiological event" prompted by lack of oxygen, the structure of the brain's visual cortex, and other factors. She recognizes that the experiences are hallucinations—albeit, seemingly, exceedingly real. And she points out that one does not actually have to be near death to have such an experience, that "many very similar experiences are recorded of people who have taken certain drugs, were extremely tired, or, occasionally, were just carrying on their ordinary activities."

Many of the DBVs reported by Wills-Brandon (2000) and others are similar to NDEs and are probably hallucinations produced by the dying brain. Some of the effects are similar because people share similar brain physiology. For example, the "tunnel" effect "probably lies in the structure of the visual cortex" (Blackmore 1991b, 39–40). Other effects are probably psychological and cultural. Wills-Brandon (2000, 115) concedes: "I agree that when the dying are passing, they are visited by those who will comfort them during their travel to the other side. For a dying Christian, that might mean Jesus; a Buddhist may see Buddha. For others, an angel, a beautiful woman or Druid priest would bring more comfort." But she rationalizes, "If I'm following a particular philosophy of religion, wouldn't it make sense for me to be visited at the moment of my death by an otherworldly escort who is familiar with my belief system?" Perhaps, but of course the simpler explanation is that people see what their expectations prompt them to see.

And that is the problem with the anecdotal evidence for "visitations." The experiencer's will to believe may override any temptation to critically examine the occurrences. Some proponents of after-death contact adopt an end-justifies-the-means attitude. One (quoted in Voell 2001) states:

"Whether any of the connections or feelings or appearances are true or not, I've finally figured out it doesn't make a damn bit of difference. If it has any part in healing, who cares?" The answer is that, first of all, people who value truth care. While magical thinking may be comforting in the short term, over time estrangement from rationality can have consequences, both on individuals, who may suffer from a lack of closure, and on societies, which may slide into ignorance and superstition. That potential peril is why Carl Sagan (1996) referred to science as "a candle in the dark."

Figure 41.1. Poster dated 1906 depicts what would today be called "a near-death experience." (Author's collection)

PART 5
SAINTLY POWERS

CHAPTER 42

MIRACLES—OR PARABLES?

I n the New Testament, Jesus is portrayed as a miracle worker. Apart from healings, exorcisms, and resurrections (treated elsewhere), he performs numerous other alleged miracles.

THE GOSPEL ACCOUNTS

The major miracles described by Mark's Gospel—the earliest source— include Calming the Sea, two miracles of the Loaves and the Fishes (Feeding the Five Thousand, Feeding the Four Thousand), Walking on Water, and the Cursing of the Fig Tree. Matthew includes *all* of the above, with minor additions and revisions, and adds the Coin in the Fish. Luke omits Feeding the Four Thousand, Walking on Water, and the Cursing of the Fig Tree; but he adds the Miraculous Draught of Fishes. John's omissions are extensive: he excludes Calming the Sea, Feeding the Four Thousand, Cursing of the Fig Tree, and Sending the Demons into the Swine (that is, he omits the story of the demoniac at Gerasa). He includes Luke's Miraculous Draught of Fishes (but attributes it to the resurrected Jesus!) and adds one miracle: Changing Water to Wine.

If we argue that a single Gospel account of a miracle is insufficient evidence to persuade us of its reliability (that it had a number of witnesses and enjoyed a tradition of retellings), we should have to exclude Matthew's Coin in the Fish and John's Changing Water into Wine. On the other hand, if we take as our criterion the appearance of a given miracle in *all* the Gospels, then we throw out every single one except Feeding the Five Thousand!

PARABLES?

Let us pause here to consider a hypothesis, that the miracle stories *originated* as parables. A parable is a simple story intended to teach a lesson or to illustrate some moral principle.

Parables are useful in giving concrete embodiment to abstract ideas. They are also—just as poems often are—full of meaning, containing many meanings. By forcing the listener to search out the "true" meaning, parables thus involve the listener in a productive quest rather than simply delivering pronouncements. Jesus makes this clear with the Parable of the Sower: Seeds may fall on rocky ground or among weeds or in good soil, and will meet appropriate fates; so do words—he explains—when they are "sown" among different listeners. He tells his disciples (Mark 4:11–12): "Unto you is given to know the mystery of the Kingdom of God: but unto them that are without, all these things are done in parables." (Why so? The answer is somewhat cryptic: "That seeing they may see, and not perceive; and hearing they may hear, and not understand; lest at any time they should be converted, and their sins should be forgiven them." The idea here is that his teachings were foreordained to failure, just as it was part of the divine plan that he should be betrayed and crucified. The view, of course, is an editorial contrivance by Mark.)

We may gain new understanding of Jesus' supposed miracles by looking at them as parables. In fact, when the Pharisees test Jesus by asking for a sign, his response is revealing: "And he sighed deeply in his spirit, and saith, 'Why does this generation seek after a sign? Verily, I say unto you, no sign shall be given unto this generation'" (Mark 8:12). To see that parables are indeed behind the various alleged miracle stories, let us look at each in turn.

CHANGING WATER TO WINE

John calls this Jesus' "beginning of miracles," but it is related only in his Gospel (2:1–11). It occurred at a marriage in Cana of Galilee, where Jesus was a guest with his mother and disciples. As John relates, when the wine ran out, Jesus' mother called the problem to his attention. Observing six stone water pots, used for the Jewish rites of purification, Jesus had them filled with water, whereupon it was transformed into fine wine. As the steward of the wedding feast says to the bridegroom (John 2:10), "Every man at the beginning doth set forth good wine; and when men have well drunk, then that which is worse: but thou hast kept the good wine until now" (figure 42.1).

In other words, the "water" of Judaism has been transformed into the new and good wine of Christianity (Dummelow 1951, 777). The synoptics do not relate this miracle, but they do contain the Parable of the New Wine (Matthew 9:17; Mark 2:22; Luke 5:37–38). In the parable Jesus says that John the Baptist's "wine" was old, suited to old bottles; but *his* wine was new and required new bottles, else the fermentation cause the old bottles to burst (Dummelow 1951, 658). John has simply followed the common tradition of comparing a jar of wine with holy teaching, and has presented a parable as a miracle.

CALMING THE SEA

Mark (4:35–41) and Matthew (8:23–27) present this as Jesus' first nature miracle and Luke (8:22–25) presents it as his second (following the Miraculous Draught of Fishes). In each, the story is essentially the same: Jesus and his disciples get into a boat and begin to cross the lake (known in different times as Lake Gennesaret, Lake Tiberias, Sea of Galilee). It is evening and Jesus is asleep in the stern. Suddenly a great storm develops; the sea begins to spill into the boat; the disciples grow alarmed. But Jesus sleeps on until they wake him, crying, "Master, carest thou not that we perish? Mark continues (4:39): "And he arose and rebuked the wind, and said unto the sea, 'Peace, be still!' And the wind ceased, and there was a great calm." Jesus rebuked and drove out the demons of the storm just as he had the evil spirits that possessed people (Craveri 1970, 110), just as magicians and shamans have commanded the elements from the most ancient times. And the disciples were filled with wonder.

We need only look at the physical characteristics of the Sea of Galilee to find a rational explanation for the miracle. According to Connick (1974, 276–77):

The Sea is hemmed in on the east and west by mountains. The summer's sun beats down on the basin with unmitigated fury. Without warning cold air currents from the west frequently pounce on the superheated depression and provoke sudden storms. Just as suddenly the storms may subside.

But scholars are quick to question whether seasoned fishermen—as some of the disciples supposedly were—would be so amazed at such a common experience.

Enslin (1968, 156–57) and others (Connick 1974, 276–77; Craveri 1970, 109–10) instead point to a literary source for the account, one that suggests the "miracle" is derivative—in this case from Psalms 107 (23–31). However, the psalm does not describe a single miracle. Rather, it speaks of those times in which "they that go down to the sea in ships . . . see the works of the Lord. . . . For he commandeth, and raiseth the stormy wind." When they are thrown about, "they reel to and fro, and stagger like a drunken man, and are at their wit's end. Then, they cry unto the Lord in their trouble and . . . He maketh the storm a calm."

There is a point to the story in Psalms: "Then they are glad because they be quiet; so he bringeth them unto their desired haven. Oh that men would praise the Lord for his goodness, and for his wonderful works to the children of men!" (Psalms 107:30–31) In Mark's account of Calming the Sea, Jesus reflects that sentiment with the question, "Why are ye so fearful? How is it that ye have no faith?" (Mark 5:40) Most significantly, *immediately preceding* the miracle in Mark is this statement (following Jesus' Parable of the Sower): "And with many such parables spake he the word unto them, as they were able to hear it. But without a parable spake he not unto them: and when they were alone, he expounded all things to his disciples" (Mark 4:33–34).

THE CURSING OF THE FIG TREE

As told in Mark's Gospel (11:12–26), after Jesus and his disciples came from Bethany, Jesus was hungry. "And seeing a fig tree afar off having leaves, he came, if haply he might find any thing thereon: and when he came to it, he found nothing but leaves; for the time of figs was not yet." In response, Jesus commanded that "no man eat fruit of thee hereafter for ever." When they left Jerusalem in the morning, "they saw the fig tree dried up from the roots." Now, if it was not the time for figs, should not Jesus have known it?

Anyway, why not just command some suitable fruit—figs, or even oranges—to appear, rather than destroy an innocent, harmless tree that could feed others? Matthew (writing later) omits the embarrassing fact and claims the tree promptly withered (Matthew 21:18–22).

That this purported miracle actually derived from a parable is suggested by Luke's Gospel (13:6–7), which says of Jesus: "He spake also this parable; A certain man had a fig tree planted in his vineyard; and he came and sought fruit thereupon, and found none. Then said he unto the dresser of his vineyard, 'Behold, these three years I come seeking fruit on this fig tree, and find none: cut it down.'" In the parable the vine dresser begs for a stay of execution for the tree—that he may have one more year to dig around it and fertilize it with manure in hopes of saving the poor tree. How much more characteristic of Jesus is Luke's parable than is Mark and Matthew's miracle! This parable may explain why the miracle tale is "missing" from Luke, furthering the hypothesis that the miracles *originally began* as parables.

THE MIRACULOUS DRAUGHT OF FISHES

Luke (5:1–11) presents this as Jesus' first nature miracle. It is told on the occasion of his meeting Simon (Peter) and his partners James and John. Although the fishermen had toiled throughout the night but caught nothing, Jesus encouraged them to try again. He was in the boat with them already, since he found it a convenient platform from which to teach the people who were pressing close upon him. When he finished speaking, he had Simon put out into deep water and let down his nets. Lo! The catch was so great that, their nets breaking, Simon's partners had to rush to his aid with another boat.

In the account by John (21:1–14), the miracle is performed by Jesus after he has risen from the dead. Moreover, as biblical scholars well know, the entire twenty-first chapter of John is a later addition (Dummelow 1951, 810). While Matthew and Mark do not relate the miraculous catch, they do tell of Jesus' meeting the three fishermen and saying, "Follow me and I will make you fishers of men" (Matthew 4:19; Mark 1:17). In fact, Jesus says the same thing in Luke (5:10): "And Jesus said unto Simon, 'Fear not; from henceforth thou shalt catch men.'" So again, it appears that a miracle tale has been created from a story that was originally a parable.

THE COIN IN THE FISH

This miracle is related only in Matthew (17:24–27), who tells of Jesus and three followers who went to Capernaum. There the tax collectors asked Peter, "Doth not your master pay tribute?" So as not to offend, Jesus directs Peter, "go thou to the sea, and cast an hook, and take up the fish that first cometh up; and when thou hast opened his mouth, thou shalt find a piece of money: that take, and give unto them for me and thee."

Critics suggest that the money may have been simply the proceeds of Peter's sale of the fish (Dummelow 1951, 685), but I think we may much more profitably look for a parable as the true source of the miracle. We do not have to look far, for just such a parable—the story of Caesar's coin—is common to Matthew, Mark, and Luke. In this story the Pharisees came to Jesus seeking "to entrap him in his talk." Full of sarcasm, they said (Mark 12:14): "Master, we know that thou art true, and carest for no man: for thou regardest not the person of men, but teaches the way of God in truth: Is it lawful to give tribute to Caesar, or not?" Such a deceitful trap! If Jesus said yes, he would provoke the Jewish nationals to cries of betrayal; if he replied no, he would commit treason against Rome. Taxation was a passionate issue throughout Judea, but the Pharisees weren't trying to resolve the question. They were simply trying to trick Jesus. However, he was ready for them. He ordered them to bring him a coin, and when one was fetched he asked a simple question, "Whose is this image and superscription?" When they replied, "Caesar's," Jesus said (Mark 12:17): "Render to Caesar the things that are Caesar's, and to God the things that are God's." What a perfect way out of the trap!

Matthew, however, does not *replace* the parable with the miracle. He includes both. (Just as he doubles other elements: there are two blind men where Mark relates one, two demoniacs at Gerasa.)

FEEDING THE FIVE THOUSAND

This is the only miracle found in all four Gospels (Mark 6:34–44; Matthew 14:14–21; Luke 9:11–17; John 6:2–14). With minor variations, the story is the same. A great throng has gathered around Jesus in an isolated place and has listened to him teach. It is now late, and they are hungry. When Jesus tells his disciples to feed the people, they complain, "Two hundred pennyworth [denarii] of bread is not sufficient for them, that every one of them may take a little" (John 6:7). Jesus notes that they have five loaves and two fish, and he has the people sit down by groups upon the grass. He looks up to heaven, blesses and breaks the bread, and gives it to his disciples to distribute. As well, "he divided the two fish among them all." Mark (6:42–43) continues: "And they did all eat, and were filled. And they took up twelve baskets full of the fragments, and of the fishes" (figure 42.2).

Enslin (1968, 155) says of the tale:

> It is quite unnecessary to toy with the notion that one day, as he had talked
> to a multitude of listeners, his generous act in sharing his own luncheon
> had encouraged others to like generosity, with the result that all had eaten;
> and later, that a miraculous element was added to a simple story.

Enslin goes on to point out that the story derives from the Old Testament. Elisha fed a hundred men with a sack of food containing twenty loaves of barley and some fresh ears of grain (2 Kings 4:43–44): "And his servitor [servant] said, 'What, should I set this before an hundred men?' He said again, 'Give them to the men, that they may eat, for thus says the Lord, "They shall eat and have some left."' So he set it before them. And they ate, and left thereof, according to the word of the Lord." Note the points of similarity. In each case the servant(s) ask how so little can feed so many; nevertheless the miracle is accomplished; and there is so much that some is left over. To see that, once again, Jesus' miracle is a parable, we need to look at what is, in effect, a repeat performance. Consider then the next "miracle."

FEEDING THE FOUR THOUSAND

Given in Mark (8:1–9) and Matthew (15:32–38), this miracle's plot is the same as that of the preceding story. Why then—if the disciples had just witnessed the Miracle of the Loaves and Fishes—do they query Jesus: "How can one feed these men with bread here in the desert?" Mark's Jesus does not make the obvious reply ("Just as I did before!"), but Matthew's Jesus seizes a later opportunity to remind them of both miracles of feeding the multitude.

And in so doing he makes clear that the "miracles" were actually parables (Matthew 16:11–12): "'How is it that ye do not understand that I did not speak about bread? Beware of the leaven of the Pharisees and Sadducees.' Then they understood that he did not tell them to beware of the leaven of bread, but of the teaching of the Pharisees and Sadducees."

The leaven of the Pharisees was hypocrisy; of the Sadducees, skepticism. Jesus was the true bread, in other words. He was the fish as well, for in this second version of feeding the multitude there were again "a few little fishes," which were multiplied. We may understand this to mean that just as a handful of "fishers of men" had spread the word to a larger group of willing listeners, so the "fish" were multiplied by the number of those receiving the word.

WALKING ON WATER

The image this miracle presents is of a god-man triumphantly overcoming the laws of nature (Mark 6:47–52; Matthew 14:23–33; John 6:16–21). By doing the impossible, he is performing a miracle; that is, working magic. Symbolically he is also presiding over the domain of fishes and the water of baptism. Mythologically speaking, it is yet another account of a storm-associated miraculous crossing of water—like those of Noah, Moses, and Jonah (figure 42.3). The archetype of these Hebrew myths is the God of Genesis, for we are told that before there was light "the Spirit of god was moving over the face of the waters" (see Genesis 1:2).

Jesus' nighttime stroll upon the water of Lake Gennesaret (or the Sea of Galilee) immediately follows the miraculous feeding of the five thousand. Omitted by Luke, it is told in slightly different versions in the other three Gospels (Matthew 14:22–33; Mark 6:45–51; and John 6:15–20). The earliest Gospel, Mark, says that Jesus directed his disciples to take the boat to the other side of the lake while he went upon the mountain to pray. The disciples made headway slowly, the wind being against them. Mark says:

> and about the fourth watch of the night he cometh unto them. . . . But when they saw him walking upon the sea, they supposed it had been a spirit, and cried out: For they all saw him and were troubled. And immediately he talked with them, and saith unto them, "Be of good cheer: it is

I; be not afraid." And he went up unto them into the ship; and the wind ceased: and they were sore amazed in themselves beyond measure, and wondered.

This story—the centerpiece of the miracles—fits perfectly with the symbolism of the other "miracles" (actually parables). There is a rather heavy-handed clue in Mark's account: the fact that the disciples are en route "to the other side, to Bethsaida." The root word *beth* means "house," and just as Bethlehem means "house of bread," Bethsaida translates "house of the fishers" (Asimov 1968, 191). Surely it is no coincidence that the Gospel writers thus name the destination. Jesus had just multiplied the bread and fish. (In the Gospels fish became a symbolic element—in part because the Greek letters spelling out the five-letter word for fish form the initial letters of five words: "Jesus Christ, Son of God, Savior" [Craveri 1970, 78].) Now the great fish traveled over the abode of all the little fishes in order to rescue his own "fishers of men." He calmed the storm, and finally he and his followers reached their haven, the "house of the fishers." No wonder then that Jesus' walking on water is the ultimate parable. The great depth of that fact becomes even clearer when we realize that the account actually belongs at the end of the Gospel story, that it is surely another account of an appearance of Jesus (refer again to chapter 33) after his resurrection! (Yet another, I believe, is the miracle known as the Transfiguration—see Matthew 17:1–117.)

As these examples demonstrate, I think pretty convincingly, the miracle stories of Jesus are actually parables intended to instruct his followers. Many, if not all, probably first existed as parables (like that of the Barren Fig Tree in Luke). Later, they were transformed—either accidentally by the folkloric process of telling and retelling, or by the deliberate acts of the Gospel writers, or both—into miracle stories.

Figure 42.1. Jesus transforms water to wine (mid-nineteenth-century illustration by Julius Schnorr von Carolsfeld).

Figure 42.2. Jesus feeds the multitude (mid-nineteenth-century illustration by Julius Schnorr von Carolsfeld).

Figure 42.3. Jesus walks on water (mid-nineteenth-century illustration by Julius Schnorr von Carolsfeld).

CHAPTER 43

MIRACLE WORKER
OF AMSTERDAM

While the country's official name is the Netherlands, most people elsewhere call it Holland (even though that term really applies only to two of its thirteen provinces). Just about a tenth the size of California, the Netherlands is still one of Europe's most densely populated countries (after Monaco and Malta). It has historically been a treasure trove of geniuses—from Dutch masters like Rembrandt and Vermeer to such scientific pioneers as Antoni van Leeuwenhoek (1632–1723), who first identified bacteria, and Christiaan Huygens (1629–1695), who proposed the wave theory of light. Indeed, seated in the front row during my talk at a skeptics congress in Utrecht on October 28, 2006, was Gerard 't Hooft, cowinner (with Martin Veltman) of the 2000 Nobel Prize in Physics.

Of course, like people everywhere, the Dutch can also be superstitious—hence the conference theme, "the paranormal." I spoke on the relationship between Dutch and American psychics and for several days before the event toured the country with noted Dutch skeptic Jan Willem Nienhuys investigating a number of mysteries and legends, including an Amsterdam woman's visions.

In Amsterdam, on March 25, 1945, the day of Catholicism's Feast of the Annunciation, a woman named Ida Peerdeman (1905–1996) was at home with her three older sisters. After a priest dropped in for a visit, Peerdeman was drawn to an adjoining room, where she said she beheld an intense light from which a female figure emerged and spoke to her. Thus began a series of fifty-six apparitions of the Virgin Mary, with messages from her that allegedly occurred over the next fourteen years (the last on May 31, 1959).

PROPHECY

The first twenty-five messages (1945–1950) were of a general nature, with imagery and prophecies that merely reflected the political as well as the spiritual turbulence of the period. In 1950, the Virgin, Peerdeman said, appeared atop a globe and announced, "Child, I am standing upon this globe, because I want to be called the Lady of All Nations" (*Messages of the Lady of All Nations* 1999, 75). The following year, she directed that she be depicted in that persona in a painting (see figure 43.1), and she advanced a new and "final" Marian dogma, that Mary was to be Coredemptrix, Mediatrix, and Advocate. The message (May 31, 1954) implied that the dogma would be proclaimed by the then-current pope, Pius XII, or at least sometime "in the twentieth century" (*Messages of the Lady of All Nations* 1999, 145–46). Neither was the case (Conte 2006).

Several other messages purported to predict future events. However, the statements, like those of French seer Nostradamus (1503–1566), are vague and open to various *later* interpretations—by a process called retro-fitting (that is, after-the-fact matching). For example, Peerdeman claimed publicly that in one message she had predicted the AIDS epidemic but had mistaken it for cholera (Van der Ven 2002). In fact, the actual reference (December 26, 1947) was to a torpedo-like device causing "terrible deadly diseases," including cholera and leprosy, and to faces "covered with dreadful ulcers, something like leprosy" (*Messages of the Lady of All Nations* 1999, 51). No place or time period was specified. Thus Peerdeman could subsequently claim to have predicted some chemical/biological attack or any of various epidemics, such as smallpox, or, later reaching for a more dramatic matching, AIDS. (For a debunking of other Peerdeman predictions, see Conte 2006.)

EUCHARIST MIRACLES

Peerdeman also claimed to have had a number of "Eucharistic experiences" that lasted until 1984, effectively supplanting the apparitions. That is, during the Eucharist (Holy Communion), certain visions and supernatural phenomena allegedly occurred. For example, her first experience (in 1958) involved the Catholic belief in transubstantiation (that when partaken, the bread and wine of Communion actually change into the body and blood of Jesus Christ—not merely figuratively). Speaking of the Host (the consecrated Communion wafer) Peerdeman said (*Daily Miracle* 2003, 14):

> All of a sudden the Sacred Host began to grow on my tongue, becoming larger and thicker. It seemed to expand and then suddenly it came alive. . . . It resembled a living fish, the way it moved in my mouth. I wanted to take it out of my mouth to see what it was but naturally out of reverence I did not dare.

(The fish is a symbol of Christ and Christianity [Stravinskas 2002, p. 328].)

In Amsterdam, Nienhuys and I visited the chapel of the Lady of All Nations Foundation, where the inspired painting hangs and nuns continue devotion to Ida Peerdeman and her cause. We spoke with one of the sisters, photographed the painting, and purchased copies of the messages, a biography of Peerdeman, and other materials. Nienhuys also subsequently obtained some relevant articles, which he translated for me.

Many indicators suggest Peerdeman was highly impressionable. The youngest of five children, whose mother died when she was eight, she reportedly had an apparitional experience on October 13, 1917, when she was twelve. Returning home from confession, she allegedly encountered a radiant Mary, who made a friendly gesture to her. This was repeated on two following Saturdays, although her father admonished her to keep her claims to herself lest she be "ridiculed and considered crazy" (Sigl 2005, 11).While to the credulous the date seems auspicious, to skeptics it seems suspicious, suggesting imitation: it was the day that, after much publicity, an estimated seventy thousand people gathered at Fatima, Portugal, where three children claimed the Virgin Mary would appear and work a miracle (Nickell 1993, 176–81).

POSSESSION?

On subsequent occasions at the Peerdeman home, a series of incidents occurred "that would not have been out of place in a *Poltergeist* movie." Lamps began to swing, doors opened and closed, and other phenomena occurred—all apparently without human agency (El-Fers 2002). However, time and again, when properly investigated, such "poltergeist" phenomena have turned out to be the pranks of mischief makers, typically children and teens (Nickell 1995, 79–107). The phenomena attending Peerdeman appear no different.

That Peerdeman was simply acting out repressed hostilities is suggested by certain "demonic torments" she supposedly endured as a teenager. These include a claimed street attack by a man "dressed all in black" who allegedly grabbed her arm and tried to drag her into a canal, and another incident in which an old woman supposedly lured her into the path of an approaching train. Further, she was "severely tormented by demons at home," on occasion exhibiting the typical, role-playing antics of those who are supposedly possessed: shouting, supposedly showing prodigious strength (lifting a chair over her head), and the like. Once, after "an invisible hand" allegedly choked her, an exorcism was performed, during which the family heard "Satan's revolting voice" (which is to say, Peerdeman speaking in a "changed" voice) cursing the priest (Sigl 2005, 13–14). (For more on possession see Nickell 2001.)

Peerdeman's devotees cite local bishop J. M. Punt's conclusion that "the apparitions of the Lady of All Nations in Amsterdam consist of a supernatural origin." In reaching this decision, Punt (2002) cited many reports of "healings" attributed in some way to Peerdeman. However, the "healings" thus far attributed to Peerdeman appear unexceptional. (For more on healings see part 3.)

In contrast to Punt's opinion that the apparitions had a "supernatural origin," an investigating commission found quite the opposite. Appointed by an earlier bishop in 1955, the group included a psychiatrist, psychologist, priest, seminary teachers, and a deacon of Amsterdam's parishes. According to their report, the committee was "deeply shocked.... The messages do not come from Heaven," they insisted, maintaining that the Holy Virgin had never revealed herself in such a manner. They added, "We recognize therefore that all these revelations in whatever manner have a purely natural origin."

In explaining, they observed that "gradually one sees, as it were, a shift in persons." That is, at first Peerdeman's experiences were about herself; then later she projected her own persona onto the Virgin Mary. The commission's president characterized Peerdeman's visions as "banal, brusque, and acerbic" (Van der Ven 2002) and concluded that the supposed visionary suffered from egocentricity (Van der Ven 2002).

Over the years, the Catholic press reportedly "demonized" her (perhaps appropriately, given the irony of her having acted in a demon-possessed manner), and she was often described by Catholic officials as "an hysteric" (El-Fers 2002). Objectively, there seems to be nothing in the claims of Ida Peerdeman that cannot be explained as the result of imagination, suggestion, or, possibly, pious deception.

Figure 43.1. A painting of the Virgin Mary as "the Lady of All Nations" produced at the direction of Marian visionary Ida Peerdeman. (Photo by Joe Nickell)

CHAPTER 44

MYSTERIES OF POPULAR SAINTS

While visiting Argentina for the 2005 Primera Conferencia Iberoamericana Sobre Pensamiento Crítico ("First Latin American Conference on Critical Thinking") in Buenos Aires, I was also able to take a look at some local mysteries with which I already had some familiarity. These included a haunted cemetery, tales of animal mutilation by the dreaded chupacabras, and miracles of popular saints. Here is a brief look at the latter.

UNOFFICIAL SAINTS

Until quite recently, Roman Catholicism was the official religion of Argentina, and it still dominates the daily lives of its people. In addition to their formal faith, however, Argentinians often seek help from a number of popular, unofficial saints. They represent a spreading folk Catholicism that often diverges from orthodoxy and even includes Spiritualist practices.

Like official saints, popular saints are often believed to work miracles. For instance, there is "the Robin Hood of Corrientes," the gaucho, Antonio Gil. An army deserter in the 1850s, Gil was hanged on an espinillo tree, but before dying he supposedly warned the commanding sergeant that his son would become deathly ill and could only recover by means of the sergeant praying for Gil's soul. Upon the boy's recovery, his repentant father carved an espinillo cross, which he placed at Gil's death site. Today, as many as one hundred thousand pilgrims visit the site each year on the anniversary of his death, crediting Gaucho Gil with miracles and life-transforming experiences (Bernhardson 2004, 186, 273, 606).

Even more popular than Gil is legendary Maria Antonia Deolinda Correa, known as the Difunta (meaning "Defunct," as the deceased are called in the countryside). A pious legend tells how she followed her husband, a conscript during the civil wars of the nineteenth century, and died in the desert of thirst. However, when her body was discovered by passing muleteers, her infant son was found alive, "miraculously" feeding at her lifeless breast.

Adding to the implausibility of an infant surviving on milk from a corpse is the limited evidence that the Difunta even existed. Nevertheless, the legend was so resonant among the local folk that they transformed the waterless site into a shrine. Today it is visited by pilgrims who stand in line to visit a chamber that holds an effigy of the prostrate Difunta with her infant at her breast (Bernhardson 2004, 273–74).

There are many other popular saints, including the faith healer Madre María Salomè. Sardonically, novelist Thomás Eloy Martinez has called his fellow Argentines "cadaver cultists" for being so devoted to the dead (Bernhardson 2004, 606–607). Not all of the unofficial saints, however, are widely believed to work miracles, and perhaps the most famous—or infamous—of all has had her status slip.

EVITA

Alternately reviled and beloved as "Evita," Maria Eva Duarte Perón (1919–1952) was the controversial first lady of Argentina from the election of her husband Juan Perón in 1946 until her death from cancer in 1952. A former film actress, she lent her charisma and ambition to the popular causes of assisting the poor, improving education, and helping to achieve women's suffrage. Nevertheless, Juan Perón's increasingly demagogic methods cost him the support of the Catholic Church, and his wife's death diminished his appeal among workers. He was ousted by the military in 1955.

In her last speech, she had stated, "I will be with my people, dead or alive." Perón helped the mythologizing process by having her body mummified and placed on display while a monument was being prepared. A popular movement sought to have the church make her a saint. Her followers installed altars to "Santa Evita" in their homes, and over one hundred thousand requests for her canonization flooded the Vatican, many crediting her with the requisite miracles (McInnis 2001; Fouché 2002; "Evita Biography" 2005; Mosca 2005).

Instead, after Perón was deposed in 1955, the church conspired with the new regime to spirit away her body. It was buried in Milan, Italy, by the sisters of the Society of St. Paul. There, under the false name Maria Maggi, it reposed for fourteen years. Meanwhile, the anti-Peronists attempted to efface her memory, tearing down statues of her and burning copies of her autobiography, *The Sense of My Life*.

In April 1971, however, the Argentine president ordered what has been called "the world's most beautiful corpse" returned to Perón, who was living with his third wife, Isabel, in Madrid ("Which Coffin Holds the World's Most Beautiful Corpse?" 1978). According to journalist Wayne Bernhardson (2004, 73), Perón's "bizarre spiritualist adviser" Jose López Rega—known as "The Witch"—"used the opportunity to try to transfer Evita's essence into Isabelita's body." (After Perón's brief return to power in 1973 and his death the following year, Isabel succeeded him, but she was soon deposed by the military.)

I visited several related sites, including the Museo Evita, where the controversial first lady is honored. It appears that claims of miracles have largely abated. However, one writer concludes (Morrison 2005):

> Though efforts to have her made into a saint have been turned down by the Vatican, Evita still holds near to saint status in Argentina. Slogans proclaiming *Evita Vive!* (Evita Lives!) can be seen everywhere even today in a new century. At her family crypt in the Recoleta Cemetery in Buenos Aires, supporters and pilgrims still leave flowers, and a continual guard is kept to prevent vandalism.

(See figure 44.1.)

Questions remain: Were none of the miracles by Santa Evita authentic? Were they rejected for lack of merit or dismissed out of hand for political reasons? How does the church reject her but canonize Mexico's Juan Diego? (He is the legendary—possibly fictitious—figure on whose cloak the Virgin Mary "miraculously" imprinted her image, though the image on the cloak is, in fact, painted [Nickell 2002].) Are any miracle claims credible, officially sanctioned or not?

Figure 44.1. Recoleta Cemetery in Buenos Aires—where "Evita is buried"—is a grand city of the dead. (Photo by Joe Nickell)

CHAPTER 45

TIJUANA'S MURDERER "SAINT"

Beautiful, exotic Tijuana—city of passion and mystery. My first investigative trip to Mexico's fourth-largest city was in the fall of 2003, when I attended Day of the Dead festivities there and went undercover in the persona of a terminally ill cancer patient to test a fortuneteller and to search for the bogus curative, Laetrile (Nickell 2004). I returned in mid-May 2009 as a side jaunt to an extensive California trip (and went on an expedition into Bigfoot country). This time in Tijuana, accompanied as before by Vaughn Rees, I looked into several mysteries, including the case of a dubious folk saint.

In Catholicism, certain deceased persons are officially recognized as saints, who are held to be in the glory of God in heaven and whose holiness is attested through miracles (Schreck 1984, 153–56). Among the rank-and-file faithful, however, there are also a number of popular, unofficial saints—like Argentina's controversial "Evita," as discussed in the previous chapter (Nickell 2006, 20).

"SOLDIER JOHN"

One such folk saint in northwestern Mexico, as well as in the southwestern United States, is known as *Juan Soldado* ("Soldier John"), the name given to Juan Castillo Morales by his devotees from southern Mexico. In 1938, at the age of twenty-four, he was in Tijuana, serving as a private in the Mexican army (see figure 45.1).

Late on February 13, an eight-year-old Tijuana girl, Olga Camacho, was sent by her mother to the corner grocery for meat. When she failed to return, an all-night search for her was conducted by citizens and authorities. It culminated at noon with the discovery of the child's raped and nearly decapitated body in an abandoned building not far from the police station. The neighbor who found her had been convinced Olga would be found safe, but that woman subsequently claimed she was directed to the site by "a vision" of the Virgin Mary (Vanderwood 2004, 5–6).

Tijuana smoldered with anger, a lynch mob was formed, and finally tensions exploded. The police station and municipal hall were torched, and fire trucks answering calls had their hoses slashed with machetes. Eventually soldiers fired on the crowd, killing one and wounding several. Newspapers dubbed that day, February 15, "Bloody Tuesday."

However, by February 17, just over three days after the discovery of little Olga's body, Juan Castillo Morales had been accused of the crime, taken into custody, turned over to the army, sentenced to death following a twelve-hour court martial, and transported to the municipal cemetery, where he was executed. He was dispatched by a method known as *Ley Fuga* ("flight law") in which he was ordered to flee for his life then cut down by a firing squad. He was badly wounded, and an officer finally administered the coup de grace (Maher 1997; "Juan Soldado" 2009; Vanderwood 2004, 49–50).

SANCTIFICATION

How was Juan Castillo Morales transformed from child rapist and murderer into "Juan Soldado" the popular saint? A rumor circulated that the little girl was actually killed by an army officer who framed Juan for the atrocity. Still later, more conspiracy theories were advanced (Maher 1997; "Juan Soldado" 2009). Meanwhile, there were unverified reports of "ghostly voices" near Juan's burial site. As well, some spoke of "blood seeping from his grave" ("Juan Soldado" 2009) or, alternately, claimed "that a rock by the spot where he fell kept spouting blood, calling attention to his innocence" (Maher 1997) or that blood oozed "through the rocks laid [ritualistically] at the grave site" (Vanderwood 2004, 64). Such *variants* (as folklorists call differing versions), together with the common folk *motifs* (or story elements),[1] are indicative of the folkloric process at work in the evolving Juan Soldado legend. (If real blood was actually "seeping up through the loosely packed soil" of Morales's shallow grave—his coffin was reportedly "just a foot or so below the surface"—it was attributable to decomposition gases forcing blood and tissue upward [Vanderwood 2004, 64, 190]. More simply, after a rain, a rock containing red ocher—red iron oxide—could have given the appearance of blood.)

In time, little shrines were built at the supposed execution and burial sites, as well as elsewhere in the area (see figure 45.1). Votive candles, cards, and other religious items devoted to Juan Soldado are now sold throughout the borderlands. Many people appeal to his spirit before attempting to enter the United States illegally: *"Juan Soldado, ayúdame a cruzar"* ("Soldier John, help me across"). Others pray to him for help with health problems, criminal troubles, and family matters ("Juan Soldado" 2009). Many attest to "miracles" he produced on their behalf. Although June 24, Mexico's *El Día de San Juan* ("The day of Saint John"), actually celebrates John the Baptist, whose feast day it is, cultists have appropriated it for their San Juan, Juan Soldado, and the cemetery is filled with believers and mariachis (Maher 1997).

The Catholic Church, on the other hand, understandably denies the sanctity of Juan Soldado. Before Olga's body was discovered, Juan Castillo Morales was seen loitering in the area. He was known to police as one who reportedly made sexual overtures to girls. His common-law wife came forward to say he had returned home very late, disheveled, and spattered with blood, whereupon he broke down and confessed to the crime. Newspaper reporters invited to interview him found him unrepentant, even nonchalant. A Los Angeles paper headlined its report, "Smiling Mexican Private Tells *Examiner*, 'Yes I did it'" (Vanderwood 2004, 14).

If the evidence is correct, and Juan indeed represents depravity rather than sanctity, how ironic is his transformation to solider-saint and even more so his purported ability to work "miracles" seemingly as real as those of any officially sanctioned saint.

Figure 45.1. This figure of folk-saint Juan Soldado ("Soldier John") stands in a Tijuana wax museum display that doubles as a shrine. (Photo by Joe Nickell)

CHAPTER 46

STIGMATA: WOUNDS OF CHRIST

Of reputed miraculous powers, perhaps none is more popularly equated with saintliness than stigmata, the wounds of Christ's crucifixion allegedly duplicated spontaneously upon the body of a Christian. Indeed one historical survey indicated that about a fifth of all stigmatics are eventually beatified or canonized (Biot 1962, 23).

The year 1999 brought renewed interest in the alleged phenomenon. Among the offerings were the movie *Stigmata* (which even contained a brief shot of my book *Looking for a Miracle* [Radford 1999]); a Fox television pseudodocumentary, *Signs from God*, which featured a major segment on stigmata (Willesee 1999); and the Vatican's beatification of the Italian stigmatic Padre Pío. For an in-progress television documentary, I took a new look at the subject.

EVOLVING PHENOMENON

From the death of Jesus, about 29 or 30 CE, nearly twelve centuries would pass before stigmata began to appear—unless one counts a cryptic biblical reference by St. Paul. In Galatians 6:17 he wrote, "I bear in my body the marks of the Lord Jesus." Many scholars believe Paul was speaking figuratively, but in any case the statement may have been sufficient to prompt imitation.

St. Francis of Assisi (1182–1226) is credited with being the first stigmatic—or at least the first "true" one, his affliction occurring just two years after that of a man from Oxford who had exhibited the five crucifixion wounds in 1222. That man claimed to be the Son of God and the redeemer of mankind, but he was arrested for imposture, his wounds presumed to have been self-inflicted.

In 1224 St. Francis went with some of his "disciples" up Mount Alverno in the Apennines. After forty days of fasting and prayer he had a vision of Christ on the cross, whereafter he received the four nail wounds and the pierced side. Francis appears to have sparked a copycat phenomenon, since publication of his reputed miracle was followed by occurrences of stigmata "even among people who were much lower than St. Francis in religious stature." These "have continued to occur without intermission ever since," according to Catholic scholar Herbert Thurston (1952, 122–23). He continues:

> What I infer is that the example of St. Francis created what I have called the "crucifixion complex." Once it had been brought home to contemplatives that it was possible to be physically conformed to the sufferings of Christ by bearing His wound-marks in the hands, feet and side, then the idea of this form of union with their Divine Master took shape in the minds of many. It became in fact a pious obsession; so much so that in a few exceptionally sensitive individuals the idea conceived in the mind was realized in the flesh.

Thurston believed stigmatization was due to the effects of suggestion, but experimental attempts to duplicate the phenomenon, for example by using hypnosis, have been unsuccessful—except for a related case that appears to have been a hoax. (The psychiatrist reported that bloody tears welled inside the subject's eyelids, but a photograph shows rivulets originating outside the eyes [see Wilson 1988].)

As the thirteenth century advanced, exhibitions of stigmata began to proliferate, one authority regarding it as "a sort of explosion" (Biot 1962, 18). Within a hundred years of St. Francis's death over twenty cases had occurred. The trend continued in successive centuries, with no fewer than 321 stigmatics being recorded by 1908. Not only were they invariably Catholic, but more than a third had come from Italy and the rest mostly from France, Spain, and Portugal, demonstrating that "the Roman Catholic countries, mostly with a Latin and Mediterranean influence have dominated the history of stigmata" (Harrison 1994, 9; Wilson 1988, 10).

The twentieth-century record of stigmata, however, "shows a change in pattern." Italy dominated somewhat less, and cases were reported from Great Britain, Australia, and the United States (Harrison 1994, 9). The latter included (in 1972) a ten-year-old African American girl named Cloretta Robinson, a Baptist and thus one of a very few non-Catholic Christians to have exhibited the stigmata (including at least three Anglicans) (Harrison 1994, 9, 87).

Other evidence that stigmata represent an evolving phenomenon comes from the form of the wounds. Interestingly, those of St. Francis (except for the wound in his side) "were not wounds which bled but impressions of the heads of the nails, round and black and standing clear from the flesh" (Harrison 1994, 25). Since then, although bleeding wounds have been typical, they have been exceedingly varied, showing "no consistency even remotely suggesting them as replications of one single, original pattern" (Wilson 1988, 63). For example, some wounds have been tiny, straight slits. Others have been simple crosses, multiple slash marks, or indentations—even, in the case of Therese Neumann, shifting from round to rectangular over time, presumably as she learned the true shape of Roman nails. In some instances there were no apparent lesions beneath the seepages (or possibly fake applications!) of blood (Wilson 1988, 64; Harrison 1994, 70; Nickell 1999).

Similarly, the wound in the side (representing the Roman soldier's lance [John 19:34]) has appeared at different locations in the right or left side, or has been variously shaped—as a lateral slit, crescent, cross, and so on—or has not appeared at all. Some stigmatics have exhibited wounds on the forehead (as if caused by a crown of thorns [John 19:2]), markings on the back (representing scourging [John 19:1]), or abrasions on the shoulder (as from carrying a cross), and so on, while others have not exhibited these. There are even symbolic markings, such as "a vivid cross" that twice appeared on the forehead of stigmatist Heather Woods (a phenomenon previously experienced by seventeenth-century stigmatic Jeanne des Anges). And stigmata-like skin lettering—including the names of Joseph, Mary, and Jesus—appeared and reappeared on the left hand of Jeanne des Anges (1602–1665) (Wilson 1988, 64, 131–48; Harrison 1994, 2, 52).

Another trend in the evolving phenomenon—represented for example by Virginia priest James Bruse—is the location of nail wounds in the wrists.

Others have tended to have them in the palms of the hands, so Bruse's wrist marks seem instructive. As Harrison observes (1994, 40), stigmata in the wrists have appeared only since photography "revealed the wounds so positioned in the Turin Shroud." Actually, while the hands of the figure on the shroud are folded so that a single exit wound shows, it seems to indicate the palm, although the flow of "blood" does extend to the wrist, thus giving the appearance of the wound being located there (Nickell 1993). Those who believe the shroud authentic (despite definitive scientific proof to the contrary [Nickell 1998]) have an interest in promoting the wrist site. They point to experiments with cadavers that supposedly show nailed hands could not support the weight of a body and would therefore tear away (Barbet 1950). (Skeletal remains have been discovered of only a single first-century crucifixion victim, a man known as Jehohanan. A scratch on the lower end of the right radius suggests a nail had penetrated between the radius and ulna. Interestingly, a nail had been driven through the heel bones from the side, indicating that Jehohanan had been forced into "a sort of sidesaddle position," quite unlike the familiar depiction of Jesus in Christian art [Wilson 1979, 50, illustration following page 128].)

In any event, if it is true that the hand location is anatomically untenable—notwithstanding the Gospels (John 20:25–27 and Luke 24:40)—the argument could be made that all stigmata in the hands are therefore false, a judgment that would exclude most reported instances. Certainly the shift of location to the wrists (in keeping with a modern view) is not surprising. Stigmatics in the Middle Ages likewise "produced wounds in themselves which corresponded to the pictures of Christ suffering around them" (Harrison 1994, 128). Similarly, the 1974 crucifixion vision of Ethel Chapman, during which her stigmata allegedly appeared, was "based on the images in an illustrated Bible which she'd been given" (Harrison 1994, 128; Wilson 1988, 147). Such strong connections between popular images and the nature of the stigmata are powerful evidence that the phenomenon is imitative.

STIGMATIC PROFILE

A look at stigmata as an evolving phenomenon also sheds light on the people involved. The previously mentioned census of 321 stigmatics reveals "an interesting seven-to-one proportion of women to men." Not only were almost all Roman Catholics, but "a very high proportion were cloistered priests or nuns"—as was, of course, the first stigmatic, St. Francis, along with such thirteenth-century stigmatics as the Blessed Helen of Veszprim (1237), St. Christina of Stommeln (1268), and others (Harrison 1994, 10, 27–28; Wilson 1988, 131–33). Indeed, of the 321 stigmatics, 109 came from the Dominican Order and 102 from the Franciscans—an overall percentage of 66 percent from religious orders versus 34 percent from among lay folk (Biot 1962, 20).

Many stigmatics seem—also like St. Francis—to have had an early life that might be characterized as notably "worldly," before coming to believe they had been called to serve God. As a youth, Francis, the son of a wealthy merchant, was "gay, adventurous, generous, and popular" (Coulson 1958) and spent his leisure time in "hedonistic extravagance" (Jones 1994), even being crowned "king of the revelers" by his friends ("Francis of Assisi, St." 1960). He later claimed he heard Christ's voice asking him to rebuild a church, whereupon he plunged into religious service, adopting the life of a hermit and later forming the order of friars named for him (the Franciscans) (Coulson 1958).

Others who were transformed from worldly to austere included the Blessed Angela of Foligno (1250–1309), who had married and bore several children but lost them all after her husband's death. After selling all her possessions, she gave the proceeds to the poor and joined the Third Order of St. Francis (Wilson 1988, 132). Another example is St. Catherine of Genoa (1447–1510), who married at sixteen, spent "ten years of a pleasure-seeking existence," then, with her husband, devoted her life to tending to the sick in a local hospital (Wilson 1988, 133).

A more recent example is that of Father James Bruse (the Virginia priest with the wrist wounds mentioned earlier). Bruse's preordination life included finding his way into the *Guinness Book of World Records* in 1978 for riding a roller coaster for five straight days. He became a Roman Catholic priest the following year but subsequently found he had lapsed into a routine. Then came the "dramatic" events of 1991–1992 in which he not only experienced the stigmata but discovered statues weeping in his presence (Harrison 1994, 80–87).

Also characteristic of many, if not most, stigmatics are a variety of symptoms "ranging from what have been described as the 'mystical' to the 'hysterical'" (Harrison 1994, 31). Taking the hysterical first, Marguerite of the Blessed Sacrament (Marguerite Parigot, 1619–1648) was prey to "devastating apparent diabolic attacks," while Anna Maria Castreca (1670–1736) "would hurl herself violently around the room" and revert "to the speech and manner of a child," and in his early life Padre Pío (1887–1968) was "emotionally disturbed." A few stigmatics were allegedly attended by "poltergeist phenomena" (disturbances attributed to "noisy spirits" but often found to be the pranks of adolescents); among them were Johann Jetzer (ca. 1483–1515) and Teresa Helena Higginson (1844–1905) (Wilson 1988, 131–48).

Illness is another frequent characteristic. René Biot, in his *The Enigma of the Stigmata* (1962, 57), exclaims with wonder at "how many stigmatics have been bedridden!" He notes that St. Lidwina (d. 1433) had so many alleged illnesses that she was "a sort of pathological museum," indeed a "museum of horrors." Similarly, Therese Neumann experienced alternate bouts of convulsions, blindness, deafness, mutism, paralysis, and so on—effects that appear to have been due to hysterical hypochondria or, more likely, outright fakery, since the alleged conditions evaded diagnosis (Rogo 1982, 65–66; Nickell 1993, 227–28). Given such cases, one researcher noted the parallels between stigmata and Münchausen's syndrome, an emotional disorder involving feigned or inflicted illness (Schnabel 1993).

Still other stigmatics—like St. Veronica Giuliani (ca. 1640–1727), Victoire Claire (ca. 1808–1883), along with numerous others—often lapsed into states of ecstasy (that is, apparent trance states arising out of religious fervor). Following St. Francis, who supposedly received his stigmata during a vision of Jesus' crucifixion, came several emulators, including Passitea Crogi, who, on Palm Sunday 1589, fell into an ecstasy and later described a vision of Christ bruised and bleeding. Other vision-delivered stigmata were claimed by Johann Jetzer, Therese Neumann (1898–1962), and James Bruse.

A great number of stigmatics were blessed, allegedly, with other supernatural phenomena, including the powers of prophecy and healing, levitation, bilocation (supposedly being in two places simultaneously), and inedia (the alleged ability to forgo nourishment). As an example of the latter, Angela of Foligno (1250–1309) reportedly went without food for twelve years. After death, the bodies of a few stigmatics were discovered to be "incorruptible" (that is, able to withstand decay). Also vials of blood preserved from the stigmatic wounds of Passitea Crogi purportedly reliquify on occasion (Wilson 1988, 131–48). Needless to say, perhaps, such claims are unproved and may be attributed to folklore, misperceptions and misunderstandings born of superstition, and pious fraud (Nickell 1993).

PROVEN FRAUDS

That many stigmatics were fakes is well established. For example, Magdalena de la Cruz, having become ill in 1543 and fearful of dying a sinner, confessed that her stigmata, inedia, and other phenomena were deliberate deceptions. Another, Maria de la Visitacion, known as the "holy nun of Lisbon," was accused by a sister nun who saw her painting a fake wound onto her hand. Although initially defended by doctors in 1587, she was brought before the Inquisition, whereupon her wounds were scrubbed and the coloration washed off, revealing "unblemished flesh" beneath (Wilson 1988, 26).

Another fake was Palma Maria Matarelli, who not only exhibited the stigmata but also "miraculously" produced Communion wafers on her tongue. Pope Pius IX privately branded her a fraud, stating that he had the proof in his desk drawer and adding, "She has befooled a whole crowd of pious and credulous souls" (quoted in Wilson 1988, 42). A more public condemnation awaited Gigliola Giorgini (b. 1933): discredited by church authorities, in 1984 she was convicted of fraud by an Italian court (Wilson 1988, 42, 147).

The authenticity of some stigmata may be questioned in light of the mystic's character. For example, Teresa Helena Higginson (1844–1905), an English stigmatic, was dismissed as a teacher on accusations of theft, drunkenness, and unseemly conduct. And Berthe Mrazek, a Brussels-born circus performer turned stigmatic, was first regarded seriously, but doubts came in 1924 when she was arrested for fraud and committed to an insane asylum (Nickell 1993, 223). Still other stigmatics must be viewed in light of their propensity for self-punishment and self-mutilation. These include the thirteenth-century masochist Lukardis of Oberweimar, who, before exhibiting the stigmata, "had the habit of driving her fingernails into her palms" (Wilson 1988, 132)!

Circumstances surrounding the twentieth century's two best-known stigmatics—Therese Neumann and Padre Pío (both mentioned previously)—raise further doubts about the genuineness of the phenomenon. For example, a Professor Martini conducted a surveillance of Therese Neumann and observed that blood would flow from her wounds only on those occasions when he was persuaded to leave the room, as if something "needed to be hidden from observation." He added: "It was for the same reason that I disliked her frequent manipulations behind the raised [bed] coverings" (Similar suspicions also accompanied her professed demonstration of inedia) (Wilson 1988, 53, 114–15).

Many Catholic scholars have expressed skepticism about the genuineness of stigmata. One was a neuro-psychiatrist who had personally observed thirty stigmatization cases and in none of them "was able to eliminate, absolutely and decisively, every kind of artificial action" (quoted in Biot 1962, 102–103). Although attributing most instances to suggestion rather than hoaxing, Herbert Thurston (1952, 100) found "no satisfactory case of stigmatization since St. Francis of Assisi."

Thurston and others defend Francis on grounds of his piety and character; however, his single-minded desire to imitate Jesus, his "immense capacity for self-sacrifice," and the fact that "he was a son of the church to the marrow of his bones" (Coulson 1958, 188) may have led him to foster a pious deception—something that many others have clearly been unable to resist.

A MODERN CASE

The Fox television network's 1999 special *Signs from God* heralded the Bolivian miracle claimant Katya Rivas, whose repertoire included not only stigmata, but also the production of an unusual "delta state" on an EEG, automatic writing in languages she allegedly did not know, and multicolored "glitter" on a print of the *Image of Guadalupe* in her home. (For a review see Nickell 1999.) The show was hosted by Australian journalist Michael Willesee, who, during an airplane accident in 1998, had "re-embraced his Roman Catholic faith in an instant conversion" (Randi 1999).

Rivas claimed she received a message from Jesus telling her that while she would not produce stigmata as hoped on Good Friday (the day Christians commemorate Jesus' crucifixion), patience would be rewarded. A later message announced that full stigmata would take place on the day following Corpus Christi (a Catholic festival honoring the Eucharist or Lord's Supper). The night before the stigmata were to appear, Rivas gave a sample of her blood as a control, since there was speculation that the blood from her stigmatic wounds might not be hers exclusively.

Come the appointed time, unsuspecting viewers were treated to what had all the signs of a staged event. Rivas was abed, in a fashion reminiscent of Therese Neumann, and the covers provided ample concealment if trickery were involved. No doctor was in attendance. Michael Willesee made a cursory examination of Rivas's hands and feet, and referred to scars from previous stigmata. These were seen on her feet, but it was unclear whether there were prior marks on her hands also. (This is significant in light of developments, as we shall see.)

During real or pretended suffering, Rivas exhibited, first, prick-like marks and bleeding on the forehead (as from a crown of thorns)—though apparently not on the sides or back of the head, suggesting the marks were only for show. Then there was (possibly) a pink mark on the left palm, followed by a tiny cross on the back of the hand that was initially without blood. Later there were bloody "wounds" on both sides of the hands and feet. Willesee used swabs to obtain samples of the blood for analysis. No side wound or other crucifixion markings ever appeared. At the end of the experience—or demonstration—Rivas displayed paroxysms of a death-like agony imitative of Jesus' crucifixion.

Rivas's wounds were never seen in the act of spontaneously issuing. Instead, they were shown in incremental shots *after* each appearance—just as they would if self-inflicted during periods of concealment. Among other suspicious elements were the mismatching of "entrance" and "exit" wounds, those on the left foot being far out of alignment. Also, those on the palms and soles of the feet were, as far as could be seen, only smears of blood.

Moreover, such wounds as could be distinguished did not resemble puncture wounds. Instead, they consisted of multiple cuts, including the cross on the back of the left hand (figure 46.1) and an array of slashes atop each foot. The latter are curiously in pairs (see figure 46.2), as if produced by a two-pronged implement, like the sharp-cornered, calyx-like ring Katya Rivas wore during the event.

Supposedly only twenty-four hours later, the camera recorded Willesee inspecting Rivas's wounds. Apparently those on the palms and soles had vanished completely (but were not specifically shown) and the markings that remained were seemingly in an advanced state of healing. Willesee treated this as remarkable, although another interpretation is that the vanishing of some "wounds" indicated they were never there in the first place and that most or all of the markings were old cuts from previously faked stigmata.

A genuine element of the affair was the blood itself, which was shown by DNA analysis to be Katya Rivas's. Unfortunately for the miracle-mongering journalist Willesee—who made much of the possibility that it might be Christ's blood in whole or in part—it proved to be Rivas's alone.

When I was asked to appear on a television documentary on stigmata and to discuss the Katya Rivas case, I decided to experiment beforehand by inflicting wounds on myself. I used a sharp blade to cut a cross on the back of my left hand. This shallow, superficial wound yielded enough blood to produce the effect of a larger wound (figure 46.3) and even (by transfer) create a "wound" on the palm (figure 46.4). The next day the latter had of course vanished and the cross had begun to heal. There are certain medicinal preparations one can apply to allegedly promote healing and, as I found, cosmetic creams that through their hiding power can seemingly advance the healing or eliminate the wound entirely.[1]

My examination of the video showing Katya Rivas's alleged stigmatization, and the simple experiments I performed, persuaded me that not only could her stigmata not be authenticated, but, indeed—like other instances of the alleged phenomenon throughout history—they cannot be distinguished from a pious hoax.

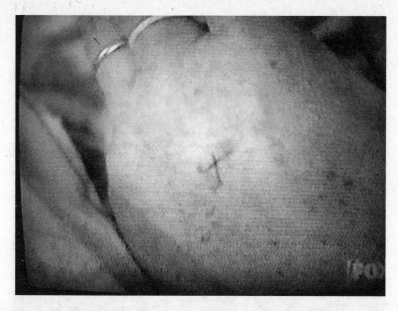

Figure 46.1. Cross-shaped wound on the back of Katya Rivas's left hand. (Photo by Joe Nickell)

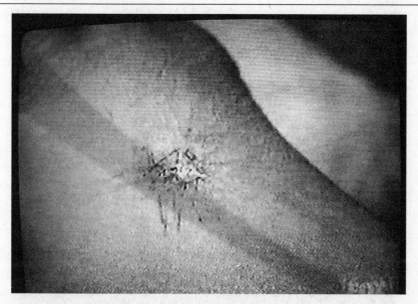

Figure 46.2. Post-stigmata marks on top of one of Rivas's feet, most or all of which are scars from previous "stigmata." (Photo by Joe Nickell)

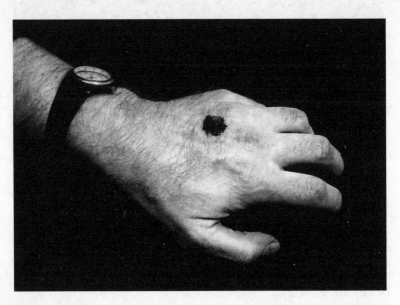

Figure 46.3. Small cuts on author's hand produce sufficient blood to simulate a sizeable wound. (Author's photo)

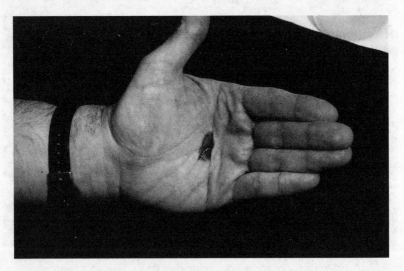

Figure 46.4. Transfer of blood from wound shown in figure 46.3 produced a fake wound on palm. (Author's photo)

CHAPTER 47

THE CASE OF PADRE PÍO

O f the twentieth century's two most famous stigmatics (those who experience the supposedly supernatural wounds of Jesus), both Therese Neumann and Padre Pío were suspected of fraud, but Pío went on to sainthood and was canonized in 2002. In April 2008 his body was exhumed and put on display in a church crypt in San Giovanni Rotondo, Italy, a move that both attracted throngs of the credulous and provoked outrage among some Pío devotees. It also renewed questions about the genuineness of the stigmata and other phenomena associated with Pío.

A CAPUCHIN FRIAR

Born Francesco Forgione on May 25, 1887, in the town of Pietrelcina, Pío grew up surrounded by superstitious beliefs and practices. His mother took him soon after birth to a fortune-teller to have his horoscope cast and at the age of two to a witch who attempted to cure an intestinal disorder by holding him upside down and chanting spells. As a boy he was tormented by nighttime "monsters," and he conversed with Jesus, the Virgin Mary, and his guardian angel. He also had other mystical experiences (Ruffin 1982, 21–23, 79) that today are associated with a fantasy-prone personality.[1] He was "frequently ill and emotionally disturbed" and claimed he was often physically attacked by evil spirits (Wilson 1988, 88, 144).

In 1903 he entered the Order of Friars Minor, Capuchin—a conservative Catholic order that traces its origin to St. Francis of Assisi (1182–1226), the first stigmatic. The new initiate was called *Fra* ("Brother") *Pío* ("Pious"), after the sixteenth-century pope, St. Pius V (Ruffin 1982, 35, 39). Pío con-

335

tinued to hear voices and experience visions, and in 1910 he began to experience the stigmata just after being ordained a priest.

As Padre Pío continued to exhibit the phenomenon, he began to attract a cult following. It was said he could look into people's souls and, without them saying a word, know their sins. He could also allegedly experience "bilocation" (the ability to be in two places at the same time), emit an "odor of sanctity," tell the future, and effect miraculous cures (Wilkinson 2008; Rogo 1982, 98–100). Village hucksters sold his credulous disciples alleged Pío relics in the form of swatches of cloth daubed with chicken blood (Ruffin 1982, 153).

The local clergy accused Padre Pío's friary of putting him on display in order to make money. They expressed skepticism about his purported gifts and suggested the stigmata were faked.

THE PHENOMENA

The claims of Padre Pío's mystical abilities are unproven, consisting of anecdotal evidence—a major source being the aptly named *Tales of Padre Pío* (McCaffery 1978). Pío's touted psychic abilities seem no better substantiated than the discredited claims of the typical fortuneteller or medium see Nickell 2001, 122–27, 197–99). Many of his "bilocations" are analogous to Elvis Presley sightings, while some are—at best—consistent with hallucinations (such as one reported during a migraine attack or others occurring when the experiencer was near sleep or in some other altered state [McCaffery 1978, 24–36]). The reputed "odor of sanctity," said Pío's accusers, "was the result of self-administered *eau-de-cologne*" ("Pío of Pietrelcina" 2008).

As to Pío's miraculous healings, they—like other such claims (Nickell 2001, 202–205)—are not based on positive evidence of the miraculous. Instead, the occurrences are merely held to be "medically inexplicable," so claimants are engaging in the logical fallacy of arguing from ignorance (drawing a conclusion based on a lack of knowledge). Faith-healing claims often have alternative explanations, including misdiagnosis, psychosomatic conditions, spontaneous remissions, prior medical treatment, and other effects, including the body's own healing ability. Cases are complicated by poor investigation and even outright hoaxing. One man's claim of instant healing of a leg wound by Padre Pío, for example, was bogus; his doctor attested it "had, in fact, been healed for six months or more" (Ruffin 1982, 159).

But it is Pío's stigmata that have made him famous. Unfortunately, some examining physicians believed his lesions were superficial, but their inspections were made difficult by Pío's acting as if the wounds were exceedingly painful. Also, they were supposedly covered by "thick crusts" of blood. One distinguished pathologist sent by the Holy See noted that beyond the scabs was an absence of "any sign of edema, of penetration, or of redness, even when examined with a good magnifying glass." Another concluded that the side "wound" *had not penetrated the skin at all* (Ruffin 1982, 147–48). Some thought Pío inflicted the wounds with acid or kept them open by continually drenching them in iodine (Ruffin 1982, 149–50; Moore 2007; Wilkinson 2008).

Nevertheless, some of the faithful were so intent on defending Pío that they made incredible claims. One was the insistence that the hand lesions, which skeptics thought were superficial injuries, were through-and-through wounds—"so much so," insisted Pío's devoted family physician, that one could see light through them." Of course, this is nonsense in view of authentic wounds in general and Pío's thickly blood-crusted ones in particular (Ruffin 1982, 146–47).

There were other problems with the "wounds," including their location. Only the Gospel of John (19:34) mentions the lance wound in Jesus' side, and John fails to specify which side. The side wound of St. Francis was on the right, whereas Padre Pío's was on the left. Also, witnesses described his side wound as in the shape of a cross; in other words, it had a stylized rather than realistic (lance-produced) form (Ruffin 1982, 145, 147).[2] Moreover, his wounds were in the hands rather than the wrists (some anatomists argue that nailed hands could not support the body of a crucified person and would tear away). When asked about this, Pío replied casually, "Oh it would be too much to have them exactly as they were in the case of Christ" (Ruffin 1982, 145, 150). (One is reminded of Therese Neumann, whose "nail wounds" shifted from round to rectangular over time, presumably as she learned the true shape of Roman nails [Nickell 2001, 278].) Moreover, Padre Pío lacked wounds on the forehead (as from a crown of thorns [John 19:2]).

For years Pío wore fingerless gloves on his hands, perpetually concealing his wounds (Ruffin 1982, 148). His supporters regard this as an act of pious modesty. However, another interpretation is that the concealment was a shrewd strategy that eliminated the need for him to maintain his wounds. Before his death, frail, weary, with "rheumy eyes seemingly fixed on another world," Padre Pío celebrated Mass. According to Ruffin (1982, 305), "For the first time in anyone's memory, he did not attempt to hide his hands at any point in the service. To the amazement of everyone there, there was no trace of any wound." At his death on September 23, 1968, his skin was unblemished.

So, were Padre Pío's phenomena genuine? Many other stigmatics—like Magdalena de la Cruz in 1543—confessed to faking stigmata. Maria de la Visitacion, the "holy nun of Lisbon," was caught painting fake wounds on her hands in 1587. Pope Pius IX himself privately branded Palma Maria Matarelli (1825–1888) as a fraud, insisting that "she has befooled a whole crowd of pious and credulous souls." Suspiciously, under surveillance, Therese Neumann (1898–1962) produced actual blood flows only when the phenomenon was "hidden from observation." And as recently as 1984, stigmatic Gigliola Giorgini was convicted of fraud by an Italian court (Wilson 1988, 26–27, 42, 53, 147).

Even a defender of Padre Pío's stigmata, C. Bernard Ruffin (1982, 145), admits, "For every genuine stigmatic, whether holy or hysterical, saintly or satanic, there are at least two whose wounds are self-inflicted." Catholic scholar Herbert Thurston (1952, 100) found no acceptable case after St. Francis of Assisi. Thurston believed the phenomenon was due to suggestion, but Padre Pío himself responded to such theorizers: "Go out to the fields and look very closely at a bull. Concentrate on him with all your might. Do this and see if horns grow on your head!" (quoted in Ruffin 1982, 150). As for St. Francis, his extraordinary zeal to imitate Jesus may have led him to engage in a pious deception (Nickell 2001, 276–83).

CANONIZATION

Not only was Padre Pío accused of inducing his stigmata with acid, he was also alleged to have misused funds and to have had sex with female parishioners—in the confessional. The founder of the Catholic university hospital in Rome branded Pío "an ignorant and self-mutilating psychopath who exploited people's credulity" ("Pío of Pietrelcina" 2008).

The faithful were undeterred, however, and after Pío's death there arose a popular movement to make him a saint. Pope John Paul II—whose papacy sped up the process of canonization and proclaimed more saints than any other in history (Grossman 2002)—heard the entreaties. Pío was beatified in 1999. On June 16, 2002, he was canonized as Saint Pío of Pietrelcina, but not before at least two statues of him wept in anticipation. Unfortunately, the bloody tears on one turned out to have been faked (a drug addict used a syringe to apply trickles of his own blood), and a whitish film on one eye of the other was determined to have been insect secretion ("Crying Statue Not a Miracle" 2002).

Interestingly, neither of the two proclaimed miracles of Pío (one used for his beatification, the other for canonization) involved stigmata. Instead, they were healings, assumed to be miraculous because they were determined to be medically inexplicable. In short, the church never affirmed Pío's stigmata as miraculous.

Of course, not everyone was happy with the canonization of Pío. Historian Sergio Luzzatto wrote a critical biography of Pío called *The Other Christ.* Luzzatto cited the testimony of a pharmacist recorded in a document in the Vatican's archive. Maria De Viot wrote: "I was an admirer of Padre Pío and I met him for the first time on 31 July 1919." She revealed, "Padre Pío called me to him in complete secrecy and telling me not to tell his fellow brothers, he gave me personally an empty bottle, and asked if I would act as a chauffeur to transport it back from Foggia to San Giovanni Rotondo with four grams of pure carbolic acid" (Moore 2007). But if the acid was for disinfecting syringes, as Pío had alleged to the pharmacist, why the secrecy? And why did Pío need undiluted acid?

Investigation shows the timing of this reported incident is significant. The previous September, Pío and some of the other friars at San Giovanni Rotondo were administering injections to boys who were ill with influenza. Alcohol not being available, an exhausted doctor left carbolic acid to be used for sterilizing needles and injection sites, while neglecting to tell the friars it had to be diluted. As a result, Pío and another friar were left with "angry red spots" on their hands. When Pío was subsequently alleged to have exhibited stigmata, the other friar at first thought the wounds were from the carbolic acid. Although Pío allegedly exhibited stigmata on his hands as early as 1910, the "permanent" stigmata appeared, apparently, not long after the carbolic-acid misuse (Ruffin 1982, 69–71, 138–43).

Sergio Luzzatto drew anger for publicizing the pharmacist's testimony. The Catholic Anti-Defamation League accused the historian of "spreading anti-Catholic libels," and the league's president sniffed, "We would like to remind Mr. Luzzatto that according to Catholic doctrine, canonisation carries with it papal infallibility" (Moore 2007).

EXHUMATION

Forty years after Padre Pío's 1968 death, his remains were exhumed from their crypt beneath a church in San Giovanni Rotondo. The intention of church officials was to renew reverence and so boost a flagging economy. Padre Pío, explained the *Los Angeles Times*, is "big business" (Wilkinson 2008).

No doubt many anticipated that the saint's body would be found incorrupt. The superstitious believe that the absence of decay in a corpse is miraculous and a sign of sanctity (Cruz 1977). In fact, under favorable conditions even an unembalmed body can become mummified. Desiccation may result from interment in a dry tomb or catacomb. Conversely, perpetually wet conditions may cause the body's fat to form a soap-like substance known as "grave wax"; subsequently, the body may take on the leathery effect of mummification (Nickell 2001, 49).

Alas, Pío's body, despite embalmment (by injections of formalin), was only in "fair condition." So that it could be displayed, a London wax museum was commissioned to fashion a lifelike silicon mask of Pío, complete with his full beard and bushy eyebrows. The "cosmetically enhanced corpse" went on display April 24, 2008, in a glass-and-marble coffin (where it was to repose until the end of September 2009) "amid weeping devotees and eager souvenir-hawkers" (Wilkinson 2008). For those who wonder: no, there was no visible trace of stigmata.

CHAPTER 48

STIGMATA OF A CONVERT

C anadian Lilian Bernas claims to exhibit—"in a supernatural state"—the wounds of Christ. On March 1, 2002, I observed one of a series of Bernas's bleedings. It was the eleventh such event that "the Lord allows me to experience on the first Friday of the month," she told the audience, "with one more to come" (Bernas 2002b). But was the event really supernatural or only a magic show?[1]

A NEW STIGMATIST

Lilian Bernas is a Catholic convert (in 1989) and one-time nursing-home worker. She first exhibited stigmata during Easter of 1992, having previously received visions of Jesus. According to one of her two self-published booklets, Jesus appears frequently to her, addressing her as "my suffering soul," "my sweet petal," and "my child" (Bernas 1999).

The Archdiocese of Ottawa, Ontario, where she then lived, established a commission to investigate Bernas's claims. "The inquiry did not make a judgment on the authenticity," stated a spokeswoman for the archdiocese, Gabrielle Tasse. Tasse told the *Buffalo News*, "It doesn't really concern the general public. It just creates propaganda." The Catholic Church often resists publicity regarding supernatural claims, noted Reverend Thomas Reese, a Jesuit priest who edits the weekly Catholic magazine *America*. "The church is very skeptical of these things," Reverend Reese explained (Tokasz 2003).

Bernas now resides in Niagara-on-the-Lake, Ontario, living with a retired couple that she asked to take her in in 1996, supposedly at Jesus' request. They are impressed with Bernas, whom they regard as a "victim soul" (one who suffers for others). In 2001 the *Ottawa Citizen* published a profile of Bernas (Wake 2001), apparently provoking displeasure from her home archdiocese in Ottawa. Their policy (according to a spokesman for the Diocese of Buffalo) is "that she is not to speak publicly because her faith journey is private" (Tokasz 2003).

However, Bernas does speak publicly, addressing the faithful and the curious at various churches. I attended a talk she gave, for example, at Resurrection Church in Cheektowaga, New York. Although she claimed Jesus guided her in her talks (she sometimes departed from her prepared text), she said that "the Devil" was at her elbow at all times and that she had to struggle with pride and self-will. She spoke of Lent, of praying the Rosary, and other Catholic topics, and claimed that Jesus had given her "a vision of aborted babies" (Bernas 2002a).

Afterward, she answered questions from those who gathered around her. Asked what Jesus looked like, she said he appeared as we did, solid. She added that he had shoulder-length hair with a beard and a mustache, and that he wore a white robe. In other words, he exhibited the conventional likeness of Jesus as it has evolved in art. Bernas's devotees exhibit a portrait of Jesus, "drawn under the inspiration of the Holy Spirit on May 20, 1994, by Lil Bernas."

MIRACLE WOUNDS?

I asked Bernas about her wounds, noting that there were reddish scars on the backs of her hands. She replied that she had also bled from the palms on occasion, but that no marks were left in those instances. She told me she was "permitted" to retain those on the backs of her hands and also on the tops of her feet. Someone asked about cross-shaped wounds (she has, for example, an apparent cruciform scar on her right jaw near the ear), and she stated that such stigmata were of the devil, that before her genuine stigmata came she had periods of possession (Bernas 2002a).

I found the absence of wounds on the palms and soles highly suspicious. A sham stigmatist might well avoid those areas, which would be subjected to additional pain and made more difficult to heal whenever one walked or grasped something. But a person truly exhibiting the nail wounds of Jesus should have his or her hands and feet completely pierced.

When I subsequently attended an exhibition of Lilian Bernas's stigmata (at Navy Hall, Niagara-on-the-Lake, March 1, 2002), my suspicions were increased. Not only was the bleeding already in progress when she appeared, but there were only the most superficial wounds. These were limited to the backs of the hands and tops of the feet, in addition to small wounds on the scalp, supposedly from a crown of thorns (John 19:2). The latter were only in the front, as if merely for show (see figure 48.1).

Significantly, there was no side wound like the one inflicted on Jesus by a Roman soldier's lance (John 19:34; 20:25, 27). Such a large wound would represent a real commitment by a fake stigmatist. It rarely appears, and then usually in a questionable fashion. Bernas exhibits a photo of an alleged wound in her left side, but it lacked rivulets of blood and—conveniently—was claimed to have soon disappeared without a trace. Bernas did say she was to receive a side wound later in the day (Bernas 2002b), but of course the crowd would not be there to witness the alleged happening.

The side wound was not the only one of Bernas's stigmata reputed to have unique properties seemingly best displayed in photographs. Bernas exhibits other photos that depict a squarish nail head emerging from a hand wound (harkening back to St. Francis), a thorn in her forehead that supposedly emerged over a week's time, and even an entire crown of thorns that allegedly materialized around Bernas's head—believe it or not!

As we watched Bernas bleed, I regretted that we were not getting to see such remarkable manifestations. I observed that her wounds soon ceased to flow, consistent with their having been inflicted just before she came out. After she had spoken to the audience for about an hour, people gathered to speak to Bernas (figure 48.2). (While shaking hands with her, one man attempted to get, rather surreptitiously, a sample of her blood, presumably as a magical "relic." He clasped his other hand, containing a folded handkerchief, against the back of her hand. Unfortunately, the blood had dried, and even rubbing did not yield a visible trace.)

Although I shook Bernas's bloody hand, I obtained a better look at a wound shortly before, when she hugged the woman in front of me and thus placed her hand virtually under my nose. I noticed that the actual wound looked like a small slit, but surrounding that was a larger red area; this appeared to have been deliberately formed of blood in order to simulate the appearance of a larger wound, like one formed by a Roman nail. (For my demonstration of a similar effect, see Nickell 2000, 27–28.)

ASSESSMENT

Bernas makes still other supernatural claims. For example, she says towels from her stigmata sessions, put away in plastic bags, allegedly "disappear within 48 hours" (Wake 2001). (I will wager they would not vanish while in my custody.)

Such outlandish and unsubstantiated claims should provoke skepticism in all but the most gullible. Yet a professor of philosophy at a Catholic college took exception to my views. I had told the *Buffalo News* that, on the evidence, I regarded stigmatics as "pious frauds," and I said of Lilian Bernas's stigmata, "Everything about it was consistent with trickery. Nothing about it was in the slightest way supernatural or intriguing" (Tokasz 2003).

Professor John Zeis (2003) replied with the astonishing statement: "Trickery is consistent with any reported miracle (including Jesus' resurrection) but that is no reason to reject belief in the miracle." He found more reasonable a priest's statement that "it is up to each person to believe or not."

CSI Public Relations Director Kevin Christopher (2003) responded: "Zeis is suggesting that objective evidence is irrelevant. What, in fact could be a more unreasonable conclusion?" Christopher also replied to Zeis's claim that "the *Skeptical Inquirer* is biased against claims concerning faith in the miraculous." Stated Christopher: "The magazine's mission is to inform its readers about the state of the evidence for paranormal and supernatural claims. When the evidence is poor or nonexistent, it is not 'biased' to report that fact. It is, in fact, a moral duty."

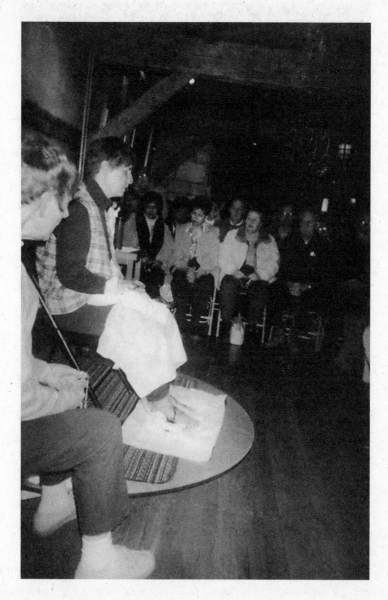

Figure 48.1. Canadian Lilian Bernas impressed many at the eleventh of twelve "first Friday" stigmata materializations. (Photo by Joe Nickell)

Figure 48.2. Although Bernas attracts the credulous, her stigmata do not convincingly replicate the wounds of Christ's crucifixion. (Photo by Joe Nickell)

CHAPTER 49

TAKING UP SERPENTS

From the snake-charming "miracle men" of the East, to their Western counterparts who "take up serpents" in certain Christian rituals or who even perform in sideshows, many have demonstrated their supposed power over the feared reptiles.[1]

ROD-TO-SERPENT MAGIC

The first biblical magic feat, performed in public, is credited to Moses' brother Aaron—one of a set of three effects based on God's instructions to Moses at the burning bush (Exodus 3:2–5). The performance occurs at the Egyptian pharaoh's court, where the brothers are attempting to convince the pharaoh to set their fellow Jews free from bondage (Exodus 7:8–12):

> And Moses and Aaron went in unto the Pharaoh, and they did so as the Lord had commanded: And Aaron cast down his rod before Pharaoh, and before his servants, and it became a serpent. Then Pharaoh also called the wise men and the sorcerers: now the magicians of Egypt, they also did in like manner with their enchantments. For they cast down every man his rod, and they became serpents.

This event was long considered to be either (depending on one's outlook) a true miracle from God or a fairy tale. If one is to hold the first position, a problem arises. How were the magicians able to work the same miracle? There are answers, of course, since theologians are very clever. But perhaps they can be spared the effort.

Surely the "enchantments" referred to are those of legerdemain, that is, sleight-of-hand. Budge (1901, 59) tells us:

The turning of a serpent into what is apparently an inanimate, wooden stick, and the turning of the stick back into a writhing snake, are feats which have been performed in the East from the most ancient period; and the power to control and direct the movements of such venomous reptiles was one of the things of which the Egyptian was most proud, and in which he was most skillful, already in the time when the pyramids were being built.

Encyclopedia Britannica (1960) says of the narrow-hooded Egyptian cobra (Naja haje), or asp, that "Egyptian snake charmers, who use it [the asp] in their street performances, are said to be able to make it rigid like a stick by a pressure on the neck, which perhaps suggests that it was the asp that served as Aaron's staff in the famous counter transformation." Gibson (1967, 73–75) says: "Photographs have been taken showing how closely the rigid snake resembles a stick, and instances have been reported where modern Egyptian magicians allow bystanders to handle 'charmed' snakes with impunity." He suggests that "ancient sorcerers who performed the trick probably carried staffs of a similar size and shape to the rigid Naja haje. By substituting a paralyzed snake at the proper time, it could still be shown as an ordinary stick up to the moment when it was thrown to the ground."

I have left off till now the final part of the account, which states (Exodus 7:12) that after Aaron and the sorcerers had all cast down their rods, "Aaron's rod swallowed up their rods."

Here again, a biblical author, whose purpose it is to give an account of the Good Guys, adds an imaginative touch. As with other magical "duels" in the Old and New Testaments, God's side wins. But theological legend aside, it would certainly seem that the rod-to-serpent trick was known in ancient Egypt.

EASTERN TRADITION

Figure 49.1 is a sketch from my travels, which I made in the Medina in Marrakech, Morocco, in 1971. I was drawn to the scene by the peculiar flute music. The performer was putting on a snake show while his assistant used his tambourine as a collection tray. As shown in the soft-pencil rendering, one of the charmer's stunts was to approach a cobra in a squatting position, one hand on the ground and the other holding a tangle of serpents with which he teased the cobra.

In India the itinerant *Jadu* (magic) performer occasionally does herpetological tricks. For example, he might transform a piece of rope into a snake (after wrapping the rope in cloth and in the process no doubt making the switch) (Siegel 1991, 186). My late friend Premanand, the Indian conjurer and skeptic, knew many such feats. One, described in his valuable *Science Versus Miracles* (1994, 36), is a rod-to-serpent feat like that of the pharaoh's sorcerers related in Exodus (7:9–15). The snake's mouth and tail are held in either hand and the reptile stretched straight. Firm pressure on the head between the thumb and the index finger causes the snake to stiffen. In this way it looks like a rod and is so presented, until it is thrown to the ground, whereupon it soon recovers and the rod is "transformed" into a snake.

The Indian snake charmer performs in the open air and uses his flute music to cause a deadly hooded cobra to rise and sway in rhythm to the music. A number of additional snakes, released from baskets and jute bags by his assistants, may be similarly entranced. When the music stops and the performer extends a stick toward the cobra, it strikes quickly. The snake charmer may even have the deadly reptiles crawling over his arms, and he concludes his act by dramatically capturing each snake.

Actually, although snakes do have hearing organs, it is the movements of the charmer himself swaying to the melody that the cobra follows. By ceasing to pipe, the charmer causes the cobra to pose motionless, and then, by extending the stick, he provokes it to strike. In some cases the cobras are drugged, or have their venom sacks removed or their mouths sewn shut. But skilled performers can and do handle the most lethal reptiles. From long experience, they understand how cobras behave, know their striking distance, and rely on their shortsightedness.

In concluding his act, for example, the charmer often deliberately provokes a cobra with the movements of one hand, then, as it prepares to strike, quickly grasps it behind the head with the other. By taking advantage of the snake's natural tendency to hide, he quickly puts it in a basket or bag (Gibson 1967, 70–73; Gardner 1962, 51–52).

SNAKE HANDLING

In the West, certain Christian charismatics believe their faith provides them with immunity to serpents, just as they are given the ability to speak in tongues and the power to heal by the laying on of hands. They are inspired by two New Testament passages. In Luke (10:18–19), Jesus said to some followers:

> I behold Satan as lightning fall from heaven. Behold, I give unto you power to tread on serpents and scorpions, and over all the power of the enemy: and nothing shall by any means hurt you.

And in a passage in the Gospel of Mark (16:16–18), when Jesus appeared to his disciples after his resurrection, he said:

> He that believeth and is baptized shall be saved; but he that believeth not shall be damned. And these signs shall follow them that believe; In my name shall they cast out devils; they shall speak with new tongues; they shall take up serpents; and if they drink any deadly thing, it shall not hurt them; they shall lay hands on the sick, and they shall recover.

However, the latter passage may be spurious—an addition of the second century (Larue 1990, 212).

The modern practice of snake handling seems to have originated in 1909 with one George Went Hensley, an illiterate Church of God preacher. Hensley was preaching about the Mark 16 passage in an outdoor service near Cleveland, Tennessee, when a box of rattlesnakes was overturned next to his pulpit. Hensley picked up the snakes and continued preaching—thus becoming known as "the original prophet of snake handling" (Yardley 1992).

No major Pentecostal denomination now endorses snake handling, and it has been specifically rejected by the Church of God. Even so, some rural congregations continue the practice, including the Free Pentecostal Holiness Church (with churches in Virginia, Kentucky, Tennessee, and North Carolina) and various independent churches scattered throughout Appalachia. The churches are invariably small, rural edifices like a small-town Alabama one converted from a store and filling station (Nickell 1998, 117).

Adherents of the practice insist that taking up serpents should only be done when worshippers truly feel the Holy Spirit is upon them. The urge to caution in handling snakes, however, may reflect more shrewdness than piety. While poisonous snakes are indeed dangerous and must be handled carefully, the knowledge that the rural snake handlers bring to the practice can be most helpful. For example, unless snakes are hot, hungry, or frightened, they move little and are relatively unaggressive (Parsons 1990, 15). Also, snakes raised from hatchlings can become accustomed to handling. Large snakes grasped firmly behind the neck will be unable to bite, and, "once they are off the ground they are much less likely to bite and can usually be held safely" (Mattison 1991, 56–57). In addition to these general practices, there are some that apply to different species of snakes that handlers can take advantage of (see Nickell 1998, 119).

The extent to which trickery is employed may be debated. Certainly there are occasional allegations of the use of defanged snakes.

Those who do receive snakebites are told it was their lack of faith that caused them. Yet when a devout member of the sect dies from a snakebite, the others resort to rationalization (Nickell 1998, 120–21).

Moreover, while snakebites should certainly be treated, the fact is that—fortunately—venom is rarely injected directly into a blood vessel, which would provide the most deadly threat. Also, snakebites vary in the amount of venom injected: With a *mild* snakebite, the strike is a glancing one and the result is minimal pain; a *moderate* snakebite causes some localized pain and swelling but not a general sick feeling; and a *severe* snakebite causes excruciating pain, discoloration and swelling, and a generalized sick feeling. Multiple bites are the most deadly, since venom can be injected with each bite, and the attack of several snakes could therefore be life threatening in the extreme.

Also, the effect of the snakebites varies considerably depending on the health and size of the victim, the speed of venom absorption, and the location of the bite, which fortunately is usually in the extremities. Remaining calm—since panic helps spread the venom more quickly—is essential, as snake handlers well know (Nickell 1998, 119; Smith and Brodie 1982, 9–10).

Ironically, snake handling's "original prophet," George Went Hensley, died in 1955 of a snakebite sustained during a religious service (Yardley 1992).

SIDESHOWS

Also in the West, snakes were part of circus and carnival exotica. They were included in menageries and featured in sideshows.

The standard snakes for the latter were Indian pythons and Central America boa constrictors, snakes that are dangerous "only if you let them get a coil around your neck or chest and then only if you are alone and can't find the head or tail" (Gresham 1953, 141–42).

A link with the East was sometimes acknowledged in sideshow presentations. A young Indian woman—Saidor A. Isoha—appeared in 1890s publicity photographs by Karl Hagenbeck, whose German circus was among the most important shows in Europe. Saidor had reportedly given up her cobras after watching a man suffer a terrible death from a cobra bite. She once staged public fights, pitting a cobra against a mongoose. Reported William G. FitzGerald (1897), in the London magazine the *Strand*, "This was a little costly, however, for the cobra was always killed."

Saidor, who dressed in colorful Indian costumes and wore metal bracelets on her wrists and upper arms, owned six Indian and three African pythons plus three boa constrictors, all in the eight- to twelve-foot range. Wrote FitzGerald (1897): "She has a real affection for her snakes, and they for her. One large python will form himself into a living turban about her head."

Most of the European and American sideshow snake charmers were women. The combination of the scantily clad ladies and their fang-bearing charges was a subtly erotic, beauty-and-the-beast theme that was irresistible to sideshow banner artists. In researching my book *Secrets of the Sideshows* (2005), I occasionally met one of the performers, as shown in figure 49.2. Obviously (as with eating fire, lying on a bed of nails, and similar tortures I endured for my research), I lived to tell about it.

One of the snake-charmers from the Medina with a tangle of snakes

Figure 49.1. Moroccan snake charmer teases a cobra with a tangle of snakes. (On-site sketch by author)

Figure 49.2. Author poses with sideshow snake charmer Ginger Donahue—and friend. (Author's photo by Benjamin Radford)

CHAPTER 50

ADDITIONAL PENTECOSTAL POWERS

I n addition to snake handling, certain other practices of some Christian fundamentalists also represent "supernatural gifts" of the Holy Spirit. These include the ability to drink poison, withstand fire, and "speak in tongues."

DRINKING POISON

The same biblical verse that refers to taking up serpents (Mark 17:18) also promises adherents that "if they drink any deadly thing, it shall not hurt them. Since the passage is in an apocryphal section of Mark's Gospel, there is no evidence that early Christians actually engaged in the practice. Still, some independent Pentecostal churches do combine snake handling with the drinking of strychnine, an alkaloid discovered in 1817. Strychnine is decidedly poisonous (even though it has been used medically—both in cathartic preparations and as a tonic and stimulant). In 1973 two Pentecostals died after drinking the poison during a Tennessee service (Nickell 1993, 121–22).

In fact the practice of sipping strychnine—typically from a jar of water supposedly "laced" with the poison—is not done under controlled scientific conditions, so how much poison is actually imbibed in a given instance is unknown, as is whether an antidote (commonly egg white) has been ingested. Interestingly, the poison is typically sipped prior to the snake handling—a small amount of strychnine actually being advocated to treat certain physiological effects that result from snakebites (Ditmars 1959, 124).

WITHSTANDING FIRE

Another form of invincibility some Pentecostals purportedly attain is immunity from fire. One feat involves a lit kerosene "lamp" (improvised from a bottle with a cloth wick) held to the performer's hands and feet without causing harm. But this seems little different than a sideshow performer's using a torch—kept in motion—for a similar stunt that I have performed myself on several occasions (figure 50.1). In fact, as one photograph of a Christian performer reveals, the sole of his foot is placed *beside* the flame, not over it, where the rising flame would surely do harm if it remained there (Nickell 1993, 122–25).

An elderly friend of mine related an amusing and revealing incident involving fire immunity. While attending a "Holy Roller" service, some worshipers removed and handled the hot glass chimneys from old-fashioned "coal oil" (kerosene) lamps. Actually they tossed them from hand to hand— "quite gingerly," she said. A local minister, growing angry at watching the stunt, suddenly leapt from his seat in the audience and seized one of the lamps, whereupon he duplicated the effect, which he noted anyone could perform. As the Pentecostals rushed to stop him, the "miracle" service was transformed into one of religious acrimony (Nickell 1993, 124).

Certain religious practitioners—not Pentecostals, but mystics from the East—attempt to prove their resistance to fire by walking barefoot across hot embers. I, too, have demonstrated this feat many times (see figure 50.2). Such "fire walking" depends on the facts that wood does not conduct heat well and that the time of contact is kept brief (Nickell 2005, 211–12).

SPEAKING IN TONGUES

So-called speaking in tongues is another practice of some charismatic Christians—appearing in the New Testament as a fulfillment of Jesus' promise that his apostles were soon to be "baptized with the Holy Ghost" (Acts 1:5, 2:1–4). Such incoherent utterances—known in psychological circles by the Greek term *glossolalia*—have recurred in Christian revivals through the ages, including thirteenth-century mendicant friars, the early Quakers, converts of Methodist founder John Wesley (1703–1791), the

Shakers (that is, the "Shaking Quakers"), and many other revivalists.

Some practitioners speak in languages they allegedly are unfamiliar with; that is, they supposedly practice *xenoglossy*. If this is not feigned, it may be an example of unusual recollection (as from earlier exposure to the language—what psychologists call *cryptomnesia* (or "hidden memory"). (For more on this, see Baker 1992.)

Often glossolalists simply jabber in a manner that resembles a known foreign language (much like comedian Sid Caesar's hilarious renditions of "German" and "French") that might pass as such to persons who were not actually conversant with those languages. However, linguistically, such utterances are nothing more than false languages.

Indeed, analysis of many expressions of glossolalia show it to be linguistic nonsense. An extensive five-year study of the phenomenon on several continents was conducted by Dr. William T. Samarin, a professor of anthropology and linguistics at the University of Toronto. He concluded:

> Glossolalia consists of strings of meaningless syllables made up of sounds taken from those familiar to the speaker and put together more or less haphazardly. The speaker controls the rhythm, volume, speed and inflection of his speech so that the sounds emerge as pseudolanguage—in the form of words and sentences.
>
> Glossolalia is language-like because the speaker unconsciously wants it to be language-like. Yet in spite of superficial similarities, glossolalia fundamentally is not language.

Samarin also observed that, according to more than half of the glossolalists he studied, it was actually easier to speak in tongues than in ordinary language ("Speaking in Tongues" 1972; Samarin 1972, 70).

Figure 50.1. The author performs a trick of "fire immunity" with a torch—a *moving* torch to be sure. (Author's photo by Robert H. van Outer)

Figure 50.2. Fire walking (walking on flowing embers) is a stunt demonstrated here by the author, not evidence of a supernatural agency. (Author's photo by Benjamin Radford)

CHAPTER 51

LORETTO STAIRCASE: ST. JOSEPH'S MIRACLE CARPENTRY?

The CBS television movie *The Staircase* (April 12, 1998), told how "a dying nun's wish to complete her order's chapel is fulfilled by a mysterious stranger" (Bobbin 1998). Starring Barbara Hershey as the terminally ill mother superior and William Peterson as the enigmatic carpenter, the movie is an embellishment of the legend of the "miraculous stairway" at the Sisters of Loretto Chapel in Santa Fe, New Mexico. The wooden, spiral stair is thought to be unique, and some claim its very existence is inexplicable.

PIOUS TALE

The Loretto legend begins with the founding of a school for females in Santa Fe in 1852. A combined day and boarding school, the Loretto Academy was established by the local Sisters of Loretto at the behest of Bishop John Lamy. In 1873 work began on a chapel. Unfortunately, some earthly, even earthy, events reportedly marred the work: the wife of Bishop Lamy's nephew caught the architect's eye and he was killed for his interest—shot by the nephew, who was distraught over his destroyed marriage.

At this time work on the chapel was nearing completion and, although the choir loft was finished, the architect's plans provided no means of access. It was felt that installing an "ordinary stair" would be objectionable on aesthetic grounds and because it would limit seating (Bullock 1978, 6, 8). "Carpenters and builders were called in," according to one source, "only to shake their heads in despair." Then, "when all else had failed, the Sisters determined to pray a novena to the Master Carpenter himself, St. Joseph" (the father of Jesus) (Bullock 1978, 8).

"On the ninth day," reportedly, their prayers were answered. A humble workman appeared outside, leading a burro laden with carpentry tools. He announced that he could provide a suitable means of access to the loft, requiring only permission and a couple of water tubs. Soon, he was at work:

> Sisters, going in to the Chapel to pray, saw the tubs with wood soaking in them, but the Man always withdrew while they said their prayers, returning to his work when the Chapel was free. Some there are who say the circular stair which stands there today was built very quickly. Others say no, it took quite a little time. But the stair did grow, rising solidly in a double helix without support of any kind and without nail or screw. The floor space used was minimal and the stair adds to, rather than detracts from, the beauty of the Chapel.

As the tale continues:

> The Sisters were overjoyed and planned a fine dinner to honor the Carpenter. Only he could not be found. No one seemed to know him, where he lived, nothing. Lumberyards were checked, but they had no bill for the Sisters of Loretto. They had not sold him the wood. Knowledgeable men went in and inspected the stair and none knew what kind of wood had been used, certainly nothing indigenous to this area. Advertisements for the Carpenter were run in the *New Mexican* and brought no response.
>
> "Surely," said the devout, "it was St. Joseph himself who built the stair." (Bullock 1978, 8, 10)

No doubt the legend has improved over the intervening century, like good wine. As we shall see, there is more to the story. But Barbara Hershey concedes, "Those who want to believe it's a miracle can, and those who want to believe this man was just an ingenious carpenter can" (Bobbin 1998). Evidence for the latter is considerable, but first we must digress a bit to understand spiral stairs.

WINDING STAIRS

Spiral and other winding staircases reached a high point in development in sixteenth-century England and France, with several "remarkable" examples ("Stair" 1960; "Interior Decoration" 1960). To appreciate the architectural and other problems such stairs present we must recognize that builders use *turns* in staircases to save space or to adapt to a particular floor plan. The simplest is the *landing turn*, which is formed of straight flights joined at the requisite angle by a platform. A variation is the *split landing*, which is divided on a diagonal into two steps.

Instead of a landing, the turn may be accomplished by a series of steps having tapered treads. Such staircases are called *winders* and include certain ornamental types, like that which takes the shape of a partial circle (known as "circular stair") or an ellipse. An extreme form of winding staircase is a *continuous winder* in the form of a helix (a line that rises as it twists, like a screw thread). This is the popularly termed "spiral staircase," like the example at Loretto Chapel (Locke 1992, 135–36; Dietz 1991, 340–42).

Helixes—unlike, say, pyramids—are not inherently stable weight-supporting structures. They require some kind of strengthening or support. Therefore, in addition to being secured at top and bottom, the spiral staircase is usually also braced by attachment along its height to a central pole or an adjacent wall (Dietz 1991, 342; "Stair" 1960).

Unfortunately, spiral and other winding staircases are not only problematic in design; they are also fundamentally unsafe. Explains one authority, "For safety, any departure from a straight staircase requires careful attention to detail in design and construction." Especially, "because people tend to travel the shortest path around a corner, where a winder's treads are narrowest, the traveler must decide at each step where each foot falls. This may be an intellectual and physical exercise best practiced elsewhere. In short, winders are pretty but inherently unsafe" (Locke 1992, 135, 136). Other experts agree. According to Albert G. H. Dietz, professor emeritus of building engineering at MIT, winders "should be avoided if at all possible. No adequate foothold is afforded at the angle [due to the tapering] and there is an almost vertical drop of several feet if a number of risers converge on the same point. The construction is dangerous and may easily lead to bad accidents" (Dietz 1991, 341). As a consequence, winders are frequently prohibited by building codes. That is especially true of the spiral stair, which "contains all the bad features of the winder multiplied several times" (Dietz 1991, 342).

PARTIAL MIRACLE

Such problems seem to have beset the staircase at Loretto, suggesting that, at most, the "miracle" was a partial one. Safety appears to have been a concern at the outset, since there was originally no railing. At the time the staircase was completed, one thirteen-year-old sister, who was among the first to ascend to the loft, told how she and her friends were so frightened—absent a railing—that they came down on hands and knees (Albach 1965). Nevertheless, despite the very real hazard, it was not until 1887—ten years after the staircase was completed—that an artisan named Phillip August Hesch added the railing (Loretto n. d.). No one claims it was a miracle, yet it is described as "itself a work of art" (Albach 1965) (see figure 51.1).

Over time, other problems arose relating to the double-helix form. The helix, after all, is the shape of the common wire spring. Therefore, it is not surprising that people who trod the stairs reported "a small amount of vertical movement" or "a certain amount of springiness" (Albach 1965) and again "a very slight vibration as one ascends and descends rather as though the stair were a living, breathing thing" (Bullock 1978, 14).

Some people have thought the freestanding structure should have collapsed long ago, we are told, and builders and architects supposedly "never fail to marvel how it manages to stay in place," considering that it is "without a center support" (Albach 1965). In fact, though, as one wood technologist observes, "the staircase does have a central support." He observes that of the two wood stringers (or spiral structural members), the inner one is of such small radius that it "functions as an almost solid pole" (Easley 1997).

There is also another support—one that goes unmentioned, but which I observed when I visited the now privately owned chapel in 1993. This is an iron brace or bracket that stabilizes the staircase by rigidly connecting the outer stringer to one of the columns that support the loft (see figure 51.2).

There is reason to suspect that the staircase may be more unstable and, potentially, unsafe than some realize. It has been closed to public travel since at least the mid-1970s (when the reason was given as lack of other egress from the loft in case of fire). When I visited in 1993 my understanding was that it was suffering from the constant traffic. Barbara Hershey implied the same when she stated, "It still functions, though people aren't allowed to go up it very often" (Bobbin 1998). It would thus appear that the Loretto staircase is subject to the laws of physics, just like any other staircase.

Another mystery that is emphasized in relation to the stair is the identity of the carpenter and the type of wood used. That it has not been identified precisely means little. The piece given to a forester for possible identification was exceedingly small (only about 3/4 inch square by 1/8 inch thick) whereas much larger (six inch) pieces are preferred. The wood *has* reportedly been identified as to family, *Pinaceae*, and genus, *Picea*—which is to say, spruce (Easley 1997), a type of "light, strong, elastic wood" often used in construction ("Spruce" 1960). But there are no fewer than thirty-nine species—ten in North America—so that comparison of the tiny Loretto sample with only two varieties (Easley 1997) can scarcely be definitive.

CRAFTSMAN IDENTIFIED

As to the identity of an obviously itinerant workman, it seems merely mystery mongering to suggest that there is anything strange—least of all evidence of the supernatural—in the failure to record his name. As it happens, however, the identity of the enigmatic craftsman has finally been revealed. Credit for the discovery goes to an "intrepid and highly respected amateur historian" named Mary Jean Cook. She learned of a "hermit rancher," François-Jean "Frenchy" Rochas, who lived in "godforsaken" Dog Canyon, nine miles from Alamogordo. Learning that he had left behind a collection of "sophisticated carpentry tools," Cook searched for his death notice, which she found in the January 6, 1896, issue of the *Santa Fe New Mexican.* It described him as "favorably known in Santa Fe as an expert worker in wood." He had built, the brief obituary noted, "the handsome staircase in the Loretto Chapel and at St. Vincent sanitarium."

Cook suspects that the legend of St. Joseph began with the sisters at the Loretto Academy, "probably in response to questions from their students." However, she observes that "it wasn't until the late 1930s—when the story appeared in Ripley's . . . Believe It or Not!—that the story became an icon of popular culture." Although some rued the debunking of the pious legend, Archbishop Michael Sheehan promised, "It will always be referred to as a miraculous staircase. It was an extraordinary piece to have been done in its time" (Stieber 2000).

Figure 51.1. The spiral stairway at Loretto Chapel in Santa Fe, New Mexico, is an alleged miracle of construction. (Photo by Joe Nickell)

Figure 51.2. Iron support bracket (unmentioned in published accounts) reveals the "miracle" is a partial one. (Photo by Joe Nickell)

PART 6
THE DEVIL'S WORK?

CHAPTER 52

EXORCISING DEMONS

Belief in demonic possession is getting a new propaganda boost. Not only has the 1973 horror movie *The Exorcist* been rereleased, but the "true story" that inspired it is chronicled in a reissued book and a made-for-TV movie, both titled *Possessed* (Allen 2000) (figure 52.1). However, a yearlong investigation by a Maryland writer (Opsasnik 2000), together with my own analysis of events chronicled in the exorcising priest's diary, belie the claim that a teenage boy was possessed by Satan in 1949.

PSYCHOLOGY VERSUS POSSESSION

Belief in spirit possession flourishes in times and places where there is ignorance about mental states. Citing biblical examples, the medieval church taught that demons were able to take control of an individual, and by the sixteenth century demonic behavior had become relatively stereotypical. It manifested itself by convulsions, prodigious strength, insensitivity to pain, temporary blindness or deafness, clairvoyance, and other abnormal characteristics. Some early notions of possession may have been fomented by three brain disorders: epilepsy, migraine, and Tourette's syndrome (Beyerstein 1988). Psychiatric historians have long attributed demonic manifestations to such aberrant mental conditions as schizophrenia and hysteria, noting that—as mental illness began to be recognized as such after the seventeenth century—there was a consequent decline in demonic superstitions (Baker 1992, 192). In 1999 the Vatican did update its 1614 guidelines for expelling demons, urging exorcists to avoid mistaking psychiatric illness for possession ("Vatican Updates Its Rules on Exorcism of Demons" 1999).

369

In many cases, however, supposed demonic possession can be a learned role that fulfills certain important functions for those claiming it. In his book *Hidden Memories: Voices and Visions from Within*, psychologist Robert A. Baker (1992) notes that possession was sometimes feigned by nuns to act out sexual frustrations, protest restrictions, escape unpleasant duties, attract attention and sympathy, and fulfill other useful functions.

Many devout claimants of stigmata, inedia, and other powers have also exhibited alleged demonic possession. For example, at Loudon, France, a prioress, Sister Jeanne des Anges (1602–1665), was part of a contagious outbreak of writhing, convulsing nuns. Jeanne herself exhibited stigmatic designs and lettering on her skin. A bloody cross "appeared" on her forehead, and the names of Jesus, Mary, and others were found on her hand—always clustered on her left hand, just as would be expected if a right-handed person were marking them. She went on tour as a "walking relic" and was exhibited in Paris to credulous thousands. There were a few skeptics, but Cardinal Richelieu rejected having Jeanne tested by having her hand enclosed in a sealed glove. He felt that would amount to testing God (Nickell 1998, 230–31). Interestingly enough, while I was researching and writing this chapter I was called to Southern Ontario on a case of dubious possession that also involved stigmata.

Possession can be childishly simple to fake. For example, an exorcism broadcast by ABC's *20/20* in 1991 featured a sixteen-year-old girl who, her family claimed, was possessed by ten separate demonic entities. However, to skeptics her alleged possession seemed to be indistinguishable from poor acting. She even stole glances at the camera before affecting convulsions and other "demonic" behaviors (Nickell 1998).

Of course, a person with a strong impulse to feign diabolic possession may indeed be mentally disturbed. Although the teenager in the *20/20* episode reportedly improved after the exorcism, it was also pointed out that she continued "on medication" ("Exorcism" 1991). To add to the complexity, the revised Vatican guidelines also urge, appropriately, against believing a person who is merely "the victim of one's own imagination" is actually possessed ("Vatican Updates Its Rules on Exorcism of Demons" 1999).

With less modern enlightenment, however, the guidelines also reflect Pope John Paul II's efforts to convince doubters that the devil actually exists. In various homilies John Paul has denounced Satan as a "cosmic liar and murderer." A Vatican official who presented the revised rite stated, "The existence of the devil isn't an opinion, something to take or leave as you wish. Anyone who says he doesn't exist wouldn't have the fullness of the Catholic faith" ("Vatican Updates Its Rules on Exorcism of Demons" 1999).

Unchallenged by the new exorcism guidelines is the acceptance of such alleged signs of possession as demonstrating supernormal physical force and speaking in unknown tongues. In the case broadcast by 20/20, the teenage girl did exhibit "tongues" (known as glossolalia [Nickell 1998, 103–109]), but it was unimpressive; she merely chanted: "Sanka dali. Booga, booga." She did struggle against the restraining clerics, one of whom claimed that, had she not been held down, she would have been levitating! At that point a group of magicians, psychologists, and other skeptics with whom I was watching the video gleefully encouraged, "Let her go! Let her go!" (Nickell 1995).

"TRUE STORY"

Demonstrating prodigious strength, speaking in an unknown language, and exhibiting other allegedly diabolical feats supposedly characterizes the "true story" behind *The Exorcist*. The 1973 horror movie—starring Linda Blair as the devil-plagued victim—was based on the 1971 bestselling novel of that title by William Peter Blatty. The movie, reports one writer, "somehow reached deep into the subconscious and stirred up nameless fears." Some moviegoers vomited or fainted, while others left trembling, and there were "so many outbreaks of hysteria that, at some theaters, nurses and ambulances were on call." Indeed, "Many sought therapy to rid themselves of fears they could not explain. Psychiatrists were writing about cases of 'cinematic neurosis'" (Allen 2000, viii–ix).

Blatty had heard about the exorcism performed in 1949 and, almost two decades later, had written to the exorcist to inquire about it. However, the priest, Father William S. Bowdern, declined to assist Blatty because he had been directed by the archbishop to keep it secret. He did tell Blatty—then a student at Washington's Georgetown University, a Jesuit institution—about the diary an assisting priest had kept of the disturbing events (Allen 2000, ix–x).

The diary—written by Father Raymond J. Bishop—consisted of an original twenty-six-page, single-spaced typescript and three carbon copies, one of which was eventually provided to Thomas B. Allen, author of *Possessed*, and included as an appendix to the 2000 edition of the book. The copy came from Father Walter Halloran, who had also assisted with the exorcism. Halloran verified the authenticity of the diary and stated that it had been read and approved by Bowdern (Allen 2000, 243, 301).

The diary opens with a "Background of the Case." The boy, an only child identified as "R," was born in 1935 and raised an Evangelical Lutheran, like his mother; his father was baptized a Catholic but had had "no instruction or practice" in the faith. The family's Cottage City, Maryland, home included the maternal grandmother, who had been a "practicing Catholic until the age of fourteen years" (Bishop 1949, 245).

On January 15, 1949, R and his grandmother heard odd "dripping" and scratching noises in her bedroom, where a picture of Jesus shook "as if the wall back of it had been bumped." The effects lasted ten days but were attributed to a rodent. Then R began to say he could hear the scratching when others could not. Soon a noise, as of "squeaking shoes"—or, one wonders, could it have been bedsprings?—became audible and "was heard only at night when the boy went to bed." On the sixth evening the scratching noise resumed, and R's mother and grandmother lay with him on his bed, whereupon they "heard something coming toward them similar to the rhythm of marching feet and the beat of drums." The sound seemed to "travel the length of the mattress and back again" repeatedly (Bishop 1949, 246). Was R tapping his toes against the bed's footboard?

POLTERGEISTS AND OUIJA SPIRITS

At this point the case was exhibiting features often attributed to a *poltergeist* (or "noisy spirit"). Poltergeist phenomena typically involve disturbances—noises, movement of objects, or, rarely, serious effects like outbreaks of fire—typically centering on a disturbed person, usually a child. Believers often attribute the occurrences to "psychokinetic energy" or other mystical forces imagined to be produced from the repressed hostilities of the pubescent child. Skeptics can agree with all but the mystical part, observing that one does not explain an unknown by invoking another. Skeptics have a simpler explanation, attributing the effects to the cunning tricks of a naughty youth or occasionally a disturbed adult. When such cases have been properly investigated—by magicians and detectives using hidden cameras, lie detectors, tracer powders (dusted on objects likely to be involved), and other techniques—they usually turn out to be the pranks of young or immature mischief makers.

Consider some of the "other manifestations" associated with R in the early part of the case, as recorded in the diary:

> An orange and a pear flew across the entire room where R was standing. The kitchen table was upset without any movement on the part of R. Milk and food were thrown off the table and stove. The bread-board was thrown on to the floor. Outside the kitchen a coat on its hanger flew across the room; a comb flew violently through the air and extinguished blessed candles; a Bible was thrown directly at the feet of R, but did not injure him in any way. While the family was visiting a friend in Boonsboro, Maryland, the rocker in which R was seated spun completely around through no effort on the part of the boy. R's desk at school moved about on the floor similar to the plate on a Ouija board. R did not continue his attendance out of embarrassment [Bishop 1949, 248].

It is well to consider here the sage advice of the late investigator and magician Milbourne Christopher not to accept statements of what actually happened from the suspected "poltergeist." Regarding one such case, Christopher (1970, 149–60) pointed out that all that was necessary to see the events not as paranormal occurrences but as deliberate deceptions was to "suppose that what the boy said was not true, that he was in one room when he said he was in another in some instances. Also let us suppose that what people thought they saw and what actually happened were not precisely the same." Experience shows that even "reliable witnesses" are capable of being deceived. As one confessed "poltergeist"—an eleven-year-old girl—observed: "I didn't throw all those things. People just imagined some of them" (Christopher 1970, 149). In the case of R, we must realize that the previously described events (such as the flying fruit) were not witnessed by Father Bishop, who reported them in his diary as background to the case, and so were necessarily second-hand or worse.

It was indeed trickery that was behind the poltergeist-like disturbances of 1848 that launched modern Spiritualism. As the Fox sisters confessed decades later, their pretended spirit contact began as the pranks of "very mischievous children" who, Margaret Fox explained, began their shenanigans "to terrify our dear mother, who was a very good woman and very easily frightened" and who "did not suspect us of being capable of a trick because we were so young." The schoolgirls threw slippers at a disliked brother-in-law, shook the dinner table, and produced noises by bumping the floor with an apple on a string and by knocking on the bedstead (Nickell 1995).

The Fox sisters were followed in 1854 by the Davenport brothers, schoolboys Ira and William, who were the focus of cutlery that danced about the family's kitchen table as well as other odd events. Ira sometimes claimed that, when alone, spirits had whisked him to distant spots. Soon the boys advanced to spirit-rapped messages, "trance" writing and speaking, and other "spirit manifestations." In his old age, Ira confessed to magician/paranormal investigator Harry Houdini that the brothers' spirit communication—which launched and maintained their careers as two of the world's best-known Spiritualistic mediums—had all been produced by trickery. Indeed, they had been caught in deceptions many times (Nickell 1999).

The Foxes and Davenports are not isolated examples. It should therefore not be surprising to learn that the case of R, which began as a seeming poltergeist outbreak, soon advanced to one of alleged spirit communication, before finally escalating to one of supposed diabolic possession.

R had been close to an aunt, who often visited from St. Louis. A devoted Spiritualist, she introduced R to the Ouija board. With their fingers on the planchette, they saw it move about the board's array of printed letters, numbers, and the words *yes* and *no* to spell out messages—she told him—from spirits of the dead. (Actually, as skeptics know, the planchette is moved not by spirits but by the sitters' involuntary—or voluntary!—muscular control [Nickell 1995, 58].) She also told R and his mother how, "lacking a Ouija board, spirits could try to get through to this world by rapping on walls" (Allen 2000, 2).

R had played with the Ouija board by himself. Then began the outbreak of noises, and eleven days later he was devastated by his aunt's death in St. Louis. He returned to the Ouija board, spending hours at the practice and "almost certainly" used it to try to reach his beloved aunt (Allen 2000, 2–6). As R, his mother, and grandmother lay in R's bed and listened to the drumming sound, his mother asked aloud whether this was the aunt's spirit. If so, she added, "Knock three times" (thus adopting a practice of the Fox sisters). The diary records that the three thereupon felt "waves of air" striking them and heard distinct knocks followed by "claw scratchings on the mattress."

POSSESSION?

Then, for approximately four continuous nights, markings appeared on the teenager's body, after which the claw-like scratches took the form of printed words. Whenever the scratching noise was ignored the mattress began to shake, at times violently, and at one time the coverlet was pulled loose (Bishop 1949, 246–47).

R's parents were becoming frantic. They had watched their son become unruly, even threatening to run away, and he seemed to be "on the verge of violence" (Allen 2000, 57). They sought help from a physician, who merely found the boy "somewhat high-strung," then from a psychologist, whose opinions went unrecorded. A psychiatrist found R to be "normal," but "declared that he did not believe the phenomena." A Spiritualist and two Lutheran ministers were consulted (Bishop 1949, 248). One of the latter eventually advised the parents, "You have to see a Catholic priest. The Catholics know about things like this" (Allen 2000, 24).

A young priest was called in, but the boy's condition was worsening, and R was admitted to a Jesuit hospital some time between February 27 and March 6. The priest, Father E. Albert Hughes, prepared for an exorcism as seeming poltergeist and demonic outbreaks intensified. Reportedly, the nuns "couldn't keep the bed still," scratches appeared on R's chest, and he began to curse in "a strange language." A later source said it was Aramaic, but a still later "well-documented record" failed to mention "any such language competence" (Allen 2000, 36). The attempted exorcism reportedly ended abruptly when the boy, who had slipped a hand free and worked loose a piece of bedspring, slashed Hughes's arm from the shoulder to the wrist, a wound requiring over a hundred stitches (Allen 2000, 37).

One investigator, however, doubts whether this attack—or even this first exorcism—ever occurred, having searched in vain for corroborative evidence (Opsasnik 2000). In any event, the parents considered making a temporary move to St. Louis, where relatives lived. When this possibility was discussed, the word "Louis" appeared across R's ribs; when the question arose as to when, "Saturday" was seen plainly on his hip; and when the duration was considered, "3 weeks" appeared on his chest. The possibility that R was producing the markings was dismissed on the grounds that his mother "was keeping him under close supervision," but they might have been done previously and only revealed as appropriate, or he might have produced them as he feigned being "doubled up" and screaming in pain.

According to the diary, "The markings could not have been done by the boy for the added reason that on one occasion there was writing on his back" (Bishop 1949, 247). Such naïve thinking is the reason "poltergeists" are able to thrive. A determined youth, probably even without a wall mirror, could easily have managed such a feat—if it actually occurred. Although the scratched messages proliferated, they never again appeared on a difficult-to-reach portion of the boy's anatomy.

In St. Louis, there were more poltergeist-type effects, whereupon Father Bishop (the diarist) was drawn to the case. Bishop left a bottle of holy water in R's bedroom but later—while the boy claimed to have been dozing—it went sailing across the room. On another occasion R's parents found the way into his room blocked by a fifty-pound bookcase. A stool "fell over." Initially, Bishop and another priest, Father William Bowdern, believed R could have deliberately produced all of the phenomena that had thus far occurred in St. Louis, recognizing that stories of alleged incidents in Maryland were, while interesting, hearsay (Allen 2000, 61–76).

Eventually Bowdern changed his view and was instructed by Archbishop Joseph Ritter to perform an exorcism on the boy. Bowdern was accompanied by Father Bishop and Walter Halloran (mentioned earlier as providing a copy of the diary to author Allen), who was then a Jesuit student. Bowdern began the ritual of exorcism in R's room. Scratches began to appear on the boy's body, including the word "HELL" on his chest "in such a way that R could look down upon his chest and read the letters plainly." A "picture of the devil" also appeared on the boy's leg. "Evidently the exorcism prayers had stirred up the devil," the diary states, because, after a period of sleep R "began sparring" and "punching the pillow with more than ordinary force" (Bishop 1949, 255–57).

Soon Bowdern "believed deep in his soul that he was in combat with Satan" (Allen 2000, 117). R thrashed wildly; he spat in the faces of the priests and even his mother; he contorted and lashed out; he urinated. Reports the diary:

> From 12:00 midnight on, it was necessary to hold R during his fights with the spirit. Two men were necessary to pin him down to the bed. R shouted threats of violence at them, but vulgar language was not used. R spit [*sic*] at his opponents many times. He used a strong arm whenever he could free himself, and his blows were beyond the ordinary strength of the boy. (Bishop 1949, 258)

The exorcism continued on and off for days. At times R screamed "in diabolical, high-pitched voice"; he swung his fists, once breaking Halloran's nose; he sat up and sang (for example the "Blue Danube," "Old Rugged Cross," and "Swanee"); he cried; he spat; he cursed his father; he mimed masturbation; he bit his caretakers. On March 18, there seemed a crisis: as if attempting to vomit, R said, "He's going, he's going . . ." and "There he goes." He went limp and seemed back to normal. He said he had had a vision of a figure in a black robe and cowl walking away in a black cloud (Bishop 1949, 257–62).

However, after the priests left, R claimed there were odd feelings in his stomach and cried out, "He's coming back! He's coming back!" Soon the tantrums and routine of exorcism continued. R seemed even more violent, hurling vulgarities, and he had spells of Satan-dictated writing and speech. For example: "In 10 days I will give a sign on his chest[;] he will have to have it covered to show my power." R also wrote, "Dead bishop" (Bishop 1949, 262–69). Subsequently on April 1, between disturbances, the youth was baptized in the rectory.

During all this time the markings—the random scratches and words—continued to appear on R's body. When there was talk of his going to school there, the boy grimaced and opened his shirt to reveal the scratched words, "No school" (Allen 2000, 46), a seemingly childish concern for truly diabolic forces. (The diary mentions only that "No" appeared on the boy's wrists.)

Reportedly, on one occasion R was observed using one of his fingernails (which were quite long) to scratch the words "HELL" and "CHRIST" on his chest. It is unclear whether or not he realized he was being observed at the time. Earlier, the priests reportedly "saw a new scratch slowly moving down his leg" (Allen 2000, 180). This sounds mysterious until we consider that the boy could have made a quick scratch just before the priests looked—which they did because he suddenly "yelped"—and what they observed was merely the after effect of the scratch, the skin's developing response to the superficial injury. (I have produced just such an effect on myself experimentally, observed by *Skeptical Inquirer*'s Ben Radford.)

On April 4, the family decided to return to their Maryland home due to the father's need to work and the need to relieve the strain on the Missouri relatives. But after five days R was sent back to St. Louis and admitted to a hospital run by an order of monks. He was put in a security room that had bars on its single window and straps on the bed. During the days the teenager studied the catechism and was taken on outings, but at night the "possession" continued. There were failed attempts to give him Holy Communion, "the devil" at one point saying (according to the diary), that he would not permit it (Bishop 1949, 282).

On April 18, R again announced, "He's gone!" This time, he said, he had a vision of "a very beautiful man wearing a white robe and holding a fiery sword." With it the figure (presumably Jesus) drove the devil into a pit. There were no further episodes, and Father Bishop (1949, 291) recorded that on August 19, 1951, R and his parents visited the brothers who had cared for him. "R, now 16, is a fine young man," he wrote. "His father and mother also became Catholic, having received their first Holy Communion on Christmas Day, 1950."

AFTERMATH

Was R possessed? Or did superstition mask a troubled youth's problems and invite elaborate role-playing? Interestingly, Archbishop Ritter appointed a Jesuit philosophy professor to investigate the matter. According to a reportedly informed source, the investigator concluded that R "was not the victim of diabolical possession" (Allen 2000, 234). Without wishing to make a categorical judgment, Halloran states that R did not exhibit prodigious strength, showing nothing more than what could be summoned by an agitated teenager. As to speaking in Latin, Halloran thought that was nothing more than the boy's having heard repetitious Latin phrases from the exorcising priest. (On one occasion "the devil reportedly spoke school kids' 'pig Latin'"!)

Nothing that was reliably reported in the case was beyond the abilities of a teenager to produce. The tantrums, "trances," moved furniture, hurled objects, automatic writing, superficial scratches, and other phenomena were just the kinds of things someone of R's age could accomplish, just as others have done before and since. Indeed, the elements of "poltergeist phenomena," "spirit communication," and "demonic possession"—taken both separately and, especially, together, as one progressed to the other—suggest nothing so much as role-playing involving trickery. So does the stereotypical storybook portrayal of "the devil" throughout.

Writer Mark Opsasnik (2000) investigated the case, tracing the family's home to Cottage City, Maryland (not Mount Rainier, as once thought), and talked to R's neighbors and childhood friends. According to their recollections, the boy had been a very clever trickster who had pulled pranks to frighten his mother and to fool children in the neighborhood. "There was no possession," Opsasnik told the *Washington Post.* "The kid was just a prankster" (Saulny 2000).

Of course, the fact that the boy wanted to engage in such extreme antics over a period of three months does suggest he was emotionally disturbed. Teenagers typically have problems, and R seemed to have trouble adjusting—to school, his sexual awareness, and other concerns. To an extent, of course, he was challenging authority as part of his self-development, and he was no doubt enjoying the attention. But there is simply no credible evidence to suggest that the boy was possessed by demons or evil spirits.

A Catholic scholar, Reverend Richard McBrien, who formerly chaired Notre Dame's theology department, states that he is "exceedingly skeptical" of all alleged possession cases. He told the *Philadelphia Daily News* (which also interviewed me for a critical look at the subject), "Whenever I see reports of exorcisms, I never believe them." He has concluded that "in olden times, long before there was a discipline known as psychiatry and long before medical advances . . . what caused possession was really forms of mental or physical illness (Adamson 2000). Elsewhere, McBrien (1991) has said that the practice of exorcism—and by inference a belief in demon possession—"holds the faith up to ridicule." Let us hope that the enlightened view, rather than the occult one, prevails.

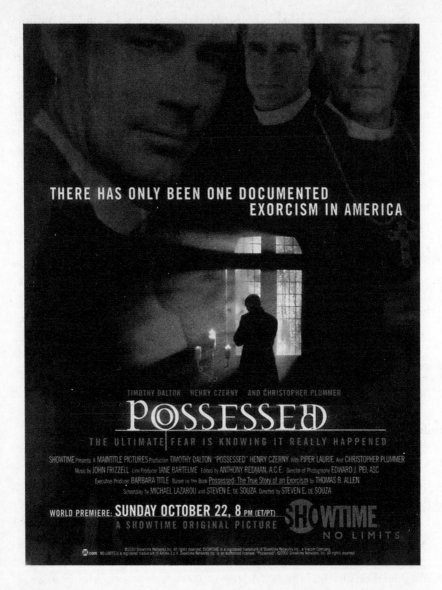

Figure 52.1. A made-for-TV movie tells the story of the case behind *The Exorcist*.

CHAPTER 53

HORROR AT AMITYVILLE

The bestselling book *The Amityville Horror: A True Story* was followed by a movie of the same title and a sequel, *Amityville II: The Possession*. Although the original event proved to be a hoax, that fact does not seem well known to the general public. Now a new book sheds new light on the sordid affair and reviews the multiple-murder case that preceded it. Written by Ric Osuna (2002), it is titled *The Night the DeFeos Died: Reinvestigating the Amityville Murders* (figure 53.1).

The saga began on November 13, 1974, with the murders of Ronald DeFeo Sr., his wife Louise, and their two sons and two daughters. The six were shot while they slept in their home in Amityville, New York, a community on Long Island. Subsequently the sole remaining family member—Ronald Jr., nicknamed "Butch"—confessed to the slaughter and was sentenced to twenty-five years to life. Just two weeks after his sentencing, late the following year, George and Kathy Lutz and their three children moved into the tragic home where—allegedly—a new round of horrors began.

The six-bedroom Dutch colonial house was to be the Lutzes' residence for only twenty-eight days. They claimed they were driven out by sinister forces that ripped open a heavy door, leaving it hanging from one hinge; threw open windows, bending their locks; caused green slime to ooze from a ceiling; peered into the house at night with red eyes and left cloven-hooved tracks in the snow outside; infested a room in midwinter with hundreds of houseflies; and produced myriad other supposedly paranormal phenomena, including inflicting a priest with inexplicable, painful blisters on his hands.

Local New York television's Channel 5 "investigated" the alleged haunting by bringing in alleged psychics together with "demonologist" Ed

Warren and his wife Lorraine, a professed "clairvoyant." The group held a series of séances in the house. One psychic claimed to be ill and to "feel personally threatened" by shadowy forces. Lorraine Warren pronounced that there was a negative entity "right from the bowels of the earth." A further séance was unproductive, but psychics agreed that a "demonic spirit" possessed the house and recommended exorcism (Nickell 1995).

In September 1977 *The Amityville Horror: A True Story* appeared. Written by Jay Anson, a professional writer commissioned by Prentice-Hall to tell the Lutzes' story, it became a runaway bestseller. Anson asserted: "There is simply too much independent corroboration of their narrative to support the speculation that they either imagined or fabricated these events," although he conceded that the strange occurrences had ceased after the Lutzes moved out.

Indeed, a man who later lived there for eight months said he had experienced nothing more horrible than a stream of gawkers who tramped onto the property. Similarly, the couple that purchased the house after it was given up by the Lutzes, James and Barbara Cromarty, poured ice water on the hellish tale. They confirmed the suspicions of various investigators that it was a bogus admixture of phenomena: part traditional haunting, part poltergeist disturbance, and part demonic possession, including elements that seemed to have been lifted from the movie *The Exorcist.*

Researchers Rick Moran and Peter Jordan (1978) discovered that the police had not been called to the house and that there had been no snowfall when the Lutzes claimed to have discovered cloven hoof prints in the snow. Other claims were similarly disproved (Kaplan and Kaplan 1995).

I talked with Barbara Cromarty on three occasions, including when I visited Amityville as a consultant to the *In Search Of* television series. She told me not only that her family had experienced no supernatural occurrences in the house, but also that she had evidence that the whole affair was a hoax. Subsequently, I recommended to a producer of the then-forthcoming TV series *That's Incredible*, who had called for my advice about filming inside the house, that they have Mrs. Cromarty point out various discrepancies for close-up viewing. For example, recalling the extensive damage to doors and windows detailed by the Lutzes, she noted that the old hardware—hinges, locks, doorknob, and so forth—were still in place. Upon close inspection, one could see that there were no disturbances in the paint and varnish (Nickell 1995).

In time, Ronald DeFeo's attorney, William Weber, told how the Lutzes had come to him after leaving the house, and he had told them their "experiences" could be useful to him in preparing a book. "We created this horror story over many bottles of wine that George Lutz was drinking," Weber told the Associated Press. "We were creating something the public wanted to hear about." Weber later filed a two-million-dollar lawsuit against the couple, charging them with reneging on their book deal. The Cromartys also sued the Lutzes, Anson, and the publishers, maintaining that the fraudulent haunting claims had resulted in sightseers destroying any privacy they might have had. During the trials the Lutzes admitted that virtually everything in *The Amityville Horror* was pure fiction (Nickell 1995; Kaplan and Kaplan 1995).

Now Ric Osuna's *The Night the DeFeos Died* adds to the evidence. Ronald DeFeo's wife Geraldine allegedly confirms much of Weber's account. To her, it was clear that the hoax had been planned for some time. Weber had intended to use the haunting claims to help obtain a new trial for his client (Osuna 2002, 282–86).

As to George Lutz—divorced from his wife and criticized by his former stepsons—Osuna states that "George informed me that setting the record straight was not as important as making money off fictional sequels." Osuna details numerous contradictions in the story that Lutz continues to offer versions of (286–89).

For his part, Osuna has his own story to tell. He buys Ronald "Butch" DeFeo's current story about the murders, assuring his readers that it "is true and has never been made public" (18, 22). DeFeo now alleges that his sister Dawn urged him to kill the entire family and that she and two of Butch's friends had participated in the crimes.

In fact, Butch maintains that Dawn began the carnage by shooting their domineering father with a .35-caliber Marlin rifle. Butch then shot his mother, whom he felt would have turned him in for the crime, but he claims that he never intended to kill his siblings. He left the house to look for one of his friends who had left the scene and, when he returned to find that Dawn had murdered her sister and other two brothers, he was enraged. He fought with her for the gun and sent her flying into a bedpost, at which point she fell unconscious. He then shot her.

Osuna tries to make this admittedly "incredible" tale believable by explaining away contradictory evidence. He accepts DeFeo's claim that he altered the crime scene and asserts that the authorities engaged in abuses and distortions of evidence to support their theory of the crimes. Even so, Osuna concedes that "Butch had offered several different, if ludicrous, versions of what had occurred" (33) and that he might again change his story. But he asserts that "too much independent corroboration exists to believe it was just another one of his lies" (370).

I remain unconvinced. Butch DeFeo has forfeited his right to be believed, and his current tale is full of implausibilities and contradictions. Osuna appears to me to simply have become yet another of his victims.

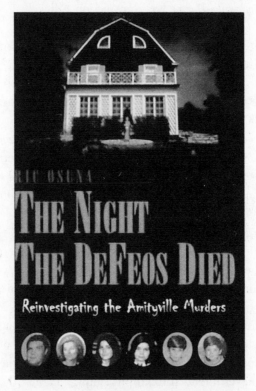

Figure 53.1. Ric Osuna's *The Night the DeFeos Died*.

CHAPTER 54

DEMON VICTIMS I HAVE KNOWN

ATTACK ON A NEW CONVERT

On October 26, 2000, a Canadian radio broadcaster invited me to Southern Ontario to investigate a case of supposed demonic possession (mentioned in chapter 52). Interestingly, it also involved stigmata.

Called to a suburban home in St. Catharines, we found a man and his girlfriend—she claiming to have experienced certain bouts of "possession," none of which we witnessed. She also exhibited various superficial wounds, including a scratched cross that extended down her left arm. (Although such markings are not duplications of the wounds of Christ [see chapter 46], they are still often referred to by extension, as stigmata.)

The couple was Catholic—he a devout doctrinaire sort, who appeared to us quite domineering. Contrastingly, she was a new convert who had been taking church instruction toward that end; she seemed, in a word, cowered. Indeed, she reminded me of certain other women I had seen, who had been battered or bullied, or who otherwise appeared to lack self-esteem.

I have no doubt that she was indeed a "disturbed" person and may genuinely have experienced outbursts of hysteria. However, I suspect neither heaven nor hell had anything to do with her situation other than to stimulate her imagination.

It was difficult to escape the thought that she was going to great lengths to please her lover—even to the point of consciously feigning possession, which she appeared to withstand, no doubt as a supposed indication of her faith, and perhaps inflicting the markings on her body that seemed signs of divine approval. (The markings were no more than scratches and were located just where a right-handed person, like her, could have made them.)

It is even possible she was directed to feign the phenomenon by her boyfriend—hence, perhaps, their having invited the media to their home. I could not help but note the timing: it was only days before Halloween.

DEVIL IN THE GRAVEYARD

A more sensational—or sensationalized—case of alleged demonic attack was the subject of a 1991 book titled *The Black Hope Horror*. I was asked to look into the claims of the authors, Ben and Jean Williams, in preparation for my appearance on *The Maury Povich Show* (taped March 2, 1992).

Reportedly, in 1980, after the Williamses moved into their Texas home in a subdivision at Crosby, Texas, they learned that their house site had once been a cemetery for poor blacks—the abandoned Black Hope Graveyard. After neighbors began to suffer from stress and to experience some strange happenings, suing developers for $2 million on the grounds that (as the *Houston Chronicle* reported) the developers failed to inform them about the graveyard and that their disturbing of the graves had agitated the spirits of the dead. The *Chronicle* added: "The story told in court sounded like the script for a low-budget remake of the movie *Poltergeist*, which concerned a family's struggle to cope with ghosts who revolted because the family's home had been built over their graves" (Tutt 1987).

After a neighbor's court case was underway, the Williamses began to report even more extensive and persistent paranormal phenomena (which, they claimed, extended back to the time they moved in). Every odd occurrence—snakes in the backyard or an infestation of ants in the house, for instance—was interpreted as further evidence of demonic activity. So was the simple malfunction of their automatic garage door. When their eight-year-old granddaughter came to live with them and often saw "shadowy presences," this was considered more proof, even though the girl loved to "daydream" and "pretend" and had "imaginary playmates" that she talked with (Williams, Williams, and Shoemaker 1991, 33, 60–61, 124).

Of all the phenomena they attributed to "the force"—which they equated with "the Devil"—the most profound was the death of their daughter Tina. However, although tragic, her death need not be attributed to the supernatural. She suffered from Hodgkin's disease, which had been in remission, but she then acquired a virus that caused her immune system to attack her heart muscle. She died, in fact, of "a massive heart attack" (Williams, Williams, and Shoemaker 1991, 172–73, 223, 227–29).

In fact, the Williamses were emotional, religious people, given to outbursts—Jean to crying and Ben to shouting at whomever would challenge him—as they demonstrated on *Maury Povich*. Jean Williams avidly read books on "supernatural and paranormal phenomena" and at times almost wished she were a Catholic so she could "attempt an exorcism." When it became awkward to carry a Bible throughout the house, she bought a crucifix, and "the time came when she was walking the halls . . . , reciting prayers aloud, carrying the crucifix in one hand and a thirty-eight pistol in the other." Ben Williams, an asthmatic with elevated blood pressure, sometimes attributed his experiences to "nerves" (Williams, Williams, and Shoemaker 1991, 32, 43, 71, 179, 203, 204).

Ida Ruth McKinney, the then seventy-nine-year-old ranch owner whose father had once owned the subdivision property, said, "I think it's a hoot. Just ridiculous." Insisting that she had never so much as heard a "boo" on the property, she added, "I think somebody's a little off in the head or wants a little money" (Horswell and Friedman 1987). Referring to the case's similarity to *Poltergeist*, McKinney said, "Maybe we'll see a sequel from this." Indeed, on March 3, 1992, CBS aired a made-for-TV movie based on the Williamses' story called *Grave Secrets: The Legacy of Hilltop Drive*. However, as one reviewer observed, "The ghosts aren't as convincing as they should be, and the movie is not scary enough to quicken your pulse" ("Grave Doubts" 1992). (For more on this case, see Nickell 1995, 139–48.)

THE SNEDEKERS' DEMONS

In 1986 the family of Allen and Carmen Snedeker (respectively a stonequarry foreman and former bowling alley cocktail waitress) moved into a former funeral home, the Hallahan House, in Southington, Connecticut. Bizarre phenomena soon began with the oldest son, Philip. He reported seeing spirits, and his personality changed drastically: for example, he reportedly broke into a neighbor's home, telling his mother he wanted a gun so he could kill his stepfather. A seventeen-year-old niece who lived with the Snedekers claimed an unseen hand fondled her on occasion as she lay abed. Other phenomena were reported: strange noises, and even alleged demonic attacks on Carmen Snedeker.

At this point the Snedekers brought in notorious "demonologist" Ed Warren and his "clairvoyant" wife Lorraine. The pair made a business—some would insist a racket—of spirits. They came to be called many things, ranging from "passionate and religious people" to "scaremongers" and "charlatans" (Duckett 1991). Already having helped promote the Amityville "horror" and a similar West Pittston, Pennsylvania, "nightmare" (Curran 1988), the Warrens continued their modus operandi of arriving at a "haunted" house and transforming it into one of a "demonic" nature, in keeping with their own medieval-style Catholic beliefs.

Soon the Snedekers were repeating their claims on national TV shows—notably on *Sally Jessy Raphael*—to promote their book with the Warrens, *In a Dark Place* (Warren et al. 1992). This was written with professional horror-tale writer Ray Garton and its release was timed for Halloween promotion, 1992. I had earlier appeared with Carmen Snedeker on *The Maury Povich Show* (previously mentioned). My investigation intensified when *Sally Jessy Raphael* producers sent me an advance copy of the book by the Warrens and Snedekers, and invited me on the show. Still later I visited Southington as a guest of one of the Snedekers' neighbors, whom I met on the show.

She was Kathy Altemus, and she shared with me her journal of events relating to the Hallahan House, beginning in mid-July 1988. The journal (written records alternating with news clippings) was revealing. For example, a TV program mentioned the sound of chains clanking in the house, but Altemus's journal shows that the noise was most likely from a passing truck that had made a sound like it was "dragging a chain." Other events also had credible explanations, some attributable to various passersby mentioned in the journal as "pulling pranks on the 'haunted house'" (Nickell 1995, 137).

The Snedekers' landlady—who had served them with an eviction notice for failing to pay their rent—had responded to the supernatural claims. She said that she and her husband had owned the property for two and a half years and had experienced no problems with it. Similar views were expressed by the Snedekers' upstairs neighbor, who called the Warrens "con artists." And still more information came to light—regarding Philip Snede-ker's drug use and other misbehavior. As to the "unseen hand" that the niece had reported, Philip was actually caught fondling her while she slept, and he had attempted to have sex with his twelve-year-old cousin. The police took him to a juvenile detention center, where he was diagnosed as schizophrenic (Warren et al. 1992, 145–47).

Several knowledgeable people labeled the Warren-Snedeker-Garton book fiction. The landlady's husband said, "It's a fraud. It's a joke. It's a hoax. It's Halloween." He added, "It's a scheme to make money." Those comments appeared in a newspaper article (Schmidt 1992), brilliantly titled "Couple Sees Ghost; Skeptics See through It." Given the publicity-seeking actions in the case and the timing of the book for Halloween promotion, one may doubt the motives of those involved. If the case did not actually originate as a hoax, I concluded from my original investigation (Nickell 1995, 139), one could hardly be blamed for thinking it was transformed into one.

Indeed, some of the coauthors of the Warrens' books have report-edly admitted that Ed Warren (d. 2006) told them to make up incidents and details to create "scary stories" (Nickell 2006). And Garton has now effec-tively repudiated the book, saying that family members—who had serious problems "like alcohol and drug addiction"—were unable to give a consis-tent account and told "different stories" ("Ray Garton" 2009).

CHAPTER 55

SATAN'S STEP

Munich's twin-towered *Frauenkirche* ("Church of Our Lady")— erected between 1468 and 1488—has a curious legend. It stems from an impression in the foyer's pavement that is said to be *Der Teufelstritt*, or "the Devil's step."

LEGENDS

Supposedly the architect, Jörg von Halspach, made a pact with Satan, who agreed to supply money for the church's construction so long as it was built without a single window in view; otherwise the builder would forfeit his soul. When the church was completed, the architect led the devil to a place where he could view the well-lit nave, yet where no windows could be seen due to their being hidden by the great pillars. Furious, the devil stamped his foot, "leaving his black hoofed footprint in the pavement" (McLachan 2001).

Actually the imprint (see figure 55.1) is not a hoofed one at all, but rather "a footprint of a human being," as it is correctly described in a church flyer ("Black Footprint" n. d.).

One could write an entire treatise on footprints in stone. In addition to those of fairies are footprints of various holy persons, including the Buddha, Jesus Christ, angels, Christian saints, and others, notably the devil (see, for example, Thompson 1955, 1:178–79). Of these, some may have been the effect of imagination applied to natural markings in rock, while others may have been pious frauds.

As to the folktale of the Teufelstritt, it exists in a number of *variants* (as folklorists say) that give evidence of the oral tradition behind it.

The greatest divergence in the varied tales is whether Satan stamped his foot in anger or out of triumph and glee. The latter versions, including the church's own flyer, tend to omit any interaction between the builder and devil and instead have Satan sneaking a view of the newly built church. Standing on the spot from which no windows can be seen and thinking that a windowless building is laughable, "in triumphal happiness he stamped into the floor, where he left this footprint in the ground." But as he took a further step, he saw the many windows: "Out of an anger he changed himself into a great wind and hoped he could blow the building down. But he failed; and since that time there is always a wind blowing around the towers" ("Black Footprint" n. d.).

Despite the variations, all of the accounts focus on the concept of a vantage point from which none of the huge windows can be seen. This is a very real effect, but only if we ignore the great stained-glass window on the opposite end of the church. While that is a replacement (the church was largely destroyed during World War II bombings but later underwent years of restoration), unfortunately for the legend makers there was a window there at the time of the church's completion in 1488. The legend of the nonvisible windows must therefore have originated after 1620, when the window was blocked by a baroque high altar (remaining so until 1858 [*Die Frauenkirche in Munchen* 1999, 10]), thus completing the illusion of no windows.

EXAMINING THE SITE

Moreover, examining the Frauenkirche's legendary footprint, I concluded that it was itself incompatible with its accompanying folktale. Whereas the foyer's pavement is a checkerboard pattern of red and gray marble, the imprint is not in one of those paving stones. Instead (as shown in figure 55.1) it is in a smaller *inset* square—apparently made of concrete and covered over (except for the footprint) with a hard, mustard-colored material that has suffered some cracking and breaking.

The next morning, while I examined and photographed the spot more extensively, Martin Mahner—executive director of the Center for Inquiry Europe—was able to strike up a conversation with the churchwarden. He admitted that the imprint was not genuine, stating that the floor had been restored and that the Teufelstritt was merely a reconstruction.

The churchwarden was uncertain whether the "original" footprint had been destroyed or perhaps was in a museum or in storage somewhere. However, the other evidence of a post-1620 creation still demonstrates that the Teufelstritt and its attendant legend are apocryphal.

A possibly innocent explanation is that the original footprint was put there by a stonemason when the floor was reportedly redone in 1671 (Schmeer-Sturm 1998). It could have been placed merely to mark the spot from which churchgoers could observe what was, after all, an intriguing little illusion. Then, after that purpose was no longer remembered, the legend could have been coined—by that notorious legend maker, Anonymous.

Figure 55.1. "The Devil's footprint" in the foyer pavement of a Munich cathedral. (Photo by Joe Nickell)

CHAPTER 56

FOOTPRINTS OF THE DEVIL?

The case of "The Devil's Footprints" is a classic of the "unsolved" genre, having been featured in Rupert T. Gould's *Oddities: A Book of Unexplained Facts* (1928, 1964); Frank Edwards's *Stranger Than Science* (1959); C. B. Colby's *Strangely Enough* (1971); Rupert Furneaux's *The World's Most Intriguing True Mysteries* (1977); Martin Ebon's *The World's Greatest Unsolved Mysteries* (1981); and many other anthologies and compendia of the unexplained. The fullest account, complete with the original source material, is given by Mike Dash in *Fortean Studies* (1994).

THE TALE

Colby tells the story in concise form:

> There was no denying the footprints in the snow on the morning of February 9, 1855. The odd tracks appeared in several towns in South Devon, England. Residents of Lympstone, Exmouth, Topsham, Dawlish, and Teignmouth all reported the same thing. During the night some weird and uncanny creature had raced in a straight line through these towns, covering a hundred miles and more and leaving behind the tracks nobody could identify.
>
> Each track, about 4 inches in length and 2¾ in width, was exactly 8 inches apart. They were roughly shaped like a hoofprint and were promptly christened "The Devil's Footprints" by all who saw them. Even the conservative *London Times* printed a report of the footprints in the snow. . . .

Going straight across country, the tracks never swerved. They were found upon the top of 14-foot walls and they crossed the roofs of barns and houses, went up and over snow-covered piles of hay and even appeared on the tops of wagons which had been left out all night.

It was as if the creature had leaped up or down, for the tracks showed no apparent change of pace or speed. In many places it was reported that the snow had been "branded" away or melted from the ground where the "feet" had touched. . . .

Over the hundred-mile course, the distance between the tracks never varied from the regular 8 inches, yet how could anyone or anything travel that far in a single night without varying its stride?

Too many people saw the tracks for it to have been a joke or a local phenomenon. In some instances the prints vanished at the edge of unfrozen ponds or rivers, and appeared again exactly in line on the opposite side, to race away in that straight and mysterious flight across the sleeping countryside. And in all that distance, no one saw it, no one heard it. Only the tracks remained as evidence of the creature's passing.

(See figures 56.1–56.3.)

Some sources, like Edwards (1959), incorrectly give the date as February 7, 1855, the confusion resulting from early reports mentioning the night of the eighth. By the seventeenth the story had reached the national newspapers, which published correspondents' accounts through mid-March. Experts from the Zoological Gardens in Regent's Park and from the British Museum were silent, but others offered theories that postulated everything from an escaped kangaroo to birds, rats, cats, foxes, and other creatures. No kangaroo was on the loose, but the naturalist Sir Richard Owen (1855) claimed the solution to the mystery was a badger, based on his interpretation of published drawings and descriptions of some of the tracks. But Owen's solution, like those of others, failed to account for all of the reported factors. As one writer noted, a badger could not have "jumped a fourteen-foot wall or squeezed through a six-inch drain pipe, let alone have left clear marks on the sill of a second-storey window!" (Brown 1982).

So what is the solution? It begins with the acknowledgment that "no one explanation will cover all the reported factors" (Brown 1982). But that statement is meant to imply some further, unknown source—perhaps, as many of the mid-nineteenth-century rural South Devon folk thought, the devil himself.

CONTAGION

Suppose, however, we postulate that the various reports are manifestations of what psychologists call *contagion*—a term I like to define by an example: in 1978, in Holland, a media alert regarding a small panda that had escaped from a zoo in Rotterdam resulted in some one hundred panda sightings made all over the country, yet, as it turned out, the panda had been killed by a train a few yards from the zoo and obviously no one had seen the rare animal (Van Kampen 1979). How do we explain the many sightings? The answer is contagion: an idea or concept that is spread by suggestion, somewhat analogous to a contagious disease. In other words, people's anticipations can lead them to misinterpret what they have actually seen. One person perceives out of the corner of his or her eye a dark shape crossing a yard; thus a dog becomes a "panda." Someone driving in the countryside sees a rustling in some bushes, and so what is actually a native wild animal triggers another panda sighting. Soon, hoaxers will get in on the act and phone in bogus reports. Not surprisingly, contagion is easily recognizable in many paranormal events such as certain UFO and monster "flaps" (Nickell 1995).

Just as there were many sightings attributed to a single panda on the loose in the case in Holland, many factors must surely have been involved during that brief period of near hysteria in February 1855 in South Devon. In fact, although Furneaux (1977) continued to treat the case as a mystery, he briefly suggested the basic explanation of the case:

> On 8 February there had been a slight thaw; more snow fell that night and a freezing wind got up at dawn, enlarging and distorting, perhaps, the prints of hundreds of badgers, otters, rats and cats.
>
> The prints were discovered over a wide area and they were observed by hundreds of people. No one observer tracked them all. Everyone needed to rely on the reports of others. The stories told agreed as to size and shape, because everyone tried to fit his or her observations into the general pattern.

VARIED DESCRIPTIONS

On this last point, however, Furneaux is partially in error. Many of the early descriptions were clearly contradictory, thus helping establish that there were indeed multiple creatures involved. Some drawings showed hoof marks that were "plainly made by a pony-shoe" (Brown 1982), while others described tracks that were "cloven." Some reported "claws" and "toes" in the tracks (Brown 1982; Furneaux 1977).

By no means did all correspondents report tracks of exactly the same size and spacing. For example, the account published in the *Times* (London) of February 16, 1855, stated that the tracks varied from $1\text{-}^1/_2$ to $2\text{-}^1/_2$ inches in width, and while their spacing was "generally" eight inches (Gould 1928, 1964), other sources represented the stride as up to twice that distance (Dash 1994). Nor were the tracks in a straight, unbroken line, as shown by various sources, including a dossier kept in a parish church by Reverend H. T. Ellacombe, who had been vicar in 1855. Says Brown (1982):

> He made careful drawings of the tracks and had found that the marks were *not* continuous, but appeared sporadically, e.g. suddenly in the middle of a field, with a flurry surrounding them, as though made by a large ice-laden bird struggling to take off. It was noticed in the estuary that many of the birds seeking water were liable to become frozen into the water, as has happened in some more recent frosts this century. So birds with ice on their feet seem part of the solution, but not all.

Moreover, Gould (1928, 1964) dismissed as "in the last degree unlikely" that any one person had followed the tracks continuously for the alleged hundred or more miles.

As for Colby's (1971) claim that "the tracks never swerved," that is simply not true. First of all, there is the *Times* report (February 16, 1855): "The creature seems to have approached the doors of several houses and then to have retreated." Indeed, Dash (1994) correctly notes: "Contemporaries reported meandering lines of prints crisscrossing gardens and churchyards," and a map of the area shows the large-scale zigzagging that is necessary to connect all the villages where the tracks were reported (Gould 1928, 1964).

The notion of the unswerving line seems to have originated from accounts that mention that the tracks appeared in a straight line, with one print directly in front of the next. And various animals, such as the donkey, fox, and cat, for example, can leave trails that resemble a single line of imprints. As well, rabbits, hares, rats, and squirrels can leave hopping tracks that not only appear in a straight line but, with their four feet held together, "can form a pattern similar to a hoofmark" (Dash 1994). In any case, one newspaper reported that the tracks were "alternate of each other like the steps of a man and would be included between two parallel lines six inches apart" (Knight 1950).

I believe we can rule out hoaxed tracks like those Brown (1982) mentions at Woodbury, which he says "were obviously manufactured by practical jokers with a hot shoe, since they were said at the time to look like this, the shoe pressed cleanly down to the ground as if made by a hot iron." Surely an iron would not have remained hot for the production of many tracks, thus making the supposed method impractical; and the description seems consistent only with the effect of melting and refreezing that took place.

However, there is ample evidence, in addition to the variety of track descriptions, that multiple creatures were involved. A number of cats, for example, were responsible for many of the tracks in one village, as was explained in 1923 by a woman who had been a young girl there in 1855. As Furneaux (1977) relates:

> She recalled that the footprints were all over the town of Dawlish where her father was Vicar. He and his curates, she said, carefully examined the tracks which ran from the Vicarage to the vestry door, and came to the conclusion that they had been made by the paw-marks of many cats which had been partly washed away by the slight thaw, and expanded into the shape resembling hoofmarks by the early-morning frost. An explanation which, she says, was vehemently rejected by the townspeople who preferred to think they had been visited by the Devil himself. A widespread conviction which the Vicar of Lympstone, the Rev. Musgrave, also found himself unable to dislodge.

In another village, Torquay, a man followed a line of tracks that led from his garden to a tree stump, beneath which he discovered the putative track maker: a large toad! Gordon Stein (1985) has made a very good case for Devonshire foxes making many of the tracks, although he conceded they would have had difficulty scaling fourteen-foot walls or walking on roofs. He suggests that swans might be responsible in the latter instances, except that their footprints do not match those reported. But can we not expect that tracks on roofs, and no doubt in many other out-of-the way locations, were seen at a distance, which would have left their exact appearance to the imagination, a collective imagination it would seem?

CONCLUSION

Clearly, as most writers on the topic agree, no one creature—not even a paranormal one—left all the reported "Devil's Footprints." As Stein (1985) points out, "When no explanation will exactly fit, either we need an additional explanation, or else some of the 'facts' may need to be discarded as weak." I suggest that we need both. We have seen that many of the alleged facts are indeed weak, and only the concept of contagion seems capable of explaining the overall case.

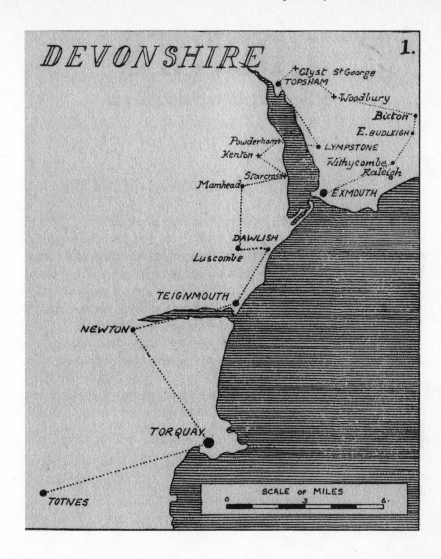

Figure 56.1. Map showing the Devonshire, England, localities in which the "Devil's Footprints" were observed in early February 1855. Contrary to some reports, the trail did not extend in a straight line but zigzagged as shown. (*Illustrated London News*)

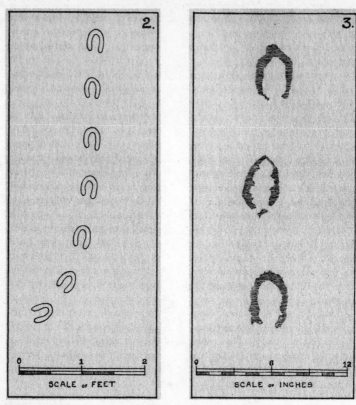

Figure 56.2 (*left*): A sketch of the strange tracks that appeared in the *Illustrated London News*, February 24, 1855. Figure 56.3 (*right*): Another sketch, portraying "hoofmarks," published in the *Illustrated London News*, March 3, 1855.

CHAPTER 57

FIRE FROM HEAVEN— OR HELL?

T he specter of death by inexplicable burning has haunted much of history. In earlier times it was attributed to the supernatural— either "by the visitation of God" (LeCat 1813) or by the legendary "hell's fire" (Arnold 1982, 60).

OCCULT CAUSES?

Apparently spontaneous fires that pseudoscientists today link to *poltergeists* (German for "noisy spirits") might in earlier times have been attributed to witchcraft. Charles Fort (1874–1932)—who made a career of taunting "orthodox" scientists with things they supposedly could not explain—suggested that "'poltergeist disturbances' are witchcraft under a new name" (Fort 1941, 983).

Indeed, in 1744 a sixty-year-old wife of an Ipswich fishmonger, Grace Pett, was found dead with her body still burning. Her daughter extinguished the fire by pouring water on it. Later, some said that Mrs. Pett was a witch and that she had died as one—through what folklorist today call sympathetic magic: she supposedly perished on the same night a farmer's wife had one of their sick sheep burned alive to end what she believed was a spell of bewitchment (Randles and Hough 1992, 20–23). (In fact, Pett had died on the hearth, apparently having ignited her clothes—either as she attempted to light the fire or as she smoked her pipe or as she brushed against a nearby candle. That she had drunk "a large quantity of spirituous liquor" no doubt helped cause the accident [Nickell with Fischer 1988, 152, 168].)

Fort also opined (1941, 662), after describing some mysterious burning deaths, "I think that our data relate not to 'spontaneous combustion of human bodies,' but, like werewolves, or alleged werewolves, mostly pick out women." However, most sources that offer a supernatural explanation attribute such deaths not to sinister, hellish fires but to divine retribution.

HEAVEN SENT?

In the Old Testament, those who engaged in some wickedness might be consumed by "a fire from the Lord" (Numbers 16:35). Leviticus tells how such holy fire consumed two sons of Aaron. One may wonder if this was a real event, but if so, the statement that the pair were using incense and "offered strange fire before the Lord," together with the prohibition against using "strong drink" within the tabernacle in future (Leviticus 10:1–9), suggests that the two men may have had an accident. Perhaps they had been playing with fire, attempting to stage some pyrotechnic effect.

In fact, the second-century Greek traveler Pausanias described how priests in Lydia—under the domination of the Persians—would place on their altars "ashes" of an unusual color, whereupon "the wood soon lights of itself without fire" (Hopkins 1976, 213). Again, a work entitled *Philosophumena* (presumably by St. Hippolytus) explains how ancient priests created illusions by rigging altars: in place of ashes, calcined lime was used, mixed with powdered incense, and it was "only necessary to throw a little water on the lime, with certain precautions, to develop a heat capable of setting on fire incense or any other combustible, such as sulfur and phosphorus" (Hopkins 1976, 213).

SPONTANEOUS COMBUSTION?

If such chemical spontaneous combustion could account for some instances of mysterious burning death, is it possible that spontaneous *human* combustion (SHC) could occur, produced by the body itself in some inexplicable manner? Consider a case discussed by Doctor Claude Nicholas LeCat (1813), who concluded that a victim of 1725 had died "by the visitation of God," but whose death others have attributed to other causes, both scientific and pseudoscientific.

The fiery death was that of a Madame Millet, of Rheims. In February 1725, her burned remains—a portion of the head, a few vertebrae, and lower extremities—were found upon the kitchen floor, a portion of which had also been burned. Her husband was convicted of murdering her; the motive is alleged to have been "an intrigue with a female servant." He was freed, however, after a higher court decided this was a case of spontaneous combustion. But neither assumption is necessary, since the wife reportedly "got intoxicated every day" and was last seen when, unable to sleep, she went to the kitchen "to warm herself." Her remains were found only "a foot and a half's distance" from the fire on the kitchen hearth. Stevenson (1883) suggested that her clothes had been "accidentally ignited" (see also Beck and Beck 1835; Lewes 1861).

The Millet case is typical of many that indicate a correlation between drunkenness and instances of SHC. The temperance movement promoted the notion that alcohol-impregnated tissues were rendered highly combustible. However, scientific experiments easily refuted the notion. Besides, one would die of alcohol poisoning long before imbibing enough alcohol to have even a slight effect on the body's flammability (Lewes 1861, 398).

INVESTIGATING THE CASES

In 1984, after forensic analyst John F. Fischer and I investigated some famous SHC cases, we compiled abstracts of thirty claimed instances of the alleged phenomenon (Nickell and Fischer 1984). Using also a much larger set of abstracts from Randles and Hough (1992), I have since extracted and tabulated data for 120 reported cases from the eighteenth, nineteenth, and twentieth centuries.

The results showed that the alleged phenomenon occurred disproportionately to females (61 percent), who generally live longer than men and are therefore are more likely to be elderly and to live alone. Indeed, victims did tend to be elderly (over sixty years old), or they were ill, infirm, or suspected of intoxication or other diminished capacity (60 percent). Such persons might be more careless with fire and/or less able to effectively respond to an accident.

Also, victims tended to be alone or at least unobserved (90 percent), and the events occurred largely indoors (84 percent), at night (72 percent), and during winter months (46 percent). These conditions would be such as to cause fire victims to encounter matches, candles, oil lamps, coal heaters, stoves, fireplaces, and similar hazards. The conditions would also provide ample opportunities for persons to fall asleep while smoking.

Specific cases are instructive. That of Mary Reeser in St. Petersburg, Florida, in 1951, for instance, involved the plump, sixty-seven-year-old woman wearing a flammable night dress and smoking a cigarette after having taken sleeping tablets. She was sitting in an overstuffed chair that probably burned slowly, fueled by melted body fat in a cyclical process known as the *wick effect.* (For a full study of this case, see Nickell with Fischer 1988, 149–57.)

In another gruesome case, which took place in Chorley, England, in 1980, a crime-scene reconstruction (see figure 57.1) showed that the elderly lady fell into the fireplace (as confirmed by the displaced grate), causing flaming embers to shower upon the body, igniting her clothing. As the fire progressed, once again the wick effect contributed to the destruction. (For a step-by-step reconstruction, see Nickell 2012, 44–45. For additional detailed cases of the alleged phenomenon, under a variety of different circumstances, see Nickell 2001, 2004, and 2012; see also Nickell and Fischer 1984, and Nickell with Fischer 1988.)

In cases of supposed spontaneous human combustion—or earlier heaven- or hell-sent fire—arguments for a paranormal or supernatural cause are invariably based on the logical fallacy of arguing from ignorance: "We don't know what caused the body to burn; therefore we do know: it was SHC." Actually, except in those cases wherein crucial data is lacking, careful investigation and analysis typically yielded plausible, naturalistic explanations. This would appear true of other supernatural or "miracle" claims as well.

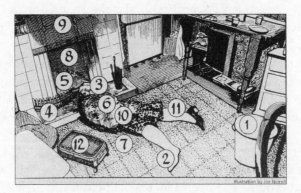

Figure 57.1. Forensic illustration reconstructing an English woman's death that is attributed by some to "spontaneous human combustion." (Drawing by Joe Nickell)

NOTES

Introduction. Toward a Science of Miracles

1. Hume is here using the principle of Occam's razor, which I explain presently.

Chapter 5. The Painting That Performs a Miracle

1. Vaughn Rees used a handheld ultraviolet lamp (both short-wave and long-wave) to examine the area around the cross but the UV showed nothing remarkable.

2. One source claims that any known luminous paint should have ceased to be phosphorescent by now due to oxidation (*Shadow* n. d.). Be that as it may, paintings are often given a protective coat of varnish (Laurie 1967, 169–71), which can improve the longevity and brightness of luminous paints ("Phosphorescent Pigments" 2003).

Chapter 22. In Search of the Emerald Grail

1. St. Lawrence was a deacon of the Roman Church, martyred during the persecution of Valerian in 258 CE.

2. Another source reports that the bowl was booty from Almeria, Spain, taken in 1147 (see Marica 2007, 7).

Chapter 23. St. James's Miraculous Relics

1. The usual Latin word for cemetery is *sepulcretum* (or *sepulcrum*, a place of interment). However, *compono* (with forms *compostus*, *compositum*, and so forth) means "to lay out for burial, place in an urn, bury" (see *Oxford Latin Dictionary* 1969).

Chapter 27. The Belgian Lourdes

1. States Adrien Delcour (1987): "At the price of slight hip dislocation certain rather supple persons (the author of the present lines, for example) can manage without effort to turn their foot around, with the great toe almost to the back by rotation [of] the ankle. This exercise should have been easier for De Rudder because he had lost the extender tendon of the big toe."

Chapter 28. Miracle Dirt of Chimayó

1. Finally, I ran a battery of standard analyses using a commercial soil-test kit, determining that the pH was 7.0 (neutral) and that nitrogen, phosphorous, and potash were at insignificant levels.

Chapter 31. Spiritist Healer: "John of God"

1. At the event I attended in Atlanta on April 4, 2006, at the Renaissance Waverly Hotel, a staffer told me the water could be replenished by refilling the bottle when the level gets low, using ordinary tap water—the original water energizing the newly added.

Chapter 33. Jesus' Resurrection Apparitions

1. For a comparison of the resurrection narratives with ancient ghost stories, see Riley's *Resurrection Reconsidered* (1995, 7–68). He observes that among the ancient Mediterraneans generally, ghosts lacked fleshly substance, yet they still exhibited the phantom wounds that caused their death, thus being recognizable to the living (50–51).

2. Craveri (1967, 219) argues that the story is only a "myth . . . designed to stress the power of faith" and not a misplaced account "based on a subsequent 'vision.'"

3. At the close of Matthew (28:16–17) is an account of the disciples having an apparent vision of the resurrected Jesus at a mountain site, similar to the story of the Transfiguration.

Chapter 35. Eucharistic Signs

1. For an updated discussion of the Shroud of Turin, see Nickell 2007, 122–79.

2. Another version of Luke is in Codex Bezae (Price 2003, 298).

3. In the first instance the man is not stated to be a Jew, but it is implied by his being a "non-Christian" and, stereotypically, a "pawnbroker," and it is further indicated by the similar tale specifically involving Jews assembled in a synagogue.

4. Examination with a 10× Bausch & Lomb illuminated Coddington magnifier reveals that the parchment's text was penned with a quill, in an ink that has the appearance of an age-browned (oxidized) iron-gallotannate variety, and in an italic hand known as cancellaresca (i.e., "chancery" script) because it was widely disseminated by scribes of the papal chancery in the fifteenth and sixteenth centuries (Whalley 1984, 22, 41, 181; Nickell 2003, 123, 131, 140).

Chapter 36. The Secrets of Fatima

1. For a discussion of fantasy proneness, see Wilson and Barber 1983.

Chapter 45. Tijuana's Murderer "Saint"

1. See, for example, Thompson (1955, 403–58), including motifs "The Unquiet Grave" (E410), "Revenant as Blood" (E422.1.11.5), "Ineradicable Bloodstain after Bloody Tragedy" (E422.1.11.5.1), and so on.

Chapter 46. Stigmata: Wounds of Christ

1. I also discovered that one could produce the opposite effect—renewing the bleeding of a cut that was many hours old—by applying hydrogen peroxide. This has implications to cases of stigmata in which bleeding was reported over an extended time, although there are many ways of accomplishing such an effect.

Chapter 47. The Case of Padre Pío

1. For a discussion of fantasy proneness, see Nickell 2001, 84–85, 298–99.

2. The three-inch side wound was seen relatively rarely, and though "most witnesses" said it was cruciform, others described it as being "a clean cut parallel to the ribs" (Ruffin 1982, 147).

Chapter 48. Stigmata of a Convert

1. I am grateful to Martin Braun for advising me of a lecture by Lilian Bernas. Benjamin Radford (*Skeptical Inquirer*) and Jenny Everett (*Popular Science*) accompanied me to witness Bernas's stigmata, and they shared valuable notes and observations. I also received very useful material from John Zachritz.

Chapter 49. Taking Up Serpents

1. Portions of this article were adapted from the author's *Looking for a Miracle* (1998) and *Secrets of the Sideshows* (2005).

Chapter 57. Fire from Heaven—or Hell?

1. Larry Arnold (1995, 338) considers the deaths of Aaron's sons to have been "a double SHC."

REFERENCES

Introduction. Toward a Science of Miracles

Hume, David. 1777. "Of Miracles," included in the posthumous edition of *Enquiries Concerning the Human Understanding and Concerning the Principles of Morals*. 2nd ed. Reprinted London: Oxford University Press, 1902, pp. 109–31.

Lewis, C. S. 1947. *Miracles: A Preliminary Study*. Reprinted New York: Macmillan, 1988.

McGlynn, Hilary, ed. dir. 1997. *Webster's New Universal Encyclopedia*. New York: Barnes & Noble.

Nickell, Joe. 1993. *Looking for a Miracle: Weeping Icons, Relics, Stigmata, Visions, and Healing Cures*. Amherst, NY: Prometheus Books.

Chapter 1. Miracle Idols

Gibson, Walter. 1967. *Secrets of Magic: Ancient and Modern*. New York: Grosset & Dunlap.

Hero of Alexandria. N.d. *The Pneumatics*, reprinted as *The Pneumatics of Hero of Alexandria*, facsimile of 1851 Woodcraft ed., introduced by Marie Boas Hall. New York: American Elsevier, 1971.

Nickell, Joe. 1993. *Looking for a Miracle: Weeping Icons, Relics, Stigmata, Visions, and Healing Cures*. Amherst, NY: Prometheus Books.

Stavroudis, Orestes N. 1979. Letter to author from the Optical Sciences Center, University of Arizona, Tucson, October 24.

Chapter 2. Miracle Statue of Belgium

Mullen, Peter. 1998. *Shrines of Our Lady*. New York: St. Martin's Press.

Nickell, Joe. 1993. *Looking for a Miracle: Weeping Icons, Relics, Stigmata, Visions, and Healing Cures*. Amherst, NY: Prometheus Books.

———. 2004. *The Mystery Chronicles: More Real-Life X-Files*. Lexington: University Press of Kentucky.

Scherpenheuvel: Famous Shrine of Our Lady. N.d. Pilgrimage information sheet in English, provided at the basilica.

Scherpenheuvel-Zichem. N.d. Large, color folder with text in four languages. Brabant, Belgium: Hageland.

Smith, Jody Brant. 1983. *The Image of Guadalupe.* Garden City, NY: Doubleday.

Chapter 3. The Idol of Pachacamac

Pachakamaq: Cíudad sagrada. N. d. An archaeological guide sold on site.

Rachleff, Owen S. 1971. The Occult Conceit: A New Look at Astrology, Witchcraft, and Sorcery. Chicago: Cowles.

Wehner, Ross, and Renée Del Gaudio. 2004. Moon Handbooks Peru. Emeryville, CA: Avalon.

Chapter 4. The Holy *Image of Guadalupe*

Brading, D. A. 2001. *Mexican Phoenix: Our Lady of Guadalupe.* Cambridge, UK: Cambridge University Press.

Callahan, Philip Serna. 1981. *The Tilma under Infrared Radiation.* Washington, DC: Center for Applied Research in the Apostolate.

"El Vaticano." 2002. *Proceso* (May 19): 29–30.

Nickell, Joe. 1997. "Image of Guadalupe: Myth-Perception." *Skeptical Inquirer* 21, no. 1 (January/February): 9.

Nickell, Joe, and John F. Fischer. 1985. "The Image of Guadalupe: A Folkloristic and Iconographic Investigation." *Skeptical Inquirer* 9, no. 3 (Spring): 243–55.

Smith, Jody Brant. 1983. *The Image of Guadalupe.* Garden City, NY: Doubleday.

Chapter 5. The Painting That Performs a Miracle

Casper, Robert F. 2004. Telephone interview by Joe Nickell, August 25.

Chavez, Lorenzo. 2002. "Taos Mystery Painting Puzzles Scientists, Tourists." August 14. http://www.archden.org/dcr/archive/20020814/2002081415wn.htm (accessed August 10, 2004).

Colombo, John Robert. 1996. Letter (with enclosures) to Joe Nickell, July 2.

———. 1999. *Mysteries of Ontario.* Toronto: Hounslow Press.

Crystal, Ellie. 2003. "Apparitions and Miracles." February 14. http://www.crystalinks.com/apparitions.html (accessed August 10, 2004).

Duffy, Michael. 1995. *Anders Knutsson: The Experience of Light.* Available at http://ander sknutsson.com/ (accessed October 15, 2003).

Gaussoin, Helen. 1998. "Ranchos de Taos Painting Shrouded in Mystery." *New Mexico*, December 21.

Laurie, A. P. 1967. *The Painter's Methods and Materials.* New York: Dover.

"Luminescence." 1960. Chicago: Encyclopaedia Britannica.

Michell, John. 1979. *Simulacra: Faces and Figures in Nature.* London: Thames and Hudson.

Nickell, Joe. 2003. "Haunted Plantation." *Skeptical Inquirer* 27, no. 5 (September/October): 12–15.

"Phosphorescence." 1911. Chicago: Encyclopaedia Britannica.

"Phosphorescent Paint Patented." 1879. *Manufacturer and Builder* 11, no. 9 (September): 199.

"Phosphorescent Pigments." 2003. http://www.gtamart.com/mart/products/phspgmnt/ paints.html (accessed October 20, 2003).

Rawson, F. L. 1914. *Life Understood from a Scientific and Religious Point of View.* London: Crystal Press.

Shadow of the Cross. N.d. [1996]. Brochure, San Francisco de Asis, Ranchos de Taos, New Mexico.

Schick, Theodore, Jr., and Lewis Vaughn. 1999. *How to Think about Weird Things.* Mountain View, CA: Mayfield.

Spilsbury Puzzle Company. 1997. Catalog item A3101, "Sunset by the Sea," p. 80.

Chapter 6. Jesus under the Microscope

Nickell, Joe. 1993. *Looking for a Miracle: Weeping Icons, Relics, Stigmata, Visions, and Healing Cures.* Amherst, NY: Prometheus Books.

———. 1997. "In the Eye of the Beholder." *Free Inquiry* 17, no. 2 (Spring): 5.

Chapter 7. Snapshot Miracles

Nickell, Joe. 1993a. "Miracles in Kentucky." *Skeptical Inquirer* 17, no. 2 (Winter): 120–22.

———. 1993b. *Looking for a Miracle: Weeping Icons, Relics, Stigmata, Visions, and Healing Cures.* Amherst, NY: Prometheus Books, pp. 177–78, 196–97.

Chapter 8. Grilled-Cheese Madonna

Chang, Daniel, and Erika Bolstad. 2004. "Virgin Mary Sandwich? Church Won't Likely Bite." *Miami Herald.* http://www.miami.com/mld/miamiherald/living/religion/10280883. htm?template=contentM... (accessed November 29, 2004).

"It's the Son of Cod." 2004. *Daily Telegraph.* http://dailytelegraph.news.com.au/story.jsp?sect ionid=1260&storyid=2282668 (accessed November 29, 2004).

Nickell, Joe. 2004. "Rorschach Icons." *Skeptical Inquirer* 28, no. 6 (November/December): 15–17.

Nohlgren, Stephen. 2004. "Flapjack Jesus Flips along eBay." *St. Petersburg Times.* http:// www.sptimes.com/2007/11/20/state/Flapjack_Jesus_flips_.shtml (accessed November 21, 2004).

Poole, Buzz. 2007. *Madonna of the Toast.* New York: Mark Batty.

"Signs from Heaven." 2006. *Penn & Teller: Bullshit! The Complete Third Season.* Three-volume DVD set, produced by Showtime.

Stollznow, Karen. 2008. "Merchandising God: The Pope Tart." *Skeptical Inquirer* 32, no. 3 (May/June): 45–51.

Thompson, Carolyn. 2004. "Expert Explains Grilled Cheese 'Miracle.'" *Newsday,* November 17.

"'Virgin Mary' Sandwich." 2004. Available online at http://www.cnn.com/2004/us/11/23/ ebay.sandwich.ap/index.html (accessed November 23, 2004).

Chapter 9. Animated Images: The "New" Idolatry

"Idolatry." 1960. *Encyclopedia Britannica.*

"Images." 1993. *Collier's Encyclopedia.*

Kollars, Deb, and Ed Fletcher. 2005. "Weeping or Not, Mary Is a Magnet." *Sacramento Bee,* December 7.

Milbourn, Todd. 2005. "No Probe Is Planned of 'Weeping' Statue." *Sacramento Bee,* November 29.

Nickell, Joe. 1996. "Examining Miracle Claims." *Deolog,* March 4–5, pp. 14, 23.

———. 1997. "Those Tearful Icons." *Free Inquiry* 17, no. 2 (Spring): 5, 7, 61.

———. 1998. *Looking for a Miracle: Weeping Icons, Relics, Stigmata, Visions, and Healing Cures.* Amherst, NY: Prometheus Books. See this source for additional cases and sources.

———. 2002. "Moscow Mysteries." *Skeptical Inquirer* 26, no. 4 (July/August): 17–20, 24.

———. 2005. "'Winking Jesus' Statue: Mystery Solved!" *Skeptical Inquirer* 29, no. 6 (November/December): 7–8.

Rogo, Scott D. 1982. *Miracles: A Parascientific Inquiry into Wondrous Phenomena.* New York: Dial Press.

"Those Who Sway Together Pray Together." 1985. *Discover,* October 19.

Chapter 10. A Weeping Icon and the Crime Laboratory

Christopoulos, George. 1996. "Priest's 2nd 'Miracle': $800G from 'Crying' NY Icon Stolen." *Toronto Sun,* September 8.

DiManno, Rosie. 1996. "Moolah Everywhere as the Pious Mob Weeping Madonna." *Toronto Star,* September 4.

Goldhar, Kathleen. 1996. "Church of 'Weeping' Virgin Headed by Defrocked Priest." *Toronto Star,* September 4.

Kudrez, Anastasia. 1997. "Crying Foul." *Buffalo News,* August 29.

Magnish, Scot, Philip Lee-Shanok, and Robert Benzie. 1996. "Expert Unmoved by Crying Icon's 'Tears.'" *Toronto Sun,* September 4.

Nickell, Joe. 1993. *Looking for a Miracle: Weeping Icons, Relics, Stigmata, Visions, and Healing Cures.* Amherst, NY: Prometheus Books, pp. 54–55.

Chapter 11. The Case of the Miracle Oil

Fernandez, Lisa. 2001. "Pilgrimage: Many Doubt Mysterious Oil Can Heal Pain." *San Jose Mercury News,* February 3.

Nickell, Joe. 1997. "Those Tearful Icons." *Free Inquiry* 17, no. 2 (Spring): 5, 7, 61.

———. 1999. "Miracles or Deception? The Pathetic Case of Audrey Santo." *Skeptical Inquirer* 23, no. 5 (September/October): 16–18.

———. 2008. "Lourdes Medical Bureau Rebels." *Investigative Briefs with Joe Nickell* (blog). http://www.centerforinquiry.net/blogs/entry/lourdes_medical_bureau_rebels/ (accessed April 12, 2010).

Sullivan, Randall. 2004. *The Miracle Detective: An Investigation of Holy Visions.* New York: Atlantic Monthly Press.

Chapter 12. Hindu Statues That Drink Milk

Jayaraman, K. S. 1995. "India's 'Milk Miracle' Is Hard to Swallow." *Nature* 377 (September 28, 1995).

Nickell, Joe. 1996. "Milk-Drinking Idols." *Skeptical Inquirer* 20, no. 2 (March/April 1996): 7. See this source for additional news sources.

———. 2001. *Real-Life X-Files: Investigating the Paranormal.* Lexington: University Press of Kentucky, pp. 312–15.

Chapter 13. The Statues That Glow

Duvall, Edward J. 1952. *Modern Sign Painting.* Wilmette, IL: Frederick J. Drake.

Green, Mike. 2003. "Colorado Capitol Walk." June 22. http://www.angelfire.com/co3/avaconvention2003/taw/denvercapitolarticle01.html (accessed October 13, 2003).

Horton, John. 2003. "Skeptics, Believers Flock to Statues." *Cleveland Plain Dealer,* August 14.

Kubik, Maraline. 2003. "Campbell Statue: It's No Miracle, but It's Nice, Officials Say." *Youngstown Vindicator.* http://www.vindi.com/print/278677665434201.shtml (accessed August 9, 2003).

Nickell, Joe. 2001. "Adventures of a Paranormal Investigator." In *Skeptical Odysseys,* edited by Paul Kurtz. Amherst, NY: Prometheus Books, pp. 219–32.

Owen, Robert E. 1958. *New Practical Sign Painting.* Milwaukee, WI: Bruce.

"Priest Offers Explanation for Glowing Statue." 2003. http://www.onnnews.com/story.php?record=26055 (accessed August 15, 2003).

Sutherland, William. 1889. *The Art & Craft of Sign-Writing.* Reprinted New York: Crescent Books, 1989.

Swierz, Michael. 2003. Interview with Joe Nickell, August 16.

Chapter 14. The True Cross: Chaucer, Calvin, and Relic Mongers

Bella, Francesco, and Carlo Azzi. 2002. "14C Dating of the 'Titulus Crucis.'" *Radiocarbon* 44, no. 3, pp. 685–89.

Calvin, John. 1543. *Treatise on Relics.* Translated by Count Valerian Kasinski, 1854. 2nd ed. Edinburgh: John Stone, Hunter, 1870, pp. 217–18; reprinted, with an introduction by Joe Nickell. Amherst, New York: Prometheus Books, 2009, pp. 49–112.

Chaucer, Geoffrey. Ca. 1386–1400. *The Canterbury Tales.* Various editions (e.g., trans. by Coghill [2003] and Tuttle [2006]; see also *No Fear Literature* [2009] and Dunn [1952]).

Coghill, Nevill, trans. 2003. *Geoffrey Chaucer:* The Canterbury Tales. London: Penguin Books.

Cruz, Joan Carroll. 1984. *Relics.* Huntington, IN: Our Sunday Visitor.

Dunn, Charles W., ed. 1952. *A Chaucer Reader: Selections from* The Canterbury Tales. New York: Harcourt, Brace and World.

Encyclopedia Britannica. 1978. Chicago: Encyclopedia Britannica.

Marica, Patrica. 2007. *Museo del Tesoro di San Lorenzo.* Genoa, Italy: Sagep Edditori Srl.

"Museum of the Treasury of the Cathedral of St. Lawrence of Genoa." N. d. Four-page guide text in English, provided by the museum.

Nickell, Joe. 1990. *Pen, Ink, and Evidence: A Study of Writing and Writing Materials for the Penman, Collector, and Document Detective.* Lexington: University Press of Kentucky.

———. 2007. *Relics of the Christ.* Lexington: University Press of Kentucky.

———. 2009. "Introduction." In *Treatise on Relics* (1543) by John Calvin. Amherst, NY: Prometheus Books, pp. 7–48.

No Fear Literature: The Canterbury Tales *by Geoffrey Chaucer.* 2009. New York: SparkNotes.

Thiede, Carsten Peter, and Matthew d'Ancona. 2002. *The Quest for the True Cross.* New York: Palgrave.

Tuttle, Peter, trans. 2006. The Canterbury Tales, *by Geoffrey Chaucer.* New York: Barnes and Noble Classics.

Chapter 15. The Holy Blood

Aspeslag, Pierre. 1988. *Chapel of the Holy Blood, Bruges.* Ostend, Belgium: s.v. Van Mieghem A.

Bruges Tourist Guide. 1998. Brussels, Belgium: Editions THILL S. A.

Calvin, John. 1543. *Treatise on Relics.* Translated by Count Valerian Kasinski, 1854. 2nd ed.

Edinburgh: John Stone, Hunter, 1870, pp. 217–18; reprinted, with an introduction by Joe Nickell. Amherst, New York: Prometheus Books, 2009.

Catholic Encyclopedia. 1913. New York: Encyclopedia Press.

Coupe, Alison, ed. 2009. *Michelin Belgium Luxembourg* (travel guide). Watford, Herts, England: Michelin Apa.

Kirk, Paul L. 1974. *Crime Investigation.* 2nd ed. New York: John Wiley and Sons.

McDonald, George. 2009. *Frommer's Belgium, Holland & Luxembourg.* 11th ed. Hoboken, NJ: Wiley.

Nickell, Joe. 2007a. "The Netherlands: Visions and Revisions." *Skeptical Inquirer* 31, no. 6 (November/December): 16–19.

———. 2007b. *Relics of the Christ.* Lexington: University Press of Kentucky.

World Desk Reference. 3rd ed. 2000. New York: Dorling Kindersley.

Chapter 16. The Image of Edessa Revealed

Humber, Thomas. 1978. *The Sacred Shroud.* New York: Pocket Books.

"Image of Edessa." 2008. *Wikipedia,* http://enwikipedia.org/wiki/Image_of_Edessa (accessed September 5, 2008).

"Mandylion of Edessa." 2008. In *Vatican Splendors: From Saint Peter's Basilica, The Vatican Museums, and the Swiss Guard.* Vatican City State: Governatorato, pp. 55–58.

Nickell, Joe. 1998. *Inquest on the Shroud of Turin: Latest Scientific Findings.* Amherst, NY: Prometheus Books.

———. 2007. *Relics of the Christ.* Lexington: University Press of Kentucky.

Sox, H. David. 1978. *File on the Shroud.* London: Coronet Books.

Wilson, Ian. 1979. *The Shroud of Turin: The Burial Cloth of Jesus Christ?* Rev. ed. Garden City, NY: Image Books.

———. 1991. *Holy Faces, Secret Places: An Amazing Quest for the Face of Jesus.* New York: Doubleday.

Chapter 17. The Holy Mandylion: A Déjà-View

Bozzo, Collette Dufour. 1974. *Il "Sacro Volto" di Genova.* Rome: Instituto Nazionale d'Archeologia e Storia dell' Arte; summarized in Wilson 1991, pp. 88, 113–14, 138.

"Church of St. Bartholomeo degli Armeni." 2009. In *The Holy Face* (official brochure, in English).

"Mandylion of Edessa." 2008. In *Vatican Splendors: From Saint Peter's Basilica, the Vatican Museums and the Swiss Guard.* Vatican City State: Governatorato, pp. 55–58.

Nickell, Joe. 1998. *Inquest on the Shroud of Turin: Latest Scientific Findings.* Amherst, NY: Prometheus Books.

———. 2007. *Relics of the Christ.* Lexington: University Press of Kentucky.

———. 2009. "The Image of Edessa Revealed." *Skeptical Briefs* 19, no. 2 (June): 9–10, 15.

Turner, Jane, ed. 1996. *The Dictionary of Art.* Vol. 20 of 34 vols. New York: Grove's Dictionaries, p. 251, s.v. "Mandylion of Edessa."

Wilson, Ian. 1979. *The Shroud of Turin: The Burial Cloth of Jesus Christ?* Rev. ed. Garden City, New York: Image Books.

———. 1991. *Holy Faces, Secret Places: An Amazing Quest for the Face of Jesus.* New York: Doubleday.

Wolf, Gerhard. 2005. "Circulation of Artifacts in the Mediterranean Area until the 15th Century: The Genovese Mandylion and Its Paleologic Framework." http://www.mpg .de/840449/forschungsSchwerpunkt1 (accessed February 14, 2013).

Chapter 18. Miracle or Fraud? The Turin Shroud

Antonacci, Mark. 2000. *The Resurrection of the Shroud: New Scientific, Medical, and Archeological Evidence.* New York: M. Evans.

Binga, Timothy. 2001. "Report in Progress from the Director of the Center for Inquiry Libraries," June 19.

D'Arcis, Pierre. 1389. *Memorandum to the Avignon Pope, Clement VII*, translated from Latin by Rev. Herbert Thurston, reprinted in Wilson 1979, 266–72.

Garza-Valdez, Leoncio A. 1993. *Biogenic Varnish and the Shroud of Turin.* Cited in Garza-Valdez 1999, p. 37.

———. 1999. *The DNA of God?* New York: Doubleday.

Gove, Harry E. 1996. *Relic, Icon, or Hoax? Carbon Dating the Turin Shroud.* Philadelphia: Institute of Physics.

Humber, Thomas. 1978. *The Sacred Shroud.* New York: Pocket Books.

Larhammar, Dan. 1995. "Severe Flaws in Scientific Study Criticizing Evolution." *Skeptical Inquirer* 19, no. 2 (March/April): 30–31.

McCrone, Walter C. 1993. Letters to Joe Nickell, June 11 and 30.

———. 1996. *Judgement Day for the Turin "Shroud."* Chicago: Microscope.

Nickell, Joe. 1989. "Unshrouding a Mystery: Science, Pseudoscience, and the Cloth of Turin." *Skeptical Inquirer* 13, no. 3 (Spring): 296–99.

———. 1998. *Inquest on the Shroud of Turin: Latest Scientific Findings.* Amherst, NY: Prometheus Books. (Except as otherwise noted, information in this chapter is taken from this source.)

Pickett, Thomas J. 1996. "Can Contamination Save the Shroud of Turin?" Skeptical Briefs 6, no. 2 (June): 3.

Shafersman, Steven D. 1982. "Science, the Public, and the Shroud of Turin." *Skeptical Inquirer* 6, no. 3 (Spring).

Van Biema, David. 1998. "Science and the Shroud." *Time,* April 20, pp. 53–61.

Whanger, Mary, and Alan Whanger. 1998. *The Shroud of Turin: An Adventure of Discovery.* Franklin, TN: Providence House.

Wilcox, Robert K. 1977. *Shroud.* New York: Macmillan.

Wilson, Ian. 1979. *The Shroud of Turin: The Burial Cloth of Jesus Christ?* Rev. ed. Garden City, New York: Image Books.

———. 1998. *The Blood and the Shroud.* New York: Free Press.

Chapter 19. Artistry and the Shroud

Chevalier, Ulysse. 1900. *Etude Critique sur l'Origine du Saint Suaire de Lirey-Chambéry-Turin.* Paris: A. Picard.

Damon, P. E., et al. 1989. "Radiocarbon Dating of the Shroud of Turin." *Nature* 337: 611–15.

Davidson, J. Leroy, and Phillipa Gerry, eds. 1939. *The New Standard Encyclopedia of Art.* New York: Garden City, pp. 226–27.

Janson, H. W. 1963. *History of Art.* New York: Harry N. Abrams, pp. 267, 286.

McCrone, Walter. 1996. *Judgment Day for the Shroud of Turin.* Chicago: Microscope.

Nickell, Joe. 1998. *Inquest on the Shroud of Turin.* Amherst, NY: Prometheus Books.

Polidoro, Massimo. 2010. "The Shroud of Turin Duplicated." *Skeptical Inquirer* 34, no. 1 (January/February): 18.

Chapter 20. Oviedo's Holy Sudarium

Anderson, Mary Jo. "Scientists: Relic Authenticates Shroud of Turin." *World Net Daily.* http://www.wnd.com/2000/10/4279/ (accessed February 14, 2013).

Guscin, Mark. 1998. *The Oviedo Cloth.* Cambridge, UK: Lutterworth Press.

Humber, Thomas. 1978. *The Sacred Shroud.* New York: Pocket Books.

McCrone, Walter C. 1993. Letters to Joe Nickell, June 11 and 30.

———. 1996. *Judgment Day for the Shroud of Turin.* Chicago: Microscope.

Nickell, Joe. 1998. *Inquest on the Shroud of Turin.* Amherst, NY: Prometheus Books.

———. 2001. "Scandals and Follies of the 'Holy Shroud.'" *Skeptical Inquirer* 25, no. 5 (September/October): 17–20.

———. 2007. *Relics of the Christ.* Lexington: University Press of Kentucky.

Whanger, Mary, and Alan Whanger. 1998. *The Shroud of Turin: An Adventure of Discovery.* Franklin, TN: Providence House.

Wilson, Ian. 1979. *The Shroud of Turin: The Burial Cloth of Jesus Christ?* Rev. ed. Garden City, New York: Image Books.

———. 1998. *The Blood and the Shroud.* New York: Free Press.

Chapter 21. Miraculous Relics

Baigent, Michael, Richard Leigh, and Henry Lincoln. 1996. *Holy Blood, Holy Grail.* London: Arrow.

Barber, Richard. 2004. *The Holy Grail.* Cambridge, MA: Harvard University Press.

Bernstein, Amy D. 2004. "Decoding the Da Vinci Phenomenon." In *Secrets of the Da Vinci Code: The Unauthorized Guide to the Bestselling Novel.* 2004. N.p.: *U.S. News & World Report,* pp. 7–15.

Brown, Dan. 2004. *The Da Vinci Code.* New York: Doubleday.

Calvin, John. 1543. *Traité des Reliques,* reprinted in Jean Calvin, *Three French Treatises,* edited by Francis M. Higman. London: Athlone, 1970, pp. 47–97.

"Christian Relics." 2004. *ReligionFacts.* http://www.religionfacts.com/Christianity/things/ relics.htm (accessed February 28, 2005).

Coulson, John, ed. 1958. *The Saints: A Concise Biographical Dictionary.* New York: Hawthorn.

Cruz, Joan Carroll. 1984. *Relics.* Huntington, IN: Our Sunday Visitor.

Frazier, Kendrick. 2005. "In the Land of Galileo, Fifth World's Skeptics Congress Solves Mysteries, Champions Scientific Outlook." *Skeptical Inquirer* 29, no. 1 (January/February): 5–9.

Garlaschelli, Luigi, et al. 1991. Letter published in *Nature* 353 (October 10): 507.

———. 2004. Personal communications, October 15–16; typescript, "Miraculous Italian Blood Relics," n. d.

Jepson, Tim. 2001. *National Geographic Traveler: Italy.* Washington, DC: National Geographic Society.

Lowenthal, David. 1998. "Fabricating Heritage." *History & Memory* 10, no. 1 (Spring). http:// iupjournals.org.history/ham10-1.html (accessed March 7, 2005).

McCrone, Walter. 1996. *Judgment Day for the Shroud of Turin.* Chicago: Microscope.

Nickell, Joe. 1993. *Looking for a Miracle: Weeping Icons, Relics, Stigmata, Visions, and Healing Cures.* Amherst, NY: Prometheus Books.

———. 1998. *Inquest on the Shroud of Turin.* Amherst, NY: Prometheus Books.

Nickell, Joe, and John F. Fischer. 1992. *Mysterious Realms.* Amherst, NY: Prometheus Books, pp. 145–64.

Olson, Carl E., and Sandra Miesel. 2004. *The Da Vinci Hoax.* San Francisco: Ignatius Press.

Pick, Christopher, ed. 1979. *Mysteries of the World.* Secaucus, NJ: Chartwell Books.

Picknett, Lynn, and Clive Prince. 1998. *The Templar Revelation.* New York: Touchstone.

Polidoro, Massimo. 2004. "What a Bloody Miracle!" *Skeptical Inquirer* 28, no. 1 (January/February): 18–20.

"Relics." 1967. *New Catholic Encyclopedia.*

"Relics." 1973. *Encyclopedia Britannica.*

Secrets of the Da Vinci Code: The Unauthorized Guide to the Bestselling Novel. 2004. N.p.: U.S. News & World Report.

Chapter 22. In Search of the Emerald Grail

Baigent, Michael, Richard Leigh, and Henry Lincoln. 1996. *Holy Blood, Holy Grail.* London: Arrow.

Barber, Richard. 2004. *The Holy Grail: Imagination and Belief.* Cambridge, MA: Harvard University Press.

Brown, Dan. 2003. *The Da Vinci Code.* New York: Doubleday.

Calvin, John. 1543. *Treatise on Relics.* Translated by Count Valerian Kasinski, 1854. 2nd ed. Edinburgh: John Stone, Hunter, 1870, pp. 217–18; reprinted, with an introduction by Joe Nickell. Amherst, New York: Prometheus Books, 2009.

Cox, Simon. 2004. *Cracking the Da Vinci Code.* New York: Barnes and Noble.

Encyclopedia Britannica. 11th ed. 1910. New York: Encyclopedia Britannica.

"'Holy Grail' Shattered." 1914. *New York Times,* April 18.

Kunz, George Frederick. 1971. Reprint of *The Curious Lore of Precious Stones.* New York: Dover, 1913.

Lottero, Fabio. 2010. "The Dish of the Last Supper." *CICAP,* available online (in Italian) at http://www.cicap.org/new/articolo.php?id=102013 (accessed January 26, 2010).

Marica, Patrizia. 2007. *Museo del Tesoro.* Genoa, Italy: Sagep Editori Sri.

"Museum of the Treasury of the Cathedral of St. Lawrence of Genoa." N.d. Museum handout in English. Copy obtained by author, October 31, 2009.

Nickell, Joe. 2007. *Relics of the Christ.* Lexington: University Press of Kentucky. (Additional sources given in this source.)

Chapter 23. St. James's Miraculous Relics

Attwater, Donald. 1983. *The Penguin Dictionary of Saints.* London: Penguin, p. 179.

Baker, Robert A., and Joe Nickell. 1992. *Missing Pieces: How to Investigate Ghosts, UFOs, Psychics, and Other Mysteries.* Amherst, NY: Prometheus Books, pp. 221–26.

Blackmore, Susan. 1991. "Lucid Dreaming: Awake in Your Sleep?" *Skeptical Inquirer* 15, no. 4 (Summer): 362–70.

Cavendish, Richard, ed. 1989. *Legends of the World.* New York: Crescent Books, p. 251.

Coulson, John, ed. 1958. *The Saints: A Concise Biographical Dictionary.* New York: Hawthorne Books, p. 237.

El Camino de Santiago. 1990. Travel booklet. N. p., Spain: Ministerio de Transportes, Turismo y Comunicaciones.

Gies, Joseph, and Frances Gies. 1969. *Life in a Medieval City.* New York: Harper Colophon Books, p. 128.

Gitlitz, David M., and Linda Kay Davidson. 2000. *The Pilgrimage Road to Santiago.* New York: St. Martin's Griffin.

Guiley, Rosemary Ellen. 1991. *Harper's Encyclopedia of Mystical and Paranormal Experience.* New York: HarperCollins, s.v. "Karma," "Leys."

Hauck, Dennis William. 2000. *The International Directory of Haunted Places.* New York: Penguin Books, pp. 133–34.

Howatson, M. C., ed. 1989. *The Oxford Companion to Classical Literature.* 2nd ed. Oxford: Oxford University Press, pp. 582–83.

Jones, Alison. 1994. *The Wordsworth Dictionary of Saints*. Hertfordshire, UK: Wordsworth Reference, p. 144.

Kennedy, Richard. 1984. *The Dictionary of Beliefs*. London: Ward Lock Educational, p. 93.

Kurtz, Paul. 1991. *The Transcendental Temptation: A Critique of Religion and the Paranormal*. Amherst, NY: Prometheus Books, pp. 23–26.

MacLaine, Shirley. 2000. *The Camino: A Journey of the Spirit*. New York: Pocket Books.

McBirnie, William Steuart. 1973. *The Search for the Twelve Apostles*. Wheaton, IL: Tyndale House, pp. 87–107.

Neville, Anne. 2000. "Walking a Mile in the Pilgrim's Shoes." Review of MacLaine's *The Camino: A Journey of the Spirit*. *Buffalo News*, July 5.

Nickell, Joe. 1998. *Looking for a Miracle*. Amherst, NY: Prometheus Books, pp. 19–29, 73–77.

———. 2000. "Haunted Inns: Tales of Spectral Guests." *Skeptical Inquirer* 24, no. 5 (September/October): 17–21.

Nooteboom, Gees. 1997. *Roads to Santiago: A Modern-Day Pilgrimage through Spain*. New York: Harcourt.

Oxford Latin Dictionary. 1969. Oxford: Clarendon.

Pick, Christopher, ed. 1929. *Mysteries of the World*. Secaucus, NJ: Chartwell Books, pp. 101–102.

"Santiago de Compostela." 1960. *Encyclopedia Britannica*.

Wilson, Sheryl C., and T. X. Barber. 1983. "The Fantasy-Prone Personality: Implications for Understanding Imagery, Hypnosis, and Parapsychological Phenomena." In *Imagery: Current Theory, Research and Application*, edited by Anees A. Sheikh. New York: Wiley, pp. 340–90.

Woodward, Kenneth L. 1990. *Making Saints*. New York: Simon and Schuster, p. 63.

Chapter 24. "Incorruptible Corpses"

Cruz, Joan Carroll. 1977. *The Incorruptibles*. Rockford, IL: Tan.

Geberth, Vernon J. 1993. *Practical Homicide Investigation*. Boca Raton, FL: CRC Press.

Gonzales, Thomas A., et al. 1954. *Legal Medicine*. 2nd ed. New York: Appleton-Century-Crofts.

MacDougall, Curtis D. 1958. *Hoaxes*. New York: Dover.

Nickell, Joe. 1993. *Looking for a Miracle: Weeping Icons, Relics, Stigmata, Visions, and Healing Cures*. Amherst, NY: Prometheus Books.

———. 1994. "Historical Sketches: Petrified Girl." *Licking Valley Courier*, November 3. (Except as otherwise noted, information on this case is taken from this source, which provides much more detailed documentation.)

———. 2011. *Tracking the Man-Beasts: Sasquatch, Vampires, Zombies, and More*. Amherst, NY: Prometheus Books.

Spitz, Werner U., ed. 1993. *Spitz and Fisher's Medicolegal Investigation of Death*. 3rd ed. Springfield, IL: Charles C. Thomas.

Stein, Gordon. 1993. *Encyclopedia of Hoaxes*. Detroit: Gale Research.

Ubelaker, Douglas, and Henry Scammell. 1992. *Bones: A Forensic Detective's Casebook*. New York: HarperCollins.

Wilson, Colin, and Damon Wilson. 1992. *Unsolved Mysteries Past and Present*. Chicago: Contemporary, pp. 368–400.

Chapter 25. Jesus' Healings

Allegro, John M. 1970. *The Sacred Mushroom and the Cross*. Don Mills, ON, Canada: Paperjacks.

Asimov, Isaac. 1968. *Asimov's Guide to the Bible*. Vol. 1, *The Old Testament*. New York: Avon.

Baker, Robert A. 1990. *They Call It Hypnosis*. Amherst, NY: Prometheus Books.

Budge, E. A. Wallis. 1901. *Books on Egypt and Chaldea*. Vol. 2, *Egyptian Magic*. London: Kegan Paul, Trench, Trubner.

Carroll, Davod. 1975. *The Magic Makers: Magic and Sorcery through the Ages*. Scarborough, ON: New American Library of Canada.

Craveri, Marcello. 1970. *The Life of Jesus*. New York: Grove Press.

Dummelow, Rev. J. R., ed. 1951. *A Commentary on the Holy Bible*. New York: Macmillan.

Enslin, Morton Scott. 1968. *The Prophet from Nazareth*. New York: Schocken Books.

Graham, Lloyd M. 1975. *Deceptions and Myths of the Bible*. Secaucus, NJ: University Books.

Hines, Terence. 1988. *Pseudoscience and the Paranormal*. Amherst, NY: Prometheus Books.

Larue, Gerald. 1990. *The Supernatural Occult and the Bible*. Amherst, NY: Prometheus Books.

Randi, James. 1987. *The Faith Healers*. Amherst, NY: Prometheus Books.

Spraggett, Allen. 1970. *Kathryn Kuhlman: The Woman Who Believed in Miracles*. New York: Signet.

United Church. 1967. *Sickness and Health*. Report by Canada's largest Protestant group. Cited in Spraggett 1970, pp. 64–65.

Chapter 26. Lourdes and Other Healing Waters

"Fountain of Youth." 2005a. *Web Gallery of Art*. http://www.wga.hu/html/c/cranach/lucas_e/8/0fountain.html (accessed July 1, 2005).

"Fountain of Youth." 2005b. Available at http://www.fountainofyouth.com (accessed July 7, 2005).

"Fountain of Youth." 2005c. http://tfn.net/Springs/FountainofYouth.html/c/cranach/ (accessed July 1, 2005).

Gonzalez, David. 1992. "At Lourdes of Bronx, Where Cooling Hope Flows." *New York Times*, May 27.

Jones, Alison. 1994. *The Wordsworth Dictionary of Saints*. Ware, UK: Wordsworth Editions.

Morris, Linda. 2004. "Priest Offers $5,000 to Disprove Miracles of Lourdes." *Sydney Morning Herald*, August 30.

Nickell, Joe. 1998. *Looking for a Miracle: Weeping Icons, Relics, Stigmata, Visions, and Healing Cures.* Amherst, NY: Prometheus Books.

Ponce de León, Juan. 2005. Available at http://library.thinkingquest.org/J0002678F/ponce_de_leon.htm (accessed July 1, 2005).

Swanner, Grace Maguire. 1988. *Saratoga: Queen of Spas.* Utica, NY: North Country Books.

"Who Wants to Live Forever?" 2000. *Economist,* December 23, pp. 23–24.

Chapter 27. The Belgian Lourdes

Delcour, Adrien. 1987. "A Great 'Lourdes Miracle': The Cure of Pierre de Rudder or, What Is the Value of Testimony?" A paper by Delcour, of Brussels, Belgium. Translated by Jan Willem Nienhuys.

De Meester, Canon A. 1957. "Report of the Holy See of Bruges." Cited in Delcour 1987.

Nieman, Carol. 1995. *Miracles: The Extraordinary, the Impossible, and the Divine.* New York: Viking Studio Books.

Nickell, Joe. 2007. *Adventures in Paranormal Investigation.* Lexington: University Press of Kentucky.

Notre Dame de Lourdes a Oostakker. 1975. Souvenir booklet in French ("Imprimature Gradae, 7–4–1975, O. Schelfhout, vic. Gen."), distributed at the shrine.

Chapter 28. Miracle Dirt of Chimayó

Del Monte, Steven. 2000. Personal communication, October 20.

Eckholm, Eric. 2008. "A Pastor Begs to Differ with Flock on Miracles." *New York Times,* February 20.

El Santuarió . . . a Stop on the High Road to Taos. 1994. Silver Spring, MD: Sons of the Holy Family.

Hamm, Elizabeth Catanach. 2006. "It's a Miracle: Hope, Faith Bond at El Santuario de Chimayó." *New Mexico* (March), pp. 40–45.

Harrington, John Peabody. 1916. Cited in Kay 1987, p. 14.

Hines, Terence. 1988. *Pseudoscience and the Paranormal.* Amherst, NY: Prometheus Books.

"Holy Dirt of Chimayó." 2011. *The Miracle Detectives.* Aired April 10.

Kay, Elizabeth. 1987. *Chimayó Valley Traditions.* Santa Fe, NM: Ancient City Press.

Kutz, Jack. 1988. *Mysteries and Miracles of New Mexico.* Corrales, NM: Rhombus.

Nealson, Christina. 2001. *New Mexico's Sanctuaries, Retreats, and Sacred Places.* Englewood, CO: Westcliffe, pp. 61–63.

Nickell, Joe. 1988. *Secrets of the Supernatural.* Amherst, NY: Prometheus Books, pp. 103–17.

———. 2004. *The Mystery Chronicles: More Real-Life X-Files.* Lexington: University Press of Kentucky, pp. 51–55.

———. 2007. *Relics of the Christ.* Lexington: University Press of Kentucky.

———. 2008. "Lourdes Medical Bureau Rebels. *Investigative Briefs with Joe Nickell* (blog).

http://www.centerforinquiry.net/blogs/entry/lourdes_medical_bureau_rebels/ (accessed February 15, 2013).

Russell, Inez. 2004. "Saving El Santuario: Preservation Process Almost a Miracle." *New Mexico* (December): 36–41.

Chapter 29. Peter Popoff's "Gift of Knowledge"

Alexander, David. 1987. "Peter Popoff's Broken Window." *Free Inquiry* 7, no. 4 (Fall): 47–49.

Asimov, Isaac. 1969. *Asimov's Guide to the Bible. Vol. 2, The New Testament.* New York: Avon Books, pp. 337–39.

Basil, Robert. 1987. "James Randi and *The Faith Healers.*" *Free Inquiry* 7, no. 4 (Fall): 49.

"Benny Hinn" 2002. Biblical Discernment Ministries. http://www.rapidnet.com/~jbeard/bdm/exposes/hinn/general.htm (accessed February 15, 2012).

Garrison, Greg. 1991. "Unmasking Fake Miracles." *Birmingham News*, January 11.

Hines, Terence. 1988. *Pseudoscience and the Paranormal.* Amherst, NY: Prometheus Books.

Kazenske, Donna. 2003. "Spiritual Gifts: The Gift of the Word of Knowledge." *Christian Online Magazine.* Available at http://sites.silaspartners.com/cc/CDA/Content_Blocks/CC_Printer_Friendly_Version_Utility/1,,PTID42281_CHID147904_CIID933680,00.html (accessed February 15, 2013).

Nickell, Joe. 1993. *Looking for a Miracle: Weeping Icons, Relics, Stigmata, Visions, and Healing Cures.* Amherst, NY: Prometheus Books.

———. 2002. "Benny Hinn: Healer or Hypnotist?" *Skeptical Inquirer* 26, no. 3 (May/June): 14–17.

Popoff, Peter. 2001. Letter to Joe Nickell, July 26. (Previously published in *Adventures in Paranormal Investigation*, by Joe Nickell [© 2007 the University of Kentucky Press].)

———. 2002a. Letter to Joe Nickell, n. d. (before June 2).

———. 2002b. Toronto "Miracle Crusade" (live).

———. 2002c. Paid program, BET. November 11.

———. 2003. Paid program, Court TV. April 10.

Randi, James. 1987. *The Faith Healers.* Amherst, NY: Prometheus Books.

Stein, Gordon. 1993. *Encyclopedia of Hoaxes.* Detroit, MI: Gale Research, pp. 219–20.

Steiner, Robert A. 1986. "Exposing the Faith-Healers." *Skeptical Inquirer* 11, no. 1 (Fall): 28–31.

———. 1989. *Don't Get Taken!* El Cerrito, CA: Wide-Awake Books, pp. 124–26.

Chapter 30. Benny Hinn's Miracle Crusades

Baker, Robert A. 1990. *They Call It Hypnosis.* Amherst, NY: Prometheus Books.

"Benny Hinn" 2002. *Biblical Discernment Ministries.* http://www.rapidnet.com/~jbeard/bdm/exposes/hinn/general.htm (accessed February 15, 2012).

Condren, Dave. 2001. "Evangelist Benny Hinn Packs Arena." *Buffalo News,* June 29.

Frame, Randy. 1991. "Best-Selling Author Admits Mistakes, Vows Changes." *Christianity Today,* October 28, pp. 44–45.

Hinn, Benny. 1990. *Good Morning, Holy Spirit.* Nashville: Thomas Nelson.

———. 1999. *Kathryn Kuhlman: Her Spiritual Legacy and Its Impact on My Life.* Nashville: Thomas Nelson.

Nickell, Joe. 1993. *Looking for a Miracle: Weeping Icons, Relics, Stigmata, Visions, and Healing Cures.* Amherst, NY: Prometheus Books.

Nolen, William A. 1974. *Healing: A Doctor in Search of a Miracle.* New York: Random House.

Randi, James. 1987. *The Faith Healers.* Amherst, NY: Prometheus Books, pp. 228–29.

Spraggett, Allen. 1971. *Kathryn Kuhlman: The Woman Who Believed in Miracles.* New York: Signet.

Thomas, Antony. 2001. *A Question of Miracles.* HBO special, April 15.

Underdown, James. 2001. Personal communication, October 23.

Chapter 31. Spiritist Healer: "John of God"

Bragdon, Emma. 2002. *Spiritual Alliances: Discovering the Roots of Health at the Casa de Dom Inácio.* Woodstock, VT: Lightening Up Press.

"Controversial Faith-Healer Schedules Atlanta Visit." 2006. WSB-TV. http://www.wsbtv .com/print/7257434/detail.html (accessed April 4, 2006).

Guiley, Rosemary Ellen. 2000. *The Encyclopedia of Ghosts and Spirits.* 2nd ed. New York: Checkmark Books.

"Is 'John of God' a Healer or Charlatan?" 2005. ABC News, February 8. Available at http:// www.religionnewsblog.com/print.php?p=10253 (accessed April 4, 2006). (The ABC *Primetime Live* broadcast on which this article is based aired February 10, 2005.)

"John of God in Atlanta." 2006a. Available at http://www.johnofgodinatlanta.com (accessed March 15, 2006).

———. 2006b. Personal communication from donjenna@johnofgodinatlanta.com. March 8.

Lucas, Richard. 1972. *The Magic of Herbs in Daily Living.* West Nyack, NY: Parker.

"Miracle Cures." 2006. *Is It Real?* National Geographic Channel. October 9.

Nickell, Joe. 1998. *Looking for a Miracle: Weeping Icons, Relics, Stigmata, Visions, and Healing Cures.* Amherst, NY: Prometheus Books.

———. 2005. *Secrets of the Sideshows.* Lexington: University Press of Kentucky.

Pellegrino-Estrich, Robert. 1995. "John of God." Available at http://www.johnofgod.com/ article.htm (accessed February 21, 2006).

Chapter 32. Healings by a "Victim Soul"

"Desperate Measures." 1999. *48 Hours.* CBS. June 24.

Harrison, Ted. 1998. "Miracle Child." *Fortean Times* (December): 40–41.

"'Little Audrey' Dies after Being in a Coma Since 1987." 2007. Available online at http://www1.whdh.com/news/articles/local/B049239 (accessed April 16, 2007).

Nickell, Joe. 1999. "Miracles or Deception? The Pathetic Case of Audrey Santo." *Skeptical Inquirer* 23, no. 5 (September/October): 16–18.

———. 2006. "The 'New' Idolatry." *Skeptical Inquirer* 30, no. 3 (May/June): 18–21.

Sherr, Lynn. 1998. "The Miracle of Audrey." *20/20.* ABC News transcript no. 1848. October 4.

"Victim Soul." 1999. Episode 4 of *Judging Amy*, CBS, aired October 5. See http://www.tv.com/judging-amy/victim-soul/episode/1754/summary.html?tag=ep_list;ep_title;3 (accessed April 17, 2007).

Weingarten, Gene. 1998. "Tears for Audrey." *Washington Post*, July 19.

Yeuell, Paul. 1999. E-mail to Barry Karr, July 8.

Chapter 33. Jesus' Resurrection Apparitions

Brunvand, Jan Harold. 1978. *The Study of American Folklore: An Introduction.* New York: W. W. Norton.

Budge, E. A. Wallis. 1901. *Books on Egypt and Chaldea.* Vol. 2, *Egyptian Magic.* London: Kegan Paul, Trench, Trubner.

Carroll, David. 1975. *The Magic Makers.* Scarborough, ON, Canada: New American Library of Canada.

Craveri, Marcello. 1967. *The Life of Jesus.* New York: Grove Press.

Dummelow, J. R., ed. 1951. *A Commentary on the Holy Bible.* New York: Macmillan.

Enslin, Morton Scott. 1968. *The Prophet from Nazareth.* New York: Schocken Books.

Fuller, Reginald H. 1971. *The Formation of the Resurrection Narratives.* New York: Macmillan.

Graham, Lloyd M. 1975. *Deceptions and the Myths of the Bible.* Secaucus, NJ: University Books.

Houran, James, and Rense Lange, eds. 2001. *Hauntings and Poltergeists: Multidisciplinary Perspectives.* Jefferson, NC: McFarland.

Nickell, Joe. 2001. "Phantoms, Frauds, or Fantasies? In *Hauntings and Poltergeists: Multidisciplinary Perspectives*, edited by James Houran and Rense Lange. Jefferson, NC: McFarland, 2001, pp. 214–23.

———. 2004. *The Mystery Chronicles: More Real-Life X-Files.* Lexington: University Press of Kentucky.

Price, Robert. 2003. T*he Incredible Shrinking Son of Man: How Reliable Is the Gospel Tradition?* Amherst, NY: Prometheus Books.

Riley, Gregory J. 1995. *Resurrection Reconsidered: Thomas and John in Controversy.* Minneapolis: Fortress Press.

Stravinskas, Peter M. J., ed. 2002. *Catholic Dictionary.* Huntington, IN: Our Sunday Visitor.

Southwell, David, and Sean Twist. 2004. *Conspiracy Files.* New York: Gramercy Books.

Tyrrell, G. N. M. 1973. *Apparitions.* London: Society for Psychical Research.

Wilson, Sheryl C., and T. X. Barber. 1983. "The Fantasy-Prone Personality: Implications for Understanding Imagery, Hypnosis, and Parapsychological Phenomena." In *Imagery: Current Theory, Research and Application,* edited by Anees A. Sheikh. New York: Wiley, pp. 340–90.

Chapter 34. "Visions" behind *The Passion*

Ashton, Joan. 1991. *The People's Madonna: An Account of the Visions of Mary at Medjugorje.* London: Fount, p. 29.

"Book That Inspired . . ." 2004. *Passion-Movie.com.* http://www.passion-movie.com/promote/book.html (accessed February 19, 2013).

Brentano, Clement. 1833. "Life of Anne Catherine Emmerich, Religious of St. Augustine, at the Convent of Agnetenberg, Dulmen, Westphalia." In Emmerich 1904.

Craveri, Marcello. 1967. *The Life of Jesus.* New York: Grove Press.

Doherty, Earl. 2001. *Challenging the Verdict: A Cross-Examination of Lee Strobel's "The Case for Christ."* Ottawa, ON, Canada: Age of Reason.

Emmerich, Anne Catherine. 1904. *The Dolorous Passion of Our Lord Jesus Christ.* 20th ed. Transcribed by Clement Brentano (1833). Reprinted El Sobrante, CA: North Bay Books, 2003.

Gibson, Mel. 2004. Quoted in "The Making of Mel Gibson's *The Passion of the Christ.*" PAX. February 24.

Jensen, Jeff. 2004. "The Agony and Ecstasy." *Entertainment Weekly,* February 20.

Neff, David. 2004. "The passion of Mel Gibson." *Christianity Today* (March): 30–35.

Nickell, Joe. 1993. *Looking for a Miracle: Weeping Icons, Relics, Stigmata, Visions, and Healing Cures.* Amherst, NY: Prometheus Books.

———. 2000. "Stigmata: 'In Imitation of Christ.'" *Skeptical Inquirer* 24, no. 1 (July/August): 24–28.

———. 2004. "The Stigmata of Lilian Bernas." *Skeptical Inquirer* 28, no. 2 (March/April): 17–19.

Price, Robert M. 2003. *The Incredible Shrinking Son of Man: How Reliable Is the Gospel Tradition?* Amherst, NY: Prometheus Books.

Thomas, Cal. 2004. Appearing on *Fox News,* February 21.

Tokasz, Jay. 2004. "With 'Passion.'" *Buffalo News,* February 25.

Wilson, Ian. 1988. *The Bleeding Mind: An Investigation into the Mysterious Phenomenon of Stigmata.* London: Weidenfeld and Nicolson.

Wilson, Sheryl C., and T. X. Barber. 1983. "The Fantasy-Prone Personality: Implications for Understanding Imagery, Hypnosis, and Parapsychological Phenomena." In *Imagery: Current Theory, Research and Application,* edited by Anees A. Sheikh. New York: Wiley, pp. 340–90.

Chapter 35. Eucharistic Signs

Borg, Marcus J., and John Dominic Crossan. 2006. *The Last Week*. New York: Harper San Francisco.

Brunvand, Jan Harold. 1978. *The Study of American Folklore: An Introduction*. 2nd ed. New York: W. W. Norton.

Cruz, Joan Carroll. 1987. *Eucharistic Miracles and Eucharistic Phenomena in the Lives of the Saints*. Rockford, IL: Tan.

Dummelow, J. R., ed. 1951. *A Commentary on the Holy Bible by Various Writers*. New York: Macmillan.

"Eucharistic Miracles of the World." 2007. *Therealpresence.org*. http://www.therealpresence .org/eucharist/mir/engl_mir.htm (accessed September 7, 2007).

Greenler, Robert. 1999. *Rainbows, Halos, and Glories*. Milwaukee, WI: Peanut Butter, pp. 23–64.

Il Miracolo di Torino. 1997. Turin, Italy: Metropolitan Curia of Turin.

McAndrew, James. 1997. *The Roswell Report: Case Closed*. Washington, DC: US Government Printing Office.

McGaha, James E. 2008. Personal communication, February 1.

Nickell, Joe. 2003. *Pen, Ink, and Evidence: A Study of Writing and Writing Materials for the Penman, Collector, and Document Detective*. New Castle, DE: Oak Knoll Press.

———. 2007. *Relics of the Christ*. Lexington: University Press of Kentucky.

Price, Robert M. 2003. *The Incredible Shrinking Son of Man: How Reliable Is the Gospel Tradition?* Amherst, NY: Prometheus Books.

Shapcote, Emily Mary. 1877. *Legends of the Blessed Sacrament*. New York: Burus and Oates.

Stravinskas, Peter M. J. 2002. *Catholic Dictionary*. Huntington, IN: Our Sunday Visitor.

"Turin Cathedral." 2007. *Wikipedia*. http://en.wikipedia.org/wiki/Cathedral_of_Saint_ John_the_Baptist_(Turin) (accessed September 7, 2007).

Valle, Thomaso. N. d. Parchment account of 1453 "miracle" of Turin in the Historical Archives of the City of Turin (part of archive catalog no. 936, in loose papers collection); personally examined October 14, 2004.

Whalley, Joyce Irene. 1984. *The Student's Guide to Western Calligraphy*. Boulder, CO: Shambhala.

Chapter 36. The Secrets of Fatima

Alban, Francis. 1997. *Fatima Priest*. Pound Ridge, NY: Good Counsel Publications.

Arvey, Michael. 1990. *Miracles: Opposing Viewpoints*. San Diego, CA: Greenhaven Press.

Barss, Patchen. 2000. "The Sundance Secret." *National Post* (Canada), May 13.

Dacruz, Rev. V. N. d. Quoted in Rogo 1982, pp. 224–25.

Fleishman, Jeffrey. 2000. "Vatican Says 'Third Secret' Speaks of Renewal." *Buffalo News*, June 27.

Gruner, Nicholas. 2006. "Living Our Daily Lives in Light of the Fatima Secret." Excerpts from interview in *Fatima Crusader* 82 (Spring): 5–10, 40–51. Available online at the *Fatima Network*, http://www.fatimacrusader.com/cr82/cr82pg5.asp (accessed February 15, 2012).

Kramer, Paul. 2006. "The Third Secret Predicts: World War III and Worse?" Fatima Crusader 82 (Spring): 11–13, 52–62. Available online at the *Fatima Network*, http://www.fatimacrusader.com/cr82/cr82pg11.asp (accessed February 15, 2012).

Larue, Gerald A. 1990. *The Supernatural, the Occult, and the Bible*. Amherst, NY: Prometheus Books.

"Lúcia Santos." 2008. *Wikipedia*. http://en.wikipedia.org/wiki/Lucia_dos_Santos (accessed September 3, 2008).

Long, Becky. 1992. "The Conyers Apparitions." *Georgia Skeptic* 5, no. 2 (March/April): 3.

Nickell, Joe. 1989. *The Magic Detectives*. Amherst, NY: Prometheus Books.

———. 1993. *Looking for a Miracle: Weeping Icons, Relics, Stigmata, Visions, and Healing Cures*. Amherst, NY: Prometheus Books. (The present discussion is largely abridged from this work—pages 176–81—and expanded to include revelation of the Third Secret.)

Oliveira, Mario de. 1999. *Fátima Nunca Mais* (*Fatima Never Again*). Porto, Portugal: Campo des Letras.

Rogo, Scott D. 1982. *Miracles: A Parascientific Inquiry into Wondrous Phenomena*. New York: Dial Press.

Sebastian, Don. 2008. "50 People Looking for Solar Image of Mary Lose Sight." *DNA*. http://www.dnaindia.com/dnaprint.asp?newsid=1152984 (accessed March 12, 2008).

Valpy, Michael. 2000. "The Vatican, Devotees Clash over Third Secret of Fatima." *Toronto Globe and Mail*, June 27.

"Visions: Messages from the Virgin Mary or Delusions?" 1989. *Los Angeles Times*, April 9.

Wilson, Sheryl C., and T. X. Barber. 1983. "The Fantasy-Prone Personality: Implications for Understanding Imagery, Hypnosis, and Parapsychological Phenomena." In *Imagery: Current Theory, Research and Application*, edited by Anees A. Sheikh. New York: Wiley, pp. 340–90.

Zimdars-Swartz, Sandra L. 1991. *Encountering Mary*. Princeton, NJ: Princeton University Press.

Chapter 37. The Medjugorje Phenomenon

Nickell, Joe. 1995. *Entities: Angels, Spirits, Demons, and Other Alien Beings*. Amherst, NY: Prometheus Books. (See this source for additional references.)

Prather, Paul. 1992. "Cold Spring Wasn't Visited by Virgin Mary, Bishop Says." *Lexington Herald-Leader*, September 2.

Sheler, Jeffrey L., et al. 1990. "What's in a Vision?" *U.S. News & World Report*, March 12.

Sudetic, Chuck. 1990. "Do 4 Behold the Virgin? Bishop Is Not a Believer." *New York Times International*, September 28.

Chapter 38. Guardian Angel Encounters

Baker, Robert A. 1995. "Afterword" in Nickell 1995, pp. 275–85.

Brunvand, Jan Harold. 2000. *The Truth Never Stands in the Way of a Good Story!* Chicago: University of Illinois.

Burnham, Sophy. 1990. *A Book of Angels.* New York: Ballantine Books.

Clarke, David. 2004. *The Angel of Mons: Phantom Soldiers and Ghostly Guardians.* Chichester, UK: John Wiley & Sons.

"Experts Call 'Hugo Christ' Photo Fake." 1990. *Charleston Evening Post*, April 12.

Graham, Billy. 1975. *Angels: God's Secret Agents.* Garden City, NY: Doubleday.

Guiley, Rosemary Ellen. 1991. *Harper's Encyclopedia of Mystical and Paranormal Experience.* New York: HarperCollins.

———. 1993. "A Radiance of Angels." *Fate* (December): 60–68.

"Headline News." 1993. *CNN/Time/Newsweek* poll cited December 18.

Holzer, Hans. 1993. *America's Restless Ghosts.* Stamford, CT: Longmeadow Press.

Larue, Gerald A. 1990. *The Supernatural, the Occult, and the Bible.* Amherst, NY: Prometheus Books.

Malz, Betty. 1993. Photograph and letter to Joe Nickell, March 17.

Nickell, Joe. 1995. *Entities: Angels, Spirits, Demons, and Other Alien Beings.* Amherst, NY: Prometheus Books. (A portion of the material for this chapter was taken from this source.)

———. 2001. *Real-Life X-Files: Investigating the Paranormal.* Lexington: University Press of Kentucky.

———. 2007. *Adventures in Paranormal Investigation.* Lexington: University Press of Kentucky.

———. 2011. "The Doctor's Ghostly Visitor: Tracking 'The Girl in the Snow.'" *Skeptical Briefs* 21, no. 2 (Summer): 5–7.

Stark, Rodney. 2008. *What Americans Really Believe: New Findings from the Baylor Surveys of Religion.* With Christopher Bader, et al. Waco, TX: Baylor University Press.

Van Biema, David. 2008. "Guardian Angels Are Here, Say Most Americans. *Time.* Available online at http://www.time.com/time/printout/0,8816,1842179,00.html (accessed September 19, 2008).

Willin, Melvyn. 2008. *The Paranormal Caught on Film.* Cincinnati, OH: David & Charles.

Woodward, Kenneth L., et al. 1993. "Angels." *Newsweek*, December 27, p. 54.

Chapter 39. Heaven's Stenographer

"About Vassula Ryden." 1995. Publisher's cover copy for Ryden 1995.

Bernas, Lilian. 1999. *This Is the Home of the Father—This Is Your Home—This Is Heaven: A Glimpse.* Poole, UK: privately printed.

Carroll, Robert J. 1995. "I Am Your Guardian Angel and My Name Is Daniel." In Ryden 1995, ix–xiv.

Christopher, Milbourne. 1970. *ESP, Seers, and Psychics: What the Occult Really Is.* New York: Crowell.

Fowler, Nancy. 1990–93. Purported messages from Jesus (3–8), in *Journal of Reported Teachings and Messages of Our Lord and Our Living Mother* at Conyers, Georgia, USA 1993. ("Compiled by Our Loving Mother's Children," PO Box 309, Conyers, GA 30207), December.

Guiley, Rosemary Ellen. 2000. *The Encyclopedia of Ghosts and Spirits.* New York: Checkmark Books.

Hilton, Ordway. 1982. *Scientific Examination of Questioned Documents.* Rev. ed. New York: Elsevier Science.

Nickell, Joe. 1990. *Pen, Ink, and Evidence: A Study of Writing and Writing Materials for the Penman, Collector, and Document Detective.* Lexington: University Press of Kentucky.

———. 1993. *Looking for a Miracle: Weeping Icons, Relics, Stigmata, Visions, and Healing Cures.* Amherst, NY: Prometheus Books.

———. 1996. *Detecting Forgery: Forensic Investigation of Documents.* Lexington: University Press of Kentucky.

———. 1997. "A Study of Fantasy Proneness in the Thirteen Cases of Alleged Encounters in John Mack's Abduction." In *The UFO Invasion,* edited by Kendrick Frazier, Barry Karr, and Joe Nickell. Amherst, NY: Prometheus Books, pp. 237–44.

———. 2007. *Adventures in Paranormal Investigation.* Lexington: University Press of Kentucky.

———. 2008. "Linguist." *Joenickell.com.* http://www.joenickell.com/Linguist/linguist1.html (accessed April 3, 2010).

Osborn, Albert S. 1978. *Questioned Documents.* 2nd ed. Montclair, NJ: Patterson Smith.

Randi, James. 1995. The Supernatural A–Z. London: Brockhampton Press.

Ryden, Vassula. 1995. My Angel Daniel. Independence, MO: Trinitas.

———. 2004. Lecture at St. John Maronite Rite Catholic Church. Amherst, NY, May 31.

Tokasz, Jay. 2004. "Controversial 'Messenger' to Speak." *Buffalo News,* May 31.

"Vassula Ryden." 2010. *Wikipedia.* http://en.wikipedia.org/wiki/Vassula_Ryden (accessed April 30, 2010).

Wilson, Sheryl C., and T. X. Barber. 1983. "The Fantasy-Prone Personality: Implications for Understanding Imagery, Hypnosis, and Parapsychological Phenomena." In *Imagery: Current Theory, Research and Application,* edited by Anees A. Sheikh. New York: Wiley, pp. 340–90.

Chapter 40. The Mormon Seer

Brodie, Fawn M. 1993. *No Man Knows My History: The Life of Joseph Smith.* 2nd ed. New York: Alfred A. Knopf.

Hansen, Klaus J. 1995. "Joseph Smith." *Encyclopedia of Religion.* Vols. 13–14. New York: Simon and Schuster.

Naiefeh, Steven, and Gregory White Smith. 1988. *The Mormon Murders.* New York: Weidenfeld & Nicholson.

Nickell, Joe. 1997. "The Two: A Fantasy-Assessment Biography." *Skeptical Inquirer* 21, no. 4 (July/August): 18–19.

Persuitte, David. 2000. *Joseph Smith and the Origins of the Book of Mormon.* 2nd ed. Jefferson, NC: McFarland.

Taves, Ernest. 1984. *Trouble Enough: Joseph Smith and the Book of Mormon.* Amherst, NY: Prometheus Books.

Wilson, Sheryl C., and T. X. Barber. 1983. "The Fantasy-Prone Personality: Implications for Understanding Imagery, Hypnosis, and Parapsychological Phenomena." In *Imagery: Current Theory, Research and Application,* edited by Anees A. Sheikh. New York: Wiley, pp. 340–90.

Chapter 41. Visits from the Beyond

Alvarez, Luis W. 1965. "A Pseudo Experience in Parapsychology." Letter in *Science* 148:1541.

Baker, Robert A. 1990. *They Call It Hypnosis.* Amherst, NY: Prometheus Books, pp. 179–82.

Barrett, Sir William. 1926. *Death-Bed Visions: The Psychical Experiences of the Dying.* Reprinted Wellingborough, UK: Aquarian Press, 1986.

Blackmore, Susan. 1991a. "Lucid Dreaming: Awake in Your Sleep?" *Skeptical Inquirer* 15, no. 4 (Summer): 362–70.

———. 1991b. "Near-Death Experiences: In or Out of the Body?" *Skeptical Inquirer* 16, no. 1 (Fall): 34–45.

Falk, Ruma. 1981–1982. "On Coincidences." *Skeptical Inquirer* 6, no. 2 (Winter): 24–25.

Finucane, R. C. 1984. *Appearances of the Dead: A Cultural History of Ghosts.* Amherst, NY: Prometheus Books, p. 195.

Hansel, C. E. M. 1966. *ESP: A Scientific Evaluation.* New York: Scribner's, pp. 186–89.

Jahoda, Gustav. 1970. *The Psychology of Superstition.* Baltimore: Penguin, p. 118.

Jung, C.G. 1960. "Synchronicity: An Acausal Connecting Principle." In *The Collected Works of C. G. Jung,* edited by Sir Herbert Read et al. Bollingen Series, no. 20. New York: Pantheon, pp. 418–519.

Kübler-Ross, Elizabeth. 1973. *On Death and Dying.* London: Tavistock.

Nickell, Joe. 1993. *Looking for a Miracle: Weeping Icons, Relics, Stigmata, Visions, and Healing Cures.* Amherst, NY: Prometheus Books, pp. 34–41.

———. 1996. "Investigative Files: Ghostly Photos." *Skeptical Inquirer* 20, no. 4 (July/August): 13–14.

———. 2001a. *Real-Life X-Files: Investigating the Paranormal.* Lexington: University Press of Kentucky.

————. 2001b. "John Edward: Hustling the Bereaved." *Skeptical Inquirer* 25, no. 6 (November/December): 19–22.

Randles, Jenny, and Peter Hough. 1993. *The Afterlife: An Investigation into Life after Death.* London: BCA; reprinted 1995.

Sagan, Carl. 1996. *The Demon-Haunted World: Science as a Candle in the Dark.* New York: Random House.

Skretny, Judith. 2001. Quoted in Voell 2001.

Steiger, Brad. 2000. Promotional blurb in Wills-Brandon 2000.

Theisen, Donna, and Dary Matera. 2001. *Childlight: How Children Reach Out to Their Parents from the Beyond.* Far Hills, NJ: New Horizon Press.

Voell, Paula. 2001. "Visitations." *Buffalo News,* May 27.

Wills-Brandon, Carla. 2000. *One Last Hug before I Go.* Deerfield Beach, FL: Health Communications.

Wilson, Ian. 1987. *The After Death Experience: The Physics of the Non-Physical.* New York: William Morrow.

Wortman, Camille B., and Elizabeth F. Loftus. 1981. *Psychology.* New York: Knopf, p. 380.

Chapter 42. Miracles—or Parables?

Asimov, Isaac. 1968. *Asimov's Guide to the Bible.* Vol. 2, *The New Testament.* New York: Avon.

Connick, C. Milo. 1974. *Jesus: The Man, the Mission, and the Message.* Englewood Cliffs, NJ: Prentice-Hall.

Craveri, Marcello. 1970. *The Life of Jesus.* New York: Grove Press.

Dummelow, Rev. J. R., ed. 1951. *A Commentary on the Holy Bible.* New York: Macmillan.

Enslin, Morton Scott. 1968. *The Prophet from Nazareth.* New York: Shocken Books.

Chapter 43. Miracle Worker of Amsterdam

Conte, Ronald L. 2006. "Claims of Private Revelation: True or False?" *Catholic Planet.* http://www.catholicplanet.com/apparitions/false01.htm (accessed June 22, 2007).

Daily Miracle: The Eucharistic Experiences, a Summary. 2003. Amsterdam: Lady of All Nations Foundation.

El-Fers, Mohammad. 2002. "The Seeress of Mary in Amsterdam." *Groene Amsterdammer,* June 29.

Messages of the Lady of All Nations. 1999. Amsterdam: Lady of All Nations Foundation.

Nickell, Joe. 1993. *Looking for a Miracle: Weeping Icons, Relics, Stigmata, Visions, and Healing Cures.* Amherst, NY: Prometheus Books.

————. 1995. *Entities: Angels, Spirits, Demons, and Other Alien Beings.* Amherst, NY: Prometheus Books.

————. 2001. "Exorcism: Driving Out the Nonsense." *Skeptical Inquirer* 25, no. 1 (January/February): 20–24.

Punt, Jozef Marianus. 2002. *Statement as Bishop of Haarlem*, May 31. In Sigl 2005, pp. 4–5.

Sigl, Fr. Paul Maria. 2005. *Ida Peerdeman*. Civitella del Tronto, Italy: Family of Mary.

Stravinskas, Peter M. J. 2002. *Catholic Dictionary*. Huntington, IN: Our Sunday Visitor.

Van der Ven, Pieter. 2002. "Van half-gek tot Zalig Is maar een kleine stap" ("From Half-Mad to Beatified Is Just a Small Step"). *Trouw*, June 20.

Chapter 44. Mysteries of Popular Saints

Bernhardson, Wayne. 2004. *Moon Handbooks Argentina*. Emeryville, CA: Avalon Travel.

"Evita Biography." 2005. Available online at http://papercamp.com/biog21.shtml (accessed September 9, 2005).

Fouché, Gwladys. 2002. "Eva Peron." *Guardian*, July 26.

McInnis, Judy B. 2001. Review of Marta Raquel Zabaleta's *Feminine Stereotypes and Roles in Theory and Practice in Argentina before and after the First Lady Eva Perón* (2002). *Delaware Review of Latin American Studies* 2, no. 2 (July 15). Available online at http://www.udel.edu/LAS/Vol2-2McInnis-ZabaletaRev.html (accessed November 7, 2005).

Morrison, Eddy. 2005. "The Colourful Career of Eva Peron." *Spearhead*. http://www.spearhead.com/0412-em.html (accessed November 7, 2005).

Mosca, Alexandria Kathryn. 2005. "The Enduring Legacy of Eva Peron." Available online at http://www.google.com/webhp?sourceid=toolbarinstant&hl=en&ion=1&qscrl=1&rlz=1T4ADRA_enUS435US435#hl=en&tbo=d&qscrl=1&rlz=1T4ADRA_enUS435US435&output=search&sclient=psyab&q=The%20Enduring%20Legacy%20of%20Eva%20Peron&oq=&gs_l=&pbx=1&fp=5a810d94e64ac590&ion=1&bav=on.2,or.r_gc.r_pw.r_qf.&bvm=bv.42553238,d.aWM&biw=1093&bih=445 (accessed September 9, 2005).

Nickell, Joe. 2002. "'Miraculous' Image of Guadalupe Painted." *Skeptical Inquirer* 26, no. 5 (September/October): 13.

"Which Coffin Holds the World's Most Beautiful Corpse?" 1978. In *Out of This World*, edited by Perrott Phillips. Paulton, UK: Phoebus, pp. 115–20.

Chapter 45. Tijuana's Murderer "Saint"

"Juan Soldado." 2009. *Wikipedia*. http://en.wikipedia.org/wiki/Juan_Soldado (accessed May 25, 2009).

Maher, Patrick. 1997. "After They Shot Juan." *San Diego Reader*, December 4. (Refurbished January 30, 2008. Available online at http://www.sandiegoreader.com/news/2008/jan/30/after-they-shot-juan/ [accessed May 25, 2009].)

Nickell, Joe. 2004. "Mythical Mexico." *Skeptical Inquirer* 28, no. 4 (July/August): 11–15.

———. 2006. "Argentina Mysteries." *Skeptical Inquirer* 30, no. 2 (March/April): 19–22.

Schreck, Alan. 1984. *Catholic and Christian.* Ann Arbor, MI: Servant Books.

Thompson. Stith. 1955. *Motif-Index of Folk Literature.* Rev. ed. Vol. 2 of 6 vols. Bloomington: Indiana University Press.

Vanderwood, Paul. 2004. *Juan Soldado: Rapist, Murderer, Martyr, Saint.* Durham, NC: Duke University Press.

Chapter 46. Stigmata: Wounds of Christ

Barbet, Pierre. 1950. *A Doctor at Calvary.* Fr. ed.; Eng. trans. Garden City, NY: Image Books, 1963, pp. 103–20.

Biot, René. 1962. *The Enigma of the Stigmata.* New York: Hawthorn Books.

Coulson, John, ed. 1958. *The Saints: A Concise Biographical Dictionary.* New York: Hawthorn Books, pp. 187–88.

"Francis of Assisi, St." 1960. *Encyclopedia Britannica.*

Harrison, Ted. 1994. *Stigmata: A Medieval Phenomenon in a Modern Age.* New York: St. Martin's Press.

Jones, Alison. 1994. *The Wordsworth Dictionary of Saints.* Ware, UK: Wordsworth Editions, pp. 116–18.

Nickell, Joe. 1993. *Looking for a Miracle: Weeping Icons, Relics, Stigmata, Visions, and Healing Cures.* Amherst, NY: Prometheus Books.

———. 1998. *Inquest on the Shroud of Turin.* Amherst, NY: Prometheus Books, pp. 61–63.

———. 1999. "Thumbs Down on Fox's 'Signs from God.'" *Skeptical Inquirer* 23, no. 6 (November/December): 61.

Radford, Ben. 1999. Film review of *Stigmata. Corrales Comment,* September 25.

Randi, James. 1999. Randi's Archive, James Randi Educational Foundation, July 30.

Rogo, D. Scott. 1982. *Miracles: A Parascientific Inquiry into Wondrous Phenomena.* New York: Dial Press.

Thurston, Herbert. 1952. *The Physical Phenomena of Mysticism.* Chicago: H. Regnery.

Schnabel, Jim. 1993. "The Münch Bunch." *Fortean Times* 70 (August/September): 23–29.

Willesee, Michael (executive producer). 1999. *Signs from God,* Fox, July 28.

Wilson, Ian. 1979. *The Shroud of Turin.* Rev. ed. Garden City, NY: Image Books.

———. 1988. *The Bleeding Mind: An Investigation into the Mysterious Phenomenon of Stigmata.* London: Weidenfeld and Nicolson.

Chapter 47. The Case of Padre Pío

Cruz, Joan Carroll. 1977. *The Incorruptibles.* Rockford, IL: Tan.

"Crying Statue Not a Miracle." 2002. Available online at http://www.ananova.com/news/story/sm_542662.html (accessed March 12, 2002).

Grossman, Cathy Lynn. 2002. "John Paul II Is History's Champion Saintmaker." *USA Today,* October 3.

McCaffery, John. 1978. *Tales of Padre Pío: The Friar of San Giovanni*. Kansas City: Andrews and McMeel.

Moore, Malcolm. 2007. "Italy's Padre Pío 'Faked His Own Stigmata with Acid.'" *Telegraph*. http://www.telegraph.co.uk/news/worldnews/1567216/Italys-Padre-Pío-faked-his -stigmata-with-acid.html (accessed October 24, 2007).

Nickell, Joe. 1993. *Looking for a Miracle: Weeping Icons, Relics, Stigmata, Visions, and Healing Cures*. Amherst, NY: Prometheus Books.

———. 2001. *Real-Life X-Files: Investigating the Paranormal*. Lexington: University Press of Kentucky.

"Padre Pío da Pietrelcina." 2008. *Vatican News Services*. http://www.vatican.va/news_services/ liturgy/saints/ns_lit_doc_20020616_padre-Pío_en.html (accessed April 28, 2008).

"Pío of Pietrelcina." 2008. *Wikipedia*. http://en.wikipedia.org/wiki/Pío_of_Pietrelcina (accessed April 28, 2008).

Rogo, D. Scott. 1982. *Miracles: A Parascientific Inquiry into Wondrous Phenomena*. New York: Dial Press.

Ruffin, C. Bernard. 1982. *Padre Pío: The True Story*. Huntington, IN: Our Sunday Visitor.

Thurston, Herbert. 1952. *The Physical Phenomena of Mysticism*. Chicago: H. Regnery.

Wilkinson, Tracy. 2008. "Padre Pío's Body Attracts Thousands." *Buffalo News*, April 25.

Wilson, Ian. 1988. *The Bleeding Mind: An Investigation into the Mysterious Phenomenon of Stigmata*. London: Weidenfeld and Nicolson.

Chapter 48. Stigmata of a Convert

Bernas, Lilian. 1999. *This Is the Home of the Father—This Is Your Home—This Is Heaven: A Glimpse*. Poole, UK: privately printed.

———. 2002a. Talk at Resurrection Church, Cheektowaga, NY, February 17.

———. 2002b. Remarks to audience at Navy Hall, Niagara-on-the-Lake, Ontario, March 1. (Transcript by Jenny Everett of *Popular Science*.)

Christopher, Kevin. 2003. Letter to editor, *Buffalo News*, July 7.

Nickell, Joe. 1993. *Looking for a Miracle: Weeping Icons, Relics, Stigmata, Visions, and Healing Cures*. Amherst, NY: Prometheus Books.

———. 2000. "Stigmata: In Imitation of Christ." *Skeptical Inquirer* 24, no. 1 (July/August): 24–28.

Thurston, Herbert. 1952. *The Physical Phenomena of Mysticism*. Chicago: H. Regnery.

Tokasz, Jay. 2003. "In Apparent Stigmata, a Question of Belief." *Buffalo News*, June 15.

Wake, Ben. 2001. "The Crucifixion of Lilian Bernas." *Citizen's Weekly* (magazine of the *Ottawa Citizen*), July 8, pp. C7–C9.

Wilson, Ian. 1988. *The Bleeding Mind: An Investigation into the Mysterious Phenomenon of Stigmata*. London: Weidenfeld and Nicolson.

Zeis, John. 2003. Letter to editor, *Buffalo News*, June 27.

Chapter 49. Taking Up Serpents.

Budge, E. A. Wallis. 1901. *Books on Egypt and Chaldea.* Vol. 2, *Egyptian Magic.* London: Kegan Paul, Trench, Trubner.

Encyclopedia Britannica. 1960. Chicago, IL: Encyclopedia Britannica, s.v. "Asp."

FitzGerald, William G. 1897. "The Fabulous Creation." *Strand* (London). Reprinted in *James Taylor's Shocked and Amazed!—On and Off the Midway* by James Taylor and Kathleen Kotcher. Guilford, CN: Lyons Press, 2002, pp. 90–113.

Gardner, Dick. 1962. *The Impossible.* New York: Ballantine Books.

Gibson, Walter. 1967. *Secrets of Magic: Ancient and Modern.* New York: Grosset & Dunlap.

Gresham, William Lindsay. 1953. *Monster Midway.* New York: Rinehart.

Larue, Gerald A. 1990. *The Supernatural, the Occult, and the Bible.* Amherst, NY: Prometheus Books.

Mattison, Chris. 1991. *A–Z of Snake Keeping.* New York: Sterling.

Nickell, Joe. 1998. *Looking for a Miracle: Weeping Icons, Relics, Stigmata, Visions, and Healing Cures.* Amherst, NY: Prometheus Books.

———. 2005. *Secrets of the Sideshows.* Lexington: University Press of Kentucky.

Parsons, Alexandra. 1990. *Amazing Snakes.* New York: Alfred A. Knopf.

Premanand, B. 1994. *Science versus Miracles.* Delhi, India: Indian CSICOP.

Siegel, Lee. 1991. *Net of Magic: Wonders and Deceptions in India.* Chicago: University of Chicago Press.

Smith, Hobart M., and Edmund D. Brodie, Jr. 1982. *A Guide to Field Identification: Reptiles of North America.* New York: Golden Press.

Yardley, Jim. 1992. "Mark of the Serpent, and Poison and Pulpit." *Atlanta Constitution,* February 9.

Chapter 50. Additional Pentecostal Powers

Baker, Robert A. 1992. *Hidden Memories: Voices and Visions from Within.* Amherst, NY: Prometheus Books.

Ditmars, Raymond L. 1959. *Reptiles of the World.* New York: Macmillan.

Nickell, Joe. 1993. *Looking for a Miracle: Weeping Icons, Relics, Stigmata, Visions, and Healing Cures.* Amherst, NY: Prometheus Books.

———. 2005. *Secrets of the Sideshows.* Lexington: University Press of Kentucky.

Samarin, William J. 1972. *Tongues of Men and Angels: The Religious Language of Pentecostalism.* New York: Macmillan.

"Speaking in Tongues 'Linguistic Nonsense,' Says U of T Professor." 1972. *Toronto Star,* August 26.

Chapter 51. Loretto Staircase: St. Joseph's Miracle Carpentry?

Albach, Carl R. 1965. "Loretto Chapel Museum Staircase Wood Analysis: Miracle or a Wonder of Construction?" from *Consulting Engineer*. Photocopy in author's files.

Bobbin, Jay. 1998. "The Staircase." Review in *Buffalo News*, April 12.

Bullock, Alice. 1978. *Loretto and the Miraculous Staircase*. Santa Fe, NM: Sunstone Press.

Dietz, Albert G. H. 1991. *Dwelling House Construction*. 5th ed. Cambridge, MA: MIT Press.

Easley, Forrest N. 1997. *A Stairway from Heaven?* Privately printed.

"Interior Decoration." 1960. *Encyclopaedia Britannica*.

Knight, Christopher. 1997. "Just What Kind of Wood Would a Woodchuck Chuck?" *Wall Street Journal*, October 22, p. B1.

Locke, Jim. 1992. *The Well-Built House*. Rev. ed. New York: Houghton Mifflin.

Loretto Chapel. N. d. Text of display card, photographed by author, 1993.

"Spruce." 1960. *Encyclopaedia Britannica*.

"Stair." 1960. *Encyclopaedia Britannica*.

Stieber, Tamar. 2000. "Loretto Staircase Mystery Unravels." *New Mexico* (January): 62–66.

Chapter 52. Exorcising Demons

Adamson, April. 2000. "Ancient Rite Generates Modern-Day Skepticism." *Philadelphia Daily News*, October 3.

Allen, Thomas B. 2000. *Possessed: The True Story of an Exorcism*. Lincoln, NE: iUniverse.com.

Baker, Robert A. 1992. *Hidden Memories: Voices and Visions from Within*. Amherst, NY: Prometheus Books.

Beyerstein, Barry L. 1988. "Neuropathology and the Legacy of Spiritual Possession." *Skeptical Inquirer* 12, no. 3 (Spring): 248–62.

Bishop, Raymond J. 1949. Typescript diary of an exorcism, April 25; reprinted in Allen 2000, 245–91.

Christopher, Milbourne. 1970. *ESP, Seers & Psychics*. New York: Thomas Y. Crowell.

"Exorcism." 1991. *20/20*, ABC. April 5.

McBrien, Richard. 1991. Interview on Nightline, ABC, April 5.

Nickell, Joe. 1995. *Entities: Angels, Spirits, Demons, and Other Alien Beings*. Amherst, NY: Prometheus Books, pp. 79–82, 119–20.

———. 1998. *Looking for a Miracle: Weeping Icons, Relics, Stigmata, Visions, and Healing Cures*. Amherst, NY: Prometheus Books.

———. 1999. "The Davenport Brothers." *Skeptical Inquirer* 23, no. 4 (July/August): 14–17.

Opsasnik, Mark. 2000. "The Haunted Boy." *Strange Magazine* 20 (serialized on strangemag.com, http://www.strangemag.com/exorcistpage1.html [accessed February 15, 2013]).

Saulny, Susan. 1999. "Historian Exorcises Mount Rainier's Past." *Washington Post*, March 24.

"Vatican Updates Its Rules on Exorcism of Demons." 1999. *Arizona Daily Star*, January 27.

Chapter 53. Horror at Amityville

Anson, Jay. 1977. *The Amityville Horror: A True Story*. New York: Bantam Books.

Kaplan, Stephen, and Roxanne Salch Kaplan. 1995. *The Amityville Horror Conspiracy*. Lacyville, PA: Belfrey Books.

Moran, Rick, and Peter Jordan. 1978. "The Amityville Horror Hoax." *Fate* (May): 44–46.

Nickell, Joe. 1995. *Entities: Angels, Spirits, Demons, and Other Alien Beings*. Amherst, NY: Prometheus Books, pp. 122–29. (Background for the present article has been abridged from this source.)

Osuna, Ric. 2002. *The Night the DeFeos Died: Reinvestigating the Amityville Murders*. N.p.: Xlibris.

Chapter 54. Demon Victims I Have Known

Curran, Robert, with Jack Smurl, Janet Smurl. Ed Warren and Lorraine Warren. 1988. The Haunted: One Family's Nightmare. New York: St. Martin's.

Duckett, Jodi. 1991. *Morning Call* (Lehigh Valley, PA). November 5.

"Grave Doubts." 1992. *Louisville* Courier-Journal, March 3.

Horswell, Cindy, and Steve Friedman. 1987. "'Nothing but Hell There' Says Man Who Fled 'Haunted House.'" *Houston Chronicle*, June 26.

Nickell, Joe. 1995. *Entities: Angels, Spirits, Demons, and Other Alien Beings*. Amherst, NY: Prometheus Books.

———. 2006. "Death of a Demonologist: Ed Warren Dead at 79." *Skeptical Inquirer* 30, no. 6 (November/December): 8.

"Ray Garton." 2009. *Wikipedia*. http://www.en.wikipedia.org/wiki/Ray_Garton (accessed February 27, 2009).

Schmidt, Karen. 1992. "Couple Sees Ghost; Skeptics See through It." *Hartford Courant*, October 30.

Tutt, Bob. 1987. "Ghost Trial Opens Grave Discussion of Fears That Won't Die." *Houston Chronicle*, July 4.

Warren, Ed, Lorraine Warren, Al Snedeker, and Carmen Snedeker, with Ray Garton. 1992. *In a Dark Place: The Story of a True Haunting*. New York: Willard Books.

Williams, Ben, Jean Williams, and Bruce Shoemaker. 1991. *The Black Hope Horror: The True Story of a Haunting*. New York: William Morrow.

Chapter 55. Satan's Step

"Black Footprint." N. d. Flyer from Frauenkirche, Munich, Germany.

Die Frauenkirche in Munchen. 1999. Regensburg, Germany: Schnell & Steiner.

McLachan, Gordon. 2001. *The Rough Guide to Germany.* London: Rough Guides, p. 75.

Schmeer-Sturm, Marie-Louise. 1998. *Die Schwarzen Führer: Munchen, Oberbayern.* Freiburg, Germany: Eulen Verlag.

Thompson, Stith. 1955. *Motif-Index of Folk-Literature.* 6 vols. Bloomington: Indiana University Press.

Chapter 56. Footprints of the Devil?

Brown, Theo. 1982. *Devon Ghosts.* Norwich: Jarrold Colour, pp. 47–53.

Colby, C. B. 1971. *Strangely Enough.* New York: Scholastic, pp. 174–75.

Dash, Mike, ed. 1994. "The Devil's Hoofmarks: Source Material on the Great Devon Mystery of 1855." In *Fortean Studies* 1, pp. 71–151.

Dingwall, Eric J. Cited in "The Devil's Footprints," pp. 102–106, in Ebon 1981.

Ebon, Martin, ed. 1981. *The World's Greatest Unsolved Mysteries.* New York: Signet.

Edwards, Frank. 1959. *Stranger Than Science.* New York: Ace Books.

Furneaux, Rupert. 1977. *The World's Most Intriguing True Mysteries.* New York: Arc Books.

Gould, Rupert T. 1928. *Oddities: A Book of Unexplained Facts.* 3rd ed. New York: Bell, 1964, pp. 9–22.

Knight, W. F. Jackson. 1950. Cited in Dash 1994, pp. 107–109.

Nickell, Joe. 1995. *Entities: Angels, Spirits, Demons, and Other Alien Beings.* Amherst, NY: Prometheus Books. (See index entries for *contagion,* *"copycat" effect,* and *hysteria.*)

Owen, Richard. 1855. Letter to editor, *Illustrated London News,* March 3, quoted in Gould 1928, pp. 16–17.

Stein, Gordon. 1985. "The Devil's Footprints." *Fate* (August): 88–95.

Van Kampen, Hans. 1979. "The Case of the Lost Panda. *Skeptical Inquirer* 4, no. 1 (Fall): 48–50.

Chapter 57. Fire from Heaven—or Hell?

Arnold, Larry E. 1982. "Did Jack Angel Survive Spontaneous Combustion?" *Fate* (September): 60–65.

————. 1995. *Ablaze! The Mysterious Fires of Spontaneous Combustion.* New York: M. Evans.

Beck, Theodric R., and John B. Beck. 1835. *Elements of Medical Jurisprudence.* 5th ed. Vol. 2. Albany, NY: O. Steele et al., pp. 60–68.

Fort, Charles. 1941. *The Complete Books of Charles Fort.* Reprinted New York: Dover, 1974.

Hopkins, Albert A., ed. 1976. *Magic, Stage Illusions, Special Effects, and Trick Photography.* New York: Dover.

LeCat, Dr. Claude Nicholas. 1813. Quoted in Arnold 1995, 29.

Lewes, George Henry. 1861. "Spontaneous Combustion." *Blackwood's Edinburgh Magazine* 89 (April): 385–402.

Nickell, Joe. 2001. *Real-Life X-Files: Investigating the Paranormal.* Lexington: University Press of Kentucky, pp. 28–36, 240–44.

———. 2004. *The Mystery Chronicles: More Real-Life X-Files.* Lexington: University Press of Kentucky, pp. 10–13, 162–64, 339–40.

———. 2012. *CSI Paranormal.* Amherst, NY: Inquiry Press.

Nickell, Joe, and John F. Fischer. 1984. "Spontaneous Human Combustion." *Fire and Arson Investigator* 34, no. 3 (March): 4–11; no. 4 (June): 3–8.

Nickell, Joe, with John F. Fischer. 1988. *Secrets of the Supernatural.* Amherst, NY: Prometheus Books, pp. 149–57, 161–71.

Randles, Jenny, and Peter Hough. 1992. *Spontaneous Human Combustion.* London: Robert Hale.

Stevenson, Thomas. 1883. *The Principles and Practice of Medical Jurisprudence.* 3rd ed. Philadelphia: Lea.

INDEX

Note: *Italicized* page numbers indicate images.

Aaron's rod, 347

Abadiania, Brazil, 213

Abgar (Edessan king), 105–06, 109

adipocere. *See* grave wax

Adler, Alan, 124

Alberto, Marlene, 74

Allen, Thomas B., 372

Altemus, Kathy, 388

Alvarez, Luis, 286

Amityville Horror, The (book), 381, 382

Amityville "horror" hoax, 381–84

Ananias, 105–06, 111

Andrew, St., 139

anecdotal evidence, 293

"Angel, Cloud," 266

Angel of Mons, 265–66

angels, 261–67, *267*, 269

animated images, 57–63, *63. See also* "glow-ing" statues; milk-drinking statues; "weeping" effigies

Anson, Jay, 382

Anthon, Charles, 280

apparitional experiences, 165–66, 227–230, 289–90

argument from ignorance, 74, 216

defined, 74

Arthur, King, 149

Atahualpa (Inca king), 29–30

Augustine, St., 91, 139

Ault, Henri, 35, 38

automata, magical, 22

automatic writing. *See* Ryden, Vassula

Baal. *See* Bel

Bader, Christopher, 261

Baker, Robert A., 207, 265, 288, 370

Barber, Theodore X., 275, 281. *See also* fantasy-prone personality

Barnum, P. T., 169

Bel

idol of, 19–20, *22*

fire miracle and, 20

"Belgian Lourdes," 187–190

belief tales, 225, 228

defined, 228

Benedict XVI, Pope, 254

Bernadette, St. *See* Lourdes

Bernas, Lilian (stigmatist), 341–44, *345, 346*

Besançon, Shroud of, 110

Binga, Timothy, 114, 119

Bishop, Raymond J., 371–72

Blackmore, Susan, 293

Blatty, William Peter, 371

Blavatsky, Madame Helena P., 281–82

Blood, Holy. *See* Holy Blood

Bollone, Pierluigi Baima, 135

Book of Mormon, 279

Borromeo, St. Charles, 170

Bowdern, William S., 371

Brodie, Fawn, M., 279–80

Brown, Dan, 142, 153

Bruge, Holy Blood of. *See* Holy Blood

Brunvand, Jan, 262

Bruse, James, 325

burden of proof, 15

Burnham, Sophy, 261, 264–65

Caiaphas, 236
Calming the Sea, 299–300
Calvin, John, 91, 94–95, 141, 151,
Camino pilgrimage, 159–166
Canterbury Tales, The, 91–94
carbon-14 dating, 126
Carson, Johnny, 199
Cayce, Edgar, 280
Changing Water to Wine, 298–99, *306*
charismatic movement, 202
Charney, Geoffroy de, 120
Charney, Margaret de, 120
Chaucer, Geoffrey, 91–94, 98
Chevaliér, Ulysse 128
Chimayó (healing shrine), 191–96, *196*
Chrétien de Troyes, 142, 150
Christopher, Kevin, 344
Christopher, Milbourne, 373
Church of Jesus Christ of Latter-day
    Saints, 277
Cipac, Marcos, 32
Clement V (pope), 102
Clement VII (Avignon pope), 120
"Cloud Angel," 266
Coin in the Fish, 302
Colby, C. B., 395–96, 398
Cold Spring, Kentucky, 258, 259
Colombo, John Robert, 37
Columbus, Christopher, 149
confabulation, 245
confirmation bias, 137
Constantine the Great, 96
contagion, psychological, 229–30, 397, 400
    defined, 397
Conyers, 185, 258–59
Cook, Mary Jean, 363
Cox, Robert G., 73
Craveri, Marcello, 229
Cromarty, Barbara, 382

Cromarty, James, 382
Crookes, William, 35
cross. *See* True Cross
Crossan, John Dominic, 241
Crowdery, Oliver, 282
Cursing of the Fig Tree, 300–301

D'Arcis, Pierre, 120–21
Davenport brothers, 374
da Vinci, Leonardo, 142
Da Vinci Code, The (book), 142–43, 153
deathbed visions, 291–94
DeFeo, Ronald "Butch," 381, 383–84
DeFeo family murders, 381
Delcour, Adrien, 189
Della Sala, Sergio, 144
demons, 208, 369–79, 381–84, 385–89
Devonshire, England, *401*
Diego, Juan. See *Guadalupe, Image of*
Dietz, Albert G. H., 361
dirt, blessed. *See* Chimayó
DNA evidence, 61, 124
Doctrine of Addai, The (book), 105
Donahue, Ginger, *354*
dowsing, 280
dream contacts, 288–89
Duyser, Diana, 51
Duyser, Greg, 51

Edamaruku, Sanal, 80
Eddy, Mary Baker, 281
Edessa, Image of. *See* Mandylion of Edessa
Embriaco, Guglielmo, 151, *154*
emerald grail, 149–155, *153–55*
Emmerich, Anne Catherine, 233–39
"entities, healing," 214
epilepsy, 369
Eucharistic miracles, 221, 241–46, 310–11
Evans, William, 63

Evita. *See* Peron, Eva

exorcism, 369–79

    Vatican guidelines, 369–70

Exorcist, The (movie), 369

"extraordinary proof" maxim, 15

exuding effigies, 60–62, 65–69, 71–78. *See also* "weeping" effigies

Falk, Ruma, 286–87

Falmouth, Kentucky, 258, 259

fantasy-prone personality, 165, 211, 229, 233, 264, 275, 281–82, 335

    traits of, 281

Fatima, Portugal

    influence of, 311

    "miracles" and "secrets," 249–55

Feeding the Five Thousand, 302–03, *306*

Feeding the Four Thousand, 303–04

fire immunity, 356, *358*

Fischer, John F., 32, 124, 405

folklore, 162–63, 245–46, 320–21

folk saints. *See* saints, popular

Fowler, Nancy, 185, 273–74

Fox sisters, 374

France, Anatole, 184, 195

Francis of Assisi, St., 323–24

Frauenkirche (Munich), 391

Frei, Max, 124–26, 136

Furneaux, Rupert, 397–98

Gallemore, Ronald P., 74

Garlaschelli, Luigi, 130–31, 144–45, *148*

Garton, Ray, 389

Garza-Valdez, Leoncio, 124

generalization technique, 200–01

Geoffroy de Charney. *See* Charney, Geoffroy de

ghostlore, 228

ghost photographs, 287

ghosts, 165–66, 227–30. *See also* apparitional experiences

Gibson, Mel, 233, 235, 239

Gil, Antonio, 315–16

glossolalia, 202, 230, 356–57

"glowing" statues, 83–87, *87*

"golden door" photos, 45, *48*, 259

Golden Legend (book), 152–53

Gora, Vikas, 81

Gordon, Henry, 80

Graham, Billy, 206, 261, 262

grave wax, 170

Greffe, Dr. Brian, 194–95

Gregory, Father Archimandrite, 67–68

grilled-cheese Madonna, 51–54, *55–56*

Guadalupe, Image of, 31–33, 72, 192, 317

    forensic illustration of, 34

guardian angels. *See* angels

Guscin, Mark, 134, 135, 137

Halahan House (Southington, CT), 387–88

Halley's Comet, 245

hallucinations, 229, 265. *See also* "waking dream"

handwriting evidence, 270–72

Harris, Martin, 280

Healing Oils of the Bible (book), 74

healings, miraculous, 175–222

    by Jesus, 175–80, *181*

        See also "Belgian Lourdes"; Chimayó; Hinn, Benny; Lourdes; Popoff, Peter; Santo, Audrey

Heatherington, Dale, 46

Helena, St., 96, 97, 141

Heller, John, 124

"hell's fire," 403

herbal remedies, 216

Herod Agrippa I, King, 158

Hero of Alexandria, 21–22

Hershey, Barbara, 359, 360, 362
Hindu deities, 79
Hines, Terence, 195–203
Hinn, Benny, 203, 205–11, *212*
Holy Blood
    at Bruge, 101–03, *103*
    on Shroud of Turin, 122–23
    on Sudarium of Oviedo, 135–36
    other, 141, 142–43, *146*, 150
Holy Blood, Holy Grail (book), 142, 153
Holy Grail, 142–43, 147, 152–53. *See also*
    emerald grail
Hornby, Sir Edmund (judge), 289–90
Hosts, 241–43
    defined, 242
    Turin "miracle," 243–46, *247*
    See also Eucharistic miracles
Houdini, Harry, 374
Hough, Joseph C., 211
Hough, Peter, 292, 405
Hughes, E. Albert, 375
Hugo, Victor, 142
"Hugo Christ" photo, 266–67
"Human Blockhead" (sideshow act),
    215–16
Hume, David, 13–14
hypnosis, 207–09
"hysteric," 313

iconoclasts, 57–58
iconography, 32, *34*, 109–10, 112, 131
ideomotor effect, 271
idolatry, 57–58
    versus veneration, 57
Image of Guadalupe. See Guadalupe, Image of
"Incorruptible" corpses, 169–72, *172*
infrared photography, 32
Irene, St. (weeping icon of), 67

Jacopo da Voragine, 152–53
Jahoda, Gustav, 286
James, St. (Santiago)
    miraculous relics of, 157–66
    statue of, *168*
Januarius, St., 102, 143–45, *148*
Jeanne des Anges, 370
Jerome, St., 139
Jesus
    apparitions of, 227–30
    burial of, 119, 149
    healings by, 175–80, *181*
    miracles of, 242, 297–305, *306–07*
    See also Holy Blood; resurrection of
        Jesus; Shroud of Turin; True Cross
Joan of Arc, 281
"John of God," 213–18, *218*
John Paul II, Pope, 184, 254
John the Baptist, St., 139, 149, 150, 244
Jordan, Peter, 382
Joseph of Arimathea, 149, 151
Josephus, 238
Judging Amy (TV show), 221

Karr, Barry, 157, 221
Katseas, Rev. Ieronimos, 66, 67
Kennedy, Anson, 46
Kübler-Ross, Elizabeth, 291
Kuhlman, Kathryn, 205, 206, 209, 211
Kunz, Geroge Frederick, 151
Kurtz, Paul, 9, 11, 157, 166
Kushner, Rabbi Harold S., 211

Labouré, St. Catherine, 171
Lawrence, St. (San Lorenzo), 149
Lazarus, 180, *181*
Le Cat, Dr. Claude Nicholas, 404
Leonard, Gladys Osborne, 281
leprosy, 177

Lewis, C. S., 13, 14
ley lines, 166
Long, Becky, 252
Looking for a Miracle (book), 15, 47, 171
Lorenzo, Cora, 71, 77
Lorenzo, St., 145
Loretto staircase, 359–363, *364, 365*
"Lourdes, Belgian," 187–190
Lourdes (healing shrine), 183–86, *186,* 216
"Lourdes of the Bronx," 185–86
lucid dreams, 288
luminescence, 36–38, *40*
Luther, Martin, 175
Lutz, George, 381–83
Lutz, Kathy, 381

Machen, Arthur, 265
MacLaine, Shirley, 159–161, 165
Magi, tomb of, 140–41
Magnish, Scot, 65, 67
Mahner, Martin, 392
Malory, Sir Thomas, 149
Malz, Betty, 266
Mandylion of Edessa, 105–10, *110,* 111–17, *116*
"Marianity," 238
Marian sites, 252
"Mariolatry," 238
Mark, St., 140
Marlboro Township, NJ, 258
Mary (mother of Jesus)
    apparitions of, 183, *186,* 249–55, 257–59, 273, 309–10, *313*
    effigies of, 23–25, 31–33, *34,* 51–55, *56,* 61, 63, 65–68, *69,* 73, 78, 83–86, *186*
Mary Magdalene, 143, 149, 226–27
"Master of the 'Shroud' of Lirey," 132
Maury Povich Show, The (TV show), 386
McBrien, Rev. Richard, 379

McCrone, Walter, 123–26, 130, 135
McGaha, Major James, 245
McKinney, Ida Ruth, 387
Medjugorie, Yugoslavia, 219, 257–59
Michell, John, 35
migraine, 369
milk-drinking statues, 79–81
Millet, Madame, 405
Miracle Detectives (TV show), 71, 72, 74, 75, 193
Miracle of Turin (painting), *247*
miracles
    defined, 13
    evidence for, 14–15
    as parables, 297–305
    types of, 15–16
    See also miracles of Jesus
miracles of Jesus
    Calming the Sea, 299–300
    Coin in the Fish, 302
    Cursing the Fig Tree, 300–01
    exorcisms, 177
    Feeding the Five Thousand, 302–03
    Feeding the Four Thousand, 303–04
    healings, 175–78, *181*
    Miraculous Drought of Fishes, 301
    raising the dead, 178–180, *182*
    Walking on Water, 304–05
Miraculous Drought of Fishes, 301
misdiagnosis, 176, 209, 216
Mitchell, S. Weir, 262
"mock sun," 245
Moran, Rick, 382
"Mormon" church. *See* Church of Jesus Christ of Latter-day Saints
Moroni (angel), 279–80
Morte d' Arthur (book), 149
Mother Cabrini Shrine, 258
Mother Teresa, 52

mummification, 170, 171
Murphy, Rev. James, 62
myrrh, 62

Napoleon I, 152
National Geographic Television and Film,
    213, 215
near-death experience (NDE), 293–94, *294*
Neumann, Therese, 325, 331
Newton, Isaac, 142
Nickell, Joe, 15, *43*, 77, *103*, *116*, *128*, *153*,
    196, *217*, *218*, 221, 270, *334*, *354*, 405
Nicodemus, 153
Nienhuys, Jan Willem, 101, 309, 311
Nolen, Dr. William A. 209, 211

Occam's razor, 15
oil, 66–69, 71–78, *78*
    testing, 74–75
    See also exuding effigies
Oostakker, Belgium, 187, 189, 190
Opsasnik, Mark, 379
Osuna, Ric, 381, 383–84, *384*
Ouija board, 374
Oviedo cloth. *See* Sudarium of Oviedo
Owen, Sir Richard, 396

Pachacamac
    idol, 27–30
    oracle of, 27–28, 30
    pyramids at, *30*
Palaeologan style, 113, 115
Palmyra, New York, 279
parables, 298. *See also* miracles, as parables
pareidolia
    defined, 52
    See also simulacra
Passion of the Christ, The (movie), 233–39
Paul, St., 139

Peerdeman, Ida, 309–13
"Pentecostal Power," 202
Peron, Eva, 316–17
"petrified" people, 169–170
phosphorescent paint, 37–38
photographs, 287
Picknett, Lynn, 142–43
Pío, Padre, 335–40
    canonization, 338–140
    exhumation, 340
    phenomena, 336–38
Pius XI Pope, 252
Pizarro, Francisco, 29–30
placebo effect, 177
Plantard, Pierre, 143
Plogojowitz, Peter, 171
poison immunity, 355
Polidoro, Massimo, 140, 143
Pollen
    on Shroud of Turin, 124–26
    on Sudarium of Oviedo, 136
Poltergeist (movie), 387
poltergeist phenomena, 311–12, 372–74,
    376
Popoff, Peter 197–203, *204*
Posner, Dr. Gary P., 203
Possessed (movie), *380*
possession, 311–13, 369–379
    defined, 369
    poltergeists and Ouija spirits, 372–75
    and psychology, 369–71
    story behind *The Exorcist*, 371–79
power, going under the, 202, 208–09
Pozzuoli Stone, 145, *148*
Presley, Elvis, sightings of, 230
Price, Robert, 238
Prince, Clive, 142–43
Priory of Sion (hoax), 143
prophecy, 197–98, 252–55, 310. *See also*

Fatima, "miracles" and "secrets"
provenance, 103, 109–110, 113, 133
    defined, 133
"psychic surgery," 214
psychosomatic conditions, 176–77, 216

Radford, Ben, 378
Ramaccini, Franco, 144
Randi, James, 53, 198–99, 200
Randles, Jenny, 292, 405
Recoleta Cemetery (Buenos Aires), 317, *318*
Rees, Vaughn, 36, 193
Reeser, Mary, 406
reflectographic photographs, 108, 113
Rega, Jose López, 317
relics, miraculous, 91–172. *See also specific
    relics, e.g.,* Holy Grail
Rennes-le-Château, 143
resurrecting the dead, 178–80, *182*
    by Elijah and Elisha, 225
    by Jesus 178–180
    See also resurrection of Jesus
resurrection of Jesus, 122, 225–230, *230*, 231
"retrofitting," 255
Ripley's . . . Believe It or Not, 363
Rivas, Katya, 330–32, *333*
Robertson, Craig, 66
Robinson, Cloretta (stigmatist), 325
Rochas, François-Jean, 363
Rogo, D. Scott, 60
Rosales, José Sol, 32
rosaries, transmutation of, 47, 259
Rubio, Maria, 41
Rudder, Pierre De, 187–90, *190*
Runciman, Sir Steven, 106–07
Ryden, Vassula, 269–75

Sagan, Carl, 294
saints, popular, 315–17, 319–321

Samarin, Dr. William T., 357
San Francisco de Asis (church), 35, *39*
"Sangraal," 153
sangreal
    san greal ("holy grail"), 142
    sang real ("royal blood"), 142
Santiago. *See* James, St.
Santiago de Compostela, 157–168
Santistevan, Corina, 36
Santo, Audrey, 219–222
Santo, Linda, 219, 222
Santos, Lucia, 249–55
Satan
    "Devil's step," 391–93, 93
    footprints, 395–400, *402*
    voice of, 312
    See also exorcism
Saunière, Bérenger, 142
Schafersman, Steven D., 125
Scherpenheuvel, 23–25
schizophrenia, 369
Schulemburg, Guillermo, 33
scrying, 280
serpents, 347–52, *353*
    eastern tradition, 348–49
    rod-to-serpent, 347–48
    sideshow features, 352, *354*
    snake handling, 350–51
"Shadow of the Cross," 35–40, *40*
Shaw, Steve, 53
Sheehan, Michael, 363
Shermer, Michael, 53
Sherr, Lynn (ABC), 220
"shotgun" technique (faith healing), 206,
    207
Shroud of Turin, 109, 119–28, *128*
    artist of, 120–21, 129–132
    "blood" on, 122–24
    C-14 dating, 126

image of, 122, *128*

image replication, 129–31

pollen claims, 124–26

scandal at Lirey, 120–21

secret study, 122–23

shrouds, bogus, 119–120. *See also* Besançon, Shroud of

"shroud science," 123–24

Siffrin, Msgr. Robert, 85

"signs," 285–87

photographic, 287

simulacra, 32, 41–44, 52–56, *55–56*, 287

defined, 41

pareidolia and, 52

Skeptical Inquirer (magazine), 81, 83, 140, 216, 344

"slain in the spirit." *See* power, going under the

"sleep paralysis," 289. *See also* "waking dream"

Smith, Joseph Jr., 277–83

fantasizer, 280–82

snake charming, 348–49. *See also* serpents

snake handling, 350–51. *See also* serpents

Snedeker, Allen, 387–89

Snedeker, Carmen, 387–89

Snedeker, Philip, 387–89

Soldado, Juan ("Soldier John"), 319–321, *322*

"Soldier John." *See* Soldado, Juan

spiritism, 214

Spiritualism, 214, 281, 285, 374

spontaneous human combustion, 403–406, *406*

spontaneous remission, 176, 216

staircase, miracle. *See* Loretto staircase

Steiger, Brad, 291

stereomicroscope, 41, *43*

Stewart, David, 74

stigmata, 234, 323–32

defined, 323

evolving phenomenon, 323–26

proven frauds, 329–30

stigmatic profile, 326–29

See also stigmatists

Stigmata (movie), 323

stigmatists

Bernas, Lilian, 341–44, *345, 346*

Francis of Assisi, 323–25

Neumann, Therese, 325, 331

others, 323–330

Pío, Padre, 334–40

Rivas, Katya, 33–32, *333*

Sudarium of Oviedo, 133–38

suggestion, 209

Sullivan, Randall, 71, 73, *76*

"sun dog," 245

sun miracles, 251–52, 259

"surgeries, invisible," 214

"Swami Yomahmi." *See* Walker, Stephon

Swank, Hilary, 15

Swierz, Rev. Michael, 84, 85

syncretism, 31

Taylor, Glenn, 32

Taylor, James, 215

Templar Revelation, The (book), 142, 143

testimonials, faith-healing, 203

Theiller, Dr. Patrick, 185

thermographic photographs, 108, 113

thixotropy, 144, 145

Thomas, Cal, 238

Thomas, St. (the doubter), 139

Titulus Crucis, 95–96, *98*

tomography, 113, 203

Tonatzin (Aztec goddess), 31

tongues, speaking in. *See* glossolalia

Tourette's syndrome, 369

Trachet, Tim, 101

Transfiguration (of Jesus), 228–29

transmutation. *See* rosaries, transmutation of

Transubstantiation, 241, 242, 311. *See also* Eucharistic miracles

True Cross, 91–99, *99*, *146*, 149

Tryon, Victor, 124

Turin, Eucharistic miracle of, 243–46, *247*

Turin Shroud. *See* Shroud of Turin

Tyrrell, G. N. M., 229

Unsolved Mysteries (TV show), 45, 47

Valley Hill, Kentucky (miracle site), 45

vampires, 171

"vaporography," 122, 129

veneration (of images), 57. *See also* idolatry

Veronica's Veil, 106, 111–12, 235–36

"victim soul," 219

Vigilantius of Talouse, 139

Vignon, Paul, 129

Virgin Mary. *See* Mary (mother of Jesus)

"visitations," 285–294

Vískontas, Indre, 71, 72, 73, *76*. See also *Miracle Detectives*

Voragine, Jacopo da. *See* Jacopo da Voragine

"waking dream," 228–29, 230, 264, 279

Walker, Stephon, 215–16

Walking on Water, 304–05, *307*

Warren, Ed, 381–82, 288–89

Warren, Lorraine, 382, 388–89

Weber, William, 383

"weeping" effigies, 23–25, *25*, 58, 60–62, 65–69, *69*, 71–78, 259

weeping icon kit, 65–66, 68

Whanger, Alan, 127, 136

Wheeler, Nancy, 170

William of Tyre, 151

Williams, Ben, 386–87

Williams, Jean, 386–87

Willin, Melvyn, 267

Wills-Brandon, Carla, 291, 293

Wilson, Ian, 109, 127, 135, 235

Wilson, Sheryl C., 275, 281. *See also* fantasy-prone personality

winding stairs. *See* Loretto staircase

Woodward, Kenneth L., 159

X-rays, 108, 113, 210

Yavorsky, John, 84

Zanic, Bishop Pavao, 257–58

Zeis, John, 344

Zimdars-Swartz, Sandra L., 252, 253–54